Chartered Banker

STUDY TEXT

Contemporary Issues in Banking

In this 2014/15 edition

- A **user-friendly format** for easy navigation
- **Updated** on recent developments
- A **chapter review** at the end of each chapter
- A full **index**

Chartered Banker
Leading financial professionalism

BPP
LEARNING MEDIA

Published July 2014

ISBN 978 1 4727 0500 6

British Library Cataloguing-in-Publication Data
A catalogue record for this book
is available from the British Library

Published by

BPP Learning Media Ltd
BPP House, Aldine Place
London W12 8AA

www.bpp.com/learningmedia

Printed in the United Kingdom by Ricoh UK Limited

Unit 2
Wells Place
Merstham
RH1 3LG

Your learning materials, published by BPP Learning Media Ltd, are printed on paper sourced from sustainable, managed forests.

A note about copyright

Dear Customer

What does the little © mean and why does it matter?

Your market-leading BPP books, course materials and e-learning materials do not write and update themselves. People write them: on their own behalf or as employees of an organisation that invests in this activity. Copyright law protects their livelihoods. It does so by creating rights over the use of the content.

Breach of copyright is a form of theft – as well as being a criminal offence in some jurisdictions, it is potentially a serious breach of professional ethics.

With current technology, things might seem a bit hazy but, basically, without the express permission of BPP Learning Media:

- Photocopying our materials is a breach of copyright
- Scanning, ripcasting or conversion of our digital materials into different file formats, uploading them to facebook or e-mailing them to your friends is a breach of copyright

You can, of course, sell your books, in the form in which you have bought them – once you have finished with them. (Is this fair to your fellow students? We update for a reason.) But the e-products are sold on a single user license basis: we do not supply 'unlock' codes to people who have bought them secondhand.

And what about outside the UK? BPP Learning Media strives to make our materials available at prices students can afford by local printing arrangements, pricing policies and partnerships which are clearly listed on our website. A tiny minority ignore this and indulge in criminal activity by illegally photocopying our material or supporting organisations that do. If they act illegally and unethically in one area, can you really trust them?

CONTENTS

INTRODUCTION

The aim of this module is to provide an extensive, detailed and critical knowledge and understanding of contemporary issues in the banking industry and develop the practitioner's ability to make professional judgements and informed decisions in relevant work situations.

Learning Outcomes

The main learning outcomes associated with this module should enable you to:

- Examine the role of the bank as a financial intermediary and deposit creator
- Critically analyse economic theories, trends and the UK economic environment
- Examine the impact of monetary policy on banks, inflation, the housing market and the economy
- Critically review the involvement of banks in the international money, credit and bond markets
- Examine and analyse international factors impacting on banks
- Examine the ways in which public finance issues in the economy affect banks and critically analyse the implications of government shareholdings in banks
- Critically analyse the regulatory framework and the competitive environment in which banks operate
- Critically review the latest trends in innovation and technology in banking

Assessment structure

Your online extended response examination will be worth 70% of your overall result and your summative assignment will make up the remaining 30%.

Introduction to your study text

It is essential for a qualified banker to have a detailed and critical knowledge and understanding of contemporary issues within the banking industry. This Study Text aims to develop the practitioner's ability to make professional judgements and informed decisions about contemporary issues relevant to their work situations.

As a banker it is essential to understand the role of the financial intermediaries in an economy. A banker must also be able to critically analyse economic trends in the UK and global economies so that he or she can properly assess the likely demand for loans and other bank services. Economic knowledge as presented in this module will also assist in the proper assessment of loan risks, which is so essential in minimising losses and maintaining the financial soundness of banks.

A key factor in such knowledge is a proper understanding of monetary policy and its impact on banks, the economy and the housing market which this module seeks to address. In addition, a banker must have a thorough knowledge of bank operations in the global financial markets and the risks associated with such activities. All aspects of securitisation and globalisation must be understood along with the creation of the EU single banking market and its likely impact on competition in the banking sector.

A banker must also understand the major public finance issues being debated in most countries and how these impact on national economies and banks. In many countries the recent financial crisis and ongoing recession has forced governments to acquire stakes in banks in order to maintain financial stability. The Eurozone crisis has also added to the problems of bankers as regards actual and potential debt write-offs which have resulted in demands for banks to have additional capital and liquidity adequacy ratios against their assets.

Against such financial maelstrom and international bank regulatory agencies are new rules and guidelines for balance sheet management, corporate governance and competition. As this Study Text will explore, the latter has the potential for a major restructuring of the banking sectors in many countries and it is against such a background that banks have to decide their operational and marketing/product strategies in the future. To this potential mix is added the impact of new technology in the delivery of bank services and internal management of banks.

It is against the above financial and economic background that this Study Text seeks to explain and critically analyse major contemporary issues in UK and global banking.

chapter 1

FINANCIAL ASSETS, LIABILITIES AND INTERMEDIARIES

Contents

Learning outcomes

On completion of this chapter, you should be able to:

- Explain the concept of the national balance sheet and sector surpluses and deficits
- Explain the domestic recycling of funds and the creation of direct and indirect financial claims
- Evaluate the role of financial intermediaries in the economy and how banks serve savers' and borrowers' needs
- Comment on the personal sector balance sheet and explain fluctuations in the personal sector savings ratio
- Examine the role of the bank as a deposit creator and analyse the concept of the bank deposit multiplier

Introduction

Understanding the concepts of the national balance sheet and financial wealth are essential in order to appreciate the role of financial intermediaries. By a process of aggregation, maturity and risk transformations, these institutions create primary and secondary financial claims which suit the asset and liability portfolio requirements of all economic agents in a country. The personal sector, by its steady accumulation of financial wealth via unspent income, encourages financial institutions, companies and the government to adapt and provide a wide range of financial products. A modern economy requires a flexible and adaptable financial system.

In this chapter, we will consider some key aspects of financial wealth and intermediation:

- Sector surpluses and deficits
- Domestic recycling of funds
- Financial claim classification
- The personal sector savings ratio/net worth
- Personal financial products
- Deposit creation and its limitations

These aspects and others will be considered in the context of each economy's need for the optimum utilisation of the nation's savings resources in order to maximise economic welfare.

To aid in the understanding of such concepts as financial wealth and intermediation, we will examine a country's financial system. The first step is to consider the national balance sheet.

1 The national balance sheet

This lists all the assets and liabilities (the claims held and claims due) on a particular date for an economy.

National Balance Sheet of Utopia (£billion)
as at 31 December 20XX

A	Physical Assets			150
B	Financial Assets			
	1	Money	20	
	2	Loans	50	
	3	Shares	90	
	4	Life Policies	20	180
				330
C	Financial Liabilities			
	1	Money	20	
	2	Loans	50	
	3	Shares	90	
	4	Life Policies	20	– 180
D	Net Worth (A + B – C)			150

The balance sheet for the hypothetical country of Utopia emphasises the fact that physical assets, such as land, buildings, roads and machinery, represent the real wealth of a nation. These physical (or capital) assets play a major role in the generation of income within an economy by assisting in the production of goods and services. Note that financial assets and liabilities cancel one another out, thus making net worth equal to the value of physical assets.

The reason for this equality of values arises from the fact that a financial claim is simultaneously an asset to one economic unit and a liability to another, linking the two economic units. For example, bank notes held by an individual are an asset to the holder, whereas to the issuing authority – the central bank – they are a liability.

A bank deposit is an asset to the individual as the holder of the claim, but it appears as a liability in the bank's balance sheet. The same applies if you hold shares or make a loan to a friend or relative. The financial system is in effect a superstructure built on the real wealth of a nation – its physical assets.

An economy can be divided into various sectors and the net worth of each one – physical *plus* financial assets *minus* financial liabilities – can be ascertained:

- The public sector incorporates central and regional governments along with various state agencies, such as Scottish Water
- The industrial/commercial sector constitutes private corporations which produce the goods and services in a market economy
- In most economies the bulk of net worth is attributable to the personal sector, i.e. private individuals

For the sake of simplicity, the overseas sector is omitted. Thus we are examining a closed or domestic economy.

QUICK QUESTION

Why do you think private individuals hold most net worth?

Write your answer here before reading on.

The net worth of any sector in an economy can be calculated by adding up all the assets it holds *minus* financial liabilities to other sectors. The net worth of the personal sector of Utopia will be equal to the physical assets *plus* financial assets held, *less* any financial liabilities it has to other sectors.

The personal sector may be in the following position:

	£billion
Physical Assets	50
Financial Assets	100
	150
Less Financial Liabilities	– 60
	90

QUICK QUESTION

What is the net worth of the other sectors in Utopia?

Write your answer here before reading on.

Thus, the personal sector of Utopia has a net worth of £90 billion. You would generally expect the personal sector of an economy to be in a net credit position. Equally you would expect the public sector to be in a net deficit position because its financial liabilities to other sectors in most cases will far exceed its financial assets. The public sector has a tendency to spend more than it receives in tax receipts and thus is forced to borrow from other sectors of the economy, thereby creating and adding to the national debt.

QUESTION TIME 1

Ascertain the net worth of the following sectors in Utopia from the figures below and the National Balance Sheet data as at 31 December 2013.

£ billions	*Industrial/Com. Sector*	*Public Sector*	*Personal Sector*	*Total*
Physical Assets	25	?	50	?
Financial Assets	?	30	100	?
Financial Liabilities	25	– ?	– 60	– ?
Net Worth	?	?	90	150

Write your answer here then check with the answer at the back of the book.

Let us now take our analysis one step further to see how financial claims are created and the role played by financial institutions in this process.

2 Funds flow analysis

This measures financial transactions between various economic sectors in a country. A sector has a financial surplus if total receipts exceed total expenditure for a particular time period, and *vice versa* for a financial deficit. The key problem of finance arises because saving does not equal investment for each economic sector.

The surplus sector must acquire or purchase financial claims (assets), and/or pay off outstanding debts, i.e. claims held against it. Obviously, a deficit necessitates the opposite course of action – the issue of financial claims (debt) or a run-down in financial assets held. The act of borrowing and lending gives rise to financial claims. The holders (savers) of assets and suppliers (borrowers) of claims create a financial market in some form.

One of the main aims of all financial institutions, including banks, is to channel funds from financial surplus to financial deficit units in an economy. Banks borrow money (surplus) from the personal sector, i.e. take deposits, not to finance their own deficits, but in order to finance other sectors' deficits. This is sometimes referred to as the domestic recycling of funds within an economy.

A simplified annual funds flow statement is shown below.

Utopia Sector Analysis (£billion)

	Public Sector	*Industrial and Commercial Sector*	*Personal Sector*	*Total*
Year 1	– 10	– 2	+ 12	0
Year 2	– 8	+ 2	+ 6	0
Year 3	– 6	+ 1	+ 5	0

The figures indicate that the financial system enables the personal sector to put its financial surplus at the disposal of the other two sectors in the form of increased holdings of bank notes, bank deposits and shares. Some people save for short periods of time, perhaps receiving their income at the beginning of the month and spending it later. Others may save for longer periods in order to make an expensive purchase or investment. In some cases, it might be a matter of principle to save income in excess of needs.

Some of the surplus might pass through financial institutions, such as banks and insurance companies, rather than holding direct claims, such as share or loan certificates, on other sectors. Note that the figures zero out in each year as financial assets and liabilities are opposite sides in the creation of a financial claim.

In most economies, the public sector is invariably a net borrower due to its expenditure being in excess of its tax revenues, so it is obliged to issue financial claims, i.e. bank notes, government stock, national savings certificates, premium bonds. Such action increases a country's national debt. On the other hand, the private sector in most economies is nearly always a net lender via increased holdings of various types of financial assets.

QUICK QUESTION

Why do economic sectors have deficits and surpluses?

Write your answer here before reading on.

3 Financial claims

A financial claim arises whenever an act of lending or borrowing takes place in an economy. Financial institutions and markets channel funds from surplus sectors to deficit sectors. Financial intermediaries borrow, not to finance their own deficits, but the deficits of other units.

Most financial claims (excluding bank notes) carry an obligation on the issuer to make periodic income payments and to redeem (repay) the claim at a stated value to the holder. This might be fixed, such as a loan with a fixed interest rate and repayment date, or variable, such as dividends on ordinary share capital (common stock), the latter in most cases not being subject to repayment by the issuer, as the corporation will be in existence indefinitely; for example, BP plc or General Motors.

In most cases, if the holder of shares wishes to recover the money balance paid to the company which issued the shares, then the shares must be sold in a secondary market, i.e. a stock exchange, to some other party. The existence of such a market guarantees the reversibility of such a claim, but not the disposal price or value. The ability to dispose of financial assets enables the holders of such claims to indulge in asset switching to suit their own needs, such as selling shares to increase bank deposit balances.

Every financial claim has some degree of risk attached to it. With a bank deposit it is relatively easy for the holder to recover the money balance, risk is low and so also is the rate of return. The greater the risk, as with ordinary shares, the higher the rate of return expected by the holders of such claims. Financial claims are generally classified according to the degree of liquidity associated with each claim – notes, bank deposits, government bonds, shares, life policies, etc (highly liquid to least liquid).

For the personal sector, most financial assets thus provide some form of return, are marketable and can be converted into cash at minimal expense and inconvenience. It is the convertibility aspect that attracts people to hold a certain proportion of their wealth in financial assets. The alternative is the ownership of physical assets – land, houses, cars, etc – which might appreciate or depreciate in value, incur maintenance costs and require to be insured against theft or accidents. The disposal of physical assets sometimes might involve considerable expense and inconvenience, such as legal documentation associated with land and property transactions.

Each year in the UK, the personal sector increases its holdings of various financial assets – bank notes/deposits, national savings certificates and shares – and also contributes to life assurance policies and pension schemes, which in turn acquire financial assets, such as domestic and overseas bonds and shares.

QUICK QUESTION

What do you understand by the term financial intermediation?

Write your answer here then check with the answer at the back of the book.

4 Financial intermediaries

Financial intermediaries, such as banks and insurance companies, acquire direct or primary claims on deficit units and issue to the public their own secondary claims to finance such acquisitions. Let us now consider claims on a bank and how they are created.

BANK INTERMEDIATION

Personal Sector Bal Sheet (£m)		**Albion Bank Bal Sheet (£m)**		**British Petroleum Plc Bal Sheet (£m)**	
Liability	***Asset***	***Liability***	***Asset***	***Liability***	***Asset***
Capital or Net Worth	Albion Bank A/C	Personal Sector Deposits	Loan to BP	Albion Bank Loan	North Sea Oil Field
100	100	100	100	100	100

Issue — Indirect/Secondary Claim

Issue — Direct Claim/Primary Claim

In this simplistic illustration of the creation of financial claims, the personal sector has an asset in the form of a secondary claim issued by Albion Bank. Albion Bank has both a financial asset and a liability. Its financial asset is the direct primary claim it holds on British Petroleum while its financial liability is the secondary claim issued to the personal sector.

In most cases, secondary claims are more attractive to surplus units (the personal sector) than direct claims on deficit units because they can get their money back when it suits them – they have liquidity. Intermediation costs (financial institutions' operating costs) must be paid from the bank's margin between borrowing (deposit) and lending interest rates. Such costs are reduced by the scale of their operations.

Most financial intermediaries are thus involved in a process known as asset or maturity transformation, whereby deposits generally have a shorter term than have their loans – banks borrow short and lend long.

The liabilities of financial institutions are quite willingly accepted as financial assets by their holders, i.e. bank depositors and insurance policy holders. Because the holder has faith in the financial intermediary, risk is reduced and convenience achieved, as some financial return on savings is derived without the need to investigate the ultimate borrower. A financial intermediary also helps by taking everyone's savings and aggregating them to make a large pool from which large borrowings or investments can be made. If the intermediary, in aggregate, has large inflows of savings deposited for varying periods of time, it can mismatch the maturities of its liabilities (what it owes to savers) and its assets (what it is owed by borrowers). This means that it can use short term deposits of savings to finance long term borrowings because it is confident that, throughout the life of long term borrowings, short term deposits will normally always be coming in to finance them.

Let us now consider claims on an insurance fund (pension fund, unit trust).

INSURANCE FUND INTERMEDIATION

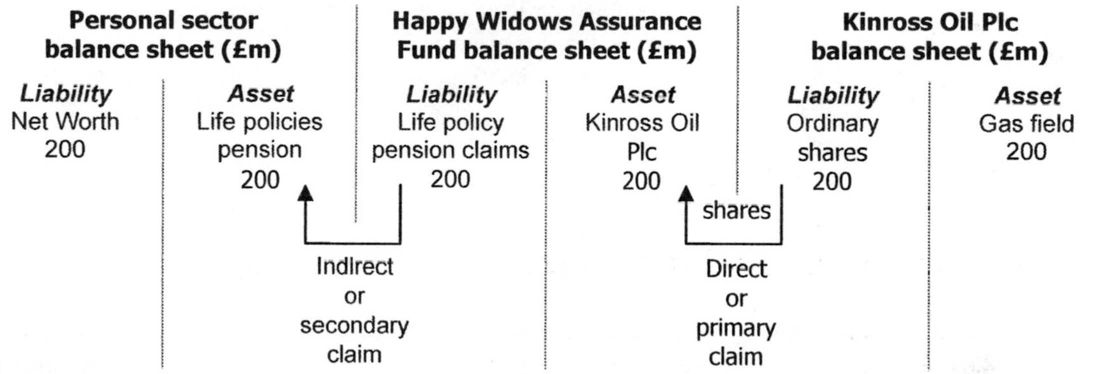

In this situation the Happy Widows Assurance Fund has life policy claims of £200m outstanding. It holds £200m worth of ordinary shares issued by Kinross Oil plc which has used the money raised to invest in a gas pipeline. The share holding is a direct claim held by the Happy Widows. These shares can be converted into cash by selling them on the stock exchange to other investors.

Financial intermediaries thus provide a link between lenders and borrowers and channel funds from those with a financial surplus to those in deficit. Many savers will save only relatively small amounts for varying time periods and do not know how to get in contact with potential borrowers. Even if they did, they would not want to incur the risk of non-repayment. Such people make use of the services of financial intermediaries – e.g. banks, insurance companies, pension funds. There may be more than one link in a chain which channels funds through a number of financial intermediaries before the link between the ultimate lender and ultimate borrower is complete, such as the inter-bank market.

QUICK QUESTION

Without financial intermediaries, how could individuals spend more than their income?

Write your answer here before reading on.

The ability to borrow allows some groups to spend more than their income by tapping the surplus financial funds of other groups. Without this facility, people could only spend in excess of their income by:

- Running down money balances previously acquired
- Selling off physical and financial assets for money

Competition, particularly between deposit takers, i.e. banks and non-banks, is based primarily on deposit and loan interest rate differentials, access to funds, the size of the branch network, opening hours and provision of ancillary services. However, despite any differences, all financial intermediaries must manage their balance sheets to ensure that no fundamental mismatch arises between deposits and loans as regards maturity and interest cost. Sufficient liquid assets must be held at all times to meet sudden fund withdrawals by customers.

5 Other aspects of financial intermediation

Financial intermediaries minimise the risk of loss by the lender(s) through the potential default by the ultimate borrower by spreading the risks through making a large number of loans (or investments) of varying degrees of risk, return and maturity. The institution reduces its own risk and thereby that of the ultimate lender(s). At the same time, the capital and reserves of the institution should enable it to sustain any possible loan or investment losses, without jeopardising the financial position of the lender(s).

As already mentioned, lenders prefer short term claims, whereas borrowers prefer long term funds. Financial intermediaries resolve this problem by maturity transformation – borrowing short and lending long. Institutions can do this because the sheer scale of their operations ensures that daily withdrawals will be matched by new deposits. Experience also enables institutions to deal with seasonal flows and make adjustments in returns to deal with the ebb and flow of funds made available by lenders and requested by borrowers.

Financial intermediaries also minimise borrowers' risks. Direct sources of funds might not be available when required. Through their deals with many lenders, intermediaries should be in a position to supply funds under agreed terms at most times. Their diversified asset portfolios enable them to consider a wide range of lending options which will meet the needs of most borrowers.

Finally, financial intermediaries, due to the scale and diversification of their lending operations, can minimise their transaction costs, which should benefit borrowers via lower interest charges or cheaper equity.

Summarising this section on financial intermediation, financial institutions – e.g. banks, building societies, insurance companies:

- Provide financial services at a low cost
- Assist lenders and borrowers
- Encourage saving and investment, thereby
- Promoting a higher rate of economic growth (in most countries)

In a narrower context, banks act to the advantage of both savers and borrowers while hopefully making a profit for their owners, the shareholders.

Savers' interests

- To find a safe place for savings with the minimum risk of default
- To have ready access to their money should they need it earlier than expected
- To diversify savings as a way of further reducing risk and spreading liquidity
- To maximise the return on savings while minimising the cost of finding a reliable borrower

Borrowers' interests

- To find an institution willing to make a loan
- To obtain a mortgage or loan at minimum cost
- To obtain the necessary funds at the time required
- To have the use of the funds for the period required without the risk of demands for early repayment

QUICK QUESTION

Distinguish between physical assets and financial assets.

Write your answer here before reading on.

6 Financial assets and physical assets

So far we have considered how certain sectors will have financial surpluses while other sectors will have financial deficits. We have seen how financial claims arise and that financial intermediaries exist to channel funds from surplus units in the economy to deficit units. Before moving on to study financial institutions and the products they offer, we will clarify the differences between financial and physical assets and why sectors hold each kind of asset.

A financial asset should provide some form of return, either as a dividend or an interest payment. To count as a financial asset, a claim must not be conditional. A life assurance policy is a financial asset because the money is paid either on death or on survival at a specified date. A fire insurance policy is not a financial asset because it is only paid in the event of a fire actually occurring, as covered by the policy. In most cases, a financial asset is marketable and can be converted into cash at minimal expense. It is this convertibility aspect which attracts people to hold financial assets, such as bank deposits, building society share and deposit accounts, certificates of deposit, government stock and ordinary shares.

Most people hold financial assets – bank notes and coins, bank account balances – to meet their immediate needs for the purchase of essential consumer goods. The more liquid the financial asset, the lower the rate of return; in the case of bank notes, no return is paid.

The degree of risk associated with each financial claim varies. As a result, the return is related to this risk factor. If a company goes into liquidation, then its financial claims – ordinary share certificates held by the owners – become virtually worthless. No secondary market exists for worthless shares. Even if a company is basically sound, the value of its financial claims – ordinary shares and debenture stock – will fluctuate in the stock market according to demand and supply, which is influenced by a large range of diverse financial/economic factors operating in the economy. As opposed to a company's shares, building society share accounts offer a lower return in exchange for less risk and greater stability of value.

Physical assets, such as houses, cars and computers, can yield utility in the form of pleasure from use. In some cases, physical assets can generate a financial return if rented or hired out to other parties. Some physical assets can be sold in a secondary market. Unfortunately, their second-hand value may be well below the initial purchase price, mainly due to depreciation (cars, washing machines, computers, etc). Other physical assets, such as houses and land, tend to appreciate in value over time.

It is not so easy to convert physical assets into financial claims (bank deposit or cash), as is the case with shares. To sell a house, a market must exist for it, and considerable expense is associated with the legal fees incurred in buying or selling property. Unlike a share certificate or a government stock certificate, a property is not transportable and must be sold in a limited local property market.

Physical assets also require to be insured against risks such as theft or fire. Total loss resulting from physical asset ownership is less likely than is the case with shares owned in a liquidated company, although ultimately a car or a washing machine will cease to function and thus be worthless.

It is for these reasons that individuals prefer to hold a combination of physical and financial assets. Some physical assets, such as a house, may retain their value in real terms during times of inflation, whereas financial assets, such as bank notes and deposits, become worth less in real terms, yet the latter must be held to retain maximum convertibility and be capable of meeting daily transactions.

QUESTION TIME 2

List and explain the reasons why people save money.

Write your answer here then check with the answer at the back of the book.

7 Development of a financial system

From a general perspective, a financial system develops in the following stages.

1 The initial stage is the introduction of money to replace a barter system.

2 The next major development is that of borrowing between the various economic sectors and units. Units with a net financial deficit may borrow from units with a surplus. Generally the deficit unit issues an interest-bearing financial claim, such as a loan or bond. These claims become financial assets for the surplus units. This stage has been initiated in many countries by governments having to borrow funds to meet expenditures in excess of tax revenues.

3 Deficit units and surplus units must now be brought together so that financial claims may be created which may also be traded, leading to the development of stock markets.

4 This leads to the development of financial intermediaries who are able to provide maximum liquidity to surplus units, such as bank deposits, while also providing loans and longer term finance to other units. They are therefore meeting the needs of both surplus and deficit units while making profits for themselves by lending at a higher rate of interest than they pay the surplus units.

5 Also a system develops whereby, through the purchase of equity securities, surplus units may gain control of a public company without having to manage it. Such equity securities are bought and sold on the stock exchange.

6 The final stage of development relates to asset switchers and liabilities switchers. The former are those units that change the composition of their portfolios by selling one claim and buying others with the proceeds. Financial intermediaries may fall into this category. The switching of assets in this manner indicates a high degree of substitutability between financial assets. Governments are the major liability switchers through the various methods used to obtain finance; for example, national savings certificates, premium bonds, Treasury bills or bonds.

QUICK QUESTION

What are portfolio institutions?

Write your answer here before reading on.

Personal sector balance sheet

Utopia Personal Sector
Balance Sheet as at 31 December 2013 (£billions)

Tangible Assets			
Residential Buildings		40	
Vehicles & Other Assets		10	50
Financial Assets			
Notes/Coin	10		
Bank Deposits	25		
National Savings	5		
Government Stock	5		
Company Securities	10		
Life Assurance	20		
Pension Funds	25	100	
Less Financial Liabilities			
Bank Loans	10		
Mortgages	40		
Other	10	– 60	40
Net Worth			90

(*Note:* The statistics in this and subsequent tables do **not** require to be memorised for exam purposes.)

The personal sector's balance sheet indicates that residential buildings are the main asset held by people in Utopia. It also accounts for the main financial liability, i.e. house loans, in the balance sheet. Among the financial assets, although bank deposits are important, company securities, life assurance and pension funds combined are more than double in value. Bank loans and other credit are associated with purchases of consumer durables, e.g. cars, TVs, washing machines. As to be expected, the personal sector has an overall net worth position. The above hypothetical balance sheet is representative of most western countries, subject to national differences in the relative importance of particular physical and financial assets.

If Utopian net personal sector wealth was £80 billion at the end of the previous year, this would imply a £10 billion or 12$^1/_2$% increase over the course of one financial year. However, it might be that most of this increase was due to inflation in the housing market rather than an increase in the value of financial assets and/or decline in financial liabilities. In other words, the increase in net worth is not due to increased savings out of disposable income.

In 2010, the UK's net worth was estimated at £6.6 trillion. Housing was the most valuable asset with a value of about £4 trillion, or 60% of the country's net worth. Civil engineering works, e.g. roads, railways, accounted for around £700 billion, or 10% of net worth.

QUESTION TIME 3

Compare and contrast the main attributes of physical and financial assets using a Ford Focus and National Savings Certificates as examples.

Write your answer here then check with the answer at the back of the book.

QUICK QUESTION

Why do people switch their holdings of financial assets?

Write your answer here before reading on.

People switch their holdings of financial assets for a number of reasons. It might be to enhance the potential yield or reduce the element of risk associated with holding a particular financial asset. Liquidity preference might be another determining factor. A person may prefer to hold a savings account balance rather than a long term bond. Shares might be sold so as to raise cash for some specific purpose, such as house improvements or a world tour.

8 Personal sector savings ratio

This ratio examines the relationship between personal sector savings and total personal disposable income, i.e. gross income *minus* compulsory deductions such as tax.

The formula for calculating this ratio is:

$$\textbf{Saving ratio} = \frac{\textbf{Personal savings}}{\substack{\textbf{Total personal disposable income} \\ \textbf{(Salaries − Tax and NIC deductions)}}} \times \textbf{100}$$

In most economies, figures for the personal sector's savings ratio are available in the form of a time series. As to be expected, it is not a constant ratio; instead, it fluctuates over time due to underlying economic and social developments in a country.

Figures for the hypothetical state of Utopia are:

Personal sector: Savings ratio

Year 1	5.7
Year 3	8.6
Year 5	12.5
Year 7	10.1
Year 9	9.0

In the UK, the main use of available funds each year has been the ongoing high level of investment in life assurance and pension funds. The personal sector appears to prefer secondary claims via institutions, such as life companies, to primary claims in the securities markets. This is the continuation of a long term trend that has not been reversed in spite of government privatisation of formerly publicly-owned companies by means of share issues.

Personal financial products

We will now switch our attention briefly to the main personal financial products made available by financial institutions, companies and the government.

In the UK, over 50% of financial assets held by the personal sector are in the form of financial claims issued by life assurance companies and pension funds. It is, therefore, hardly surprising that banks and building societies have increased their presence in this financial product sector.

The main financial liability consists of home loans provided by banks and building societies. Bank lending is also an important source of finance to a large number of households. Most of these funds are used to finance consumer expenditure, such as the purchase of cars.

Banks and building societies are the main providers of liquid assets to the UK private sector, so that competition between them for market share of current, deposit and investment accounts, etc, is likely to remain intense in the future.

Personal sector holdings of UK company securities as financial assets have declined in recent years due to the increased volatility in share prices. This encouraged the personal sector to reduce the number of shares held and to invest the sale proceeds in various low-risk savings facilities.

QUESTION TIME 4

(a) Suggest possible reasons for the rise in Utopia's personal sector's savings ratio from Year 1 to Year 5 and its subsequent decline by Year 9.

(b) Comment on the UK's personal savings ratio rising from about 2% in 2005 to 6% in 2010.

Write your answer here then check with the answer at the back of the book.

9 Bank deposit creation and money supply

The Bank of England can try to influence the level of economic activity and inflation rate by altering interest rates or money supply. Such a strategy is known as monetary policy, which requires the Bank to control bank deposit growth in the economy by the various means at its disposal.

9.1 Bank deposit creation

Money deposited by customers

Bank deposits can be used for the discharge of debts by means of a cheque. Bank deposits are thus regarded as much a part of the country's money supply as bank notes and coins. Bank deposits are initially created by customers depositing cash in a bank which opens an account in their name and credits it with the deposit amount. In simple balance sheet terms, the bank has an asset, cash, and a liability, a deposit claim against it, for an equal amount.

Loans granted by banks to customers

Bank money can come into existence not only because people deposit money with a bank, but also because banks grant loans to their customers. In such cases, it would be inconvenient if the bank had to pay out cash. Instead, the bank adds the sum to the account of the customer to whom the money is being advanced.

The customer can now draw, in cash or by cheque, not only that part of their account which constitutes money actually paid in by them, but also that part of the account which has been advanced by the bank. The granting of the loan has increased the spending power of the customer – money has been created.

Overdraft facilities granted to customers

Overdraft facilities also create money as soon as the customer draws cheques against these facilities, because the cheques must be paid into a bank account somewhere, thus raising the total level of bank deposits.

In the case of a customer loan, the creation of money takes place when the granting bank credits its customer. In the case of an overdraft, money is created as soon as the cheques drawn against the overdraft facilities are paid in, either to the same bank or to other banks. This is the explanation of the sentence, often used to explain credit/deposit creation: every advance creates a deposit.

These three methods of deposit creation are now illustrated by a simple balance sheet in a single bank economy.

Albion Bank

	Liabilities		Assets	
1	Bank Deposits	1,000	Cash	1,000
2	Bank Deposits	2,000	Cash	1,000
		2,000	Loan	1,000
3	Bank Deposits	3,000		2,000
			Cash	1,000
			Loan	1,000
			Overdraft	1,000
		3,000		3,000

QUICK QUESTION

How might a bank's ability to create credit be limited?

Write your answer here before reading on.

9.2 Limitations on bank deposit creation

The creation of bank deposits (money) by the banking system, which generates more profits for individual banks, is subject to important limitations. Briefly, these are:

- **Sufficient demand for loans and overdrafts, i.e. advances**

  Demand must come from safe, creditworthy customers with the ability to repay advances. In the early 1990s one of the factors contributing to the depth and length of the economic recession was the lack of the right sort of bank borrowers. Banks could not find safe borrowers offering adequate collateral security.

- **The liquid asset position of banks must be adequate**

  UK banks must maintain adequate liquid assets – e.g. cash, bills, money at call – to meet repayment of deposits. Through money/securities market operations, the Bank of England can adjust the amount of liquid assets available to the UK banking system.

- **The need for banks to keep in line**

  No individual bank can afford to expand its lending faster than the other banks in the system unless it can attract extra deposits from the public. In a five bank system, a bank with only 20% of the market would expect 80% of the loans it made to be re-deposited with other banks and this would require a transfer of cash from it to other banks. There would, of course, be transfers back as the loans created by competitors were re-deposited with it. If the bank created loans at a faster rate than its competitors, there would be an imbalance in these transfers and a loss of cash liquidity for the bank.

- **The total amount of cash in the country**

  The amount of cash available to the banks to support the expansion of their deposits will be influenced partly by the total amount of cash in the country – the more cash there is, the more cash is likely to be left with the banks. The desire of the public to hold money in the form of cash, rather than as bank deposits, will also influence deposit creation in the economy.

9.3 Deposit creation and liquid assets

- **The effect of granting a loan**

  A loan given by a bank to one of its customers will raise advances on the assets side and deposits on the liabilities side of the bank's balance sheet. As the bank's liquid assets are unaltered while its deposits (and assets) have risen, its overall liquidity will decline. Each bank must maintain a minimum level of liquidity to retain customer (and shareholder) confidence. If liquidity falls below this level, the bank cannot grant further loans (or any form of advances) to customers.

- **The effect of granting overdraft facilities**

  Overdraft facilities granted by a bank to one of its customers will have a similar effect on the bank's liquid assets as soon as the facility is drawn upon. If the customer draws cash, the bank's holding of cash falls and advances rise as the customer's cheques are debited to their new overdraft account; the composition of the asset side on the bank's balance sheet thus alters.

If cheques are drawn to pay bills and these are paid in at other banks and then presented for payment through the clearing system, the bank granting the overdraft must transfer part of its Bank of England operational balance to the presenting bankers in settlement. These cheques are then debited again to the customer's new overdraft account.

In both cases, the bank's cash has fallen, while advances have risen. As deposits have remained unchanged (assuming recipients of such funds have accounts with other banks), the proportion of liquid assets may fall below the required minimum.

Summary

Individual commercial banks create money when they grant loans and overdraft facilities to their customers. This power is conditioned by several factors, such as the monetary authorities' requirements concerning minimum liquid assets and their policy concerning bank lending, the maintenance of liquid assets by the banks themselves and their willingness to undertake bank lending.

10 Liquidity ratio

Let us now assume that banks have to maintain a 10% liquidity ratio against deposits. Liquid assets might be comprised of:

- Cash
- Bank of England operational balances
- Money at call
- Bills discounted
- Government stock (gilts), with less than a year to maturity

At this stage it will be obvious to you that the requirement to maintain a 10% liquidity ratio against deposits reduces a bank's ability to make loans (advances), as such action increases its deposits, against which must be held the 10% liquidity ratio. If we further assume that the Bank of England controls the supply of liquid assets included in the ratio, then control of the growth of advances, deposits and money supply is within its grasp. As we shall see (in Chapter 3), control of the supply of liquid assets is one of the main levers of monetary control used in the UK economy.

Simplified Illustration of One Commercial Bank Economy

Stage I **B/S (£)**

Deposits	500	Liquid Assets	100
		Advances	400
	500		500

Liquidity ratio: $\frac{\text{Liquid assets}}{\text{Deposits}} \times 100$

$$\frac{100}{500} \times 100 = 20\%$$

Stage II **B/S (£)**

Deposits	700	Liquid assets	100
		Advances	600
	700		700

Liquidity ratio: 14.3%

Stage III **B/S (£)**

Deposits	1000	Liquid Assets	100
		Advances	900
	1000		1000

Liquidity ratio: 10%

Note: Assume

1 A single bank system, i.e. there is only one bank in the country

2 No leakages, i.e. bank deposits are generally acceptable as a means of payment, and people who receive bank deposits are perfectly happy to hold them and do not attempt to turn them into cash

3 A fixed supply of liquid assets in the country of £100

4 A constant level of demand for cash

5 The bank decides to keep a 10% liquidity ratio

In the three stages, you can see how a commercial bank could expand its advances from £400 to £900, and still comply with the 10% liquidity ratio. It is also apparent that, if the Bank of England reduced the supply of liquid assets, then the volume of advances, deposits and thus money supply, would decline in the economy.

Stage IV **B/S (£)**

Deposits	980	Liquid assets	80
		Advances	900
	980		980

Liquidity ratio: 8.2%

Stage V **B/S (£)**

Deposits	800	Liquid assets	80
		Advances	720
	800		800

In Stage IV, the Bank of England, via money market operations, reduces the liquidity ratio to 8.2%. In order to restore the ratio to 10%, the total level of advances is reduced by £180 to £720, with a consequential contraction in deposits of £180.

11 Credit creation in a multi-bank system

Credit creation in a multi-bank system (an economy in which there is a number of banks) is more complicated, but the final result is much the same. In a multi-bank system, when bank X makes a loan (and creates a matching deposit) there is no guarantee that a cheque drawn on that deposit will be re-deposited with bank X. It may go to bank Y or bank Z which would mean that bank X would need to transfer funds to bank Y or bank Z and so would lose cash.

If banks Y and Z are also making loans, there is likely to be transfer of funds in the opposite direction. These movements tend to cancel each other out, so that in practice the banks are only concerned with settling their net imbalances.

In a multi-bank system:

- There is need for a clearing house to resolve inter-bank differences. Each clearing bank keeps a current account at the central bank (the Bank of England). Payments and settlements of imbalances are made from one bank to another by cheques drawn on their operational accounts at the central bank.
- Banks are aware that the creation of loans can lead to a leakage or loss of cash.

12 Bank deposit multiplier

In the example, liquid assets of £100 were used to support total bank deposits of £1,000 (Stage III). This is known as the bank deposit multiplier process. The original deposit of liquid assets has been multiplied to total deposits of £1,000 via the granting of £900 of advances. The multiplier value in this case is 10.

Assume the government needs to borrow £200, which it partly finances by issuing more notes or cheques drawn on its account at the Bank of England. If the notes and cheques are deposited by private sector recipients in our bank, both assets and liabilities increase by £200 from the Stage V position.

Stage VI — **B/S (£)**

Deposits	1,000	Liquid assets	280
		Advances	720
	1,000		1,000

Liquidity ratio: 28%

The bank is now in a position to expand its advances/deposits as it has adequate liquid assets.

Stage VII — **B/S (£)**

Deposits	2,800	Liquid assets	280
		Advances	2,520
	2,800		2,800

Liquidity ratio: 10%

The bank has expanded its advances by £1,800. Deposits have also grown by a similar amount. The liquidity ratio is at the statutory minimum of 10%.

This relationship can be shown by the equation:

$$\text{Bank deposit multiplier} = \frac{1}{\text{Liquidity ratio}} = \frac{1}{1/10} = 10$$

Or, to put it another way, the multiplier is the reciprocal of the liquidity ratio. So a liquidity ratio of 10% (or $^1/_{10}$) gives a bank deposit multiplier of 10. A 20% ratio would give a multiplier of 5.

The amount of bank deposit multiplier process depends on the amount of cash (notes) and Bank of England cheques deposited and retained at the bank. It also depends on the multiplier's value.

QUICK QUESTION

What determines how much cash is deposited with banks?

Write your answer here before reading on.

The amount of cash deposited with the bank will be influenced by the total amount of cash available and the public's desire to hold cash. Some Bank of England cheques may be deposited in the bank and then be transferred back to the Bank if private individuals decide to purchase national savings certificates or gilts.

The amount of cash deposited with banks will be influenced by:

- The total amount of cash available
- The public's desire to hold cash
- The public's trust in the banking system

The bank deposit multiplier concept helps us to understand the deposit creation process in a country's banking system. However, cash and deposits can leak out of the banking system due to changes in people's liquidity preference or by transfers to the government. As a result, the deposit multiplier is less stable and predictable in the real world than textbook examples imply.

QUESTION TIME 5

(a) Calculate the bank deposit multiplier for liquidity ratios of 12.5%, 6% and 4%.

(b) Taking Stage VI balance sheet, draft a new Stage VII balance sheet assuming a liquidity ratio of 4%.

Write your answer here then check with the answer at the back of the book.

KEY WORDS

Key words in this chapter are given below. There is space to write your own revision notes and to add any other words or phrases that you want to remember.

- Physical assets
- Capital assets
- Real wealth
- Net worth
- Public sector
- Industrial/commercial sector
- Personal sector
- Financial surplus
- Financial deficit
- Domestic recycling of funds
- Rate of return
- Liquidity asset or maturity transformation
- Intermediation
- Financial claims
- Personal sector savings ratio
- Bank deposit creation
- Bank deposit multiplier

REVIEW

The main learning points introduced in this chapter are summarised below.

Go through them and check back to the learning outcomes at the beginning of the chapter. Only move on when you are happy that you fully understand each point.

- The concept of the national balance sheet enabled us to distinguish between physical assets and financial assets and introduced the concept of net worth for economic sectors.
- The role of financial intermediaries includes aggregation, maturity and risk transformations. The ultimate importance of intermediation is to ensure that savings are put to good use, that investment and output are increased and that the total utility and welfare of society are greater than they otherwise would be.
- We examined the personal sector in order to identify the main sources and uses of funds, along with the computation of its overall net worth.
- We considered deposit creation by banks and the limitations imposed on this activity by balance sheet constraints and the maintenance of an adequate liquidity ratio. We also examined the bank deposit multiplier.

In summary, we looked at:

- The national balance sheet and funds flow analysis
- The main aspects of financial intermediation
- Differences between physical and financial assets
- The main items included in the personal sector's balance sheet
- The personal sector savings ratio
- The bank deposit creation and its control
- The bank deposit multiplier

chapter 2

NATIONAL INCOME

Contents

Learning outcomes

On completion of this chapter, you should be able to:

- Critically analyse the circular flow of income in an economy and explain the basic concept of national income
- Comment on the problems of national income measurement, determinants of its size and the usefulness of such data to economic management
- Explain the income multiplier and investment accelerator together with their influence on total demand in an economy

Introduction

We'll start by examining the total flow of economic activity within a country and the basic division between production and consumption. The latter is organised around households, while work or production is organised around firms. Such analysis will help us to view the whole process of production in terms of a circular flow of output or income.

We shall then examine how the national income of a country is measured in nominal and real terms and consider measurement problems, along with determinants of overall national income size.

We'll review the main components of aggregate demand in the economy as well as two important macroeconomic concepts – the multiplier and accelerator. This will involve an examination of injections and leakages in the circular flow of income and output, together with those factors which influence the level of investment in an economy.

We'll also consider some key concepts in relation to the national income of an economy:

- Circular flow of income
- National income measurement
- National income determinants
- Marginal propensity to consume
- Income multiplier
- Investment accelerator

1 National income flow

Income is derived from two main sources:

- The performance of personal services such as work
- The ownership of factors of production providing impersonal services – land and capital

Inequality of income arises from differences in payments made for personal services (wage differentials) and differences in the amount of property owned by individuals. Most people derive the bulk of their income from the provision of personal services for which they receive a wage or salary which is supplemented, possibly, by investment income from a building society or bank account. Inequalities in income and wealth can be reduced by progressive taxation. Income can take the form of wages, rent, interest and profit, and all income in an economy is received by someone. Total income depends upon the total volume of production. Expenditure for one person or household becomes income for others in the economy providing the goods or services.

The following diagram of the circular flow of income in the economy shows the provision of the factors of production to firms. In return for their effort, income is paid to households. This money is spent in the economy on consumer and investment goods which are supplied by the firms.

In other words, this diagram emphasises the basic economic concept:

National income = Total production = Total expenditure

With the use of money as a unit of account, it is possible to measure these flows in an economy.

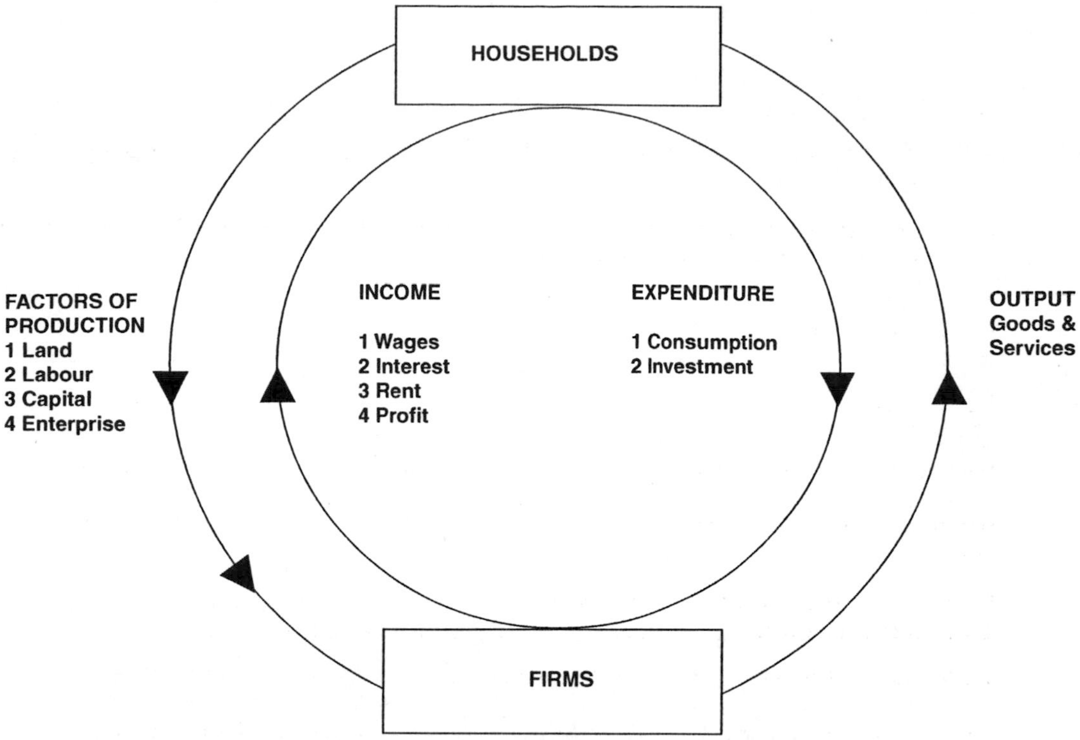

2 Circular flow leakages and injections

This equality of product, expenditure and income is based on some rather big assumptions, that:

- There is no time gap between earning and spending
- All income is spent
- No goods and services are removed from the flow

In practice these provisos cannot, of course, be sustained. Nevertheless, if it is possible to show that leaks from the circle can be balanced by injections back into it, then we can see that the total flow can still be maintained in a state of equilibrium, i.e. the condition when the flow remains the same from one time period to the next.

If we consider the flow in terms of money, then the following leakages can occur:

2.1 Savings

These are personal or household savings from income. In our definition of savings, we must include all income that is not immediately spent. Savings are seen, then, as 'non-consumption', at least for a measurable period of time.

2.2 Taxation

This is deducted either from income in the form of direct taxes, such as income or corporation tax, or deducted from expenditure in the form of VAT or duties on petrol and tobacco.

2.3 Imports

Money spent on imported goods, such as food or cars, or services, such as foreign holidays, is leaked out of the domestic circular flow of income.

However, to offset these leakages there are three types of injections that increase the circular flow of income:

Investment

This is money spent by firms in acquiring additional means of production. It is an increase of total spending in addition to that brought about by consumer spending on final goods and services.

Ideally, it would probably be desirable to distinguish genuine increases in production capacity from that investment expenditure which merely represents the replacement of existing machines and factory building. In practice, when we are dealing with broad national figures, this is just not possible. We also have to remember that firms rarely replace an old machine with one that is exactly similar – they usually buy better and more productive equipment, so that we have to assume that all investment spending is productive whilst recognising that there must always be some investment that is just replacement.

In national income analysis, increases in stocks of finished goods, i.e. inventories, which are yet to be bought, are regarded as investment, although it is always kept separate in the national accounts.

Government expenditure

Spending on defence, education, health and social services, etc is largely financed from taxation and not from charging a price in the market place. Factors of production have to be employed to provide government services – their income becomes part of the circular flow.

Exports

Money received for selling goods and services to foreign countries enters the circular flow of income in the form of a reward to those factors of production engaged in such export activities.

QUICK QUESTION

Explain what you think national income equilibrium means.

Write your answer here before reading on.

3 National income equilibrium

It is now possible to incorporate these leakages and injections into the circular flow of income diagram.

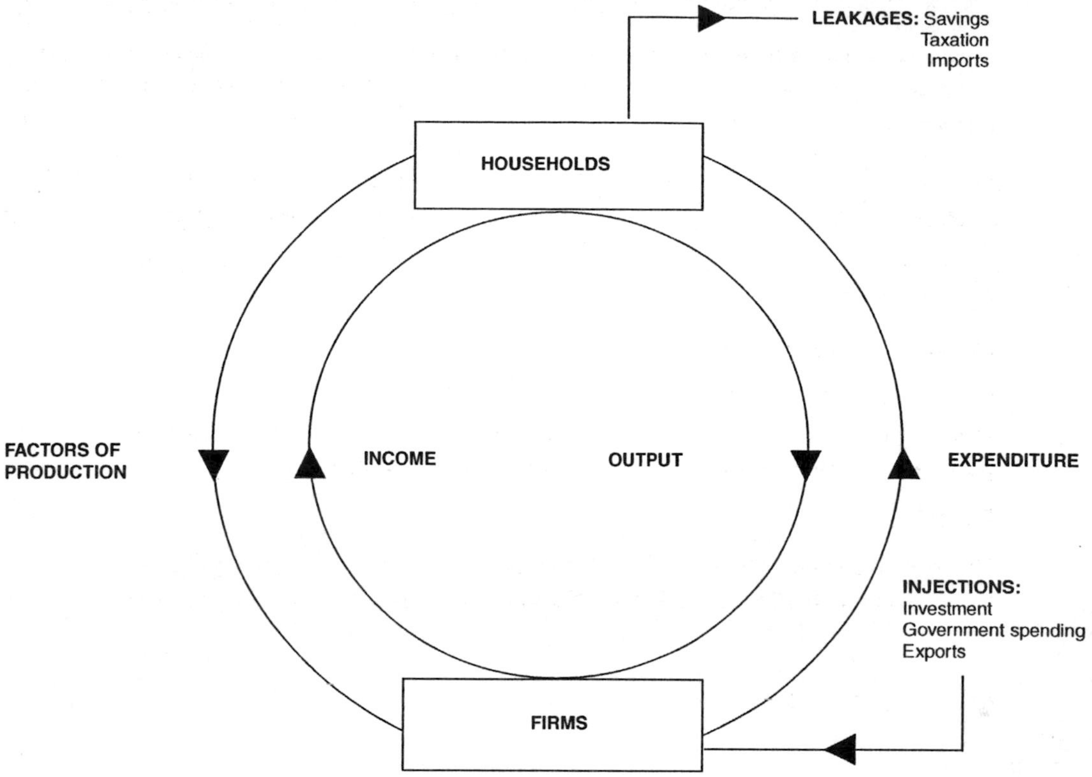

As the narrative and diagram indicate, each leakage is apparently offset by an associated injection:

Savings – Investment

Taxation – Government expenditure

Imports – Exports

However, this does not imply that each pair must be in balance. If total leakages *equal* total injections from one time period to the next, then it is possible to state that total national income – product – expenditure flow is in equilibrium. In the event of leakages exceeding injections, national income is contracting, whereas if injections exceed leakages, the national income is expanding from one time period to the next.

Using this simplistic economic model, if we assume the national income is in equilibrium and taxation plus imports is offset by government expenditure plus exports, then savings must always equal investment.

OUTPUT	=	CONSUMER GOODS + INVESTMENT
INCOME	=	CONSUMPTION + SAVING
therefore C + I	=	C + S
therefore I	=	S

In most economies there is a tendency for savings and investment to come together and thus ensure national income is in equilibrium.

Suppose intended investment is greater than intended savings. This means that intended production for consumption is likely to be less than desired consumption (income which people wish to spend on consumption). The immediate result is that people are buying more than is being made, so stocks of goods fall (reducing actual investment according to our definition). Producers will find goods easier to sell and will seek to raise production; and these developments will tend to bring actual investment and savings together as increased income will generate higher savings.

As regards taxation and government expenditure, whether or not they are balanced depends on government economic policy and/or the state of the economy. Up to the 1980s, governments ceased to attempt to balance taxation and spending as a matter of necessity, but tried to adjust each in accordance with their opinion of whether total demand needed to be stimulated or curtailed. Taxation was increased to reduce total demand, and reduced to stimulate consumer spending, and so total demand. The government's own spending intentions were adjusted for similar demand management requirements.

More recently there has been a belief that government expenditure should be restrained by the amount of tax revenue collected, but most governments do have deficits and finance these by borrowing savings from the personal sector.

There is no automatic way of maintaining a balance between imports and exports. Imports are the result of spending intentions and income levels in the home country, and exports are the result of similar intentions and income levels in other countries. The resultant external imbalance is offset by changes in the level of income and production in a country.

In general, we can see that there are likely to be forces tending to bring total national income and production into equilibrium and other forces tending to produce disequilibrium. Understanding these forces and the efforts of governments to control them are the basic themes in subsequent chapters.

QUESTION TIME 6

Describe the circular flow of income.

Write your answer here then check with the answer at the back of the book.

4 National income terms and measurement

Some of the basic terms used when explaining national income statistics are:

Gross Domestic Product (GDP) at market prices

This is the total market value of all the goods and services produced in a country.

Gross National Product (GNP) at market prices

This is the GDP after account is taken of net property income from abroad; for example, investment income from overseas assets minus interest paid on domestic government debt to non-residents.

Net National Product - Income - Expenditure

This equals GNP at factor cost *less* an estimate of capital consumption in the economy, i.e. depreciation of the existing stock of capital. A similar adjustment is made to national income and expenditure figures.

The table shown next relates to the fictional state of Utopia for a given year. The national income figures are measured in three separate forms:

- National product
- National income
- National expenditure

The final total of all three calculations is the same: £4,000 million

National Income Measurements Utopia (£ million)

Total Output		**Total Income**		**Total Expenditure**	
Agriculture	130	Wages	2,700	Personal Consumption:	
Mining	60	Rent	200	Food	630
Manufacture	1,400	Profits	700	Clothing	260
Transport	350	Interest	300	Rent/rates	470
Services	2,000			Others	1,700
				Total	3,060
GDP at mkt. price	3,940	Net income overseas	460	Govt. expenditure	900
		Other income	40		
Net income overseas	460	Gross nat. income	4,400	Capital formation	880
GNP at mkt. price	4,400	Less cap consumption	– 400	Exports	700
					5,540
Less capital consumption	– 400	NET NATIONAL INCOME	4,000	Imports	– 1,140
NET NATIONAL PRODUCT	4,000			Gross national Expenditure	4,400
				Less capital consumption	– 400
				NET NATIONAL EXPENDITURE	4,000

Notes:

1 OUTPUT – This indicates the value of output of the main economic sectors in Utopia. From total GNP at market price £4,400m a deduction for capital consumption (depreciation) is made of £400m in the economy. This part of total output is not available for consumption.

2 INCOME – Pensions and social security payments are omitted, as these represent transfers payments from mostly wage earners to non-earners, e.g. pensioners, in Utopia. Direct tax or income tax is also ignored in net national income figure.

3 EXPENDITURE – Personal consumption equals £3,060m, on to which is added government expenditure, capital formation (investment in plant and machinery) and exports. From a total expenditure figure of £5,540m, a deduction of £1,140m is made for imports to provide gross national expenditure of £4,400m.

4 You are not required to memorise these figures for examination purposes.

QUICK QUESTION

Why measure Gross Domestic Product?

Write your answer here before reading on.

5 Other aspects of the national income

5.1 Why measure the national income?

The national income is measured in order to assist governments with their economic policy making and thus hopefully the attainment of full employment and economic growth. National income statistics can also be used to measure improvements in living standards and for making comparisons between various countries.

For comparisons to be meaningful over a period of time, inflation must be taken into account and national income must be measured in constant (real) prices.

Utopia National Income (£ million)

	Market prices	*Constant prices*
Year 0	4,000	4,000
Year 4	8,000	4,800

The first column illustrates the measurement of national income in market prices. It provides a nominal growth rate of 100% over four years, or 25% per annum. In other words, assuming a constant population and distribution of income, the standard of living has doubled. The second column, which measures the national income in constant or real prices, thus removing the element of inflation, reveals a growth rate of 20% or 5% per annum. This is a more realistic measure of the national income for time comparisons, and is sometimes referred to as the real national income.

For international comparisons, national income is divided by the total population to derive *per capita* income for individual countries. China's GNP is larger than that of Norway but the difference in population size of approximately 1.4 billion and 4 million respectively, results in a higher living standard in Norway.

Even *per capita* income figures have to be treated with a fair degree of caution before any value judgements are made on such statistics. It is necessary to take account of the cost of living in each country – low prices for goods and services in China in comparison to Norway – along with the extent of subsistence agriculture in the economy.

Useful international comparisons must take account of the distribution of income in an economy between the rich and poor, which influences the level of economic welfare. Another factor is the level of expenditure on armaments in each country. International comparisons are complicated by the rates of exchange of the various currencies of the world.

Thus, it is important to understand what the GDP *cannot* tell us. It might tell us that the average citizen of a country is better or worse off in terms of goods and services *per capita* but it does not capture things deemed important to general well-being. For example, increased output may come at the cost of environmental damage, depletion of natural resources or reduced leisure time. So GDP figures must be treated with caution as regards their interpretation.

QUICK QUESTION

How might a country's capital stock influence the national income's size?

Write your answer here before reading on.

5.2 What determines national income size?

As to be expected, the quantity and quality of the four factors of production are important in determining the size and growth rate of a country's national income.

1 **Labour**

The age distribution of the population will determine the size of the available work force; an ageing population might reduce the labour force size. Apart from numbers of workers, consideration must also be given to the education, skills and health of the labour force. The latter play an important part in determining overall labour productivity which greatly influences national income size.

2 **Land**

This cannot be increased to any great extent by man. Climate, water supplies and mineral endowment are gifts of nature or God. The only way in which this factor can contribute to increasing national income is by the better utilisation of existing resources, which generally entails the use of more capital to produce higher returns.

3 **Capital**

More plant and machinery per head generally results in a higher level of output per head in an economy. The best prospects for increasing national income may thus be found in a policy of promoting more capital investment in an economy. Not only is it important to increase the amount of equipment for labour, but it is also necessary to replace existing capital assets fairly rapidly to ensure that workers in all economic sectors are always using the most up-to-date equipment possible.

4 **Enterprise**

Management which uses the most up-to-date techniques of organisation and control should be able to employ combinations of the other three factors in the most productive manner possible. Obviously the use of modern technology by enterprises will tend to accelerate economic growth and add to total output.

QUICK QUESTION

How does inflation complicate GDP measurement?

Write your answer here before reading on.

5.3 Why is national income measurement not precise?

Calculation of the national income statistics for a country is not as precise as an accountancy exercise. The following points, although not exhaustive, provide some indication of the measurement problems associated with national income statistics.

1 **Incomplete information**

Income information relies on completed tax returns which often do not disclose a person's total income. Many people perform services for which they receive a cash payment that is not entered in their tax return. Such income, output and expenditure is excluded from national income statistics.

2 **Unpaid services**

Work performed by people in their own domestic situations is excluded from national income calculations in most countries because no payment of money income takes place. If someone were employed to perform these services and wages paid, this would be included in the national income, as income and output.

3 **Value added**

National output figures must consider only value added at each stage of production. From the gross value of a firm's output must be deducted the cost of inputs acquired from other firms, otherwise double counting could result in a grossly inflated figure for total output.

4 **Estimates**

National income statistics involve the use of estimates for capital consumption, stock valuation and imputed rents for owner-occupied houses. Although such information is not entirely accurate, it does not detract from the overall value of drawing up national income statistics.

5 **Inflation**

The depreciation of money via inflation can artificially boost the resultant national income figure. Unfortunately, no other method of measurement is available for national accounting purposes. The use of real GNP figures enables realistic comparisons to be made over a period of time. Despite these problems, national income accounting is a useful aid in the management of a country's economy.

QUICK QUESTION

What is meant by consumption in economic terms?

Write your answer here before reading on.

6 Influences on the national income

We now need to look a little more closely at the main elements in the national product or income, and try to understand how these are likely to change in response to the influences operating on them.

6.1 Consumption

This is the main objective of all economic activity. There are two main classes of consumption:

- Household consumption, usually known as consumer expenditure, accounts for approximately 70% of total expenditure in most advanced economies. Any small percentage fluctuation in this type of expenditure has important implications for the overall level of economic activity.
- Community consumption (defence, education, etc) is expenditure undertaken by the government and other agencies on behalf of the whole community.

There is a fundamental difference between the two. Government spending is the result of political and administrative decisions. Changes may take place, therefore, for reasons that are not strictly economic, in the sense that they are *not* the result of considerations of cost and the availability of finance. Nevertheless, governments now find increasingly that they have to operate subject to various cost (economic) constraints.

Personal consumption is assumed to be purely economic in nature and responsive to economic pressures. We assume, fairly reasonably, that consumption rises with disposable income, i.e. income left to the consumer after deduction of direct taxes, national insurance and pension contributions. We can also regard certain other regular payments as having a similar effect to tax, such as house mortgage interest payments.

Any change in direct or income tax will change disposable income and thus influence consumption. A reduction in income tax or mortgage interest rates would be expected to increase consumption and *vice versa*. Consumption is thus a function of income.

However, it is important to recognise that other factors also influence consumer intentions. People's spending patterns may depend partly on their expectations of the future. If they expect to be earning more in the future, if there is confidence and a feeling that the economy is expanding, then they are likely to be prepared to spend more now, perhaps with the help of consumer credit. They are not afraid to commit future income to instalment payments. On the other hand, if consumers are fearful about the future and expect an economic recession or overtime income to be cut, then they may reduce present consumption and seek to save more for the uncertain future.

Price expectations can also influence consumption – a rise encourages spending now, whereas an expected price fall will lead to the postponement of major spending decisions, such as car purchase or new furniture.

6.2 Saving

Saving is income not consumed. It is a residual which is influenced and determined by consumption decisions – out of a given level of income, if people consume less, then savings increase. Alternatively, if incomes increase, then in most circumstances so also will savings. Savings, like consumption, are a function of income, as are imports and tax revenues. Higher incomes encourage the consumption of more foreign goods, while for the government, as incomes and spending rise, more tax is collected.

Marginal propensity to consume (or save)

The marginal propensity to consume is that proportion of any change in disposable income that will be spent on consumption of goods and services. When we think in terms of disposable (after-tax) income, we see that any disposable income not consumed must then be saved. Thus, the marginal propensity to consume (mpc) *plus* the marginal propensity to save (mps) is equal to one or unity, i.e. equal to the change in disposable income.

6.3 Injections into national income

We have so far concluded that consumption is a function of the level of income. However, three important injections – investment, government expenditure, exports – into the circular flow are subject to separate considerations and thus initially may not change in response to domestic income level changes.

Investment expenditure is influenced by a range of factors such as utilisation of existing productive capacity, expected future levels of demand, new technology and the availability/cost of finance. Business firms do not alter investment decisions directly in response to income changes. Investment in short term economic models is not regarded as a function of income.

Government expenditure depends on political decisions and thus in the short run is not directly related to the level of income, while exports are a function of income levels in other countries.

QUESTION TIME 7

National income can be measured by three methods. Explain each method and some of the problems of measurement.

Write your answer here then check with the answer at the back of the book.

7 Equilibrium level of national income

We can now say that aggregate demand in an economy is determined by:

- Consumption (C)
- Investment (I)
- Government expenditure (G)
- *Plus* exports (X) *minus* imports (M)

It is assumed that investment and government expenditure offset saving and taxation. As we saw in the circular flow of income, total aggregate demand (expenditure) will equal total national income or output in an economy.

AGGREGATE DEMAND = C + I + G + (X – M) = NATIONAL INCOME

Given the above, if there is free movement of the factors of production and some are underutilised in the economy, what will happen if government expenditure increases without a corresponding increase in taxation?

Assuming such expenditure is used to pay for goods and services, it becomes income for firms and their employees. This will increase the general level of income in an economy; national income will be at a new higher equilibrium level, assuming other injections and leakages remain constant.

There is likely to be a natural balance between the levels of saving and investment, as defined for purposes of national income calculation. If saving is greater than investment, given that the other injections and withdrawals are in balance, then people are not consuming all the goods and services available for consumption. The immediate effect is for stocks (inventories) of goods to rise, bringing total investment (which includes stocks) back into balance with saving.

However, firms will not continue to produce stocks that are difficult to sell, so they will cut back production. This will involve both a reduction in real productive investment and a reduction in income. As the income level falls, actual saving will be reduced, thus restoring equality between saving and investment, but this relationship only holds when other injections and leakages balance and there is free movement of the factors of production.

QUICK QUESTION

Consumption 50; Exports 10; Investment 15; Imports 20; Government Expenditure 25. Calculate total aggregate demand, i.e. national income.

Write your answer here before reading on.

QUESTION TIME 8

How might national income statistics be misleading as an indicator of living standards?

Write your answer here then check with the answer at the back of the book.

8 The multiplier

Any increase in government spending will result in a more than proportionate change in national income. This is because there is a multiplying effect created when any given amount of new spending power enters into an economy. If the government spends money on a building contract, contractors and their employees will receive additional income. Most will be spent in the form of consumer expenditure and will then become someone else's extra income, and so on.

Thus, if there is unemployment, an increase in government expenditure (or investment or exports) will lead to more people being employed. Increased expenditure will have not only primary effects on employment and expenditure but also secondary effects. However, the multiplying effect will not continue indefinitely, as leakages – savings, taxation, imports – will reduce each successive additional income round.

The way in which an initial increase in expenditure is magnified as it is dispersed through the economic system can be measured by the multiplier. The employment multiplier, for example, is the ratio of the increment of total employment which is associated with a given increment of primary employment in the economy. Thus, if increased government expenditure on the nation's infrastructure generated 250,000 jobs in the building and road construction industries which in turn increased total employment by 750,000, this would imply a value of three for the employment multiplier.

One of Britain's most influential economists in the inter-war period, John Maynard Keynes, produced a formula in 1936 for the measurement of the income multiplier:

$$\text{Income multiplier (k)} = \frac{\Delta I}{1 - c}$$

where c = marginal propensity to consume

ΔI = increase in investment

It follows that the larger the marginal propensity to consume (i.e. the greater the proportion of an increment of income which people are likely to spend), the greater the multiplier will be in an economy. Alternatively, a high propensity to save reduces the multiplier effect on income (and employment).

CASE STUDY

Assume an increase in investment in Utopia of £100 million. The marginal propensity to consume is 9/10. No other leakages or injections take place in the economy.

Key to symbols

I = Investment (real capital formation in the economy)
Y = National income
C = Consumption; c = marginal propensity to consume
S = Saving; s = marginal propensity to save
⦚ = Continuation of calculation
Δ = Increase (e.g. ΔI = increased investment)

Arithmetic method

Increased investment of £100m will increase national income by £100m. Of the latter, $^{9}/_{10}$ will be spent on consumption – £90m – and $^{1}/_{10}$ – £10m – will be saved. The spending generates £90m of income of which $^{9}/_{10}$ – £81m – is spent and $^{1}/_{10}$ – £9m – is saved, and so on.

Y	=	C	+	S
I = 100	=	90	+	10
90	=	81	+	9
81	=	73	+	8
	=		+	
⦚		⦚		⦚
1,000	=	900	+	100

Results: National income rises by £1,000m as a result of the £100m investment. Savings increase by £100m which is equal to the initial investment. Income generation brings saving and investment into equilibrium.

Mathematical method

$$\Delta Y = \frac{\Delta I}{(1-c)}$$

$$\Delta Y = \frac{\Delta I}{s}$$

i.e. $$\Delta Y = \frac{100}{\left(1-\frac{9}{10}\right)} = \frac{100}{\left(\frac{1}{10}\right)} = \frac{100\times10}{1}$$

therefore ΔY = 1,000m

The multiplier in this case study has a value of 10, i.e. $\frac{1}{\frac{1}{10}}$

Provided that resources are unemployed in the economy, the rise in investment will generate employment. If the economy is near full employment, then an increase in investment will result in demand pull inflation which will stimulate a wage price spiral. However, Keynes, in his book *The General Theory of Employment, Interest and Money* (1936) was interested in the economic problems of a depressed economy in the 1930s, when prices were stable or declining – a state of deflation – together with high unemployment. Note that a rise in government expenditure, or consumption as the result of a tax cut, or increased exports of £100 million rather than increased investment in Utopia would have exactly the same effect on income, consumption and saving.

QUICK QUESTION

Marginal propensity to save (mps) = 1/5; increased government spending = £50 mil. Calculate the increase in Utopia's national income.

Write your answer here before reading on.

9 Is the multiplier dynamic?

Even Keynes admitted that the multiplier might not be as dynamic as was believed at first sight. A series of lags exist in an economy. A consumption lag might exist; as extra income generated might not result in an immediate increase in consumption, it might be saved or used to pay off past debts. An investment lag might exist between planned investment and the actual expenditure in the economy. Finally, increased consumption might be satisfied initially from existing excess inventories accumulated during a recession, thus an output lag might exist.

As shown, some of the extra income generated at each round in the multiplier process is lost to savings, which prevents the income generation process continuing forever. In addition, some of the income generated will be spent on imports and this will become income in foreign countries. A high propensity of import will therefore reduce the overall size of the multiplier.

Another leakage is direct and indirect taxation which also siphons off some of the increased income. Higher personal income means greater tax liability and thus higher tax deductions. Also, most luxury and semi-luxury goods are subject to VAT or customs/excise duty. Although this increases government tax revenue which could cover some of the initial expenditure from this source (public works), it does of necessity reduce the size of the multiplier. This is sometimes referred to as fiscal drag.

CASE STUDY

Assume an increase in investment in Utopia of £100m. The marginal propensity to save (mps) is $^1/_{10}$, the marginal propensity to import (mpm) is $^3/_{10}$, the marginal propensity to tax (mpt) is $^1/_{10}$. The final equation for the multiplier is:

$$\Delta Y = \frac{\Delta I}{\text{mps} + \text{mpm} + \text{mpt}}$$

$$= \frac{\Delta I}{\frac{1}{10} + \frac{3}{10} + \frac{1}{10}}$$

$$= \frac{100}{5/10}$$

= £200m

The multiplier has a value of 2 in this case study, which makes it a less dynamic element in the workings of an economy. Obviously alterations in the values of the above propensities will change the value of the multiplier.

This more conservative estimate of the multiplier's size means that a huge increase in government expenditure might be needed in an economy to solve unemployment. In most cases this is not possible due to budgetary constraints, worries over the size of the national debt and possible inflation, together with an increase in imports, which might have a negative impact on economic activity and employment.

QUICK QUESTION

What factors may influence the level of investment in an economy?

Write your answer here before reading on.

10 Investment

As we have seen, additional investment (capital expenditure) in an economy via the multiplier process can generate increased income and employment. It is therefore important for a government to try and ascertain those factors which influence the level of investment in an economy.

Traditional economics states that interest rates, i.e. cost of borrowed funds, is the main determinant of investment, so that if the government wants to raise the level of economic activity (cut unemployment) it might lower interest rates to cut the cost of borrowing for firms, which are then expected to increase investment. In the opposite situation, if the government wishes to reduce inflation, it might increase interest rates.

Some studies have indicated that the influence of interest rates is rather limited, especially where firms have adequate internal funds from accumulated profits. This does not mean that interest rates are unimportant in investment decisions, but it is thought that expectations of businesses about potential returns from an investment are the key factor.

Firms or entrepreneurs base investment decisions on their feeling about economic prospects. These can be influenced by the prevailing level of interest rates in an economy. In modern economics the question as to what induces businesses to invest is far from settled. We have only rather vague references to the 'state of expectations of firms'. At the present time this is as precise as we can be.

Keynes stated that a firm will only invest if the marginal efficiency of investment (MEI), i.e. the expected yield on a piece of machinery etc, exceeds the current rate of interest. Otherwise, the investment will not proceed unless it is vital to the firm's continuing operations. If investment is to be increased, it will take place either through a reduction in the rate of interest or through an increase in the marginal efficiency of investment.

10.1 Investment accelerator

In our analysis of the multiplier we assumed there was no direct link between consumption and investment. Consumption and savings decisions were made by households while investment decisions were made by business firms. However, if we assume that firms exist to satisfy consumer demand, then there must be a link between consumption and investment: it lies in the expectations of firms about future consumer demand.

In the first case study, increased investment resulted in a rise in national income and consumption. As firms endeavour to satisfy consumer wants, more investment will be undertaken to increase productive capacity. This in itself will result in a further rise in national income. In other words, investment may not be completely autonomous of changes in the level of income.

However, the process can also operate in the reverse direction. The accelerator can be a decelerator. Suppose firms feel that consumer spending is likely to remain at its current level; they can produce for this demand level without investment, so the level of investment falls.

The reduction in new investment reduces the real equilibrium level of national income, thereby producing a decline consumption which could lead to a further fall in investment as firms implement planned cut-backs in productive capacity. If unchecked, all this can lead to further falls in investment, consumption and income, with resultant high unemployment.

In light of the above, we can appreciate the importance that some economists and politicians give to the level of government spending. If investment is indirectly the result of consumer spending and anticipated future spending, and if exporting is a result of changes outside the economy, then the one part of the total injection mechanism that the government can influence is its own spending. This is not only an important part of the total injection and national-income-increasing process in itself, it also has a psychological impact on business.

The knowledge that government spending is being increased and will have a future multiplying effect on income and consumer demand may build up precisely that expectation of future demand expansion that will persuade firms to increase investment and so further strengthen the tendency for income levels to rise.

Q QUESTION TIME 9

(a) Explain what is meant by the multiplier in national income analysis.
(b) Why is the multiplier concept important in economic analysis?
(c) What is the investment accelerator?

Write your answer here then check with the answer at the back of the book.

KEY WORDS

Key words in this chapter are given below. There is space to write your own revision notes and to add any other words or phrases that you want to remember.

- Leakages
- Injections
- National income
- Equilibrium
- Gross domestic product
- Gross national product
- Net national product
- Real national income
- Per capita income
- Consumer expenditure
- Marginal propensity to consume/save
- Aggregate demand
- Demand pull inflation
- Deflation
- Marginal efficiency of investment
- Multiplier
- Accelerator

REVIEW

The main learning points introduced in this chapter are summarised below.

Go through them and check back to the learning outcomes at the beginning of the chapter. Only move on when you are happy that you fully understand each point.

- We have examined the circular flow of income in a national economy.
- We considered injections and leakages associated with this circular flow along with the concept of national income equilibrium.
- National income measurement techniques were reviewed along with the potential uses of such data; those factors determining the size and growth of national income and the limitations associated with such statistics were also considered.
- Aggregate demand and its components were explained, along with how any change in a component via the multiplier and accelerator effect can influence the level of economic activity and employment in an economy.

In summary, we looked at:

- The circular flow of income
- National income concepts, measurements and uses
- Aggregate demand and the impact of injections and leakages
- The employment and income multiplier
- The determinants of investment in an economy and the accelerator concept

chapter 3

ECONOMIC TRENDS AND MANAGEMENT POLICIES

Contents

Learning outcomes

On completion of this chapter, you should be able to:

- Analyse the concept of full employment and types of unemployment along with trade cycles and why output fluctuates in economies over time
- Critically evaluate UK economic management and the adoption of Keynesian, monetarist and supply-side policies along with the current economic environment

Introduction

In the previous chapter we examined various national income concepts including some of the factors underlying long term economic growth. Now we have to consider the dynamics of the national income and try to explain how changes in national income and output take place over time – booms and recessions.

We shall look at the various types of unemployment that can arise in a market economy, demand-deficiency unemployment being the most serious type. We'll then examine the business cycle and the various theories expounded to explain this phenomenon of the market economy.

We conclude by considering the concept of full employment in a free society and how demand management policies were used for over 30 years to secure this objective, although less successfully with the passage of time. Their subsequent replacement by monetarist/supply-side policies is reviewed, together with the implementation of current economic policies.

We will consider some key theories in relation to management of the national economy:

- Full employment in an economy
- Unemployment – causes and remedies
- Trade or business cycle theories
- Economic philosophies on how to manage an economy
- Economic management at present

1 Full employment level of national income

So far we have assumed that factors of production enter and exit the production process freely and we have ignored factor limitation or unemployment, so we will now have to modify those assumptions as regards the real economy or national income.

It was once believed that the natural equilibrium of national income would be at a level where all factors desiring employment were fully employed. It was thought that pressure to obtain work would produce a competitive market for labour (and land and capital), so that a full employment equilibrium could be achieved by adjustments in wages and prices.

If there was unemployment, then this was likely to be caused by the refusal of workers to take wage reductions, or firms creating uncompetitive market conditions via price fixing or oligopolies. Unemployment was seen as a market imperfection which necessitated government action to ensure that normal market forces were working as freely as possible.

Some economists, particularly in the 1930s, pointed out that there is no practical reason why an equilibrium level of national income should equate with a condition of full employment in an economy. Total aggregate demand (C + I + G + X – M) could be less than potential output and a deflationary gap could exist – some factors would be unemployed.

Now think of this situation in the light of our earlier reasoning concerning the multiplier and the investment accelerator or decelerator. There is no automatic mechanism that can lift an economy out of a recession caused by the public's unwillingness to consume up to the level required to meet the conditions for full employment. If people try to save more in order to protect themselves from the consequences of a recession and out of fear of possible unemployment, the position will get worse. This is sometimes referred to as the paradox of thrift.

Here we can see the importance of government expenditure as a potential means of closing a deflationary gap. If the government knows the value of the multiplier and can estimate the amount of additional income likely to reduce unemployment to an acceptable level, then it can also work out the amount of injection spending it must create to close any deflationary gap in order to avoid the economic and social consequences of prolonged unemployment.

The reverse possibility is that aggregate demand might exceed potential supply in an economy and an inflationary gap might exist where there will be full employment of all the factors of production. An inflationary gap can result in postponed spending due to shortages, a diversion of spending on imports or a rise in prices of goods and services in the economy. The latter is the most likely outcome, as excess demand results in higher money prices and incomes.

Excess demand, which may be the result of excessive consumption, investment, government spending or exports, invariably results in cost push inflation. This is when incomes begin to rise in order to offset higher prices and thereby create an inflationary spiral. Once such a situation has arisen, a government will curtail its own planned expenditure and that of consumers by increasing taxation. Consumer expenditure might be further compressed by higher interest rates and tighter credit market conditions.

Government expenditure (or taxation) is viewed by some politicians and economists as a means to offset fluctuations in private sector demand. If consumer spending and business investment are at a high level which results in an inflationary gap, government expenditure should be reduced to ease pressure on the economy. A deflationary gap should prompt higher government expenditure.

In practice, government attempts to manage or fine-tune the economy have encountered a number of problems which will be considered later in this chapter, but next we'll review unemployment and the trade cycle.

QUICK QUESTION

Give one example of a cause of unemployment.

Write your answer here before reading on.

2 Unemployment

There are various types of unemployment, with different causes and possible cures.

2.1 Residual unemployment

The residual unemployed are all those people who, on account of physical or mental disability, are unable to find employment. The government provides them with social security benefits and may also set up various initiatives to provide them with employment.

Another type of residual unemployment arises where some members of society refuse to work and are content to live on unemployment/social security benefits for an indefinite time period. In recent years, governments have attempted to reduce this type of voluntary unemployment by withdrawing or reducing some state benefits. This has only been partially successful as such people make themselves unemployable either by appearance or attitude, while the state is reluctant to make any of its citizens completely destitute. One solution might be to link community work for state benefits.

2.2 Seasonal unemployment

This form of unemployment arises because of climatic conditions which reduce the demand for labour in certain industries, such as agriculture, fishing, tourism and construction. This type of unemployment accounts for only a small proportion of total unemployment and can be partially cured by, for example, extending the tourist season, using new techniques in construction work and banks providing working capital loans to assist with seasonal cash flows.

2.3 Frictional unemployment

This arises from the bankruptcy or liquidation of private firms which is part of the dynamic process of the market system. It refers to the temporary unemployment people may experience when changing jobs. If there is a break between the end of one job and the start of another, a person may register as unemployed in order to receive unemployment benefit. If people are moving from work where they are not required to work where they are, frictional unemployment may be considered a sign of a dynamic economy and an indication of increasing efficiency.

Frictional unemployment may be reduced by shortening the time people spend searching for work. This is often a matter of improving the flow of information through job centres and the media, plus government grants to improve the geographical and occupational mobility of labour.

QUICK QUESTION

What impact have Asian imports had on the UK textile industry?

Write your answer here before reading on.

2.4 Structural unemployment

Structural unemployment is a much more serious form of unemployment and is the result of long term changes in the economy's structure. There are three main underlying causes.

1 A reduction in demand owing to changes in consumer tastes or the success of a rival product or service, e.g. coal/oil, cotton textiles/artificial fibres.

2 A technological development resulting in a reduced demand for certain forms of labour, e.g. in agriculture, steel, heavy engineering – technological unemployment (same or more output with fewer workers).

3 Foreign competition resulting in cheaper or better quality goods being offered on the domestic market.

This type of unemployment is made worse if the declining industries are concentrated in certain regions of the country. The west of Scotland around Glasgow experienced a rapid decline of coal mining, shipbuilding and steel production, thereby creating a regional unemployment problem.

Over the years successive governments have tried to introduce new industry and service activities into depressed regions. For example, UK banks such as Santander have opened customer call centres in the north of England. This has been done via UK and EU grants, tax allowances and improvements in the social/economic infrastructure. Despite such regional aid, considerable variations in unemployment rates still exist between the various regions of the UK. Regional decline or stagnation remains a major problem in the UK economy. For Scottish-based banks it encouraged an acquisition/expansion strategy to broaden and diversify their customer base to England and overseas.

2.5 Demand-deficiency or cyclical unemployment

This type of unemployment is associated with the trade or business cycle in a market economy. During a recession, the general deficiency in demand affects nearly all industries. It is the most serious type of unemployment and if it persists for a prolonged period of time it can cause extreme social and economic distress. At the depth of the Great Depression in 1932, registered unemployment in the USA and UK reached approximately 25% and 20% respectively of the then available workforce. It is this type of unemployment that Keynesian demand management policies sought to avert in the British and other advanced economies in the post-1945 era.

QUESTION TIME 10

Using text information and media reports, briefly describe the main types of unemployment in your own UK region and how they may be remedied.

Write your answer here then check with the answer at the back of the book.

3 Trade or business cycle

The capitalist or market economy system is basically unstable and fluctuates between periods of high economic growth/full employment and low (nil) economic growth/high unemployment. This trend has been evident in all industrialised economies since the 19th century. The Great Depression in the 1930s was the most severe economic downturn yet experienced in global economic activity (although it could be argued that current global economic conditions are rivalling that period).

It was the resolution of the economic and social distress caused by the trade cycle that led to the use of demand management policies in many economies and the establishment of international institutions, such as the International Monetary Fund, in the post-1945 period. However, economies have continued to experience recessions which in recent times have become more severe, thus providing evidence of the continuing existence of the trade cycle. Demand management or supply-side economic policies have apparently only moderated swings in economic activity.

QUICK QUESTION

During a recession, most asset prices ... ?; unemployment ...?; economic growth ...?; and tax revenues ...?

Write your answer here before reading on.

3.1 Trade or business cycle phases

The business cycle is typified by peaks and troughs in economic activity. Although not all cycles are of the same length or range of fluctuations, there are generally four phases.

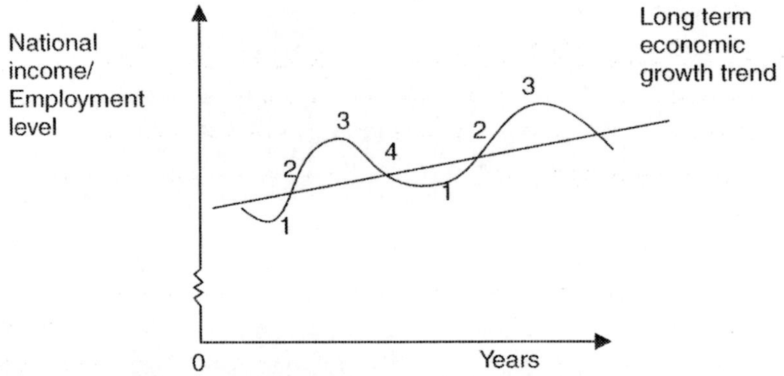

1 **Slump**

This is typified by high unemployment and a lack of investment in an economy. Firms will be disposing of excess inventories and will not be replacing depreciated machinery. In extreme cases, a slump may result in nominal wages and prices declining. The price of houses, land and most assets declines.

Output and employment fluctuations tend to be most severe in the capital goods industries, such as steel/engineering and construction, due to a collapse in investment in new productive capacity.

In recent times, minor slumps are sometimes referred to as a recession. Such an event was experienced in the UK in the early 1990s due to a collapse in the housing market. The banking/financial crisis in 2008 also created a recession and a fall in house prices. Some East Asian economies felt the onset of a severe recession in 1997-98 which was triggered by excessive budget deficits, collapsing currency and bank solvency problems. Similar problems in the Eurozone in 2010-12 reduced economic growth and prolonged an already existing recession in Europe.

During this business cycle phase, banks experience increased loan losses, reduced profits and perhaps an erosion of their capital base. This can make banks more reluctant to lend to cash-strapped customers. There is also a reduction in the number of viable loan propositions available to banks due to the reduced level of economic activity.

2 **Recovery**

An upturn in economic activity could arise due to a number of factors:

- Demographic and social factors increasing housing demands
- Government spending programmes on defence, roads, schools etc, and/or the provision of cheap money, i.e. low interest rate policy or more money via quantitative easing, i.e. open market operations
- Recovery in business confidence which leads on to higher investment in plant and machinery; this might come about due to lower interest rates, improved profits or the need to replace worn-out equipment. Such investment via the multiplier and accelerator generates increases in national income, employment and wages
- Government actions to encourage more enterprise via tax breaks, less regulation and state-guaranteed bank loans to businesses

3 **Boom**

The economy reaches full capacity, output and employment are at a maximum and increased demand results in higher prices, which stimulates demand for higher wages, although this might be tempered by foreign worker immigration. Profits may come under pressure. Due to resultant inflation, interest rates rise and business confidence might decline in the expectation of an economic crisis. The accelerator effect 'peters out' owing to production (and income) being at a maximum.

4 **Recession**

Falling income and expectations results in investment being curtailed, which causes redundancies in the capital goods/construction industries. The multiplier and accelerator are working in a perverse manner and speed the economy towards a slump.

The official definition of a recession in the UK is two consecutive quarters of a year of declining GDP.

It might be the case that each boom carries the seeds of a slump (or recession). Sometimes bankers and politicians have tended to ignore the business cycle phenomenon in a market economy, with resultant large loan losses and huge budget deficits. Gordon Brown, who was Chancellor of the Exchequer (1997-2007), used to state at regular intervals that his economic management had ended the boom – bust cycle!

4 Trade cycle theories

A number of theories have been put forward over the years to explain business cycles in market economies. A summary of some of the main ones follows.

4.1 Psychological theories

Insofar as economic behaviour is a facet of human behaviour, it must have certain psychological mainsprings. Economic theory admits as much, since it postulates expected human reactions to given conditions. It is possible for a country to talk itself into a deep recession or to indulge itself in the belief that the good times will last forever.

With regard to the psychological explanation of trade cycles, investment decision makers are said to be influenced by waves of confidence in future prospects, or by waves of loss of confidence. After a slump/recession has continued for a while, they begin to assume that things must get better and start to invest in plant and machinery; or, when a boom has run its course, they start to feel that it must soon end and prefer to postpone investment decisions.

Business confidence in future prospects is certainly a vital psychological factor in the complex pattern of causes behind the trade cycle. Confidence is affected by objective phenomena such as developments in international markets, energy prices, government fiscal and monetary policies and by technological breakthroughs such as computers or digital television systems.

4.2 Investment theories

These theories relate to the irregularities in the flow of orders for capital goods on account of their durability and the fact that other producers must encounter or anticipate a demand at a certain level for their products before they invest in capital goods to meet it. Temporary increases in the flow of orders for capital goods upset the rhythm of production and create a long term distortion in the flow of work.

It is for these reasons that capital goods and construction industries tend to feel the worst effects of fluctuations in trade. The acceleration principle shows that changes in the demand for consumer goods bring about wider fluctuations in the production of capital goods required by the consumer industries.

Sometimes too much investment can take place in an economy or sectors of it which, via diminishing returns, tends to depress profits and undermine business confidence. There is ample evidence of this occurrence in the UK residential and commercial property sector over the decades. This has often been aided by the lax lending practices of banks and other financial institutions.

4.3 Monetary theories

Money supply growth can influence the level of economic activity. The increased availability of credit does influence purchasing power and effective demand for goods and services. In the mid-2000s a rapid expansion of money supply in the UK economy resulted in an economic boom and real asset appreciation, i.e. a sharp rise in house and share prices.

Closely related to money supply, interest rates have been a determining factor in trade cycles. When interest rates are high, retailers and wholesalers run down their stocks, thereby discouraging output. Entrepreneurs as a whole, it is suggested, calculate the future rate of yield on a new investment, from which they deduct the rate of interest paid for the financing of the investment. Unless the yield appears to be appreciably higher than the cost of servicing any necessary loan, a decision to invest will not be made.

High interest rates in the early 1990s to reduce inflation undoubtedly triggered the deep recession experienced by the UK in 1991-92. The subsequent decline in interest rates post-1992 helped economic recovery. In 2008 the Bank of England reduced its discount rate to 0.5% in order to stimulate the economy, support the housing market and reduce funding costs for banks during the recession.

5 Full employment in a free society

In 1944 the government published a paper on *Full Employment in a Free Society* as part of its proposed post-war economic and social policies. This did not envisage that every member of the workforce would be fully employed all the time; seasonal, frictional and structural unemployment would still occur, but cyclical or mass unemployment could be almost wholly eliminated.

The paper's author, Lord Beveridge, laid down the following conditions for the maintenance of full employment, i.e. approximately 97% of the then available workforce:

- Maintenance of a high level of aggregate demand by government fiscal/monetary policy
- Controlled location of industry to help regions afflicted by declining industries
- Improved geographical/occupational mobility of labour
- A responsible attitude by workers and trade unions to prevent inflationary wage awards
- Favourable global economic conditions to be achieved via international institutions and free trade

Full employment was a basic policy objective of all UK governments between 1945 and 1976. Its abandonment by a Labour government after 1976 was in part due to large budget deficits, high inflation, a changing domestic/international environment and a revival of pre-Keynesian economic philosophy.

Q QUESTION TIME 11

(a) Describe the principal features of the trade cycle.
(b) Critically comment on any two explanations for the business cycle in market economies.

Write your answer here then check with the answer at the back of the book.

6 Managing the UK economy: 1945-1979

6.1 Economic philosophy

Until the 1930s it was accepted that the state had to balance its budget, i.e. government expenditure = tax revenues. In the depressed inter-war years, this policy meant that, although the government, for political and social reasons, might have wanted to relieve unemployment and social distress, for example by increasing expenditure on road building, its adherence to conventional economics prevented such action. It was believed that if a country did not balance its books, national bankruptcy would quickly follow – a belief re-invoked by the government in 2010 due to a huge budget deficit and rising national debt.

The essential message of the Keynesian revolution (demand management principles) was that the budget need not be balanced each year; instead the government should attempt to 'fine-tune' the economy. A government's first priority was not to balance its own books but to ensure that aggregate demand was at a high enough level to attain full employment in the economy.

6.2 Economic policy

During the 1950s and 1960s, the Keynesian view prevailed on how the economy works: by manipulating the total amount of spending in the country it was possible to smooth out the business cycle in the economy and keep it on a path of steady growth. By fine-tuning the economy and managing the overall level of demand, it was possible to strike a balance between unemployment and inflation. Keynesians considered fiscal policy – changes in government spending and taxation – as the most effective way of influencing the level of aggregate demand. Monetary policy was regarded as a secondary weapon, with the main emphasis being to keep interest rates as low as possible in order to provide cheap finance for industrial investment and housing.

6.3 Economic outcome

Keynesian demand management seemed to work well during the 1950s and 1960s and was supported by all major political parties in Britain. Unemployment averaged less than 2% compared with 13% during the 1920s and 1930s. Inflation was higher at about 4% per annum, whereas there had been a slight fall in prices between the wars. Growth at 2.8% per annum was slightly higher than before the war.

During the era of fine-tuning the economy, UK banks increased their domestic operations via an expanded branch network and new products, such as personal loans. With full employment and rising incomes, bank loan risk was reduced and the banks increased their balance sheet size without the need for additional shareholder funds. The subsequent reduction in capital-asset ratios from approximately 10% to 2% enabled banks to pay larger dividends to their ordinary shareholders. As a result, bank shares were regarded as being relatively risk free, with good dividend prospects, and therefore were included in most investment portfolios.

One problem was the balance of payments current account. If the UK economy, which had a fixed exchange rate pre-1972, expanded too rapidly, domestic supply constraints and higher inflation resulted in extra imports which led to a current account deficit, i.e. imports greater than exports, and nearly always a sterling exchange rate crisis.

In such a situation, the government had to deflate the economy – reduce the level of demand – usually by decreasing its own spending where it could, and increasing taxes. This would reduce imports and check inflation; unfortunately it also reduced employment and held back economic growth. When it was felt the balance of payments was under control, or unemployment was too high, the government would reverse the process and reflate the economy.

6.4 Stagflation

In the 1970s, Keynesian demand management policies fell into disrepute as both inflation and unemployment rates increased while output stagnated – thus the term 'stagflation'. In partial defence of fine-tuning policies, higher energy prices, volatile exchange rates and the globalisation of trade/capital flows reduced the effectiveness of demand management policies in the UK economy.

Not with standing these external factors, Keynesian demand management was widely criticised on a number of points:

- The economy had suffered from the stop-go cycle; a suspicion existed that economic policies had been destabilising due to poor economic forecasting and had accentuated the business cycle.
- The public sector's size as a proportion of the GDP increased throughout the period 1945-1976; reflationary injections of government expenditure during recessions increased public sector employment and the national debt.
- This enlarged public sector necessitated increased taxation and borrowing which acted as a disincentive and raised the cost of capital for privately-owned industry.

For the above reasons and others, Keynesian demand management policies were abandoned in the late 1970s in the UK and in most other countries.

It is interesting to note that the UK's first post-war banking crisis occurred in 1973-74. A number of small banks based in London had lent heavily to the commercial property sector via the use of wholesale funds obtained from the London money markets. A recession resulted in a collapse of commercial property prices and rents which impacted on these banks. Wholesale funding dried up and these banks had to be bailed out by the Bank of England which provided liquidity support. This became known as the secondary banking crisis. Some of the banks were liquidated, others merged and some were partially nationalised via Bank of England ownership. From an historical perspective, this crisis was a forerunner of the UK banking crisis in 2007-09.

QUICK QUESTION

What is a balanced budget?

Write your answer here before reading on.

7 Monetarism

This is a catch-all phrase which describes a return to traditional economic philosophy as regards macroeconomic policy. Monetarists believed that demand management had failed and instead recommended a balanced budget, supply-side measures to stimulate employment and specific targets for money supply growth in the economy. If the government could keep to its targets, then people would expect lower inflation and reduce their demands for higher wages.

Monetarists accept that the economy does not automatically achieve full employment but believe there is a natural rate of unemployment of, say 6%, at which it settles. The monetarist view is that, in the long run, boosting aggregate demand cannot reduce unemployment below its natural rate. Attempts to do so may have temporary success but lead to permanently higher prices and no long term decline in unemployment. This viewpoint, which became popular in the 1980s and 1990s, seriously undermined the case for Keynesian demand management.

8 Supply-side policies

Monetarists believe that the way to reduce the natural rate of unemployment, to say 3%, is to influence the supply side of the economy. Policies monetarists favour include:

- **Income tax cuts**

  It is argued that high rates of income tax are a disincentive to work, saving and enterprise. If income tax rates are cut, people are more willing to work and are likely to make a greater effort.

- **Improving the labour supply**

  Improved training should increase the productivity of workers and make them more attractive to employers. People should be given financial assistance to move out of declining occupations into those where opportunities are expanding.

- **Reducing the power of trade unions**

  If trade unions are strong, they may be able to push wage levels above the market clearing level. By limiting the powers of trade unions, it is argued that this cause of unemployment could be reduced.

- **Reducing benefits**

  If the real value of unemployment benefits is kept low, there is greater incentive to seek work.

- **Increasing demand for labour**

  If industry is made generally more efficient and able to produce the goods and services people want to buy, then as the demand for British products increases, so too does the demand for workers.

9 Economic policy in practice: post-1979 to the present

Conservative governments (1979 - 1997) attempted to put monetarist/supply-side ideas into practice. The standard rate of income tax was reduced, workers and employers were free to negotiate their own wage/salary agreements, trade union powers were reduced through changes in trade union law and, as part of the attempt to reduce the role of government, major state-owned industries such as gas, water, electricity and telecommunications were privatised.

However, the government's principal economic aim was to control inflation through an active interest rate policy while at the same time seeking to reduce the government borrowing requirement, i.e. the balanced budget concept. Thus, fiscal policy – government spending and taxation – was used to support monetary policy. This contrasts with the Keynesian approach whereby monetary policy in the form of low interest rates was secondary to fiscal policy.

Labour governments (1997-2010) did not fundamentally alter economic policy. There was no return to Keynesian demand management policies. Instead, the Bank of England was made solely responsible for interest rate policy and achieving of an inflation target of around 2% per annum in the UK economy. The Labour government continued to pursue a wide range of supply-side policies, excepting the privatisation of remaining state assets and services.

The period 1997-2008 witnessed a revolution in the UK banking and financial services industry. A number of mergers created larger banks, such as RBS absorbing NWB and the creation of HBOS, with the former also expanding its presence in the USA. Barriers between financial services providers continued to be dismantled, thereby encouraging increased competition and more financial products. The main UK banks actively participated in the securitisation and globalisation of the world's financial markets. Most became more reliant on wholesale markets to fund their ever-increasing balance sheet size and, unbeknown to most, to invest heavily in riskier assets, such as sub-prime debt. Derivative markets were used to shift risk, but many banks failed to realise such actions did not eliminate risk from the financial markets upon which banks were becoming more dependent in terms of their assets and liabilities.

Initially the government had a budget surplus up to 2001 and was able to reduce the national debt. However, from 2001-02 a budget deficit re-emerged and government borrowing increased. Thereafter, increased public expenditure plans were based on anticipated increases in tax revenues from banks and the financial services industry (the City). In 2008-09 a banking/financial crisis resulted in a fall in tax revenues and increased expenditure as the economy experienced a deep recession. Budget deficits increased at an alarming rate, along with the national debt. To deal with the deficit/debt problem the Labour government increased taxation and attempted to cut public spending programmes. Little attempt was made to fine-tune the recession-hit economy as government concerns were centred on the size of the national debt and the UK's credit rating.

The election of a new Conservative-Liberal Democrat coalition government in mid-2010 resulted in an austerity budget with increased value added tax (VAT) at 20% and substantial planned cuts in public expenditure from 2012 onwards. It must be stated that this is a tough economic policy to pursue in a recessionary environment. The government hopes various supply-side measures will assist the private sector to bring about economic recovery in the UK.

10 UK economic environment

In September 2013, total UK unemployment was 2.47 million, or 7.6% of the workforce. This is the lowest level of unemployment in three years. The fall in unemployment has been attributed to stronger than expected economic growth, which is expected to continue in 2014 . The UK economy is expected to grow by 2.4% in 2014 and 2.4% in 2015. Unemployment is forecast to fall below 7% in 2014. However, unemployment below 7% is the level where the Bank of England has stated it will consider rising interest rates, which could potentially hinder the economic recovery.

Despite the recovery in economic growth, the UK still has an astonishing National Debt of £1,211 billion (75.9% of GDP). Solving the UK's national debt problem is going to take longer than anyone expected because the credit boom up to 2007 was bigger than first realised and the 'bust' is going to be deeper. The only positive feature is that inflation is relatively low and was reported as 2.2% in October 2013.

10.1 Current developments

It is essential that you remain up to date as regards economic developments in the UK and the global economy as the consequences for banks and the financial system are major.

You should read on a regular basis the business pages of quality newspapers such as the Financial Times, The Times, The Scotsman, The Herald, The Independent and journals/magazines such as The Bank of England Quarterly Bulletin, The Economist and Chartered Banker. Television, radio and numerous internet sources also provide valuable information on current economic, financial and banking developments.

QUESTION TIME 12

(a) Contrast the economic philosophy of a balanced budget with a demand management budget.

(b) Critically evaluate the last 10 years of UK government economic management.

Write your answer here then check with the answer at the back of the book.

KEY WORDS

Key words in this chapter are given below. There is space to write your own revision notes and to add any other words or phrases that you want to remember.

- Deflationary gap
- Paradox of thrift
- Residual unemployment
- Voluntary unemployment
- Seasonal unemployment
- Frictional unemployment
- Structural unemployment
- Demand-deficiency or cyclical unemployment
- Slump
- Recovery
- Boom
- Recession
- Trade or business cycle
- Stagflation
- Balanced budget

REVIEW

The main learning points introduced in this chapter are summarised below.

Go through them and check back to the learning outcomes at the beginning of the chapter. Only move on when you are happy that you fully understand each point.

- We have examined the business cycle and unemployment in a market economy. Attempts to reduce fluctuations in economic activity and unemployment resulted in the use of demand management policies by successive post-1945 governments up to 1976. Operational problems plus questions over the basic economic philosophy underpinning this strategy led to its abandonment.
- It was replaced by supply-side policies which incorporate the balanced budget concept and a non-inflationary monetary policy. Such policies are aimed at stimulating economic activity and reducing the natural unemployment rate in the economy.
- Keynesians believed that steady growth could be achieved by controlling total spending, but there were problems with demand management. In the 1970s there was a period of stagflation – rising unemployment and inflation combined with falling output.
- Monetarists argued that if markets were made more efficient and the supply side (the productive side) of the economy improved, it would be easier for workers to find employment.

In summary, we looked at:

- The concept of full employment
- Types of unemployment
- Trade cycle theories
- Demand management and supply-side policies
- Government economic management

chapter 4

MONETARY POLICY AND INTEREST RATE THEORIES

Contents

Learning outcomes

On completion of this chapter you should be able to:

- Evaluate the main objectives and instruments of monetary policy, together with the role of the Monetary Policy Committee
- Explain the mechanics and impact on the supply of credit of credit of the discount rate, open market operations and quantitative easing
- Critically analyse interest rate theories and their relevance to economic management

Introduction

We will now examine monetary policy – interest rates and money supply – in depth. The Bank of England, which is the fulcrum of the entire UK financial system, is responsible for the implementation of monetary policy. Monetary policy is a general market policy. Its effects are felt throughout an economy, although in practice it might impact more heavily on certain economic sectors; for example, interest rate policy might have a significant influence on the owner-occupied housing market but little initial effect on non-durable consumption such as food or fuel expenditures.

We will study the implementation of monetary policy and its impact on the economy by examining the operation of:

- Monetary policy committee
- Monetary weapons
- Interest rate theories

QUICK QUESTION

What do you think are the government's main economic objectives?

Write your answer here before reading on.

1 Objectives of monetary (economic) policy

Monetary policy has four main objectives:

1 The maintenance of high and stable employment
2 Price stability (low inflation)
3 Balance of payments (currency flow) equilibrium
4 Economic growth

As we have already seen, these objectives have proved difficult to achieve simultaneously in the UK economy. Attempts to foster economic growth and full employment between 1945 and 1976 often led to balance of payments difficulties. Thereafter, attempts to reduce inflation in the economy were often accompanied by a substantial increase in unemployment.

In theory, there is no reason why an economy should not enjoy economic growth, full employment, price stability and balance of payments equilibrium. The reality is that few economies achieve all four objectives at the same time. This may be due to poor economic management on the part of the government or internal/external factors outside its control.

2 The role of money

Monetary policy is based on the view that money supply, bank credit and interest rates influence the behaviour of the real economy. Monetary policy concentrates on the control and management of one or more of these influences and is based on the belief that monetary demand has an important influence on output, employment and prices. Thus, if monetary demand increases and prices remain stable, it follows that output and employment must increase, or, if the latter remain unaffected, then prices must rise.

Pre-2008 the political/economic view was that changes in monetary demand mainly influenced prices and the value of money, and had little impact on output and employment over the long term. The objective of monetary policy was therefore to create a stable financial environment within which economic agents – consumers and companies – could make market-based decisions which determined the level of output and employment.

Post-2008 the main objective of monetary policy has been to stabilise output and employment with any increase in money supply and/or low interest rates being directed at offsetting recessionary forces in the economy.

2.1 Target variables

The controls selected to achieve a particular economic objective take the form of a monetary variable which is of importance, such as bank lending growth or money supply growth. This is referred to as a target variable.

To achieve a target, the Bank of England will not control it directly, but will use various monetary instruments or techniques such as altering interest rates, open market operations, quantitative easing, reserve ratios and directives. These instruments influence the target variable and may contribute to the achievement of a particular economic policy objective. As an example, Bank of England interest rate policy will influence monetary demand which ultimately has an impact on the country's inflation rate, output and employment.

2.2 Monetary Policy Committee (MPC)

In 1997 the UK government gave the Bank of England operational responsibility for setting interest rates. The monetary policy objective of the Bank is to deliver price stability, as defined by the government's inflation target. The Bank has operational independence and responsibility for setting short term interest rates to achieve the government's inflation target. Legislation provides that, in extreme economic circumstances, if the national interest demands it, the government has the power to give instructions to the Bank on interest rates for a limited period. This is the practice in most other countries.

The UK government has provided the Bank with operational independence and thereby has attempted to take politics out of the monetary policy process. It should in theory keep politics out of this aspect of economic management and aid the development of macroeconomic stability.

Operational decisions on interest rate policy are made by the MPC which consists of the Bank's governor, two deputy governors and six members. Two of these members, who are appointed by the governor, take management responsibility for monetary policy and market operations; the remaining four, appointed by the Chancellor, are recognised experts in monetary/financial economics.

This Committee meets monthly and any decisions on interest rates are announced immediately after its proceedings close, with the minutes released no later than six weeks after the meeting. The MPC is responsible under the legislation for approving the Bank's quarterly *Inflation Report*, and is closely involved with Bank staff in the preparation of the forecasts for the *Report*.

The Bank's monetary policy objective is set out in the Bank of England Act 1998. The Bank is to maintain price stability and, subject to that objective, to support the government's economic policy, including its objectives for growth and employment. The Treasury is responsible for defining and publishing what it means by price stability, and for specifying the economic policy of the government. In other words, the government sets the inflation target and the Bank takes the operational decisions required to reach it.

The government has told the MPC to pursue a target for consumer price inflation of 2% per annum. If inflation moves more than one percentage point either side of the target, then the governor must send an open letter to the government explaining why this has happened and what actions are to be taken to deal with it.

These detailed provisions relating to the inflation target are not contained within the Act itself, although it does specify that the Treasury must publish a statement on its price stability objective at least once every 12 months – the inflation target is confirmed in each Budget.

Post-2008 the 2% inflation target has received less attention by the Treasury with inflation rising to over 5% per annum in September 2011. It is acknowledged by the Bank and the Treasury that higher interest rates to get inflation down to 2% would threaten output and employment and thereby delay economic recovery.

QUESTION TIME 13

Critically evaluate the role of the MPC at present.

Write your answer here then check with the answer at the back of the book.

QUICK QUESTION

What do you think are the implications when it is announced in the media that the Bank has raised its interest (discount) rate?

Write your answer here before reading on.

3 The Bank of England's monetary 'weapons'

3.1 The Bank's interest (discount) rate

In a modern market economy the main instrument of monetary policy is the short term interest rate. Central banks have a variety of techniques for influencing interest rates but they are all designed, in one way or another, to affect the cost of money to the banking system. In general, this is done by keeping the banking system short of money, and then lending the banks the money they need at an interest rate which the central bank decides. In the UK, such influence is exercised through the Bank of England's daily operations in the gilt and money markets.

Interest rates in the money markets will generally be close to those at which the Bank conducts its operations. If the MPC decides that a change in short term interest rates is appropriate, the Bank will signal this by changing the level of rates at which it is prepared to relieve the shortage: any such change will normally be reflected quickly in money market rates in general, and in banks' base rates which they use to calculate their customer rates for savers and borrowers.

A change in interest rates will affect the economy through a number of routes.

- A change in the cost of borrowing will affect spending decisions. Interest rates affect the relative attraction of spending today as against spending later, in that a rise in rates will make saving more attractive and borrowing less so, and this will tend to reduce present spending, both on consumption and on investment.
- A change in rates affects the incomes of borrowers and lenders. A rise or fall in interest rates has quite a significant impact on their outgoings, and thus on their spending power. For example, if interest rates rise, individuals with large debts tend to reduce their borrowing commitments and spending, whereas pensioners with savings receive more interest and thereby increased spending power. Companies, similarly, are traditional net debtors and net borrowers from banks and thus an interest rate rise will curtail their inventory and capital investment plans.
- A change in interest rates affects the value of certain assets, notably property and stocks and shares. In the UK, a change in rates can have a particularly visible effect on house prices, and that in turn will influence people's willingness to borrow and spend money.

  All of these influences on spending will tend to affect economic activity and there will be further knock-on effects on demand from rising or falling company profits and employment. If there is lower demand and economic activity, this is likely to stabilise or reduce prices, partly because pressure on company sales encourages price reductions and partly because wage pressures will be less.
- A particular pressure on prices comes through the sterling exchange rate. For example, a rise in domestic interest rates relative to those overseas will tend to result in a net inflow of capital and an appreciation of the exchange rate. A rising pound will reduce import prices, thus increasing the downward pressure on inflation.

  The objective is to set interest rate policy in such a way as to achieve and maintain long term economic and social goals, e.g. affordable housing, economic growth and price stability.

QUICK QUESTION

If the Bank buys gilts in the market, will interest rates rise or fall?

Write your answer here before reading on.

4 Open market operations (OMO)

The Bank uses open market operations – the purchase and sale of gilts – to influence the price of gilts and interest rates. As gilt prices rise, interest rates fall and *vice versa*. This in turn influences money supply growth and overall demand in the economy. For OMO to be effective there must be an efficient, deep and liquid market in government securities (gilts).

Open market operations affect the cost and supply of money in two ways:

1 Through its operations in the gilt market the Bank is in a position to influence security prices and interest rates. If it wishes to prevent interest rates from rising, it must prevent gilt prices from falling. To achieve this it must purchase gilts at the appropriate price in any amount and thereby prevent a rise in interest rates. The Bank's actions pump additional money into the financial markets and add to money supply in the economy. The opposite approach of selling gilts will depress their price, raise interest rates and take money out of the financial markets and economy. As well as impacting on current interest rates, the Bank uses its OMO to influence expectations about future interest rates.

2 The Bank's OMO have an additional effect on the cash reserves, operational balances at the Bank and overall liquidity position of UK banks. If the Bank is buying securities, it pays the sellers by cheques which are deposited into their bank accounts at retail banks and in due course are presented through the clearing system to the Bank for payment. The Bank makes settlement by crediting the banks' accounts at the Bank, thereby increasing their operational balances. The banks can use this increase in their liquid assets (operational balances) as a basis for credit/deposit creation via the bank deposit multiplier. If the Bank sells securities to the public, it has the opposite effect and leads to a contraction in bank credit in the economy.

4.1 Quantitative easing (QE)

A variation on OMO is quantitative easing (QE) which was first used in 2009. It is an emergency measure used to boost economic growth by buying assets, such as gilts and corporate bonds, with money that is effectively created out of accounting entries at the Bank. Quantitative easing is just like printing money as the Bank creates money to buy gilts/bonds and credits the cash reserves of banks and financial institutions with new money. All things being equal, the Bank's actions should create more liquidity in the banking system and thereby enable banks to lend more money. In 2009, QE of £200 billion was undertaken by the Bank. In October 2011, the Bank undertook a further QE of £75 billion; this was nicknamed by the media as QE2. In February 2012, more QE of £50 billion was announced, which lifted total assets purchased by the Bank since the start of the financial crisis to £375 billion. In September 2013 the Bank of England Governor Mark Carney announced that he saw no further need for further QE due to the recovery of the UK economy. This decision was partly influenced by the strength of the pound against other major currencies, which Carney believed showed how the UK was leading the economic recovery of the advanced national economies. However, he has not ruled out bringing back QE should the UK economy begin to falter. Therefore QE is now an accepted economic tool that the Bank of England is prepared to use as and when they deem it necessary.

The main benefit of QE was to provide a boost to economic growth that would prevent the UK from falling into a double-dip recession. Another benefit is that it pulls down the yields on UK government debt, allowing lower borrowing rates to be offered to businesses and households. Economists also believe that QE has a positive effect on confidence. QE has resulted in a recovery in UK house prices and in stock prices, which in turn leads to people spending more money.

Some economists fear that QE could result in high inflation. Although UK inflation in 2013 was 2.2%, there is a possibility that a QE-led increase in economic growth could raise inflation to dangerously high levels. This would happen due to an increase in business and consumer borrowing, which would further increase the money supply.

A criticism of QE is that it has only benefitted banks and not businesses and the general public. Small and medium sized businesses have complained that despite QE, banks are still not lending enough money in order to meet their requirements. Some economists have claimed that banks used QE funds to bolster their own balance sheets rather than to lend to customers and benefit the UK economy as a whole.

QUICK QUESTION

What direct controls might a central bank place on bank lending?

Write your answer here before reading on.

5 Directives

Under the Bank of England Act 1946, the Bank can give directions to banks. This power has never been formally invoked; instead the Bank has issued voluntary directives of two kinds:

- **Quantitative directives** – these are concerned with the amount of lending that banks can undertake during a specific time period. The Bank could establish lending ceilings.
- **Qualitative directives** – these are concerned with the type of lending banks do. The Bank could request banks to restrict lending for property development while encouraging finance for exports or industrial investment.

Direct controls on credit are often suggested as an alternative to reliance on the price mechanism (interest rates). However, they introduce rigidities and reduce competition in the financial system. In today's world of deregulated and sophisticated international financial markets, direct controls are out of favour because they interfere with the free market and probably result in a misallocation of economic resources.

QUESTION TIME 14

How might the Bank of England attempt to restrict money supply growth?

Write your answer here then check with the answer at the back of the book.

6 The gilt repo market

Before moving on to present monetary control techniques in the UK, it might be useful to comment on the gilt repo market. There are no official restrictions on anyone reporting, lending or borrowing gilts for any purpose, either directly or indirectly through an intermediary. This extends choice and thereby increases the demand for gilts which enhances the liquidity and efficiency of the gilt market.

6.1 What is a repo?

A repo is a sale and repurchase agreement: Party A sells securities to Party B with a legally binding agreement to purchase equivalent securities from Party B for an agreed price at a specified future date, or at call. Thus, Party B has unfettered title to the securities, and may use or dispose of them as it pleases, but it has an obligation to deliver *equivalent* securities to Party A at the end of the repo.

The interest rate implied by the difference between the sale price and repurchase price is the repo rate. If Party A is selling securities to Party B in order to raise finance, the repo rate, in effect, is the cost to Party A of raising secured funds. Party B can lend money to Party A for a repo rate of interest, and take in exchange a bundle of gilts. This is a general collateral repo.

General collateral repo (in non-specific stock)

First leg of the repo:

Party A → sells £100 worth of stock → Party B

Party A ← pays for stock ← Party B

Party A now has £100 of cash, against which it has delivered £100 of stock to which Party B has full title.

Second leg of the repo:

Party A → pays £100 cash plus repo rate of interest of, say, 6½% → Party B

Party A ← sells £100 worth of stock ← Party B

The gilt repo market has developed to such an extent that it has become a modern form of secured money and therefore is an appropriate additional instrument for the Bank's open market operations.

7 Present monetary control techniques

7.1 The cash ratio

All banks with eligible liabilities (ELs) of £400 mil or more must keep 0.15% of their ELs at the Bank of England. This non-operational, non-interest balance is reset every six months in relation to outstanding ELs at each bank.

The main ELs are comprised of:

- Scottish bank notes
- Sterling sight deposits
- Sterling time deposits (maturity 2 years or less)
- Sterling certificates of deposit

ELs are reported in a uniform manner by all reporting institutions, with no artificial reduction on reporting dates permitted by the Bank. The current 0.15% of ELs in the UK has no monetary policy purpose – the intention is simply to secure the income and resources of the Bank, and the ratio is reviewed from time to time in the light of that requirement alone.

7.2 Gilt repo operations

The Bank uses gilt repos to manage daily short term interest rates and thereby ensure that interest rate changes are transmitted effectively across the economy. Overall gilt repos have enhanced the scope for banks and other sterling market participants to manage their day-to-day liquidity, plus fostering the continuing development of efficient and competitive sterling money markets.

QUICK QUESTION

What might be the purpose of daily open market operations?

Write your answer here before reading on.

8 Daily open market operations

The objective of the Bank when operating in the market is broadly to offset the cash flows between the Bank and the markets and to leave the UK banks within reach of their desired operational balances. The Bank thus provides whatever assistance is necessary to offset the daily cash position in the market. The terms (that is, the interest rates at particular maturities) at which the cash position is offset are, of course, determined by the Bank, which provides overnight lending and deposit facilities.

The Bank invites counterparties to bid for funds by means of gilt repos. The maturity for the Bank's repo operations is two weeks, although minor variations take place to smooth out daily shortages/surpluses. The range of counterparties includes banks, building societies and securities firms.

To participate in the Bank's daily operations, these institutions have to meet certain functional requirements. They must:

- Have the technical capability to respond quickly and efficiently to the Bank's operations
- Maintain an active presence in the gilt repo market, thus contributing to the distribution of liquidity around the system
- Participate regularly in the Bank's operations
- Provide the Bank with useful information on market conditions and developments

We have now discussed the main techniques of monetary control in the UK at present. The primary aim of the Bank's operations in the sterling money and repo markets is to steer short term market interest rates to the levels required to implement monetary policy. Subject to meeting that aim, it operates so as to help the banking system to manage its liquidity effectively. You should try to find out and keep up to date with current developments regarding interest rates, credit demand and money supply from the media.

QUICK QUESTION

Write your own definition of interest.

Write your answer here before reading on.

9 Interest rate theories

We have dealt with interest rates a number of times already, but we'll now consider interest rates more fully and examine some basic theories.

A definition of interest might be that it is a sum, usually expressed as a rate or percentage per annum, paid for the use of financial capital. Interest is therefore derived from the use of capital. An interest rate is the price paid for borrowing money – capital – and is determined by the interaction of supply and demand. Interest rate theories incorporate different concepts on the supply of, and demand for, funds.

We'll examine two theories: the classical theory and the loanable funds theory. The demand or investment function is common to both and therefore makes a useful point at which to start.

10 Investment demand function

The theory of the investment demand function assumes that the rate of return on investment falls as the level of investment increases. This is because entrepreneurs are likely to invest first in those areas where they get the highest return. They get a diminishing return on each extra (or marginal) pound invested.

Putting this proposition another way, the marginal efficiency of investment (MEI) diminishes because the return on each extra pound invested is less than the return on the previous pound invested. This can be illustrated in a graph.

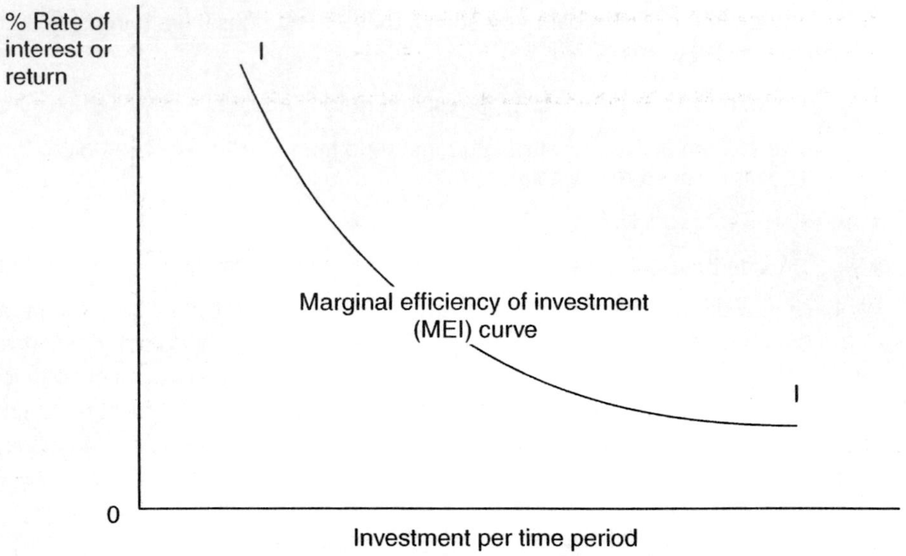

A business person considering borrowing money for an investment will compare the cost of borrowing with the expected rate of return. If this is higher than the rate of interest charged for the loan, the investment is likely to take place. Obviously, when interest rates are high, only those projects with a high rate of return are worthwhile. As these are likely to be limited, so too will be the demand for funds.

The MEI curve can be regarded as showing the underlying demand for investment funds over a period of time. The downward sloping MEI curve indicates that, as interest rates decline, more business projects will become viable and so the demand for capital – savings – will increase. House purchase loans and government borrowing also represent additional demands for capital.

The supply of loanable funds comes from individuals and firms. Individuals save for a variety of reasons such as 'for a rainy day' or to enable them to purchase some expensive item in the future. Companies save in the form of undistributed profits. It pays those with surplus funds to lend them out, provided that they obtain a rate of interest which covers the risk of the loan not being repaid.

QUICK QUESTION

How will higher interest rates affect the level of savings in the economy?

Write your answer here before reading on.

11 Classical interest rate theory

Classical theory combines the investment demand (MEI) curve with the supply of savings curve. It is referred to as a real or non-monetary theory of interest rates. If the interest rate increases, it is assumed that people will save more, and *vice versa* if it falls.

The equilibrium interest rate is the rate at which savings and investment are equal for a particular time period.

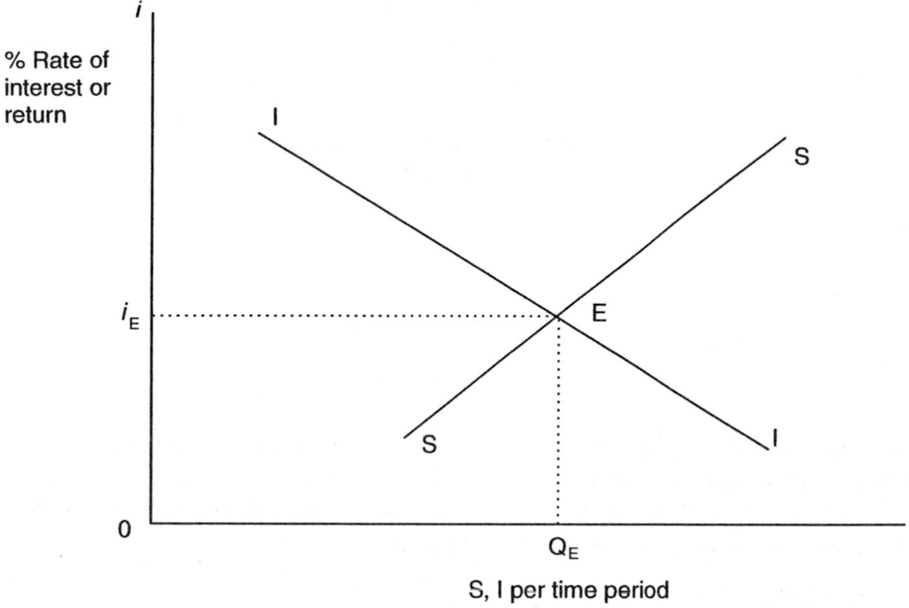

In this diagram the demand for, and supply of, capital are equal at E. The equilibrium interest rate that equates demand and supply is i_E.

Classical theory assumes that people have a time preference for money and prefer a given sum now to the same sum in the future. Interest is paid to compensate them for the loss of current purchasing power. Savings and investment are brought into equilibrium by changes in interest rates. If the economy experiences a recession due to a collapse in exports, then investment may decline. The net effect of this would be lower interest rates, savings and investment in the economy.

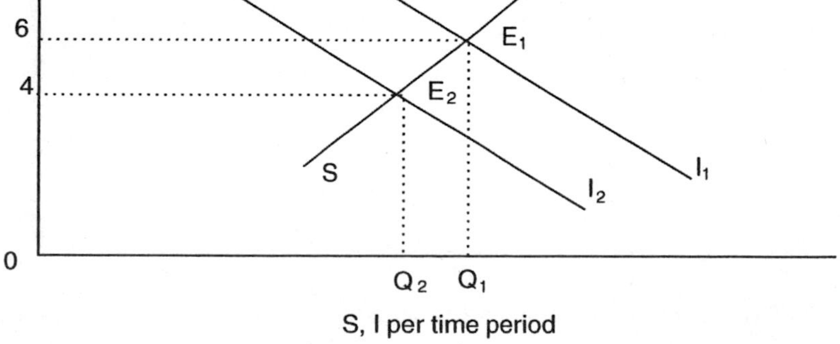

In this diagram the investment demand declines from I_1I_1 to I_2I_2. As a result, interest rates decline from 6% to 4%. The lower interest rate results in less savings being made available for investment at Q_2.

The classical theory regards savings as being influenced by interest rates, whereas modern theory believes that savings depend more on disposable income. The classical version is also concerned with flows of savings and investment over a period of time.

QUICK QUESTION

What other factors could influence the supply of capital apart from savings?

Write your answer here before reading on.

12 Loanable funds theory

The loanable funds theory is a development of the classical theory but is more realistic about what actually happens in the capital markets. The supply of funds in the capital market is not the same as savings – changes in the money supply can change the supply of funds, thus the theory is concerned with the supply of loanable funds, not just saving.

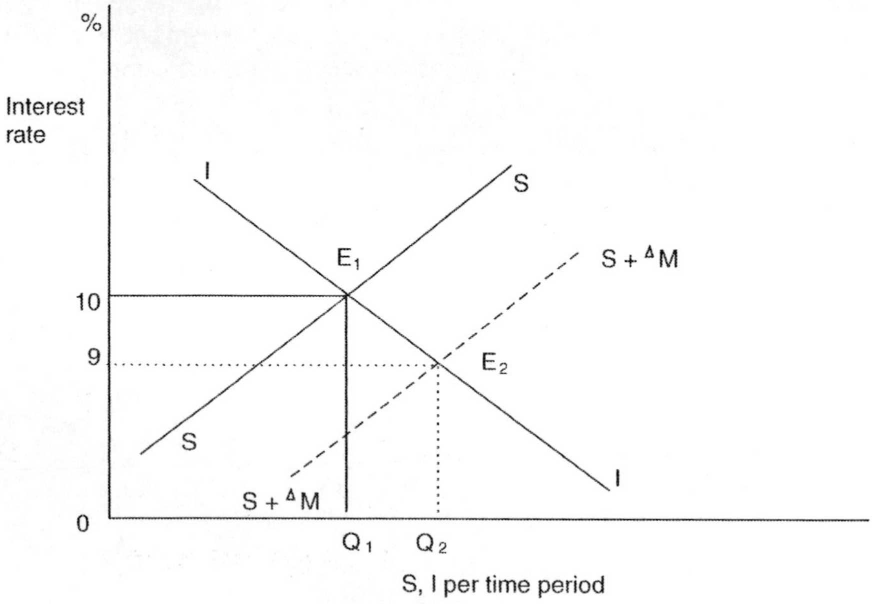

In this diagram we see the savings and investment functions of the classical version (lines S and I).

In the loanable funds version the supply of funds is modified by changes in the money supply (ΔM) thus the total supply of loanable funds is S + ΔM.

In this diagram, the increase in the money supply has led to a lower equilibrium interest rate (sometimes referred to as the natural rate) and more investment in the economy.

On the demand side there is a similar change. The demand for loanable funds is not just the demand for investment. Account must be taken of changes in people's (and a firm's) desire to hold money for purposes other than investment, such as hoarding cash balances.

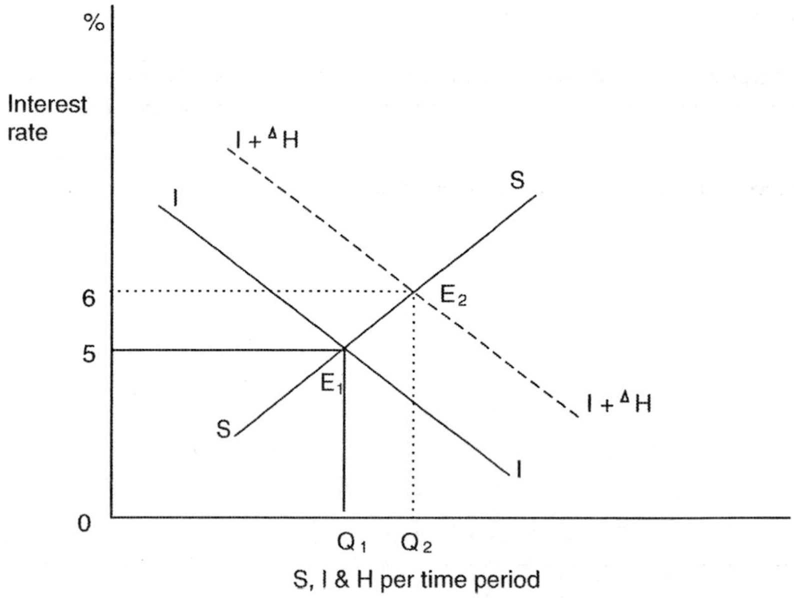

In this diagram the demand for investment funds has been augmented by an increase in (ΔH) which has led to a rise in the rate of interest and more money being saved. The equilibrium rate of interest is where the supply of, and demand for, loanable funds are equal.

It is now possible to illustrate the equilibrium interest rate that will be established under loanable funds theory.

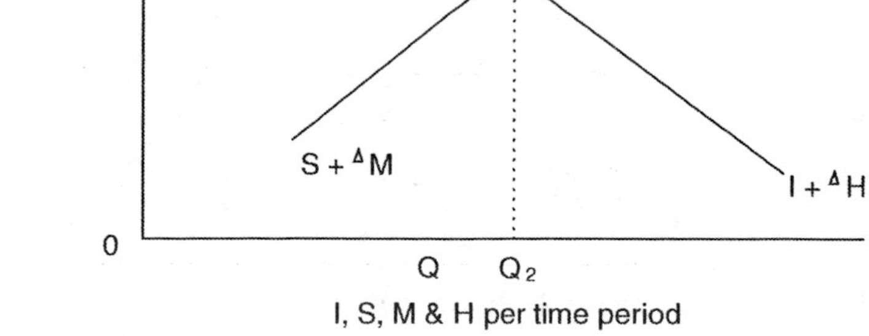

In this diagram the equilibrium interest rate (i_e) equates the demand for, and supply of, loan funds.

If the interest rate was fixed at *i*, this would increase the supply of loanable funds but would decrease the demand for such funds. In these circumstances, financial institutions would reduce interest rates to attract borrowers and thereby increase investment. This process would continue until interest rates returned to *i*.

Only a shift of either or both the curves – I + ΔH and /or S + ΔM – would bring about a new equilibrium interest rate. The former might be the result of a change in business people's expectations, while the latter results from an increased propensity to save, or perhaps an increase in money supply.

It would be tempting to state that the price of loanable funds is determined by the demand for, and supply of, loanable funds, but this is too simplistic. Often interest rates are not sufficiently free to move so as to equate the demand for, and supply of, loanable funds. For example, for administrative reasons, banks are reluctant to alter their interest rates every time the demand for loans changes.

As we have seen, the central bank, via money and gilt market operations, also exerts considerable influence over the level of interest rates.

13 Liquidity preference theory

Leading on from loanable funds theory is the fact that money is not just a medium of exchange but can also be held (or hoarded) as an asset or form of wealth. This preference for money over other kinds of assets, e.g. bonds and shares, is known in economics as liquidity preference theory. When interest rates are low (and bond prices high) liquidity preference will be high as the opportunity cost (lost interest) of holding enlarged cash/money balances is relatively low.

In this situation, efforts by the Bank to reduce interest rates by increasing money supply might be ineffective if economic agents simply accumulate 'idle' cash balances. This economic/monetary scenario is sometimes referred to as the liquidity trap.

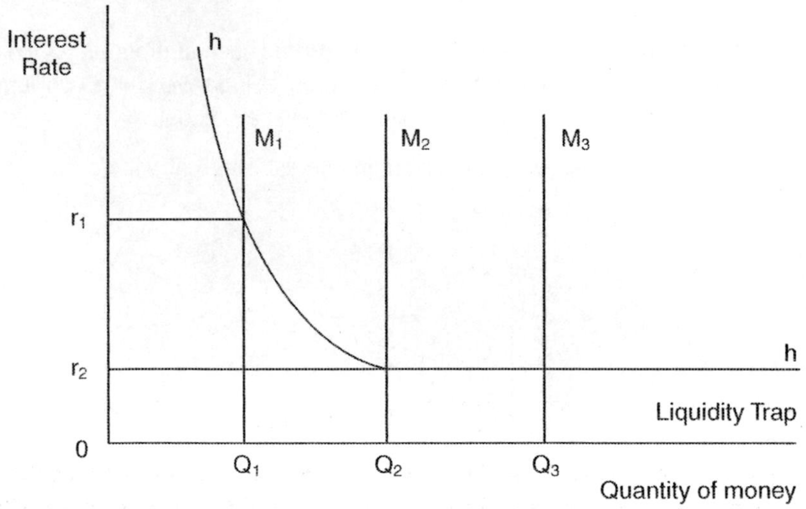

In this diagram, curve LL is the liquidity preference schedule, i.e. the demand to hold money as an asset. The Bank increases money supply from M_1 to M_2 and the interest rate falls from r_1 to r_2. If the Bank increases money supply from M_2 to M_3 it has no impact on the interest rate at r_2. This represents the liquidity trap and to a certain extent at this point interest rate management/policy ceases to be an effective demand management tool.

14 Nominal and real interest rates

A nominal interest rate is one expressed in money terms, as advertised by a bank, whereas a real interest rate is the nominal rate stated minus the inflation rate. For example, a nominal interest rate of 5% adjusted for an inflation rate of 2% is equivalent to a real interest rate of 3%. If the inflation rate was 7%, then the real interest rate is – 2%. In other words, it represents a negative return on your money or capital.

QUICK QUESTION

Why are long term interest rates higher than short term interest rates?

Write your answer here before reading on.

15 Term structure of interest rates

Interest rate term structure refers to the pattern of interest rates on similar securities with differing maturities. It is generally the case that interest rates on short term securities are lower than on long term securities. This can be illustrated by a yield curve.

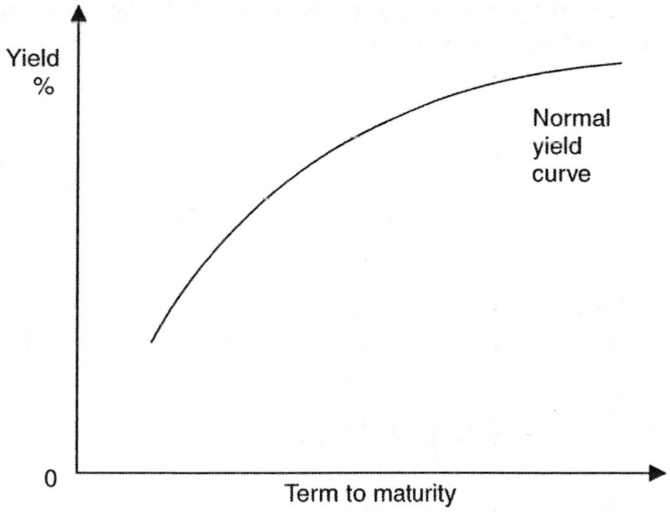

The yield curve takes this shape because the longer the term to maturity, the greater the risk and uncertainty, so the lender looks for compensation through a higher return rate. The lender also seeks compensation for lack of liquidity and flexibility associated with a longer term claim than a short term claim. The borrower is willing to pay more for longer term funds because they provide certainty of cash and cost, unlike short term borrowing which has to be constantly reviewed at uncertain interest rates.

In addition to QE, governments have attempted to change the structure of the yield curve to stimulate economic demand. The Federal Reserve in the USA embarked on 'Operation Twist' to flatten the yield curve. To do this, they sold short-dated Treasury Bonds and bought long-dated Treasury Bonds in order to lower interest rates and ease credit conditions.

QUICK QUESTION

What affects the pattern of interest rates?

Write your answer here before reading on.

16 Interest rate pattern

The pattern of interest rates is the result of such factors as risk, maturity and competition. A bank's interest rate structure is influenced by the competition for funds in the savings/money markets. On the lending side it must offer overdrafts, loans and mortgages on competitive interest rate terms in order to win business. Obviously, the interest rate charged will also be influenced by the creditworthiness of the borrower and the facility's repayment date. All other things being equal, the longer the maturity, the higher the rate of interest.

Interest rate levels are determined by the government's economic policies. The size of the budget deficit and the technique of funding can have a profound effect on interest rates. Overall monetary policy can influence interest rates, particularly short term rates which are influenced by daily intervention in the gilt repo money markets by the Bank of England which can control the marginal cost of funds to the banking system and thereby control the speed and direction of interest rate changes it desires.

In the case of longer term interest rates, a change in short term rates may influence expectations on long term interest rates, although the latter are also influenced by inflation expectations.

QUESTION TIME 15

Explain the following terms in relation to interest rates.

(a) Investment demand function
(b) Equilibrium interest rate
(c) Nominal and real interest rates
(d) Normal yield curve

Write your answer here then check with the answer at the back of the book.

KEY WORDS

Key words in this chapter are given below. There is space to write your own revision notes and to add any other words or phrases that you want to remember.

- Target variable
- Monetary Policy Committee (MPC)
- Open market operations
- Quantitative easing (QE)
- Gilt repo market
- Eligible liabilities
- Investment demand function
- Rate of return
- Marginal efficiency of investment (MEI)
- Classical interest rate theory
- Loanable funds theory
- Nominal and real interest rates
- Yield curve

REVIEW

The main learning points introduced in this chapter are summarised below.

Go through them and check back to the learning outcomes at the beginning of the chapter. Only move on when you are happy that you fully understand each point.

- We considered the main objectives of monetary policy and the operational remit of the Monetary Policy Committee at the Bank of England.
- We examined the main monetary weapons – interest rates, open market operations, and direct controls – along with the gilt repo market and quantitative easing.
- Present day open market operations were explained in order to see how the Bank influences interest rates.
- We also examined interest rate theories which incorporated the marginal efficiency of investment schedule.
- After ascertaining how the equilibrium interest rate is established under classical and loanable funds theories, we looked at liquidity preference theory and the term structure of interest rates.

chapter 5

INFLATION AND THE HOUSING MARKET

Contents

Learning outcomes

On completion of this chapter, you should be able to:

- Examine the main aspects of inflation and its impact on society and the economy along with the concept of price deflation.
- Explain the housing market's special features and evaluate the impact on abnks and the economy of house price bubbles/bursts.

Introduction

We will now examine the main causes of inflation in an economy, including analysing the importance of the budget deficit and how this is financed. Printing money or borrowing directly from banks is likely to have inflationary consequences. In order to avoid the latter, government borrowing needs must be financed by the issue of bonds or certificates to the private sector. We will consider current UK policy for controlling inflation in the economy.

We will also examine the housing market – an important market for financial institutions, while for most people a house is their most important asset in terms of need, value and potential borrowing capacity. Any national and/or regional fluctuation in house prices has substantial implications for householders' overall net wealth and their willingness to spend. A decline in the price of houses makes people feel financially vulnerable, while a house price rise, apart from potential first-time buyers, makes most people feel better off – a feel good factor.

The housing market is also important for building societies and banks as an outlet for lending funds via mortgages. Such institutions are interested in the security aspect of house loans and potential house price movements.

We will be looking at demand and supply of housing, special features of the housing market, housing tenure and recent trends in house prices, as well as negative equity. The latter has potential implications for younger mortgagees and financial institutions.

In summary, we will be examining and commenting on inflation and the UK housing market, in particular in relation to:

- Inflation problems
- Inflation causes and control
- Inflation trends and deflation
- Demand and supply in the housing market
- House price bubbles and bursts
- Negative equity and repossession

QUICK QUESTION

Write your own definition of inflation.

Write your answer here before reading on.

1 Inflation

Inflation is a rise in the general level of prices and a fall in the value of money. What concerns us most here is not so much the level of prices, but the rate at which prices change. This rate of inflation is measured by the Consumer Prices Index.

1.1 Consumer Prices Index (CPI)

In December 2003 the Chancellor of the Exchequer changed the UK inflation target from one based on the Retail Prices Index (RPI) excluding mortgage interest payments (RPIX) to the Consumer Prices Index. Like the RPI, the CPI measures the average change from month to month in the prices of consumer goods and services, but it differs in the particular households it represents, the range of goods and services included, and the way the index is constructed.

Each month, the current prices of the chosen items are collected around the country, multiplied by their respective weights and added together. The total is then divided by the sum of all the weights to produce a single figure. A base year for the index is given a value of 100 and the monthly index indicates how prices in general have changed since that date. An index of 110 would show that prices on average had risen by 10%.

The CPI is an average showing what has happened to the general level of prices. It does not show what has happened to individual prices. Over the past twenty years, prices on average have risen; some prices have risen at a faster rate than the general trend and some have actually fallen, such as personal computers. The CPI is thus a useful tool for showing the general trend of prices, but it must be used with care.

1.2 Retail Prices Index (RPI)

The RPI is the most familiar general purpose measure of inflation in the UK. It measures the average change from month to month in the prices of consumer goods and services purchased by most households in the UK. The Pre-Budget Report in December 2003 confirmed that index-linked gilts would continue to be calculated with reference to the RPI. In mid-2011 the Treasury issued a consultation paper on the possible issue of CPI index-linked gilts in the future. The Treasury has to ascertain the possible level of demand for such gilts and also its implications as regards debt service costs for the government.

In 2011 the measure used for the annual up-rating of state pensions and benefits was switched from the RPI to CPI. This step was taken by the government in order to reduce planned welfare expenditure and thereby future budget deficits.

1.3 What are the differences between the CPI and the RPI?

In terms of commodity coverage, CPI excludes a number of items that are included in RPI, mainly related to housing, including council tax and a range of owner-occupier housing costs such as mortgage interest payments, house depreciation, buildings insurance, estate agents' and conveyancing fees.

The CPI covers all private households, whereas RPI excludes the top 4 per cent by income, and pensioner households who derive at least three quarters of their income from state benefits.

Individual prices are combined in the CPI and RPI within each detailed expenditure category according to different formulae. The CPI uses the geometric mean, whereas the RPI uses arithmetic means; this lowers the CPI inflation rate relative to the RPI.

1.4 Which is the better measure of inflation – CPI or RPI?

In terms of their basic usability, there is little to choose between them. Both are published each month, to a common timescale, and are subject to minimal revisions (RPI by convention is never revised).

The RPI coverage of spending and households is based on the National Accounts, which makes for better comparisons of inflation in different countries.

A key advantage of RPI is its familiarity and credibility based on its longer history. Inevitably, it will be some time before the CPI becomes as widely recognised. The CPI's exclusion of most elements of owner-occupier housing costs lessens its relevance for some users, but this must be weighed against the significant difficulties encountered in measuring such costs appropriately, reflected in the absence of any international consensus in this area.

1.5 UK inflation trends

In the last 20 years the annual inflation rate has been as high as 10% in the 1990s and as low as 2% by the mid-2000s. At present, the Chancellor of the Exchequer still sets the CPI inflation rate target at 2% per annum.

In October 2013, RPI was reported as being 2.6% and CPI was 2.2%. This is part of a trend of falling UK inflation over the past two years. In September 2011, RPI stood at 5.6% and CPI at 5.2%. Quantitative Easing and low interest rates were resulting in the highest inflation levels of the decade, exasperated by high crude oil prices and energy. However, low interest rates have resulted in lower mortgage repayments and crude oil prices have since eased. Despite falling inflation levels, a concern for the government is the lack of the growth in wages in the UK. Because wage rises over the past five years have been outpaced by inflation, the real income available to UK households has been diminished.

Economists compare the rate of inflation against the average pay rises that workers receive to gauge if pay is keeping pace with inflation. This helps to assess if real levels of income are increasing or decreasing. Since 2008, the general trend in the UK has been for inflation to outpace pay rises. For example, in the public sector, pay rises have been capped at 1% per year since 2011.

QUICK QUESTION

Why do governments want to keep the rate of inflation low?

Write your answer here before reading on.

2 The problems of inflation

Governments are concerned to keep the rate of inflation low for a number of reasons.

2.1 Redistribution of income and wealth

Inflation leads to an arbitrary redistribution of income and wealth. People on fixed incomes suffer because their incomes buy less. This can be especially severe on those who retire on a fixed pension. Fortunately, state pensions and many company pensions are increased (or indexed) to offset inflation. Creditors (savers) also suffer because the money they receive on repayment buys less than when they lent it. On the other hand, debtors (borrowers) gain.

Inflation can change the nominal value of other physical assets such as land, property in general, jewellery, paintings, etc. In most cases a rise in the nominal value of such assets has been sufficient to maintain their real value. At the same time it may push down the real value of financial assets, particularly those with a fixed rate of return such as corporate bonds, most government securities and national savings.

The real value of bank and building society accounts would also fall unless the rate of interest after tax was greater than the rate of inflation.

2.2 Production

A moderate degree of inflation can be helpful to businesses because it may build in an added element of profit via price rises in excess of production cost rises. Too much inflation, however, can be costly and disruptive, adding a further element of uncertainty to companies' plans and making predicting future costs and revenues difficult. High levels of inflation make suppliers very wary of fixed price contracts. Such factors can result in lower investment and economic growth, which ultimately leads to higher unemployment.

2.3 Industrial relations

Inflation and expectations of inflation can lead to pay demands that are inflationary. It can also lead to poor industrial relations and conflict (strikes) between workers and employers. This results in lost output, lower profits and reduced investment, all of which damage a country's economic performance and may add to unemployment.

2.4 The balance of payments

If, as a result of inflation, UK prices rise faster than those of competing countries, export sales will decline and domestic markets will be increasingly penetrated by imports, which can lead to a deterioration of the balance of payments current account. The sterling exchange rate will ultimately depreciate against other currencies of countries with lower inflation rates. Such a development leads to higher import costs and further increases the inflation rate.

2.5 Expectations

Expectations of rising prices can make inflation self-perpetuating. If people expect prices to rise, they will seek higher wages to compensate. This adds to costs and leads to further price rises, thereby confirming their expectations. Once it reaches a high level, such an inflationary spiral is hard to control. Investors will be reluctant to lend at fixed rates of interest, making it difficult for firms to raise loans and undertake investment.

QUICK QUESTION

Does anyone benefit from inflation?

Write your answer here before reading on.

3 The benefits of inflation

Some people benefit from inflation. Those who are able to increase their income in line with, or ahead of, price rises may gain. People with real assets, such as their own home, will also benefit, providing the economy is not suffering from stagflation, whereas people with financial assets, such as bank and building society deposits, generally stand to lose. High inflation is also beneficial to those with high levels of debt, as inflation erodes away the value of the borrowing. Some commentators have suggested that high inflation would be beneficial in Europe, as it would reduce the real value of the high debt levels held by national governments.

Those who own ordinary shares may benefit because, although shares are financial assets, they represent claims over the physical assets and potential future income of companies. Inflation will tend to increase profits and thereby enable an increase in dividends to take place.

QUICK QUESTION

What do you think are some of the causes of inflation?

Write your answer here before reading on.

4 Causes of inflation

Economists identify two types of inflation:

- Demand pull inflation
- Cost push inflation

4.1 Demand pull inflation

Demand pull inflation occurs when total spending (aggregate demand) in the economy exceeds the total value at current prices of what the economy is able to produce. If there is spare capacity, such as unemployed workers and underused factories, extra demand may lead to increased production and employment without any rise in prices. However, if total spending exceeds potential supply, there will not be sufficient goods and services to meet demand at current prices. Prices will then rise to match demand with supply. It will also encourage an increase in imports.

Experience suggests that prices will start to rise before full employment is reached. Not all parts of the economy reach full employment at the same time. Production of some goods reaches its maximum while other parts of the economy are still under-employed. There may be shortages of skilled workers, although this might be partially offset by immigration, while some unskilled workers remain out of work. Bottlenecks appear in the economy and skilled workers may find their rates of pay rise as employers compete for their services.

This tends to suggest there is an inverse relationship between the annual rate of inflation and the level of unemployment in the economy. Increases in government expenditure to reduce unemployment may encourage, in certain instances, a higher rate of inflation in the economy.

4.2 Cost push inflation

Cost push inflation can occur before full employment is reached and is associated with a rise in production costs which is passed on in higher prices. Since wages account for around three quarters of total production costs in Britain, most attention is focused on the labour market and the bargaining power of trade unions. Rising costs of raw materials, food and energy (oil, gas and coal) may also lead to cost push inflation in an economy.

4.3 Explanation of inflation

Most economists, central bankers and politicians now believe that inflation is caused primarily by the excessive growth of money supply in an economy. Inflation can only occur if there is money available to finance it. Demand pull inflation can only continue if there is sufficient money to sustain it. Similarly, cost push inflation depends on people having an increasing amount of money to pay higher prices for goods and services.

QUICK QUESTION

Can you suggest one method for controlling inflation?

Write your answer here before reading on.

5 Control of inflation

Control of inflation depends on the underlying causes.

The cure for demand pull inflation would depend on what caused collective demand to rise and exceed output in the first place. A likely cause, but not the sole one, is a government spending more than its tax revenue. Governments which are always under pressure to increase the range and quality of public services have great difficulty in curtailing public expenditure growth. At the same time, nobody likes paying the taxes needed to finance the public sector. The result may be that the government spends more than it receives in taxes and borrows or prints extra money to finance the difference.

The amount the government borrows or requires is known as the Public Sector Net Borrowing (PSNB). Thus the government is putting more demand into the economy through its spending than it is taking out through taxation. Unless properly financed, such action may cause inflation.

One solution is to cut collective demand. The government could cut private sector spending by increasing taxes (not very popular) and cut its own spending by reducing services and benefits (also not popular and difficult to achieve). Increased taxes and lower government spending should reduce or eliminate the PSNB.

6 PSNB financing

The impact of the PSNB on money supply growth and inflation in the economy depends on how it is financed. If the government has a deficit, then the UK private sector must have a surplus, the bulk of which will end up as bank deposits. The PSNB will tend to increase money supply and thereby create more inflation in the economy. However, the ultimate outcome depends on how it is financed.

The most appropriate strategy is to sell an equivalent amount of long term debt to the UK non-bank private sector, which prevents any increase in bank deposits or money supply taking place.

QUICK QUESTION

How can the government encourage people to purchase gilts and national savings certificates?

Write your answer here before reading on.

Debt sales organised by the Treasury include national savings instruments and government stocks (gilts). Unless there is a budget surplus, the Treasury knows the estimated PSNB each fiscal year and develops a financing or funding programme of debt sales to offset the potential inflationary impact of the PSNB.

It will sometimes be necessary for the Treasury to adjust the interest rate on new gilts and national savings upwards in order to create sufficient buyers for the new debt in the market. The Treasury's task is eased by some of the tax privileges accorded to public sector debt, such as tax-free national savings certificates.

A PSNB financing policy based on public sector debt sales to the non-bank private sector reduces the availability of liquid assets in the banking system and curtails its lending capacity. Bank lending creates deposits and increases money supply, so PSNB debt sales influence money supply growth in the UK economy. This is important for controlling the rate of inflation.

6.1 The Funding for Lending Scheme (FLS)

The Funding for Lending Scheme (FLS) was launched by the Bank of England in 2012. The purpose of the scheme was to allow banks and building societies to borrow cheaply from the Bank of England in order to loan the funds to individuals and businesses. So far, £23.1 billion has been borrowed by banks and building societies. from FLS. In December 2012, FLS was restricted to lending to businesses only, as the Bank of England feels that sufficient consumer credit is now available without using FLS.

7 Anti-inflationary policy

Cost push and demand pull inflation may occur together. The latter encourages workers to seek wage/salary increases to maintain their living standards. This adds to costs in industry and commerce, which are then passed on to consumers in the form of higher prices, i.e. cost push inflation. The latter tends to develop a momentum of its own, with each group of workers asking for income increases to meet higher prices caused by increased awards to other groups of employees. Workers also seek awards to maintain their relative income position in relation to other crafts and skills.

QUICK QUESTION

How can any government tackle cost push inflation?

Write your answer here before reading on.

Demand pull inflation may cease to exist in the economy due to increased taxation or a deep recession, but cost push inflation may continue to exist as trade unions seek to maintain the real income of their members via annual wage/salary awards or commodity/energy prices remain high in the global economy/markets.

Cost push inflation requires different action from that of solving demand pull inflation. One approach has been to link wage/salary rises with productivity increases. If wage increases are paid out of increased output, then costs will not rise per unit of output and prices will remain stable. Such pay increases are non-inflationary. The problem with this approach is that some types of output cannot be measured; for example, the work of nurses, teachers, etc. Such workers tend to experience a decline in their relative income position in society. In the past this has led to major wage disputes and strikes in the public sector, which subsequently resulted in inflationary wage/salary awards. Another approach used by governments in the 1970s was an incomes policy, i.e. a statutory limit on wage/salary increases each year. Such policies proved to be unpopular and achieved only limited short term success but had little impact on cost push inflation in the economy. In recent years the government has sought to limit public sector wage/salary increases, not as a form of inflationary control but to reduce public expenditure.

As regards rising commodity/energy prices, the UK government can usually do little but hope that excess demand will be temporary in the global markets. Obviously, if the sterling exchange rate appreciates against the US dollar in which most commodities/energy are priced, this will reduce import prices and thereby the cost of living for UK householders. Recent developments have shown that politicians are now prepared to take direct action to tackle high energy prices. The opposition Labour Party has promised to cap UK gas and electricity prices until 2017 should they win the 2015 general election.

QUICK QUESTION

Why did inflation decline in the mid-2000s?

Write your answer here before reading on.

8 Low inflation

A number of factors contributed to low inflation in the years up to 2008 in the UK economy:

- The government set an inflation target of 2% per annum, which the Bank of England achieved via interest rate adjustments.
- Aided by deregulation, there was increased competition in manufacturing and services, which encouraged better cost control and lower prices.
- International competition depressed prices of imported goods and domestic manufacturers, due to the supply of cheap goods from emerging economies like China.
- The relatively high value of the pound reduced import prices.
- Improved productivity of goods retailing as efficient supermarkets took a larger share of the market.

Most economists believed inflation would remain low and result in lower real interest rates which would encourage investment and economic growth. There is some economic evidence this scenario did happen before the onset of the banking/financial crisis in 2008. Thereafter, economic growth stalled and unemployment increased but so also did inflation – in other words, the UK economy experienced stagflation. The key point is that we cannot stop worrying about inflation – inflation is never beaten.

9 Hyper-inflation

Fortunately, hyper-inflation is a rare occurrence and happens only when there is gross economic mismanagement by the government/central bank of a country. The most well known example was the hyper-inflation experienced by the Weimar (German) Republic in 1922-23. Before the outbreak of hostilities in August 1914, the German mark was trading at four to the US dollar. By the end of World War One it traded at 9 to the dollar. This ratio rose to over 160 to the dollar by January 1922. Between then and November 1923, inflation increased to 32,400% and the exchange rate was 4.2 trillion marks to the dollar. Paper money ceased to have any value or use in Germany. The Weimar Republic introduced a new currency – the Rentenmark – the supply of which was strictly controlled. This measure halted inflation in Germany.

QUESTION TIME 16

(a) How can inflation be controlled?
(b) What might cause the UK inflation rate to rise?
(c) How might quantitative easing impact on the UK inflation rate?

Write your answer here then check with the answer at the back of the book.

10 Deflation

Deflation – a falling price level – is the opposite of inflation. It means that fixed income instruments, including cash and bonds, can offer good real interest returns. Initially, equity shares will perform badly in a recessionary environment, but in a long term deflationary environment, with the economy growing, shares can be good investments. Property, however, would provide significantly poorer returns than in the inflationary period of recent decades; but once property prices had adjusted, they could offer decent long run returns through rental yields, provided deflation was not severe.

A move to deflation involves the same mechanism as for achieving a fall in the rate of inflation. The emergence of an output gap in the economy, i.e. spare resources, puts downward pressure on prices and wages so that the overall inflation rate finally falls so far that it turns negative. It does not necessarily require a recession, merely a long enough period of growth below trend. Once deflation has set in, taking the output gap back to zero will stabilise the rate of deflation. Thereafter, only a boom will reduce the rate of deflation.

Deflation could make economic downturns more severe than in periods of mild inflation or price stability:

- If prices are falling, people may delay spending on expensive items, or companies may delay investments, expecting to do them more cheaply later.
- Deflation means that property prices tend to fall, which reduces its value as collateral and thus may impact on the banking system.

When the price level is falling, interest rate policy is much less effective, as interest rate cuts from already low levels are unlikely to boost investment and consumer spending. Expansionary fiscal policy through an increase in government spending and tax cuts, is likely to have a muted impact on the economy. Tax cuts might just be tolerated by the citizens of a country, as happened in Japan a few years ago. Rather than issuing bonds to finance a fiscal deficit, it could be financed by printing money; the mechanism being that the government issues bonds which are bought by the central bank, i.e. quantitative easing. This can be regarded as combined fiscal and monetary policy and will be effective if done on a large enough scale.

All this might appear academic after decades of inflation. However, financial and economic problems in Japan have resulted in deflation. Similar developments in Europe due to continuing banking/financial and currency problems could bring about a fall in price levels.

11 The housing market

QUICK QUESTION

How does an increase in house prices influence housing supply?

Write your answer here before reading on.

11.1 Demand and supply in the housing market

House prices, like the prices of other normal goods, are determined by the interaction of supply and demand. If we assume other things being equal, that is, nothing else changes, as price rises, suppliers (house builders and house sellers) will be encouraged to supply more. Making the same assumptions in the case of demand for houses, we find that, as price falls, more are demanded.

QUICK QUESTION

In a free market, what happens to house prices if demand exceeds supply?

Write your answer here before reading on.

In a free market if the quantity of houses on offer does not equal the quantity demanded, price will adjust until equilibrium is achieved. If the quantity demanded exceeds the quantity supplied, price will rise. This should discourage some potential buyers and encourage suppliers (house builders) to increase output. Alternatively, if supply exceeds demand, price will fall, discouraging output and encouraging buyers. This process continues until a price is found where quantity supplied equals quantity demanded.

As the average house price adjusts, it performs three important functions:

1 **Rations out available supply**

Price rations out supply to meet demand. In the short run there is often little that can be done to increase housing supply. If demand exceeds supply, prices rise rapidly, choking off part of the demand until the remaining demand just matches the existing supply of houses.

2 **Signals**

Price and changes in price pass valuable information about the state of the housing market between buyers and sellers. Both can take account of this when making decisions.

3 **Allocates**

Price helps to allocate resources. If the price of houses rises, this encourages building firms to increase supply via new start-ups. The higher price provides additional funds to pay for extra labour and materials, plus higher profits. A fall in demand or price has the opposite effect.

Any attempt by the government for political reasons to interfere with market price prevents it from carrying out these three vital functions.

QUESTION TIME 17

Discuss the consequences for the mortgage market of a decision by banks and building societies to keep their mortgage lending rates below the market interest rate level.

Write your answer here then check with the answer at the back of the book.

11.2 Special features of the housing market

Immobility

Unlike many products we consume, houses are immobile. They cannot be moved from one part of the country where there is a surplus to another where there is a shortage. So, rather than one, single national housing market, there is a number of separate, regional markets. While house prices tend to move in the same direction across the country, there may be considerable regional/local variations in price levels and rates of change.

Lack of homogeneity

Houses are neither identical nor homogeneous. Even within a region or a locality there will be considerable variation in house types and prices. As well as bungalows and flats, houses may be terraced, semi-detached or detached. They may vary in size and style, in location and proximity to schools and other amenities. All of these will have an influence on price.

Durability

Houses are extremely durable so that, once built, a house can be expected to provide useful service for a considerable number of years. This means that a significant proportion of houses coming on to the market at any given time will be second-hand houses rather than newly constructed.

Owner-occupation

An unusual feature of the housing market is that often a seller is also a buyer. When an owner-occupier decides to move home, he or she adds to the supply of houses by putting his or her own house on the market while simultaneously adding to the demand.

Taking the long view, the factor which has correlated most closely with average house prices is average earnings, the average house costing roughly three and a half to four times average earnings of the purchaser(s). As earnings increase in the economy, so house prices can be expected to keep pace. Pre-2008, the variation was greater, i.e. average house price equal to 6 or 8 times average earnings, with financial institutions like Northern Rock providing huge mortgages to some of their customers who lacked the means to service such debt.

11.3 Factors influencing demand in the housing market

Price

The demand for houses responds to changes in price. Other things being equal, the higher the price, the fewer people are able to afford it or are willing to pay it. Price, however, is only one factor, albeit a very important one. Most house purchases are financed by mortgages, so for many purchasers the key question when buying a house is not so much price as whether or not they can afford the deposit and the monthly mortgage payment.

The cost of mortgages

An important part of the monthly mortgage payment is the rate of interest charged. A rise in interest rates would increase the monthly mortgage payment and so discourage some potential buyers. They may be forced to make a lower bid for a house or withdraw from the market completely. The effect should be to depress house prices. Falling interest rates have the opposite effect and are likely to lead to an increase in house prices unless the overall economy is in recession.

QUICK QUESTION

How does the availability of mortgages from banks and building societies affect demand?

Write your answer here before reading on.

The availability of mortgages

The availability of mortgages will depend on the flow of funds into the building societies and banks, as well as the terms on which mortgages are granted. The inflow of funds will depend on the general state of the economy and how competitive the rates are that building societies and banks offer savers.

If funds are limited, building societies and banks may restrict the availability of mortgages by lending a smaller proportion of the value of a house. They may also reduce the period of loans and lend a lower multiple of the borrower's income. If funds are readily available, a greater proportion of the price of a house may be lent for a longer period and as a greater multiple of the borrower's income. Prior to the financial crisis in 2008, lenders offered a wide variety of mortgages and were asking borrowers for deposits as low as 5%. After the financial crisis, lenders have introduced a much more stringent lending criteria (including higher deposit requirements) and have reduced the number of mortgage products on offer, including the withdrawal of interest-only mortgages.

The deregulation of the financial system has introduced new lenders into the mortgage market, such as specialist mortgage companies. This has further increased the availability of mortgages.

The level of real disposable income

Disposable income is the money left out of income after compulsory deductions such as income tax. A rise in income or a cut in taxes will increase disposable income. Real disposable income is simply disposable income adjusted for inflation.

Other things being equal, a rise in real disposable income should allow people to spend more on housing, which should lead to higher house prices. A fall in real income or a rise in tax is likely to depress house prices.

The number of households

This is influenced by various social, economic and demographic factors. A household may range from an individual living alone to a family or large group of people living together.

QUICK QUESTION

What kind of changes can affect household formation?

Write your answer here before reading on.

Household formation may be influenced by a number of trends.

- Changes in the average age for marriage/cohabiting – if people marry/cohabit at a younger age, it is likely to increase the demand for suitable accommodation and *vice versa*.
- Changes in the number of one person households – demand might rise if young, single adults earn more and decide to set up home on their own or move to other parts of the country for work.
- A rise in the divorce rate would increase the demand for housing as a divorced couple would need two homes instead of one.
- Changes in the size of the population, including changes brought about by regional migration and immigration will also be reflected in the demand for housing.
- Changes in the size of particular age groups, such as a fall in the birth rate, could affect future household formation.

Alternatives to owner-occupation

Where there are attractive alternatives to buying a house of one's own, the demand to buy a house will be reduced. The most obvious alternative is rented accommodation. If there is a good supply of low rent accommodation, fewer houses are likely to be bought. Rented housing may be provided by both the private sector and the public sector through local authorities and special housing bodies. An alternative open to elderly people is sheltered housing which may be rented.

Other associated costs

In addition to the monthly mortgage repayments, there are many other costs involved in buying and running a home. At the time of purchase there are legal fees and taxes (stamp duty) to be met and regular outgoings include insurance, maintenance and repairs. A rise in any of these expenses is likely to discourage house purchase. A potential problem facing some UK households is a proposed Mansion tax.

If approved by Parliament, this tax would introduce a yearly 1% annual levy (based on the value of the property) on properties with a market value of greater than £2 million.

11.4 Factors influencing the supply of housing

The supply of houses coming on to the market comes from three main sources:

- The stock of owner-occupied houses
- The stock of rented accommodation
- Newly built houses

Supply is influenced by the following factors:

Price

The higher the price, other things being equal, the greater the incentive for builders to build new houses and for the owners of existing houses to offer them for sale. As house prices rise, home owners have the opportunity of selling at a profit and making a capital gain. In most cases, this is balanced by the need to buy a replacement home, the price of which will also have risen.

Building costs

A rise in building costs such as land, labour and materials is a disincentive to builders to supply more houses unless these increases are matched by higher new house prices.

The availability of building land

An important factor in the cost of new houses is the price of land which is also determined by supply and demand. As the demand for houses grows, so does the demand for building land which increases in price. Building restrictions such as green belts and planning controls may exacerbate this.

Transfers from the private sector

High prices in the housing market encourage private landlords to sell rather than rent.

The economic climate

House building is a long term enterprise. A builder must finance a project from the purchase of land through to the completion of the house but only receives payment when the house is sold. This locks up considerable sums of the money for a long period.

If the money is borrowed from banks, then interest is charged. If the builder uses his own funds, he must consider the interest they could have earned if invested elsewhere. Builders also need to anticipate the state of the market on the expected completion dates of their houses.

QUICK QUESTION

About what percentage of homes in the UK are owner-occupied and why was there an increase up to 2007?

Write your answer here before reading on.

12 Housing tenure

Broadly speaking, there are two forms of housing tenure: owner-occupation and renting. The long term trend has been one of increasing owner-occupation, while the share of public rented sector has declined. At present about 70% of Britain's homes (Scottish homes 62%) are owner-occupied, up from just over 50% in 1979. This trend has been encouraged by the sale of council houses. Privately rented and housing associations' share of housing tenure has increased slightly since the mid-1980s, again the result of government policy.

Owner-occupation means that the occupier benefits fully from any capital appreciation (while bearing the risk of capital depreciation) and is able to obtain a loan secured on the house by way of a mortgage, to purchase it. With renting, the tenant has no right to capital appreciation of the dwelling, and no responsibility for maintenance of the structure.

13 House price bubbles and bursts

13.1 1986-1995

Mortgage lending grew rapidly after 1982 as the country experienced steady economic growth. Real personal disposable incomes grew moderately in the mid-1980s and then accelerated strongly towards the decade's end. At the same time, the Conservative government deregulated the UK's financial markets which enabled banks to expand their share of the house loan or mortgage market from less than 10% to over 25%. Owner-occupation was advertised as an excellent long term investment opportunity which benefited from guaranteed speculative gains. Council tenants were encouraged to buy their houses at a discount of 33% to the market price. Many people took out larger mortgages in order to move into more substantial properties. Others took out second mortgages on their existing property to finance consumption expenditure on cars and foreign holidays.

The housing market speculative bubble burst in mid-1989. Like the end of most speculative housing/financial frenzies, it was due to a change in underlying economic conditions. From 1988 onwards, increasing cost push inflation forced the government to increase interest rates to historically high levels, which resulted in a near doubling of mortgage interest payments per month for most owner-occupier households. At the same time, the overall economy slid into a deep recession with a consequential steep rise in unemployment.

House prices experienced a substantial decline of 13% from peak to trough for the first time in living memory. Nominal house prices fell in 1990, for the first time in 20 years, and fell again in each of the following five years. In real terms, house prices fell in each year during 1990-95, and it was then that many house purchasers realised that house prices could go down as well as up. In the south east of England, house prices declined by an average of 30% within a very short period of time, the main factor being a lack of adequate demand in the housing market.

It took the housing market until 1998-99 to return to the same price levels as in 1989.

13.2 2002-2011

Between 1996 and 2000, the housing market did not witness the speculative frenzy of the late 1980s. Annual house price increases fluctuated between 5% and 10%, with usual regional variations between the south-east of England and elsewhere.

House price inflation began to accelerate again in 2002, until by 2004 the annual increase in house prices was about 25%. Thereafter, annual price rises fluctuated between 5% and 20%, depending on interest rates and the availability of mortgages. The market was underpinned by high employment, rising incomes in the economy and an expansion of the buy-to-let market. In order to increase their supply of mortgage funds, banks and some building societies resorted to securitization of some of their home loan books. As a result, the average price of a house by 2005 was £125,000, compared to £80,000 in 2002.

In 2007-09 the banking/financial crisis impacted upon the supply of mortgages from banks, securitization of debt dried up and the economy drifted into a recession. By mid-2008, house prices began to decline and mortgage approvals slumped. Prices fell by 15% between 2008 and 2011, despite the Bank of England's discount rate being 0.5%.

The recessionary outlook in the final quarter of 2011 provided little optimism that house prices would stabilise or rise in the near future. Some economists predicted that a further fall of 25% in house prices was required in order to bring prices into line with the long term ratio to average earnings and rents. The National Institute of Economic and Social Research in 2011 predicted a decline of 10% in real terms in house prices by 2016. In the USA, house prices fell by about 30% between 2007-2011 due to the cycle of mortgage defaults, repossessions and distress sales. The main worry in the UK was that higher interest rates to curb inflation, public expenditure cuts, rising unemployment etc, would create a similar scenario in our housing market.

Either way, a price slowdown or price crash will impact upon the overall economy and financial system. The end of all house price 'bubbles' has generally been associated with a prolonged period of economic weakness, increased financial fragility (bank bad debts) and rising government deficits.

QUICK QUESTION

What have been the general trends in house prices in your region of the UK in the last 5 – 10 years?

Write your answer here before reading on.

You should keep up to date via the media, mortgage lenders' surveys and estate agents' reports about national and local house market developments during your studies. Trends in house prices have important implications for the overall economy and personal net worth.

QUICK QUESTION

How do you think house price declines affected the owners of houses with large mortgages?

Write your answer here before reading on.

14 Negative equity and repossessions

One of the features of the 1990s recession, apart from the decline in nominal and real terms of house prices, was the creation of negative equity. This occurs when the mortgage outstanding on a house exceeds its market value. Negative equity was particularly prevalent among first-time buyers in the south of England who purchased houses on very high loan-to-value ratios.

Negative equity had two effects:

- It made some home owners reluctant to move as a paper loss would automatically be transformed into a cash loss. This added to a decline in housing transactions and made labour less mobile geographically.
- It made people reluctant to take on new commitments or to spend

By 1993 the fall of house prices in nominal terms created a negative equity position for 1.7 million households. Only the gradual recovery in house prices in the late 1990s eliminated such negative equity positions.

Another reason driving negative equity in the early 1990's was the popularity of endowment mortgages. In 1990, these mortgages represented nearly 60% of the UK mortgage market. However, poor performance of the investment funds linked to these mortgages led to people not having enough money to pay-off the capital element of their mortgage, forcing them to either re-mortgage or sell their property. Due to these problems, endowment mortgages are seldom seen today.

The number of repossessions also increased as some owner-occupiers were unable to meet interest and principal payments. Despite the natural reluctance of financial institutions to put people out of their homes, the number of repossessions increased to almost 400,000 in the 1990s.

In mid-2011 it was estimated that over 800,000 mortgage borrowers had negative equity in relation to their houses and flats. This was approximately half the number of the early 1990s. About 40% of those with negative equity were first-time buyers who had bought their house/flat at the peak of the boom in 2006-07. This time a high proportion of negative equity was to be found in the north of England. Some believed this was due to its greater reliance on public sector employment which encouraged householders to borrow ever more funds. This trend was, perhaps, encouraged by the reckless lending policies of Northern Rock, Bradford and Bingley, and HBOS.

Although negative equity is a problem, it should not be overlooked that un-mortgaged property was estimated to be worth £1.4 trillion. Also about half of the people with mortgages had house loans equivalent to less than 70% of their house value, thereby providing them with an equity cushion of at least 30%.

As regards repossessions, it was estimated that the figure for 2011 was approximately 40,000. This was the highest number since 1992. At the same time, about 400,000 borrowers were at least three months in arrears as regards home loan payments.

QUICK QUESTION

How might repossessions create a catch 22 position for building societies and banks?

Write your answer here before reading on.

A problem for building societies and banks was that their subsequent disposals of repossessed houses simply depressed house prices further and added to the negative equity problem of their other customers.

QUESTION TIME 18

Explain the trend in house prices in your region/locality between 2001 and 2011.

Write your answer here then check with the answer at the back of the book.

14.1 New rules on mortgage provision: post 2013

In order to stop excessive and risky house lending in the future, the former Financial Services Authority (now the Financial Conduct Authority), after a two-year inquiry, published a report in December 2011. Its main recommendations were as follows:

- Interest only mortgages are to be stopped.
- A ban on self certification mortgages; self-employed applicants will have to submit fully verified accounts.
- Mortgage applicants will have to provide fuller and verifiable details on their income and spending; account must also be taken of the possible impact of interest rate rises on household budgets.
- A more robust approach is to be taken to mortgage applicants nearing retirement age in order to avoid +60 year old people taking out a 25 year mortgage to be financed by inadequate pension provisions.
- Avoidance of lending policies that rely on anticipated house price increases to repay debt and accumulated interest.
- New rules are to be introduced to permit sound customers to transfer existing negative equity on their home to another house, if changing localities for job reasons, rather than being forced to repay it on a sale and purchase of homes.

After consultation, the FSA hoped to publish its final rules on mortgage lending in mid-2012 and have them fully implemented by mid-2013. The delay in implementation is possibly due to the weak state of the housing market at present (2012). Once implemented, the Financial Conduct Authority (FCA) estimates that the new rules will have negative impact of about £3 billion on the economy as fewer people buy and sell homes. However, this might be a small price to pay for the avoidance of future boom-bust scenarios in the housing market and the economy.

14.2 Help to Buy scheme

In April 2013, the Help to Buy scheme was launched in the UK. The government scheme will underwrite £130 billion of mortgages for buyers who only have a 5% deposit. The scheme was launched to help those people who have been frozen out of the mortgage market due to lenders only offering competitive interest rates to borrowers with large deposits. The scheme has been criticised by some commentators as they believe that government-backed mortgages will lead to another housing bubble that will be guaranteed by tax-payers funds.

Help to Buy was extended in December 2013 to allow existing mortgage borrowers with low equity in their homes to re-mortgage. The major mortgage lenders in the UK have reported a strong uptake in a Help to Buy applications – RBS and Halifax alone have received applications for £365 million of mortgages.

14.3 Rising house prices in 2013

Despite most house prices in the UK still being below their 2007 peak, there are growing fears that another housing bubble is on the horizon. Halifax have estimated that house prices have risen by an average of 7.7% in 2013, the biggest annual increase in six years. With economic growth rising, UK property prices are expected to keep rising into 2014 and 2015. Having already bailed out financial institutions in 2007 due to a credit and housing bubble, the UK government is concerned that history could repeat itself – especially now that they are underwriting Help to Buy mortgages. Another concern is that the housing market is too expensive for young people and families. This could have negative demographic consequences, as people put off having children due to not being able to afford a home.

The price of housing has been particularly strong in popular cities such as London and Oxford. One of the reasons behind increases in house prices in these areas has been the influx of foreign investors buying UK property. European investors, wary of the precarious economic situation in the Eurozone have bought UK property as a safe haven for their money. Investors from across the globe invest in UK property due to the high rental yields on offer. However, in 2015, the government plans to introduce capital gains tax on non-resident foreigners selling UK property, which could help to dampen demand and prices.

KEY WORDS

Key words in this chapter are given below. There is space to write your own revision notes and to add any other words or phrases that you want to remember.

- Consumer Price Index
- Demand pull inflation
- Cost push inflation
- Deflation
- Demand and supply of housing
- Owner-occupation
- Negative equity
- Repossessions

REVIEW

The main learning points introduced in this chapter are summarised below.

Go through them and check back to the learning outcomes at the beginning of the chapter. Only move on when you are happy that you fully understand each point.

- We have examined inflation – its causes, effects and remedies – and also dealt with the importance of how the PSNB is financed.
- We noted that most economists support the view that inflation is caused by excessive money supply growth.
- We looked at the problems created by price deflation in an economy.
- We examined key aspects of the housing market and house prices, starting with the special features of the market – immobility, durability, lack of homogeneity – and then demand and supply factors.
- We also examined recent trends in house prices, along with the past/present problems of negative equity and repossessions.
- New rules on mortgage provision will be introduced by the FCA post 2013.

chapter 6

THE INTERNATIONAL MONEY MARKETS AND BANKS

Contents

Learning outcomes

On completion of this chapter, you should be able to:

- Analyse the interest rate structure and the demand/supply of funds in the international money market.
- Explain the operational activities of banks together with the key role played by the interbanks market in asset-liability management.

Introduction

Understanding the eurocurrency market's operational aspects is essential in order to appreciate the financial role of eurobanks and eurobond/securities markets. The next three chapters will build upon many of the concepts covered in this chapter. The influence of interest rate differentials will be examined, together with other key factors affecting the demand and supply of eurocurrencies. The basic features of the eurocurrency market will be discussed in detail to ensure a thorough understanding of this important international financial market.

Knowledge of the organisational form and operational aspects of eurobanks is also essential in order to understand their role in the provision of financial services, including loans. Active balance sheet management is used by eurobanks to maintain liquidity and overall profitability. We will examine these key aspects of eurobanking, and the important role played by the interbank market in providing funding for loans.

These key aspects of the eurocurrency market and eurobanks will be examined under the following headings:

- Eurodollar creation
- Operational aspects of the eurocurrency market
- Demand and supply of eurocurrencies
- Essential features of the eurocurrency market
- Eurobank organisational forms
- Eurobank balance sheet
- Eurocurrency interbank market role

The significance of these concepts will be considered against the background of the overall role of financial markets.

1 Financial markets

Before we can examine international money markets and develop the themes of intermediation and interest rates in an international context, it is essential to note a number of key distinctions as regards financial markets. Some financial markets, such as the foreign exchange market, are used as a means for making payments and settling outstanding debts. Other financial markets are primarily used in the provision of credit over specific time periods.

As noted in chapter one, financial markets, which are basically involved in the provision of credit, can be subdivided into those providing direct or indirect financing to the users of financial funds.

A final differentiation of financial markets can be made based on the location of the lending and borrowing. A domestic financial market is where the lender and borrower are located within the same national market, such as the UK. Most transactions in such a market are denominated in the national currency, in this case, sterling. A foreign financial market is where the lender and borrower are located in different countries. The financial transactions undertaken will be subject to the regulatory jurisdiction of the national market in which the funds are raised. For example, if a New Zealand corporation issues sterling bonds in the UK capital market, the issue procedures must comply with British regulations.

An external or eurocurrency market avoids national regulations by locating the credit market denominated in a particular currency outside the country of the currency's origin, e.g. US dollar deposit, loan and bond markets situated in London, Luxembourg or the Cayman Islands.

QUICK QUESTION

Which one of the following definitions of a eurocurrency do you think is correct?

A It is currency with its own individual exchange rate.

B It is held only by non-residents.

C It is a deposit of a currency held outside the country of the currency's origin.

D It is a European currency.

Write your answer here before reading on.

2 Eurocurrency market

2.1 What is a eurocurrency?

A eurocurrency is a time deposit held in a bank located outside the country (or central bank's jurisdiction) responsible for the currency in which the deposit is denominated, for example a dollar time deposit held in any bank's branch in London or a Swiss franc time deposit held in any bank's branch in Luxembourg – both financial centres are outside the USA and Switzerland respectively.

The dollar is the most important currency in the eurocurrency market, thus the term 'eurodollar market' is frequently used to describe the entire market.

2.2 What is a eurodollar?

A eurodollar deposit is a time deposit denominated in dollars in a bank (US or non-US owned) outside the United States, while a eurodollar loan is a dollar-denominated loan made by a bank outside the United States. It is different from the locational local currency of the bank making the loan, such as Barclays Bank in London (locational currency – sterling) granting a eurodollar loan to a British company. The key factor is whether the deposit or loan transaction is entered in the books of a bank based in the USA or elsewhere – the former (USA) are domestic dollar transactions, whereas the latter are eurodollar transactions.

2.3 Who can hold eurodollars?

Eurodollar deposits and loans made in London are virtually identical to domestic deposits and loans in US-based banks. Bank money managers and corporate treasurers readily switch funds between the domestic (onshore) and external (offshore) dollar markets. The important distinction between both dollar markets lies not in the nature of deposits or types of loan granted but in the fact that eurodollar banking is not subject to US domestic banking regulations.

Banks outside the USA have never been obliged to hold reserve (liquidity) requirements against or insure eurodollar deposits. No interest rate controls operate in the eurodollar market. It is essentially a wholesale deposit market with most deposits in excess of $1 million.

These factors enable the eurodollar market to offer more competitive deposit rates than the domestic market. It is the interest differential which distinguishes eurodollars from domestic dollars; both have the same foreign exchange rate against other currencies.

The above comments apply to all eurocurrency deposits such as euro-Swiss franc deposits, euro-yen deposits.

Eurodollar time deposits are held by residents and non-residents of the USA. The factor that makes dollars into eurodollars is the location of the holding bank; it does not depend on the nationality of the depositor or the bank. There is nothing to prevent a US resident transferring a time deposit denominated in dollars from Big Apple Bank's New York branch to its London branch to earn a higher interest return as a eurodollar time deposit.

The domestic dollar deposit is money within the context of the US economy, while the eurodollar deposit is near money held by a bank in an offshore money market such as London. So the eurodollar market is a place where banks outside the USA accept (borrow from customers) and place (lend) dollar deposits.

3 Nostro accounts

As there is no dollar clearing and settlement system outside the USA, all eurodollar transactions/settlements must take place through banks in New York using their clearing house system. Therefore all banks operating outside the USA and dealing in eurodollars must hold demand deposit accounts with US-based banks in New York through which receipts and payments can be effected.

These accounts, known as nostro accounts (a Latin term meaning our), are also used to settle banks' foreign exchange transactions and to enable them to conduct normal correspondent banking relationships, e.g. import/export payments. Just as you hold an account with a bank to effect cheque payments in sterling in the UK, a British bank which makes and receives payments in US dollars on behalf of its customers must hold an account in a bank in the USA. If XYZ plc requires to make a payment in US dollars, their UK bank account is debited the sterling equivalent of the draft (cheque) in US dollars drawn on the bank's nostro account in the USA.

Banks hold nostro accounts in various currencies with correspondent banks around the world to enable them to participate fully in international trade and investment transactions. Nostro accounts are also essential for conducting business in the eurocurrency (dollar) market in London and elsewhere.

QUICK QUESTION

What is the key factor in determining what is a eurocurrency deposit or loan?

Write your answer here before reading on.

3.1 Europe only?

Although the term eurodollar (or eurocurrency) might imply a market based exclusively in Europe, as was once the case, there is now an active Asian dollar market based in Singapore and Hong Kong which enables banks in the Far East to intermediate (borrow and loan) in external dollar deposits. A Middle East dollar market exists in Bahrain and Dubai, where eurodollars and other currencies are intermediated in by a number of Arab and non-Arab banks. Collectively these various regional banking centres make the eurocurrency market one of the largest money markets in the world.

Any freely convertible currency intermediated in, outside its country of origin, is a eurocurrency, e.g. euro £ in Paris. A UK bank with a Luxembourg branch holding euro Swiss franc deposits will instruct its correspondent bank in Switzerland on how to deal with its Swiss franc nostro account balance when the euro Swiss franc deposit is loaned to another bank or non-bank borrower for use.

Such eurocurrencies are held outwith the constraints of domestic banking regulations which are applicable to domestic deposits and loans in the country of origin of the currency.

Location is the key factor in determining whether a deposit is a eurocurrency deposit or not. A euro (€) deposit in the Eurozone is a domestic € bank deposit whereas a € deposit in London is a € eurocurrency bank deposit.

4 Eurocurrency market's essential features/characteristics

Being essentially free and unregulated, the eurocurrency market is governed by the principles of competition, while most domestic money markets in the past have been subject to restrictive practices which sought to secure a privileged position for certain vested parties such as government borrowers and domestic banks.

In the eurocurrency market, the avoidance of reserve requirements, insurance premiums, high volume/low value transactions has enabled the payment of higher interest on deposits (competition forced these cost savings to be passed on to depositors). Large loans, arranged in many cases by telephone, have kept operating costs to a minimum, and so the eurocurrency market provides lower-cost loans than domestic banking intermediation.

With new banks entering the market at will, competition is guaranteed in the eurocurrency market. At the same time, the eurocurrency markets provide banks with a useful pool of liquidity which helps them to match assets and liabilities within their portfolios.

Summary

Hopefully, for the international economy the eurocurrency markets bring about a more efficient allocation of investment or financial resources and increase world economic welfare.

In the final analysis it must be recognised that the eurocurrency markets are demand-determined. Their ability to provide large loans quickly and efficiently to multinational corporations, public sector corporations, international agencies and governments is the main justification for their existence. Such demand for funds brings forth a necessary supply of eurocurrency deposits.

5 Components of the eurocurrency market

5.1 Eurocurrency loan market

In this short term money market most loans mature within twelve months. It is primarily an interbank trading market where banks lend and borrow overnight, or up to one year, on an unsecured basis. This market accounts for up to 50% of the eurocurrency market's gross (total) size and provides the breadth and depth of financial resources required to enable banks to adjust their liquidity positions with relative ease.

To explain the mechanics of the interbank market, you should examine and carefully follow the sequence of fictitious transactions between banks operating in the London eurodollar market in the following case study.

CASE STUDY

EURODOLLAR INTERBANK MARKET ($M)

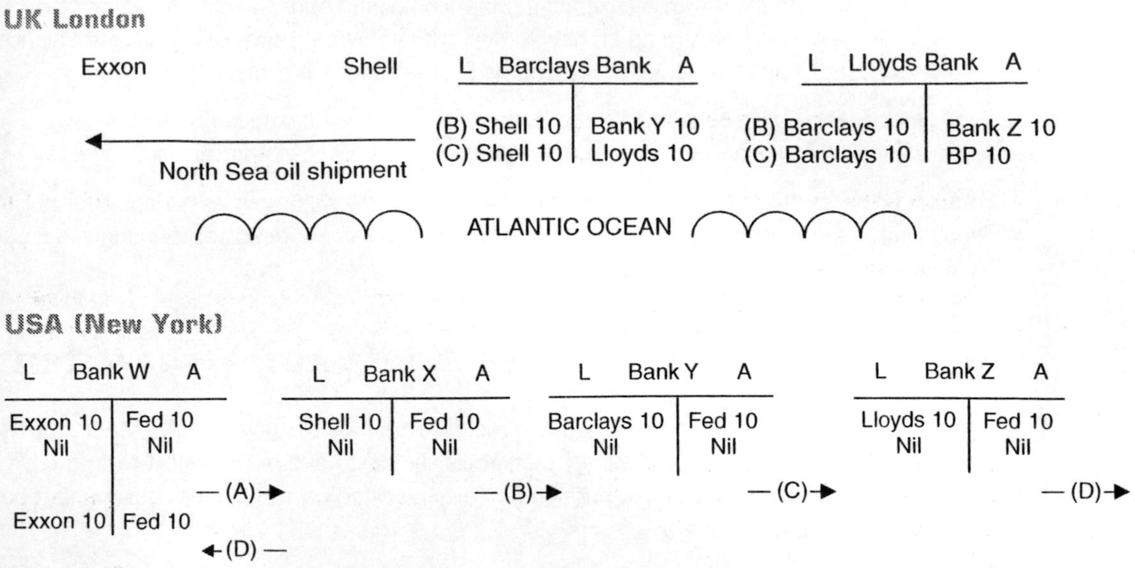

Stages

A Shell sells $10m of North Sea oil (shipment) to an Exxon refinery in the UK. Exxon, which banks with Bank W, transfers $10m from Bank W to Bank X to settle its debt with Shell. Bank X is Shell's bank in the USA. (Fed (asset) balance used for illustrative purposes only; it could be other assets, such as money market loans or Treasury bills). After transfer to Shell, Bank W (excluding all its other business) now has a nil balance on both sides of its balance sheet. The deposit and Fed balance of $10m are transferred to Bank X through the New York clearing house.

B Shell transfers $10m deposit to Barclays Bank, London. This is the initial Eurodollar deposit. Barclays' nostro account is held at Bank Y in the USA, therefore $10m is transferred from Bank X to Bank Y in New York. This transfer is effected through the New York clearing house. Note that Bank X's liability/asset balance are now nil. Shell has $10m eurodollar time deposit in Barclays Bank, London which has an asset of $10m in its name at correspondent bank, Bank Y, in New York. In Bank Y's books Barclays' balance is a liability, while the asset held against it is the original Fed balance.

C Barclays Bank lends $10m deposit to Lloyds Bank, D British Petroleum (BP) requires to make a $10m London, via the interbank market. As Lloyds payment to Exxon for gas supplied. Lloyds Bank's nostro account is at Bank Z in New York, a Bank lends BP $10m. BP's payment to Exxon in transfer from Bank Y to Bank Z takes place. Bank Y the USA results in $10m transfer from Bank Z now has nil balances. Note that in Barclays' to Bank W in the USA. Bank W, once again, has books Shell still has a $10m euro deposit, only the an Exxon deposit of $10m and a Fed balance of asset composition has changed from a balance at $10m. Meanwhile Bank Z has nil asset/ Bank Y to an interbank loan given to Lloyds Bank, liability balances. London. In Lloyds Bank, the deposit (liability) for $10m is in Barclays' name and the asset held is the $10m with Bank Z.

A summary of the final balances is:

UK (London)

Barclays Bank	
Shell $10m	Lloyds $10m

Lloyds Bank	
Barclays $10m	BP $10m

ATLANTIC OCEAN

USA (New York)

Bank W	
Exxon $10m	Fed $10m

Bank X	
Nil	Nil

Bank Y	
Nil	Nil

Bank Z	
Nil	Nil

At some future date BP must acquire dollars (from oil/gas sales) to repay Lloyds Bank, which in turn can repay its interbank loan to Barclays Bank, and if required to do so the latter can repay Shell's deposit of $10m.

The case study illustrates:

- The creation of a eurodollar deposit – by Shell
- The eurodollar interbank market – loan/deposit by Barclays Bank with Lloyds Bank in London
- The making of a eurodollar loan – Lloyds Bank loan to BP

This means that no single customer or bank via the interbank market can be sure of where its deposits will end up – Shell's deposit was loaned by Barclays to Lloyds and Lloyds used it to grant a loan to BP. A vast chain of bank intermediaries links the suppliers and users of eurocurrency market funds.

Banks use the interbank market either to finance international loans or to meet liquidity requirements, i.e. deposit repayments. Despite this market's importance to the existence and operational efficiency of the eurocurrency market, it operates on a very informal and unregulated basis. Transactions are effected by telephone or electronic means between money market dealers who must have an inherent trust in each counterparty bank's ability and willingness to repay these short term loans (deposits).

Like the foreign exchange market, no physical eurocurrency market exists; instead it consists of telecommunications between banks. Most business is handled by each bank's foreign exchange department because of the close similarity between buying/ selling bank deposits and borrowing/lending bank deposits. Both types of transactions necessitate the use of nostro accounts with correspondent banks. Also the combination of both activities enables banks to reduce overall operating costs. The main centres of eurocurrency activity are London, Luxembourg, Paris, Singapore and the Cayman Islands.

5.2 The eurocredit market

This market deals with the provision of medium and long term loans on a fixed or variable interest rate basis by banks to corporations and governments. Loans are used to finance international trade, investment and economic development programmes.

5.3 The eurobond market

Eurobonds are issued by corporations, governments and international agencies, such as the World Bank. Most bonds are listed and quoted on major stock exchanges. The bonds are placed (sold) by banks with their investment clients worldwide. Investors hold bonds (securities) issued by the ultimate borrower, unlike the eurocurrency bank market where investors hold short term claims on banks (intermediaries).

Therefore, the criteria to be met for a market to be categorised as eurocurrency are:

- It is a credit market – funds are lent and borrowed.
- It involves indirect financing, i.e. eurobanks accept deposits and grant loans, while the eurobond market provides direct financing in eurocurrencies via the issue of securities.
- It is located outside the country of the currency's origin, i.e. an external market.

5.4 Why do dollar bank transactions take place outside the USA?

Several conditions must be fulfilled for the lending and borrowing of dollars to take place in eurobanks outside the USA.

- Eurodollar deposit rates must be higher than domestic dollar deposit rates in order to induce a shift of dollar bank balances outside the USA to a foreign financial centre(s).
- Eurodollar loan rates must be more competitive than domestic dollar loan rates in order to induce non-bank borrowers to acquire dollar funds for their financial needs outside the USA.
- Eurodollar margins, i.e. loan rate *minus* deposit rate, must enable eurobanks to make a profit from their eurodollar business.

These conditions can be illustrated by a diagram:

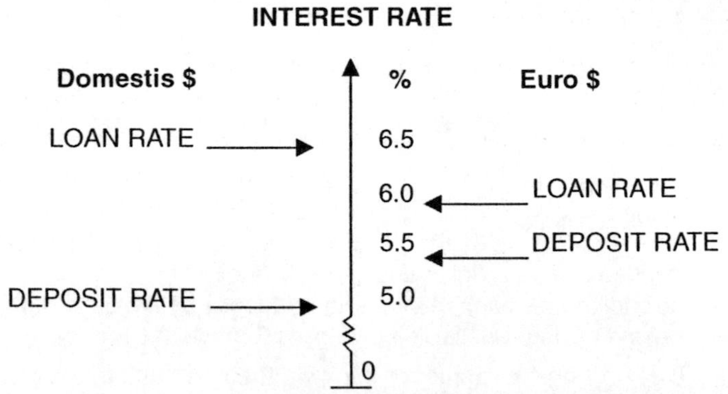

5.5 Size of the eurocurrency market

The exact size of the eurocurrency market is not known. Various estimates are published by the Bank for International Settlements (BIS). Steady and sustained growth of the eurocurrency market since the 1980s resulted in the market's estimated gross size increasing to approximately $10.0 trillion in recent years.

The gross size represents total foreign currency liabilities of banks in major financial centres including liabilities between banks within the market, as well as deposits from non-banks. It provides a gross measure therefore of the extent of eurocurrency intermediation.

In the eurodollar market there is a considerable amount of re-depositing between banks in eurocurrency market centres, so that the gross size overstates the amount on deposit from non-bank sources and made available to ultimate borrowers. Interbank deposits regularly account for up to 50% of the market's gross size.

5.6 Demand and supply of funds in the eurocurrency market

The eurocurrency market's overall size and activity is influenced, like all competitive markets, by demand and supply factors.

Demand factors

World monetary conditions, such as interest and exchange rate volatility, international trade needs and countries' external account disequilibrium, influence users' needs for finance.

Funds are required for portfolio (share/bond) investment and direct investment in projects by domestic and multinational corporations.

Some governments borrow for balance of payments purposes. Funds borrowed on a medium term basis are either added to official reserves or used for intervention purposes in the foreign exchange markets to maintain the value of a country's currency. Governments also borrow funds to finance infrastructure projects, such as new roads, in their own countries.

Supply factors

Funds are deposited in the market by governments, central banks and international banks. Central banks of countries such as China, Russia, Saudi Arabia, deposit their excess foreign currency reserves in the eurocurrency market. These funds are supplemented by transfers made by domestic banks and residents from internal (onshore) to external (offshore) money markets in their own currencies. Interest rates on offer appear to be the key factor influencing these deposit transfers.

Institutional investors, domestic and multinational corporations also deposit funds in the eurocurrency markets. Such non-bank corporations are able to reduce transaction costs by holding deposits in a currency in which they have frequent two-way dealings, e.g. BP holds a $ account in a bank in London.

The eurocurrency market's growth is also influenced by bank attitudes. Inadequate capital resources, insufficient eurocurrency intermediation profits or worries over loan exposures influence the willingness of banks to accept and lend funds.

You will now realise that the size and growth of the eurocurrency markets are influenced by a complex array of demand and supply factors. For example, nonresidents of Germany holding euro (€) deposits have a number of choices. The €s could be converted into the holder's domestic currency or another currency. If €s continue to be held, then the funds might be invested in the Eurozone's domestic money or securities markets, or alternatively the €s could be deposited in the € eurocurrency market. The non-resident's choice will depend on their needs, interest differentials and risks associated with each course of action.

5.7 Eurocurrency interest rates

Offshore interest rates are closely correlated to domestic interest rates because the eurocurrency market is a segment of the total credit market in each currency. The eurodollar market competes against the domestic dollar market for funds, just as banks compete domestically for funds. Because of interest rate arbitrage, eurocurrency interest rates are linked to domestic credit market interest rates; they are not determined in isolation. There is an obvious incentive for banks and non-banks to borrow in the cheap market and lend in the more expensive market, in order to make a risk-free profit.

Suppose 3 month domestic dollar interest rates were 6% and 3 month eurodollar time deposits generated 10%, then financial market operators/users would borrow domestic dollars and lend (deposit) them in the eurodollar market. Such action would increase onshore (domestic) interest rates and reduce offshore (euro) interest rates. Interest rates would quickly converge to about 8% in both markets. Regulatory and other factors would probably maintain a small interest rate differential in favour of the eurodollar market.

Alternatively, suppose the domestic interest rate on time deposits in the USA rose above the eurodollar rate in London, then the latter will quickly rise to a competitive level to prevent eurodollars flowing back to the USA to take advantage of higher domestic interest rates.

Such capital flows maintain a constant relationship between the onshore and offshore interest rates in each eurocurrency. Thus the eurodollar interest rate in London will reflect US domestic interest rates in New York rather than sterling interest rates.

QUICK QUESTION

Domestic dollars and eurodollars have the same spot foreign exchange rate against sterling – true or false?

Write your answer here before reading on.

6 London Inter Bank Offered Rate (LIBOR)

The interbank market in any eurocurrency determines the marginal cost of funds to banks operating in the eurocurrency markets. It is also used as a reference point for interest chargeable on variable rate loans. Major banks in the interbank eurodollar market usually quote a $^2/_{16}$% difference between bid and offer rates for interbank deposits.

As to be expected in a competitive market, LIBOR is determined by the demand and supply of eurodollar (or any other eurocurrency) funds. However, the free flow of funds between national and international money markets ensures that key domestic interest rates influence the cost of eurocurrency funds. Movements in US domestic-based banks' lending rates influence the eurodollar's LIBOR; the same applies to domestic and euro deposits and loans in other currencies.

LIBOR is the most widely used reference rate for short term interest rates. It is compiled by the British Bankers' Association and released to the market shortly after 11.00 am London time each day. The BBA maintains a reference panel of at least eight contributor banks which reflect the balance of the market in terms of country, institution, reputation, scale of market activity and perceived expertise in the currency concerned. BBA LIBOR fixings (average interest rate of the reference panel banks) are provided in nine international currencies including the dollar, euro, yen and sterling, etc. LIBOR is used as a reference interest rate for most eurocurrency loans to non-banks, e.g. governments, corporations.

Rumours began to circulate in 2008 that quoted LIBOR rates during the financial crisis did not accurately represent inter-bank lending rates. In February 2012, the US Department of Justice launched a criminal investigation into LIBOR abuse, suggesting that banks and inter-broker dealers were colluding to set LIBOR at artificial levels.

With the help of a whistleblower, regulators from both the US and the UK concluded that traders and brokers from a range of institutions had been manipulating LIBOR. The manipulation had been to serve two purposes – to increase the profits of their trading books, and to increase confidence in banks during the credit crisis.

Barclays was fined $200 million by the Commodity Futures Trading Commission, $160 million by the US Department of Justice and £59.5 million by the FSA for their part in the LIBOR scandal. Following the interest rate rigging scandal, both Marcus Agius, Chairman of Barclays, and Bob Diamond, Chief Executive Officer, resigned their respective positions. UBS was fined a total of $1.5 billion by various regulators. Rabobank also paid a $1 billion fine. Eight other banks, including RBS and Deutsche Bank, are set to be fined a total of €1.7 billion to settle LIBOR manipulation claims with European regulators.

The LIBOR scandal caused a huge shock to the global banking industry. The aftermath has resulted in the NYSE taking over the administration of LIBOR from the British Bankers Association (BBA). LIBOR itself has now become a regulated activity, overseen by the Financial Conduct Authority (FCA). However, Danish, Swedish, Canadian, Australian and New Zealand LIBOR rates have now been terminated.

QUICK QUESTION

What is a eurobank and what services does it provide?

Write your answer here before reading on.

7 Eurobank

A definition of a eurobank is:

'an international lending institution with an office in London or some other international financial centre whose principal activity is related to the taking of eurocurrency deposits and on-lending them to other banks or non-bank clients.'

To participate in the eurocurrency market, most large banks have established a presence in London, Luxembourg, Singapore, etc. Dependent on local regulations in each financial centre, major banks have established eurobank subsidiaries or branches from which to conduct eurocurrency loan business. In London, eurobanks also provide sterling loans, foreign exchange services and investment and corporate advice. They also undertake active balance sheet management in order to maintain adequate liquidity levels and overall profitability.

7.1 Organisational forms

- **Subsidiary**

  A subsidiary is a separately incorporated bank owned entirely or in major part by a foreign parent bank. The latter owns all or most of the ordinary (equity) share capital in the subsidiary bank. Such a eurobank's lending capacity is based on a multiple of its equity funds and it will probably participate in both international and domestic lending business. As it is locally incorporated, the eurobank subsidiary must comply with banking law and regulations of the host country.

- **Branch**

  A foreign bank branch in an international financial centre is legally and operationally part of the parent bank. This type of eurobank is subject to home country and host country regulation. It has its own assets and liabilities but in accounting terms these are part of the overall bank. The parent bank's net worth – capital – stands behind the branch deposits. US banks mainly operate through eurobank branches in London as they are simpler to create and staff than a subsidiary.

7.2 Other aspects

Apart from the attraction of eurocurrency market business in various financial centres, eurobanks also have a number of other roles and functions:

- Provision of banking facilities to multinational corporations and their own nationals based in a country
- Participation in foreign exchange market and domestic money market operations for clients
- Provision of banking services to resident nationals and corporations of the country hosting the eurobank

This list, by no means exhaustive, will provide you with some idea of the width and depth of eurobank activities in eurocurrency market centres.

7.3 Operational overview of a eurobank

Before examining the balance sheet of a eurobank subsidiary, it might be useful to summarise three key operational aspects relating to all types of eurobanks.

- Eurocurrency deposits mainly take the form of time deposits with fixed maturity dates, therefore low precautionary liquid asset balances are held by eurobanks.
- Non-interest bearing assets are held in nostro accounts at correspondent banks for transaction purposes in relation to foreign exchange and eurocurrency business transfers.
- Most eurobanks have no captive or natural deposit base in eurocurrencies and thus rely on wholesale money markets for funds (exceptions: US banks in eurodollar market, Swiss banks in euro Swiss franc market).

The overall objective of all eurobanks is to keep non-interest bearing assets to an absolute minimum. Assets must generate revenue to pay deposit interest, staff/administrative costs and contribute to a eurobank's overall profit.

QUICK QUESTION

What types of liquid assets might be held by a eurobank?

Write your answer here before reading on.

8 Eurobank balance sheet

The main assets and liabilities listed in the balance sheet of a typical eurobank subsidiary may look something like this.

Balance Sheet

Liabilities	*Assets*
Interbank Deposits	Nostro Account Balances
Non-Bank Time Deposits	Liquid Assets
Certificates of Deposit	Loans
Notes and Bonds	Other Assets
Parent Bank Loans	
Share Capital	

8.1 Liabilities

1 **Interbank deposits**

These funds are obtained via the eurocurrency interbank market. Eurobanks bid in or offer funds in this market, depending on whether they are short or long in available funds. The key interest rates in the London eurocurrency market are the London Interbank Bid Rate (LIBID) and the London Interbank Offered Rate (LIBOR) for each eurocurrency. Banks adjust their individual bid and offered rates in light of their funding needs. These rates are communicated to other banks in the market either directly or through money brokers. LIBID and LIBOR are quoted for overnight, 7 days or 3 months, etc funds.

2 **Non-bank time deposits**

As international banks lend in a variety of currencies other than their own, they are forced to bid in funds to support these operations. For most, no domestic deposit source exists. The competition for deposits is intense.

Depositors are concerned basically with available interest returns, liquidity and safety of funds. Interest rates negotiated on customers' wholesale time deposits are influenced by bid rates in the interbank market. Depositors may place funds with a bank for a fixed term at a fixed interest rate. To avoid penalties, such time deposits must be held for their full term.

Deposits come from a variety of sources:

- Governments
- State or private corporations
- Institutional investment funds
- Multinational corporations
- Central bank foreign exchange reserves

3 **Certificates of Deposit (CDs)**

In order to overcome the perceived inflexibility of time deposits, certificates of deposit (CDs) are used in the eurocurrency markets. A CD is a negotiable bearer instrument issued by a bank which certifies that a stated sum has been deposited for a specific time period at a particular interest rate. The key feature of a CD is that it can be sold by the holder in a secondary market, prior to maturity. It is thus an extremely liquid investment instrument. Dollar CDs issued by banks in London can have terms ranging from seven days to five years.

CDs are only issued to the customer after the dollar funds have been transferred to the issuing bank's nostro account in New York. As a CD is a bearer instrument, most are held in safe custody at banks or in many instances no certificate is issued; instead it takes the form of a book entry.

Most CDs are issued for periods of six months or less, in which case the accrued interest plus principal is repaid on the CD's maturity date.

4 **Notes and bonds**

Most notes have a variable coupon rate whilst bonds have fixed coupon rates. Notes and bonds provide medium to long term funding for eurobanks. Key aspects in relation to these financial instruments will be examined in Chapter 7.

Although not shown on the eurobank subsidiary's balance sheet, medium-term syndicated loans are sometimes used by lesser rated banks to fund loan books. Although it is more expensive than the above methods, the funds are reliable. A bank using this technique of funding must charge a higher spread on its own loans than it is paying for such funds.

Most large international banks issue floating rate notes as a major source of medium-term funding.

5 **Parent bank loans**

This represents a book transfer from the parent bank to its subsidiary; for the former it appears as an asset in its balance sheet. Funds from this source may be used where access to other sources is restricted or too expensive. Tax considerations also come into play as regard such intra-transfer of funds within the same banking organisation.

6 **Share capital**

Share capital represents a permanent source of funding for the eurobank subsidiary. The cost of such funds is determined by the size of dividend payments to the parent bank and any outside investors.

Summary

The liability items listed above will appear on the balance sheet of a subsidiary bank whilst a eurobank branch will be different due to the omission of notes/bonds and share capital; this will be offset by intra-bank transfers from the parent bank. As sources of funds become longer term and more permanent on the liabilities side, their corresponding cost for the eurobank will rise.

QUICK QUESTION

What types of liquid assets might be held by a eurobank?

Write your answer here before reading on.

8.2 Assets

1 **Nostro account balances**

Nostro accounts are held by eurobanks with correspondent banks in countries where a eurocurrency is the domestic currency of issue, e.g. US dollar in the USA. The balance in such accounts is kept to an absolute minimum as no interest is paid on these accounts by correspondent banks. This interest-free source of funds for the correspondent bank compensates it for the work undertaken on behalf of the overseas bank.

2 **Liquid assets**

These very liquid assets which earn a low return (yield) mainly take the form of interbank claims against other eurobanks. Most are in the form of short-term interbank deposits with other banks, with the balance being made up of purchased CDs which have been issued by other eurobanks requiring short-term funds. The liabilities of eurobanks seeking such sources of funds appear as an asset in eurobanks providing the financial resources required.

3 **Loans**

This asset represents funds lent by the eurobank subsidiary to non-bank users such as corporations and governments, etc. The loan price, i.e. interest cost, for an end-user is in most cases LIBOR plus a spread.

LIBOR is the loan reference rate and is similar to the use of the US prime rate or UK base rate in a domestic context. The spread compensates the eurobank subsidiary for granting the loan. Spread size is dependent on market conditions and the perceived creditworthiness of the borrower. Most spreads vary between 0.25% and 1.5%.

Most loans are re-priced every three or six months at the prevailing LIBOR plus the agreed spread. The re-pricing date is referred to as the rollover date. Thus, a one year loan with a six month rollover date would be priced at LIBOR plus spread when granted and then be re-priced six months later.

Eurobanks need to attract deposits to fund their loan book. Medium-term loans are to a large extent funded (financed) by short-term deposits which have to be repaid and then re-borrowed on a continuous basis. This necessitates the use of rollover dates in loan agreements to deal with fluctuations in the interest cost of funds. Thus, a eurobank can fund three or five year loans through three or six month borrowings on the liabilities side of its balance sheet without exposing itself to interest rate risk. The use of matched rollover dates ensures that the interest rate risk associated with a loan is borne by the end user, i.e. non-bank borrower.

EXAMPLE

10 year eurodollar loan @ LIBOR plus 1% spread; 12 month interest rollover; funded by issue of 12 month CDs.

Loan Cost to Borrower	%LIBOR	+	%Spread	=	%Total
1st Year (initial price)	15	+	1	=	6
2nd Year (re-priced)	10	+	1	=	11

If deposits are renewed at shorter time intervals than the loan rollover dates (mostly six months), a bank might increase its profits, as seven-day deposit funds are usually cheaper than six month funds. Short-term interest rates are usually lower than long-term interest rates. Due to greater liquidity, flexibility and less risk, investors (depositors) accept a lower rate of return on their funds. In this manner eurobanks can take advantage of the normal positive yield curve or on anticipated decline in market interest rates.

This practice of mismatching rollover dates for deposits and loans is known as gapping or trading in maturities. However, such practices do involve an element of risk for a bank. If during a six-month funding operation, seven-day money suddenly becomes more expensive due to higher money market interest rates, then a loss might be incurred. Loan interest received from the borrower over the six months might not be sufficient to cover the bank's own deposit (fund) interest costs.

4 **Assets**

In the eurobank subsidiary's balance sheet this item includes the cost of premises and equipment plus any long-term investments held such as bonds or shareholdings in other financial institutions, e.g. a consortium bank.

QUICK QUESTION

Can sterling deposits fund a eurodollar loan?

Write your answer here before reading on.

Summary

The major function of any eurobank is to accept deposits, i.e. interbank funds, time deposits, etc and utilise such funds to finance medium and long-term loans to non-bank customers. Most loans are re-priced on interest rollover dates, thus highlighting the crucial distinction between the loan commitment period and the applicable interest period.

At this point it is important to note that the survival of international banking and the eurocurrency loans market depends on adequate money market funds in each currency, the alternative for a bank being to purchase foreign exchange with domestic currency and thus incur a potential foreign exchange risk or lend its own domestic currency to overseas borrowers., A considerable proportion of international lending does take this latter form. US domestic-based banks do lend domestic dollars to Latin American customers, just as German banks make domestic euro loans to East European borrowers, such as Russian corporations.

Finally, on both the liabilities and assets sides of most types of eurobank balance sheets, interbank activity constitutes approximately 50% of the total gross size.

QUESTION TIME 19

Assume XYZ plc borrows $1million at LIBOR plus 0.5% spread. The loan has a three month rollover. LIBOR on 1 January, 1 April, 1 July and 1 October is 10%, 8%, 14% and 12% respectively. Calculate the total interest cost to XYZ plc of the loan for one year.

Write your answer here then check with the answer at the back of the book.

Q QUESTION TIME 20

How might a German bank subsidiary in London fund its euro Swiss franc loan book?

Write your answer here then check with the answer at the back of the book.

9 Eurocurrency interbank market

Surpluses and deficits of funds in relation to loan demand for individual eurobanks creates the need for an interbank market, enabling banks to eliminate or minimise their non-earning assets. Although little or no profit is made from interbank transactions, banks can undertake liquidity smoothing via active asset-liability management policies.

It is essential for banks to remain active in this market in order to keep abreast of market developments and to be seen as takers/suppliers of interbank funds. Banks tend to be subject to interest rate tiering in this market according to their perceived creditworthiness. This determines the overall cost of such funds in each bank.

Non-bank customers tend to do most of their banking business with prime named banks due to their credit standing, size and ability to offer large loan facilities. As a result, prime named or large international banks act as overall net suppliers of funds to the interbank market. Citibank and Bank of America tend to be net suppliers of eurodollars. The net takers tend to be smaller, less well-known banks, with lower credit ratings in the financial markets. Thus, dependence on interbank funds is a function of the nationality, size and creditworthiness of a bank.

9.1 Interest rate tiering

As noted above, some banks are net takers of interbank funds, the cost of these being related to a bank's size, nationality and reputation. Under normal market conditions the margin paid by lesser-rated banks over prime banks is about 0.25%. If the eurocurrency market experiences a financial shock and confidence declines among banks, the margin can widen to 1% or more. This could cause a small eurobank a potential problem if its loan portfolio is yielding LIBOR + 0.75% while funding costs are LIBOR + 1%. A loss of 0.25% on an entire loan portfolio could not be sustained over a prolonged time period.

9.2 Credit lines

Eurobanks have a large number of unadvised and uncommitted credit lines from other banks on both sides of their balance sheets. These lines can be tapped with the minimum of formality in order to raise or dispose of funds to other banks. Such credit lines must be diversified via a large number of banks and financial centres in order to reduce risk associated with active asset-liability management. The ability to raise required asset funding at any point of time is an absolute necessity for all eurobanks.

9.3 Information role

The interbank market assists in the transfer of deposits from non-bank lenders to non-bank borrowers. It is assumed that the end lending bank is better able to assess the creditworthiness of the end non-bank user than the intermediary banks in the interbank chain.

Also by participating in the interbank market, eurobanks can collect information on the funding needs of other banks and/or transmit information on their funding position and credit standing in the market. Thus, active participation in the market can be regarded as a form of insurance for a eurobank should it experience a temporary liquidity squeeze at any point of time.

From an information perspective, the interbank market acts as a market barometer to eurobanks by providing an accurate indication of market conditions.

9.4 Transformation role

The interbank market also initiates a number of transformations:

1 **Geographical transformation**

Eurocurrency funds deposited in London through the interbank market may eventually be lent out in Singapore. In effect the interbank market is a worldwide clearing house for funds.

2 **Credit Transformation**

Prime name banks on-lend funds to other banks and thus relieve the non-bank depositor of the need to carry credit risk assessment of lesser-known banks.

3 **Currency transformation**

A eurodollar deposit via the interbank chain might end up as a sterling loan in the books of a bank. The lending bank sells the dollars for sterling to on-lend to its customer.

4 **Maturity transformation**

Non-bank depositors prefer short-term deposits, whereas non-bank borrowers require funds over a longer timescale. Eurobanks can deal with this mismatch of requirements via the interbank market and interest rate rollovers.

5 **Market transformation**

History tends to confirm that the international banking system via the interbank market adapts speedily and efficiently to new developments and lending opportunities.

Summary

The primary function of the interbank market is to re-distribute funds within the international banking system, enabling banks to put deposits to work and reduces precautionary liquid asset balances to a minimum. The intermediation of non-bank funds are effected from depositors to borrowers through a process of transformations. The efficiency of the interbank market in no small way aids in the process of using world capital funds/savings in the most efficient manner.

9.5 Credit crunch 2007-09

The interbank market increases the number of eurobanks that might be affected by a liquidity and/or solvency problem in an individual bank. The market involves an element of credit risk and is only as strong as its weakest link. Lending between banks has sometimes been described as the 'Achilles heel' of the international financial system. This became evident during the credit crunch of 2007-09 when banks stopped lending to one another due to an overall lack of confidence in the global banking/financial system. The latter was encouraged by an increasing number of major banks incurring liquidity and solvency problems. The resultant liquidity squeeze on banks due to the drying up of interbank lending forced most central banks into providing lender-of-last resort support to their own national banks.

Interbank market problems were clearly highlighted by the key LIBORs for most currencies which reached unprecedented margins above central bank discount rates.

Again such margins indicated a lack of confidence in the global banking system. Banks with funds to lend became more risk averse and demanded premium LIBORs from other banks suffering a shortage of funds. Extreme interest rate tiering was self evident in the interbank market.

10 Asset-liability management

International banks engage in active asset-liability management to reduce risks and enhance returns. Such management necessitates a continuous review of a bank's overall balance sheet in order to avoid excessive time maturity and interest rate mismatching of assets and liabilities. It is also important to have a diversified deposit base without undue reliance on one particular economic sector or region of the world.

For non-US banks operating in the eurodollar market such precautions can be reinforced by establishing, for a small fee, domestic dollar standby facilities, i.e. borrowing agreements, with US banks in the USA. Similar standby credit facilities can be established in respect of other eurocurrencies.

Asset-liability management is assisted by computerised accountancy systems which can present information on a bank's total exposure by country or customer on a daily basis. Also in most countries (and financial centres) such operations are closely monitored by the central bank and regulatory authorities.

QUESTION TIME 21

Explain the main features and roles of the eurocurrency interbank market.

Write your answer here then check with the answer at the back of the book.

KEY WORDS

Key words in this chapter are given below. There is space to write your own revision notes and to add any other words or phrases that you want to remember.

- Eurocurrency
- Interbank market
- Nostro account
- Asset-liability management
- Certificate of deposits
- Spread
- LIBOR
- Interest rate arbitrage
- Transformation role

REVIEW

The main learning points introduced in this chapter are summarised below.

Go through them and check back to the learning outcomes at the beginning of the chapter. Only move on when you are happy that you fully understand each point.

- We have defined a eurocurrency as a time deposit in a currency intermediated in outside the country of the currency's origin.
- The creation of Eurodollar (or any eurocurrency) deposits was explained as well as the key role of nostro accounts.
- A review of eurocurrency market transactions emphasised the importance of the interbank market as a means of transferring funds.
- Two types of eurobanks – subsidiary and branch - were explained.
- Key operational aspects of a eurobank subsidiary were reviewed with the aid of a specimen balance sheet which highlighted the main assets and liabilities.
- The interbank market's role as a vital link between eurobanks and financial centres.
- Asset-liability management techniques were explained, with emphasis on the use of gapping by eurobanks to enhance their profits.

chapter 7

INTERNATIONAL LOAN AND BOND MARKETS

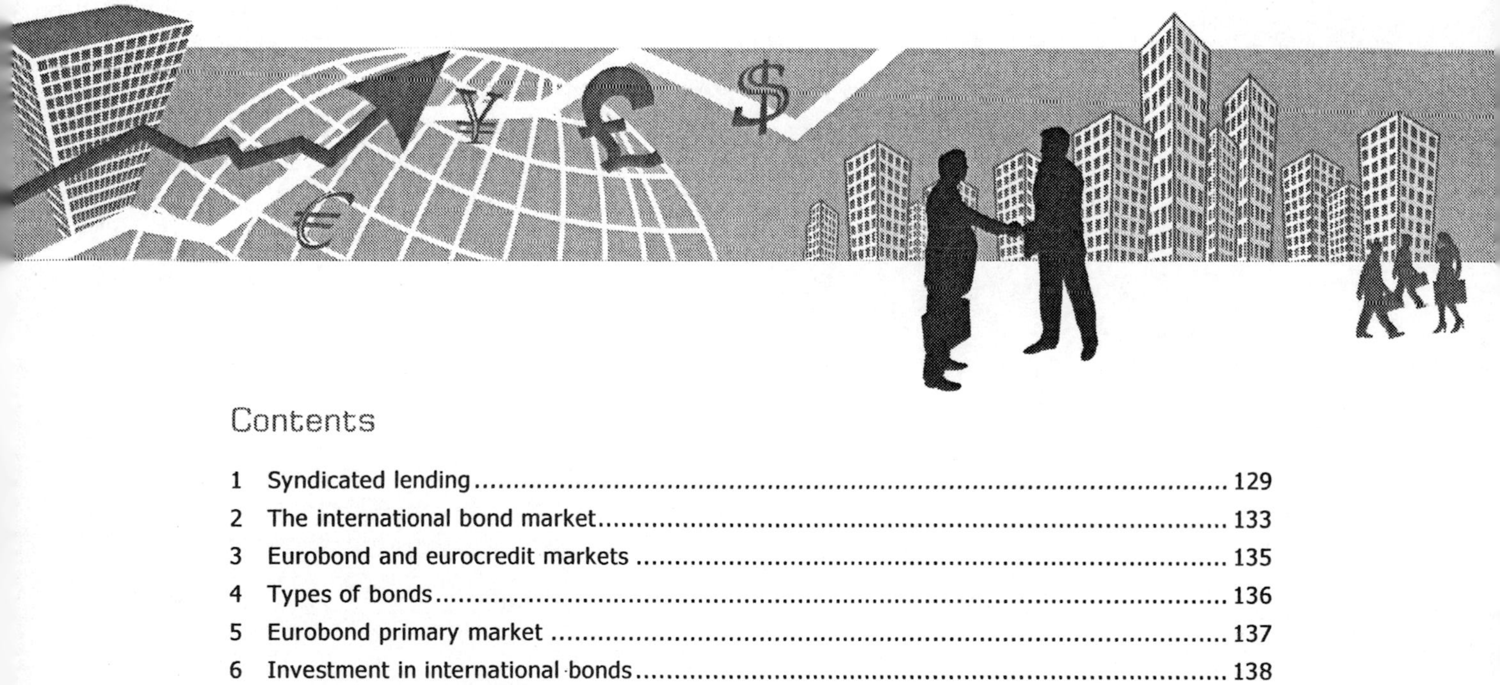

Contents

Learning outcomes

On completion of this chapter you should be able to:

- Explain the main features of the syndicated loan market, its participants and the flexibility of such loans for non-bank borrowers.
- Compare and contrast the eurobond and foreign bond markets together with the various types of bonds issued and the role of credit rating agencies.
- Critically reflect on international banking centres in particular offshore functional and shell centres along with a close examination of London as the world's leading centre.

Introduction

We are now going to examine syndicated lending and consider the roles of the main participants, including the syndicate leader. We will also look at some standard loan clauses which protect banks against money market developments and possible default.

The two main components of the international bond market are the foreign bond market and the eurobond market. We will analyse what the attractions of the various types of bonds are for investors/borrowers as opposed to syndicated loans, and we will also consider floating rate notes in relation to their use by banks as a source of funding.

Having already examined the eurocurrency market and eurobanking, we now need to differentiate between international financial centres, and in this context we will analyse the role of London as the world's main international banking centre and take into consideration new developments that could erode London's comparative advantages.

1 Syndicated lending

Most loans for financing international trade and investments are made by individual banks to their customers without the assistance of other banks. Loans can be secured or unsecured and have a floating (LIBOR) interest rate. In most cases the bank has a formal loan agreement with customers.

A considerable proportion of eurocredit lending takes this form but the granting of large loans of over $50 million encouraged banks to provide funds via loan syndication. Some sovereign government loans or loans for large projects are in excess of $1 billion and are commonly referred to as jumbo loans.

A syndicated loan might be defined as:

> **'a loan made by two or more lending institutions, on similar terms and conditions, using common documentation and administered by a common agent.'**

Multi-bank loans are common in most developed countries for large amounts because banking prudential regulations limit the size of a loan that a single bank can grant to any one customer. Multibank loan techniques were thus readily adopted in the eurocurrency markets.

For borrowers with large funding requirements, the use of syndicated loans enables the managing bank to obtain funds more quickly, in greater amounts and at a lower cost than would be the case in conducting separate negotiations with up to fifty lending banks. The terms attached to such loans are dictated by market conditions and the usual criteria of security, creditworthiness and risk.

Syndicated eurocredits also enable banks to spread their risks by having a large and diversified loan portfolio rather than being overcommitted to a few customers. Also, some banks seek the publicity associated with such large loans as well as the possibility of establishing profitable working relationships with the borrower and other banks involved in the syndication.

QUICK QUESTION

What do you think are the main functions of the syndicate manager?

Write your answer here before reading on.

1.1 Syndicate parties

A syndicate loan has four parties:

- Borrower
- Syndicate leader (or manager)
- Participating banks
- Agent bank

Borrower

The borrower seeks to obtain funds in a convenient, economic and flexible manner, as well as maintaining its financial status in the world's capital and credit markets. Details on the size, use and any security for the loan are provided by the borrower to the syndicate leader.

Syndicate leader

The syndicate leader must have adequate lending experience and high standing in the international banking community. The leader (or manager) has obligations to both the borrower and participating banks. As the financial engineer, the syndicate manager must assess the viability of the loan proposal programme or project which might require specialist knowledge in some industry or region of the world. To a certain extent, participating banks, if they wish, can avoid a detailed analysis of each loan proposal by relying on the syndicate leader's expertise and good faith. This is sometimes referred to as the comfort factor. Participation in loans by other banks is often influenced by which bank is the syndicate leader, as the latter might have specialist knowledge of a particular economic activity or sector. The syndicate leader receives management fees from the borrower for arranging the loan facility. Most syndicate leaders keep some of the loan in their own asset portfolio.

Participating banks

The participating banks rely on the integrity of the syndicate leader who has a moral obligation to ensure that the information provided by the borrower via a placement memorandum and passed on to other banks in the syndicate is correct. Whether there is a legal obligation is unclear at present. The participating banks collectively provide the bulk of the funds for most syndicated loans.

Agent bank

The agent bank, which is often the syndicate leader, acts as a communication link between the borrower and the lending banks on completion of the loan deal. The agent bank fixes the interest rate on the reference date for rollover loans, collects and distributes interest/principal payments from the borrower and has the power to renegotiate some of the loan terms. An agency fee is payable to the agent bank on an annual basis.

1.2 Other aspects of syndicated loans

Flexibility

The syndicated loan market provides one of the most flexible forms of finance available. Most eurocredits provide drawdown facilities so that funds can be accessed when required by the borrower. Prepayment and cancellation clauses with or without financial penalty are included in order to take account of alterations in the borrower's cash flow position.

Syndicated credits also provide a stable source of funds, whereas bond issues sometimes have to be postponed if the capital market is disrupted by some financial shock. Eurocredits are suitable as a means of raising finance where some form of discrete deal, such as a takeover or acquisition, is being contemplated by the borrower.

Compared with the bond market, a syndicated loan is a relatively inexpensive way of obtaining funding, offers the borrower the opportunity of developing banking relationships and can be used for a whole range of funding requirements. The syndicated market has continued to evolve with market needs.

Uses of currency loans

Fixed and floating rate eurocurrency loans can be used to finance a wide range of activities – loans to finance government infrastructure expenditure, industrial projects, trade and investment. Some governments in the past have encouraged state-owned enterprises to borrow in the eurocredit market, with the resultant foreign exchange proceeds, once exchanged for domestic currency at the country's central bank, being used for balance of payments support in order to stabilise a country's exchange rate.

Most large corporations, irrespective of their domestic base, usually seek to establish a presence overseas by direct investment in a subsidiary unit or joint venture. Foreign currency loans from banks are often used to finance such expansion and diversification. Foreign currency loans are also used extensively in foreign trade finance.

Borrower considerations

For governments, state and private corporations, foreign currency borrowing represents a departure from traditional fund sources – domestic currency borrowing from local banks, money and capital markets. This can have advantages where credit restrictions on local banks in emerging and developing economies make foreign currency borrowing the only source of finance available, or if interest rates are lower than domestic currency loan rates.

Against such benefits the borrower has to consider the possibility of domestic currency depreciation in terms of the loan's currency, which would increase overall debt service costs. The most desirable situation is to ensure, if possible, that the export or project's receipts are in the currency of a loan as this facilitates interest and principal repayments.

All borrowers must carefully weigh up the benefits and potential costs of using foreign currency loans, as opposed to domestic currency loans, to finance trade, investment and public expenditure.

QUESTION TIME 22

The total interest cost on a variable interest rate eurocredit loan is composed of LIBOR plus a spread.

(a) Explain the factors influencing LIBOR

(b) What is the significance of the spread for a bank?

(c) Why do spreads vary among borrowers?

Write your answer here then check with the answer at the back of the book.

1.3 Loan contract

The documentation for a syndicated loan is arranged and negotiated by the lead manager with the agreement of participating banks. Most loan agreements include standard clauses that can be divided into two main types:

1. Those dealing with the mechanics of the lender/borrower relationship
2. Those to protect the interests of the lenders

The latter may appear to be biased in the lender's favour but on the release of the funds, the banks in the syndicate are dependent upon the borrower for interest payments and repayment of the principal sum lent. Also, most syndicated credit facilities are unsecured, with no collateral or guarantees being provided by borrowers.

Some standard loan clauses

- **Eurodollar (or market) disaster clause**

  This clause protects banks if they are unable to fund proposed or existing loans via the eurocurrency interbank market. There are three specified circumstances.

  1. Substitute New York prime rate for LIBOR. Although unlikely ever to happen, economic and/or financial factors could prevent eurodollar market funding of a dollar loan made in London. Banks would thus be forced to fund such a loan via the New York money markets. The substitute interest rate would reflect the higher funding costs involved for the banks.

  2. Reference interest rate adjustment. It could happen that LIBOR no longer reflects the funding costs of participating banks. Volatile money markets might result in excessive interest rate tiering in the interbank market. LIBOR plus 0.5% spread on a loan is inadequate if funding costs for many eurobanks rise to LIBOR + 0.75%. Such a situation would necessitate a new reference interest rate to reflect higher average funding costs for syndicated loan participants.

3 Rollover date variations. In this situation, eurocurrency deposits for a particular time period, say 6 months, may no longer be available to eurobanks. If only 3 month funds are available, then a 6 month rollover may be changed to a 3 month rollover date.

A market disaster clause enables the borrower and lenders to re-negotiate the loan deal within 30 days and to arrange an alternative basis for the remainder of the loan's term. The syndicate leader specifies the new formula if this is rejected by the borrower, then the latter is allowed to repay and cancel the loan agreement without any penalty payments.

- **Change of circumstances clause**

  This clause relates to the lenders or borrower and covers events national or international which may increase funding costs via the imposition of reserve requirements, insurance premiums or taxes. Additional funding costs must be met by the borrower, although the latter is provided with a prepayment option without penalties.

- **Undertakings and covenants**

  An undertaking is where the borrower promises to provide half-yearly reports on their current financial position. For sovereign government borrowers this involves statements on their international reserves, budget and external account position. Covenants set down financial obligations agreed between the borrower and lenders. These might include minimum tangible net worth, limits on disposal of assets and limits on total consolidated borrowings in relation to tangible net worth of a corporation.

- **Events of default clause**

  The lending banks have the right to terminate their loan obligations and call in their loan if any of the following six events occur:

  1 Failure to pay interest or principal on the required dates
  2 Misrepresentation by the borrower in the original loan agreement, e.g. no borrowing authority exists or false accounts were presented
  3 Failure to observe undertakings and covenants
  4 Bankruptcy or liquidation
  5 Material adverse change in the borrower's financial position
  6 Default on any other debt, i.e. cross default clause sets minimum amount of default for this to be triggered

  The agent bank acts with the consent of the majority of the lenders in activating this clause.

2 The international bond market

The international (or external) bond market comprises two components: the foreign bond market and the eurobond market. We will discuss the attractions of bond issues for borrowers as opposed to eurocredits, and analyse which types of bonds are appropriate for different types of investors.

2.1 Foreign bonds

This is a bond sold by a borrower outside of their own country in another country's capital market and currency. For example, a state enterprise in Brazil might issue a dollar bond in New York or a Swiss franc bond in Zurich. Such an issue might be encouraged by low interest rates and/or the availability of funds in a foreign capital market. The funds raised might be required to meet the foreign currency import costs of a particular project. Of course, subsequent fluctuations in the exchange rate between the borrowing currency and domestic currency of the borrower will affect the interest cost and principal repayment burden.

If the Brazilian state enterprise decided to raise Swiss franc funds in Switzerland's capital market, the bond's issue (sale) would most likely be managed by a syndicate of Swiss banks, with the resultant bonds being traded and quoted on the Swiss capital market. The bonds would be held by Swiss resident and non-resident investors who are attracted by the higher yield than that available on purely Swiss domestic bond issues.

Foreign bonds are also issued on the Yankee (foreign) bond market in New York by foreign corporations. A high percentage of these bonds are purchased by US resident investors. Large foreign bond markets also operate in Japan, Germany and the UK.

2.2 Eurobonds

This is a bond sold by a borrower outside of their own country in other countries' capital markets, other than that capital market of the bond's currency denomination. For example, a Brazilian state enterprise might issue a dollar bond in London or Luxembourg, or a Swiss franc bond in Luxembourg. Such a bond will be issued for the same reasons as above, only in this case the bond issue will be managed by a syndicate of international banks and the subsequent bond holders will nearly all be non-residents of the country in whose currency the bond is denominated.

This eurobond market has certain features that distinguish it from most foreign bond (or domestic bond) markets:

- It operates with the minimum of regulations, unlike most domestic capital markets. It completely avoids the regulations, controls and queue procedures used and enforced in domestic capital markets by central banks and/or government finance departments.
- Eurobonds are not available for public subscription but instead are placed by investment banks involved in the issue with a wide geographical spread of investors who generally hold investment accounts with them. The funds held in these accounts are exempt from any form of exchange control, for example non-resident investment account holders in Switzerland.
- The interest on eurobonds is exempt from any form of withholding tax which is unlike some domestic and foreign bonds, although non-resident holders of the latter bond types can recover tax deducted from the appropriate tax authority.
- Interest rates payable on eurobonds are influenced by market conditions and investor preferences. In most cases, eurobond yields are closely correlated to domestic bond yields on similar instruments in the same currency.

  Yield is the rate of return on a bond as determined by its interest rate, market price and maturity.

  Eurobond issues regularly account for about three quarters of the international bond market's gross size each year. Dollar-denominated bond issues are the largest single component of the eurobond market (Swiss franc-denominated bonds usually constitute the main component of the foreign bond market). The eurobond market makes available to creditworthy borrowers an almost inexhaustible supply of funds in a variety of currencies.

QUICK QUESTION

Who invests in eurobonds?

Write your answer here before reading on.

2.3 Eurobond investors

- Investors in euro (and foreign) bonds can be divided into two major categories – private individuals and institutional investors. Most private individuals have bond holdings in excess of $250,000. Many of these substantial investment portfolios are held with trust departments of banks in Switzerland and Luxembourg, which offer their investment clients two types of account:

  1 Discretionary account – where the bank alone decides how to invest its clients' money in bonds and equities, etc. Such power provides Swiss banks with the ability to place a large number of eurobonds in clients' portfolios.

  2 Advisory account – where both the bank and client determine the overall investment strategy. The client might not want to invest in bonds issued by specific governments or corporations because of moral or ethical objections, such as bonds issued by a military equipment manufacturer.

With both types of account there is a tendency by the banks, with or without the consent of their clients, to invest in bonds issued by prime-rated names from the rich industrialised countries. At the same time, the issue of euro and foreign bonds denominated in various currencies enables Swiss (and other) banks to achieve maximum portfolio diversification on behalf of their investment clients.

Institutional investors, e.g. pension funds and insurance corporations, have become more important with the passage of time and now hold approximately 90% of all bonds issued. Such investors have made available a larger supply of funds to the market, which has encouraged progressively larger euro and foreign bond issues to take place. They have also brought about greater transparency to the eurobond primary (new issues) market and have actively improved the functioning of the secondary market.

QUICK QUESTION

In what ways do you think eurobonds are different from eurocredits?

Write your answer here before reading on.

3 Eurobond and eurocredit markets

Fundamentally, the eurobond market performs the same functions as the eurocredit market. Funds are gathered internationally, denominated in a variety of currencies, and made available to borrowers from various countries, largely without being influenced, allocated or regulated by national authorities.

Some casual observers have viewed the eurobond market simply as a long term extension of the eurocredit market. In fact eurobonds are quite distinct from eurocredits since bond markets enable investors to hold the securities issued by final borrowers, unlike the eurocredit market which allows investors to hold short term claims on eurobanks which transform deposits into long term riskier loans on their books to final borrowers.

No intermediaries intervene between the lender and borrower in the eurobond market. Banks are only involved in the initial bond placement, for which they receive a one-off management fee for their services.

There are several other points of contrast between eurobonds and eurocredits.

- Eurobonds generally entail a fixed coupon rate rather than a variable interest rate associated with most syndicated eurocredits, which means that the cost of funds is known to the borrower – the bond issuer – at the outset, unlike the use of bank credit, where interest charged depends on money market developments.
- In most cases, bonds are issued on an unsecured basis with no fixed or floating charge over the issuer's assets, unlike syndicated eurocredit agreements which often contain restrictive clauses on the future actions, such as asset disposals, of the borrower.
- Most eurobonds are listed and traded, whereas with syndicated eurocredits, the transfer of participations by banks is subject to various legal technicalities or problems over the transfer of legal rights and remedies.

4 Types of bonds

There are many types of eurobonds (and foreign bonds) and two of the main ones are as follows.

4.1 Fixed rate (straight) bonds

Under normal market conditions these are the most popular type of bond issue. They have a fixed interest rate and maturity date. Interest is usually paid once per annum. The minimum face value of each bond is $1,000. Fixed rate bonds are available to investors in the widest possible choice of currencies and maturities to suit their portfolio requirements. For the borrower, certainty of interest cost and a specific repayment date provide some assistance in estimating future cash flows. Bond redemption can either be a one-off payment at maturity or specific amounts at set dates. In the latter case, bonds are drawn by lot and repaid at full face value. This tends to limit the level of discount on bond prices in the secondary market.

4.2 Convertible bonds

Some fixed rate bonds have incorporated into them a convertible element which enables the investor to convert into the equity (common) stock of the issuer – the industrial corporation or bank – at a future date at predetermined conversion prices. This enables the bond holder/investor to become a shareholder in a corporation or bank and participate in its future profits. Such bonds with conversion rights can be issued with a lower coupon rate than a straight bond.

Conversion prices are generally 10 - 20% higher than the share price at the issue date of the convertible bond. If the money raised is used wisely, the corporation will prosper and with it the value of its ordinary or equity shares. This makes conversion a profitable exercise for the bond holder. In the secondary market the convertible bond's price will be closely correlated to movements in the ordinary share price.

Conversion is optional for the holder. If the ordinary shares fail to rise in price, the convertible bond holder will retain the bonds and thus will continue to benefit from annual interest payments and ultimate redemption.

QUESTION TIME 23

What are the advantages of convertible eurobonds for investors?

Write your answer here then check with the answer at the back of the book.

5 Eurobond primary market

A eurobond issue is generally handled by an international banking syndicate which has a three tier structure:

- Lead manager
- Underwriters
- Selling group

5.1 Lead manager

Like syndicated credits, the lead manager must compete with other banks for the mandate to issue bonds on behalf of a government or corporation. Success in mandate competition is often linked to a reputation for trouble-free bond issues in the past and a wide range of market contacts for placing the bonds.

For a management fee (up to 0.5% of bond issue size), the lead manager discusses with the bond issuer the bond's terms, such as the interest/coupon rate, redemption features and maturity date. Alternative sources of finance might be given consideration at this point, such as a syndicated credit.

Once it is decided to proceed with the bond issue, the lead manager assists in preparing the bond prospectus and arranging the underwriting and selling of the bonds.

5.2 Underwriters

The second tier consists of an international syndicate of US, Japanese and European banks to underwrite the bond issue. If the bonds are not placed (sold) with investors, the underwriters will take up the unsold bonds; this guarantees the borrower's expected funds. Underwriting commission (up to $^3/_8$%) is paid to these banks and they receive an assurance of a specific allocation of bonds for themselves and their investment clients.

5.3 Selling group

The third tier consists of the selling group of banks (up to fifty) which have a wide geographical spread and large numbers of investment clients. Details of the borrower, bonds and use of funds are dispatched to each selling bank. The selling group receives commission up to a maximum of 1.5% of the bond issue value allotted to it. The selling group also incorporates the underwriting banks which, via underwriting and selling fees, may receive up to 2% of the value of each bond placed with their investment clients.

Overall, front-end fees for a bond issue can amount to approximately 2.5% of the bond issue value. These are deducted from the proceeds of the bond issue and the borrower receives the net amount. The actual level of front-end fees payable is influenced by market conditions and the bond's term – longer maturities generally entail higher fees.

6 Investment in international bonds

6.1 Credit ratings

One of the first facts an investor in euro or foreign bonds will want to determine is the ability of the bond issuer to meet payment obligations. Investors know that creditworthiness varies greatly among bond issuers and that there are professional, impartial bond rating agencies which give judgements on the basic quality of bonds.

The Standard & Poor's Corporation (S&P) and Moody's Investors Services Incorporated in the USA make their investment ratings available to the public. The ratings are given to the actual debt securities issued by the borrowers, not the borrowers themselves. Fitch IBCA is Europe's largest credit rating agency.

In relation to corporations, rating agencies analyse economic and financial data such as leverage, cash flows, profits, interest cover, etc before awarding a particular grade. Bonds issued by governments are rated on the basis of economic and political risk. Bond ratings are constantly reviewed in light of new economic, financial and political data/developments becoming available to the rating agencies.

An investor in bonds must consider the relationship between yield and risk. High yielding bonds generally involve a greater degree of risk than bonds offering lower yields. The main bond risk variables include:

- The country of the issuer
- The creditworthiness of the issuer
- The economic sector of the issuer, e.g. risks vary between engineering, banking and oil

Also a fixed interest/coupon rate issue with limited return and yield must be compared with the greater risks attached to bonds with warrants or convertible bonds offering equity participation.

Rating agencies use different letter systems to classify bond issues. Standard & Poor's is noted below as a guide:

Standard & Poor's Guide to Definitions

AAA	Extremely strong capacity to pay interest and repay principal/ Best quality.
AA	Very strong capacity to pay interest and repay principal/High quality.
A	Strong capacity to pay interest and repay principal – more susceptible to adverse effects of changes in economic conditions than AAA or AA/Upper medium grade obligations.
BBB	Adequate strong capacity to pay interest and repay principal. Adverse economic conditions more likely to weaken capacity to meet obligations/Medium grade obligations.
BB, B, CCC, CC	Predominantly speculative, major risk exposures to adverse conditions/Lacks characteristics of desirable investment.

C	Income bonds on which no interest is being paid/Highly speculative.
D	In default and payment of interest and/or repayment of principal in arrears/Lowest rated class of bonds.

Issues with credit ratings agencies

The business model used by credit rating agencies has been criticised in the wake of the 2008 financial crisis. It has been suggested that ratings agencies put profit before the integrity of their ratings, which led to securities being issued with incorrect credit ratings. In particular, many Collateralised Debt Obligations (CDOs) were issued with strong credit ratings due to banks encouraging strong credit ratings in order for the ratings agencies to win more business.

This has led to US government seeking a $5 billion civil lawsuit against S&P for (allegedly) defrauding investors by claiming that their credit ratings were objective. This lawsuit has damaged the credibility of S&P and also calls into question the future of ratings agencies – the current model of issuers paying agencies fees for a credit rating may end, which begs the question of how ratings agencies will be able to operate in the future without this fee structure.

7 Secondary eurobond market

Most eurobond issues are listed in London or Luxembourg. A fee is payable by the issuer to the respective exchange. The listing of eurobonds is beneficial as it assists primary market placing of bonds and also forces issuers to meet disclosure requirements.

The secondary eurobond market is an over-the-counter market – there is no physical market as such. Instead it is a telephone online market where banks act as market makers, both buying and selling bonds on a continuous basis.

Deals are for a minimum of 25 bonds (approximately $25,000 or the equivalent in other currencies), and prices are quoted as a percentage of 100. Thus a bond quoted at 98 is standing at a discount in relation to its maturity value of 100. The normal bid-offer spread quoted by market makers is ½%; for example, Albion Bank eurobonds quoted at 97-97½.

Eurobond secondary market prices are influenced by a range of factors such as interest rate and exchange rate developments; for example, dollar interest rise results in $ straight bonds falling in price. Obviously, the financial position of the bond issuer also affects market sentiment as regards a bond's value.

The clearing of bonds traded is handled by one of two agencies – Euroclear based in Brussels and Clearstream in Luxembourg. Both have approximately 2500 participating banks and institutions. Their computerised systems are linked and thus the actual physical exchange of paper and cheques is avoided. Both agencies act as bond depositories where investors can deposit their bond certificates for safe keeping. A fee is charged for this service. This income is supplemented by bond clearing fees and interest income on loans granted against bond holdings.

8 Floating Rate Notes (FRNs)

8.1 Key features

In recent years an increasing number of FRNs, or variable interest rate eurobond issues, have been made. The coupon or interest rate is adjusted at three or six monthly intervals in line with an appropriate reference rate in the eurocurrency market for bank deposits in the currency of the note, i.e. $ LIBOR.

Like other bonds, FRNs are usually issued in denominations of $1,000 each, although some have denominations ranging from $10,000 to $500,000. The interest rate is based on a spread over six (or three) month LIBOR. This is normally 1/4% to 1% depending on the creditworthiness of the note issuer. LIBOR fluctuations result in the establishment of a new coupon rate every three or six months on the FRNs.

In some respects FRNs are the retail equivalent of eurocredits in that the notes are a floating rate asset available to individual investors, whereas eurocredits are provided by banks alone.

FRNs are a component of the international bond market. Like bonds, the notes are bearer securities that are issued in the eurobond primary market and traded in the secondary market. Issue procedures and costs are the same as for eurobonds, as are listing requirements and trading procedures.

8.2 Types of FRNs

Vanilla FRN

This involves a coupon rate linked to LIBOR plus a spread, as well as a fixed maturity date. In some cases the spread may increase near maturity.

Perpetual FRNs

Perpetual FRNs which have no redemption date can be regarded as part of the primary capital of banks, providing the following issue conditions are complied with and satisfy the needs of bank regulators:

- The FRN is subordinate to the claims of all other creditors in a bank.
- No clauses are incorporated into the FRN which trigger early repayment.
- Repayment of the FRN requires the consent of bank regulators.
- There is automatic conversion to preference stock if losses breach a prescribed level.

8.3 FRN investors

For investors, the adjustment of the FRN's interest rate to market levels tends to ensure the relative stability of the FRN's capital value (price) in the secondary market and thus minimises the risk of incurring a capital loss on disposal prior to maturity. Most FRNs trade at approximately par value, i.e. 100, unless interest payments have been disrupted, in which case they would trade at a discount in the secondary market.

FRNs also provide investors with protection against inflation. Higher inflation in any currency generally results in higher market (LIBOR) interest rates and thus higher FRN coupon rates which compensates investors for the loss in the real value of the principal sum invested.

8.4 Banks and FRNs

Most FRN issues are made by governments, large corporations and international banks. The reason why non-American banks have been the main issuers of $ FRNs is that it allows them to obtain dollar funding without using their interbank credit lines with other banks.

Funds raised in the interbank market or by CD issue do not count as capital. In some countries (including the UK) central banks are willing to consider the proceeds of FRN issues as an addition to a bank's capital, provided they are subordinated to deposit liabilities, i.e. on bank liquidation other deposit liabilities are repaid before FRNs. Another advantage for banks, as borrowers, is that they usually lend at floating rates of interest and it therefore makes sense for them to obtain funds on the same basis, whether in the form of deposits or capital.

FRNs provide a link between the international bond market and the syndicated eurocredit market. Banks also purchase FRNs to add to their own asset portfolio. Being money market instruments, FRNs are traded actively in the secondary market. Banks are major issuers and purchasers of FRNs which makes the market an alternative source of potential funding for bank asset portfolios. This close involvement of banks in FRNs means that this component of the eurobond market is bank-dominated.

QUICK QUESTION

What do you think the advantages are of medium term notes over bonds?

Write your answer here before reading on.

9 Medium Term Note market (MTN)

Euro MTNs are fixed rate notes, although some have a floating interest rate, with a term in excess of one year. The underwriting of such notes is optional. MTNs are issued at odd intervals to meet the borrower's requirements for funds; various maturities and currencies are utilised.

MTNs are a more flexible form of borrowing than straight bonds or FRNs. The use of standardised documentation makes the issue of notes easier, more flexible and cost effective than bonds. The secondary MTN market is relatively liquid, as placing agents act as market makers.

QUESTION TIME 24

A customer notes that your bank has outstanding $ floating rate notes.

(a) Why does a UK bank need to issue $ FRNs?
(b) What are the main features of FRNs?
(c) Are $ FRNs a worthwhile purchase for an investor?
(d) How do they differ from MTN facilities?

Write your answer here then check with the answer at the back of the book.

10 Other aspects of bonds

10.1 Junk bonds

Mention the word junk and most bankers will tactfully suggest that high yield is perhaps a better description for the bonds. They are speculative debt securities issued by companies which have no ratings from the international credit rating agencies or which are rated below these agencies' investment grade threshold: BBB- Standard & Poor's. In return for the higher risk, they reward investors with margins over benchmark interest rates. High yield bonds are one of the cheapest sources of financing for non-blue chip companies.

10.2 Yield and bond risks

Private and institutional investors (including banks) must consider the relationship between yield and risk. High yielding bonds generally involve a greater degree of risk than bonds offering lower yields. Bond risk variables include the following.

- **The country of the issuer:** risks will vary between countries in accordance with their different political, social and economic characteristics.
- **The creditworthiness of the issuer:** in the case of a corporate issue this is determined by the stability of its earnings and profitability. Issues with the highest credit ratings will offer lower yields to investors than poorer quality issues.
- **The economic sector of the issue:** there is a difference in risk between public sector issues made by governments or nationalised industries and issues made in the private sector by major corporations. Again risks will vary between companies, depending upon the risks associated with their industrial or commercial sector (e.g. ship-building, banking, insurance, manufacturing, oil).
- **The type of issue:** a fixed interest issue with limited return and yield must be compared with the greater risks attached to convertible bonds offering equity participation.

11 International financial centres

International financial centres can be divided into three broad categories:

- Capital exporting centres
- Entrepôt financial centres
- Offshore financial centres

11.1 Capital exporting centres

A high level of domestic savings and a balance of payments current account surplus enable a country to finance a capital outflow via foreign investment abroad. Before 1914, the UK, represented by London, was the largest net capital exporter to the rest of the world. Post-1945, the USA was the main provider of foreign investment funds. This role has now been taken over by Japan, Germany, China and Switzerland and has aided the development of international financial centres in these countries.

The above countries' capital outflows involve a real financial transfer whereby their current account surpluses are used to acquire foreign assets and thus add to the net worth of these countries, whereas the USA and UK, with large current account deficits, finance capital outflows with short term capital inflows (monetary transfer) which initially will not increase a country's net worth.

11.2 Entrepôt financial centres

In such centres the country's domestic financial markets are used by foreign lenders and borrowers. New York is a prime example of this particular role because its deep liquid money/capital markets provide unrivalled opportunities for investment and sourcing of funds. This also applies to London, Frankfurt and Tokyo, but to a lesser extent.

To be an entrepôt financial centre a country must have:

- A convertible currency, such as $, €, ¥, £, etc
- An efficient and experienced financial community
- Good communications
- Sophisticated domestic financial markets
- Economic and political stability

11.3 Offshore financial centres

These centres are basically involved in eurocurrency business. Such centres are to be found all over the world and thus embrace all time zones. Offshore financial centres can be divided into two categories:

1 **Functional centres**

In the world's main functional centres most major banks have a physical presence at which deposit taking and lending occur. Such centres are to be found in all the world's relevant time zones, e.g. London, Singapore, Bahrain and Luxembourg. These offshore centres tend to have specific natural advantages such as:

- Language
- Legal system
- Time zone
- Expertise
- Infrastructure

Along with regulatory advantages such as:

- The absence of strict reserve requirements
- No deposit insurance premiums
- No controls on non-domestic currency transactions
- No withholding tax on interest/dividends

2 **Shell centres**

Shell (paper/booking) centres are where business is booked but *no* physical presence exists apart from a brass plate at the office entrance of an accountant or lawyer. The main attractions here are:

- Regulatory advantages (as listed for functional centres)
- No stamp duties
- Secrecy
- No taxes on bank profits
- Tax avoidance or evasion

Examples of such centres are Cyprus and the Cayman Islands. These centres benefit from the sale of bank licences and employment in banks which have a limited physical presence in such centres.

Unlike entrepôt financial centres, offshore financial centres are not dependent on a sophisticated financial infrastructure and can thus be located almost anywhere in the world. Regulatory advantages, plus secrecy and tax laws, are the key factors in the development and growth of offshore shell centres.

However, in both types of offshore financial centres, prudential control implemented by the central bank or regulatory agency must be stringent enough to prevent bank failures and fraud from being a regular occurrence and yet should not impede eurobank activities.

QUICK QUESTION

List four reasons for London's role as an international financial centre.

Write your answer here before reading on.

12 London as an international financial centre

At various times London has combined all three of the above categories of financial centres. Presently, its role is mainly that of an entrepôt and functional offshore centre. As regards natural and regulatory advantages, London has most, but it is not a tax haven for banks.

At present over 200 foreign banks have deposit/lending operations in London; this is the largest concentration of banks in the world. With just under 20% of all international lending by banks 'booked' in London, it is the world's main international banking centre. This dominant position in global banking is due to the following reasons.

First, the political/social stability of the UK attracts foreign representation in London while the risk of British governmental interference has been almost minimal, so far.

Second, sterling's former role as the major international currency enabled London's financial community to accumulate vast expertise in handling foreign finance associated with trade and investment. To this was added the stability of the UK domestic banking system (pre-2008) together with supportive services, such as telecommunications.

Third, foreign banks were subject to minimal regulations on their foreign currency (non-sterling) deposit and loan business by the Bank of England. The latter pursued an open-house policy which encouraged the establishment of foreign bank branches and offices in London. It thus indirectly promoted fierce competition in international banking.

Fourth, London is situated in a favourable time zone between the Far East and North America and thus acts as a valuable/key link between various national money and foreign exchange markets.

In the rest of this section we will examine the various factors which have kept London at the forefront of international banking and also analyse what will possibly be London's future position in the global banking market, including the likely impact of the European single currency and the credit crunch.

12.1 London: international banking centre

International banking in the City of London includes not only the branches and subsidiaries of foreign banks but also British overseas banks and the international divisions of domestic UK banks.

The principal activities of London's international banking community include:

- The finance of foreign trade in sterling or other currencies
- Eurocurrency lending by single bank loans and syndicated loans
- Interbank lending, money market and foreign exchange deals to support foreign trade finance, eurocurrency lending and international investment

- Eurobond primary and secondary market activity
- International portfolio management and corporate finance
- Corporate financial services

These activities are closely integrated with the economy at large and generate significant national benefits by supporting the domestic and overseas trading activities of British industry and commerce.

QUICK QUESTION

What benefits are likely to be provided by an international banking centre?

Write your answer here before reading on.

As already noted, the benefits provided by an international banking centre are not limited to the banks themselves and their customers, but permeate throughout the national economy. The particular benefits which London, as the world's leading banking centre, imparts to the British economy are not easily quantifiable but they are undoubtedly greater than is generally appreciated.

These benefits are experienced at five distinct levels.

1. At a local level, London's banks support the activities of other City institutions and markets, providing essential services to markets such as insurance, shipping, commodity, futures trading and the Stock Exchange. By providing complementary services, it is possible to put together complete deals entirely within London, for example to purchase a commodity, finance the purchase and arrange both shipping and insurance, all within a few hundred metres. In this way the banks directly or indirectly make a valuable contribution to the City and the British economy.
2. British industry and commerce benefit as bank services and facilities are made available to domestic and overseas customers. These include foreign exchange and international payments services as well as the provision of trade finance to foreign purchasers of British goods.
3. The presence of a large and active international banking community has stimulated new lending methods and has increased the range of financial services available to British enterprise. Foreign banks in London wishing to generate some domestic sterling business have ensured that banking services to corporate customers are competitively priced.
4. The banks pay tax to central and local government, provide direct and indirect employment and make a valuable contribution via bank/financial service fees to the balance of payments current account via invisible earnings.
5. London as an international banking centre also provides a valuable stimulus to employment in other UK industries, such as legal and accountancy advice, printing, building and telecommunications.

These benefits made international banking one of the country's most valuable (and successful) economic activities. From the mid-1970s to 2008 the international financial services sector grew more rapidly than the rest of the UK economy. It was estimated to account for up to 140,000 jobs, generate approximately 3% of the UK's GDP and made a major contribution to the balance of payments current account via invisible earnings of over £20 billion in 2007. The banking/financial crisis (2007-2009) will perhaps lead to a loss of 50,000 jobs in London's financial services sector.

12.2 London's prospects

It would be a mistake to ignore the natural advantages – pleasant climate, good communications, time zone – that London enjoys mainly by virtue of its geographical position. However, these advantages are applicable to other West European financial centres so London has to remain competitive in order to maintain its dominant position in the future.

One real advantage is the English language. Having a common language with the Americans and large parts of the former British Empire is important, not only because it directly encourages American banks to come to London, but also because it makes Britain an obvious place for other American multinational companies to locate. The presence of such customers draws foreign banks to London and to the UK as a whole.

Britain's political and economic stability, reasonable personal and corporate taxation, together with a pool of trained labour in the financial markets has also aided the City's development over the last forty years. Thus, any political or social upheaval, punitive tax measures or onerous regulatory requirements would damage London's standing as an international banking and financial centre.

The main facet of all financial dealing is confidence. If confidence is in any way undermined, banks tend to move to other locations. Successive British governments have adopted a liberal attitude towards the regulation and supervision of British and foreign banks in London. This liberal climate, until the credit crunch in 2008, was unique amongst the larger industrial countries.

The Bank of England believed in persuasion and discussion. It did not believe in the rigid ratios, regulations and massive legal backup, although the Banking Act 1987 and the Financial Services and Markets Act 2000 were a move in that direction. Post-credit crunch London's comparative regulatory advantage could be further eroded.

The challenge for London-based banks will be to match on a cost basis the equally sophisticated financial services available in other banking and financial centres. Provided London does not fail to develop new technology-based service products, its relative position as a leading international banking centre should not be seriously undermined.

Throughout history, international financial activity in any given time zone appears to have gravitated towards a single pre-eminent centre. Economic forces plus natural and regulatory advantages appear to support a cluster effect which is hard for competitors to replicate. The growth of telecommunications has not led to a dispersal of financial services; if anything, it has resulted in increased centralisation. Research has indicated that regulatory costs in London are still relatively low by international standards – about half the estimated level of bank regulatory costs in New York.

12.3 Potential threats to London's dominance

1 **Effect of European Union regulations**

A potential regulatory threat to London comes in the form of possibly over-restrictive laws and regulations being introduced by European Union (EU) legislators in Brussels. It is important for them to remember that London is an international wholesale centre for banks, whereas cities like Frankfurt and Paris are more typical of regional financial centres. The UK government must ensure that Brussels takes note of this distinction.

In 2011, France, Germany and others proposed the introduction of a new EU-wide Financial Transaction Tax (FTT), sometimes referred to as a Tobin Tax. Some Eurozone leaders believed hedge funds had caused problems in the Greek and Italian bond markets and that a tax on their speculative activities would ease Europe's sovereign debt problems. It was estimated the FTT, if implemented, would generate about €60 billion per annum, mostly from the City. In December 2011, David Cameron vetoed this proposal as it would damage London's role as a major international banking and financial centre. He believed it would result in job losses and less tax revenue in the UK as financial institutions would switch business to centres outside the EU.

France and Germany still intend to introduce an FTT on a national basis. The UK government stated that it will support an FTT if it is introduced on a global basis by all countries with important financial centres. If this tax is introduced and applies to Paris, Frankfurt and Amsterdam, it will probably mean that more euro-denominated business will be conducted in London as market operators seek to avoid the FTT.

The proposed launch date of FTT is in mid-2014. This date is in doubt though, due to a legal challenge. Lawyers have argued that FTT is incompatible with the EU treaty and that it is illegal because only 11 EU states have agreed to implement FTT. The UK is the driving force behind challenging FTT, as the tax would harm the City of London. Therefore, there is continuing debate as to whether FTT will be scrapped altogether.

It must be stated that hedge funds and speculators are not the primary cause of budget and debt problems in Europe, and that in fact it is the failure of governments to adhere to the criteria for financial stability laid down in the Maastricht Treaty. Shooting a messenger (hedge funds) who bears bad news does not make the bad news (debt problems) disappear — even Roman Emperors appreciated this fact 2000 years ago when news arrived of German tribes breaching their northern frontier!

The EU has also proposed a bonus cap for banking staff to curb the excessive bonus culture that some commentators believe was instrumental in the 2008 financial crisis. The cap would limit variable to pay to being a maximum of 100% of fixed pay. The UK voted against the proposal, fearing that the cap would result in some financial services companies relocating away London to jurisdictions such as Switzerland to avoid the bonus cap.

2 Challenge from the Far East

Japan's banks, which are among the largest in the world, expanded their international banking operations, particularly in London, in the 1990s. In the UK they undertook both eurocurrency and domestic sterling business. However, also in the 1990s, domestic loan problems forced Japanese banks to curtail their international activity and concentrate on restoring profitability to their domestic operations in order to remain solvent. Such banking, financial and economic problems in Japan resulted in Tokyo being regarded as less of a threat to London's dominance. However, the rise of Singapore and Shanghai could result in new Far East challenges to London's overall position.

QUICK QUESTION

How might a single currency in most of the EU affect London?

Write your answer here before reading on.

3 **Economic and monetary union (EMU)**

The UK decided not to take part in EMU (Eurozone), unlike 17 of its EU partners. Despite recent Eurozone problems, exclusion from the single currency area which uses the euro is viewed by some politicians and financial experts as a major threat to London's position as Europe's main banking and financial centre.

It has been suggested that, in the future, the EMU area will boast huge financial markets and that investors and bankers will gravitate to Frankfurt, the financial capital of Germany and home of the European Central Bank. It would be foolish to dismiss such fears, as London's attractions might fade if Frankfurt acquired the major share of Europe's local financial business.

How might this situation fail to occur?

The City thrives on liquid markets regardless of the currency involved. Rather than posing a threat to London, the euro is viewed as providing a great opportunity for the City's markets and financial institutions. There is a vigorous euro (€) eurocurrency market in London just as there was in euroDeutsche marks or euroFrench francs prior to the establishment of the Eurozone in January 1999.

It is possible that the offshore euro market will remain more liquid than the domestic euro markets, unless or until the latter becomes one seamless market for the EMU zone. Perhaps, differences between Paris and Frankfurt will enable the UK-based euro market to thrive, as does the eurodollar market in London today.

A new threat to London's prospects is the proposed EU referendum in 2017. David Cameron has promised that a 'yes' or 'no' referendum over the UK's EU membership would be held in 2018 should the Conservative Party be in power at that time. Should Britain leave the EU, it could have disastrous effects for financial services in London. It is predicted that European banks based in London would be under pressure to move their funds back into other EU states. This would result in London losing its status as the main trading hub for the Euro and Eurobonds. Should this trading activity move out of London, the effect on jobs on London (and the tax revenues generated from their activities) would be huge.

The reality is that the location of financial activity in a currency does not depend upon the domestic market. It will be carried out in a financial centre where it is most convenient, efficient and profitable to do so.

4 **Tax and regulation**

In 2011, HSBC announced that they were considering moving their headquarters away from London due to the cost of UK regulation. HSBC estimated that UK regulation would cost them $2.5 billion a year. In light of this, HSBC announced that they were considering moving their head quarters to Hong Kong. Another difficult issue is UK corporation tax. Due to the large UK budget deficit, some politicians have suggested increasing corporation tax. There has also been public outcry over companies such as Google using UK tax loopholes to reduce their tax bill. Increasing the level of taxes for banks may result in some financial services companies moving away from London, making it a delicate issue for the government.

QUESTION TIME 25

(a) What are the main natural advantages of London as a financial centre?

(b) List the benefits derived by the UK from London being a major international financial centre.

Write your answer here then check with the answer at the back of the book.

KEY WORDS

Key words in this chapter are given below. There is space to write your own revision notes and to add any other words or phrases that you want to remember.

- Syndicated loan market
- Eurodollar disaster clause
- Events default clause
- Coupon
- Institutional investors
- Discretionary account
- Advisory account
- Fixed rate (straight) bonds
- Zero coupon bonds
- Convertible bonds
- Capital exporting centre
- Offshore financial centres
- International banking centre
- Floating rate note (FRN)
- Medium term note (MTN)

REVIEW

The main learning points introduced in this chapter are summarised below.

Go through them and check back to the learning outcomes at the beginning of the chapter. Only move on when you are happy that you fully understand each point.

- The main terms of the syndicated loan market were explained. Loan contract terms were reviewed to illustrate the legal technicalities of such credit facilities. The flexibility of syndicated loan facilities for the borrower was also reviewed.
- We have looked in detail at the international bond market which is made up of two components – the foreign bond market and the eurobond market. We examined their main aspects and reviewed different types of eurobonds.
- We differentiated between international financial centres according to their role as capital exporting, entrepôt or offshore centres.
- We examined London's dominance as an international banking and financial centre and analysed the economic benefits for the UK as a whole from London's role, as well as the challenges it faces to its primary position.

In summary, we looked at:

- The main aspects of the syndicated loan market
- The distinctive features of the international bond market
- Straight and convertible bonds
- The operational aspects of the secondary bond market
- The main aspects of FRNs and MTNs
- The role of London as an international banking centre

chapter 8

INTERNATIONAL BANKING RISK

Contents

Learning outcomes

On completion of this chapter you should be able to:

- Examine international deposit risk and the Act of State Doctrine.
- Evaluate factors influencing country risk and how banks assess such risks and manage these on their balance sheets.

Introduction

In considering the risks associated with international banking activities, we will concentrate on the various aspects of eurocurrency deposit risk in relation to eurobank branches and subsidiaries, then look at the provision of bonds (guarantees) by banks to assist UK exports of capital goods as well as foreign currency risk exposure management.

We will also examine the assessment and management of country risk in banking. Such risk is a major concern to banks involved in syndicated credits to corporations and sovereign borrowers on a global basis. We'll conclude with an analysis of how banks deal with cross-border loan defaults.

In summary, we will consider some key international banking risks under the following headings:

- Eurocurrency deposit risk
- Banks and bonds
- Foreign currency exposure
- Country risk assessment
- Country risk management in banks

1 Eurocurrency deposit risk

1.1 Legal relationship

Definitive laws are non-existent or dubious at best in the arena of international banking due to overlapping jurisdictional relationships between the parent bank's home country and the host country in which the foreign banking establishment exists. It is therefore necessary to use banking case law and analyse the actions of banks to examine the legal relationship between a parent bank and its overseas operational units.

- **Subsidiary**

  A subsidiary is a legally distinct/separate entity and can fail independently of the parent bank. For example, a parent French bank is under no legal obligation to pay off depositors in its failed eurobank subsidiary in London although, for practical and commercial reasons, it might provide support to the failed subsidiary and its depositors, in order to maintain overall confidence in the parent bank. Otherwise, its credit rating may decline and it could suffer deposit withdrawals. In other words, banks bank on their reputations, and self-interest might compel the parent bank to provide financial assistance.

  In the 1970s, the United California Bank voluntarily assumed responsibility for a Swiss bank subsidiary in which it had a 58 per cent stake; the latter had failed due to incurring a $40 million loss on unauthorised cocoa futures transactions.

  However, if a eurobank subsidiary has its assets expropriated or new exchange controls prevent deposit repayment, a parent bank can rely upon the separate entities status and decline to pay off the subsidiary's depositors. Action by the host government might reduce the practical/moral pressure on the parent bank to do something for depositors in its subsidiary.

  It is for these reasons that deposits in a eurobank subsidiary may be regarded as being riskier than those in a eurobank branch. A subsidiary may therefore have to pay a slight premium over market interest rates to attract time deposits.

- **Branch**

  The general principle of law is that the parent/home office of a bank is responsible for a foreign branch's liabilities if the latter wrongfully refuses to repay deposits to its customers. However, the exact legal position depends upon the circumstances in each case. In the case of Sokoloff v National City Bank (1928), a former Russian citizen successfully sued the US bank for repayment at its New York parent/home office for his Russian currency deposit at the bank's Petrograd (St Petersburg) branch in 1917. The Petrograd branch, anticipating nationalisation by the Bolsheviks, closed its doors without giving depositors the chance to withdraw their deposits. The US court held that the branch's assets belonged to the parent bank and thus it was responsible for the deposits.

  This case appeared to have established the principle of corporate responsibility of a parent bank for deposits placed in its overseas branches. However, subsequent case law appears to have established the principle of separate entity doctrine which implies that a branch can be regarded as a self-contained entity and thus a deposit is situated in the host country. This basic principle is strengthened by the Act of State Doctrine which means that courts in other countries must give effect to the law or Acts of a recognised host country's government where the branch is situated. Thus under the Act of State Doctrine the following acts of a recognised host government will relieve a parent bank of its liability to repay deposits of its foreign branch:

  - Imposition of exchange controls
  - Moratorium or bank holiday
  - Disturbed conditions (riots or civil unrest)
  - Seizure of assets and liabilities by the host government

  It is important to note that if a foreign branch gets into financial difficulties through making inappropriate business decisions or the doors are closed before the seizure of assets and liabilities by the host government, then depositors can demand repayment from the home office of the parent bank. During the time interval between the closure and the government's action, the deposits spring from the branch to the home office, as in the Sokoloff case.

  It thus appears that deposits in a eurobank branch are less risky than in a subsidiary in the event of mis-management in the overseas unit. However, the Act of State Doctrine appears to put deposits in any form of eurobank at risk from the actions of wayward host country governments. Such a threat, although possible, must not be over emphasised. An offshore banking/financial centre government could seize the assets and liabilities of a eurobank(s) and then find few assets (loans and investments) situated in its own (host) country. In this situation, the lenders and borrowers would simply transact existing and future business elsewhere by effecting payments and transfers in another user-friendly offshore centre. As the recording of transactions can take place anywhere, it perhaps means that most eurocurrency operations are free from expropriation threats.

1.2 Interbank deposit risk

The case Wells Fargo Asia *v* Citibank (1985) provided some guidance as to the legal position of interbank deposits. In January 1984, Citibank's Manila branch in the Philippines refused to repay maturing eurodollar deposits due to a debt moratorium announced by the Philippines' government. Citibank Manila had $500 million of interbank borrowings outstanding; the creditor banks sought repayment of these eurodollar deposits in New York.

Wells Fargo Asia sued Citibank for repayment of a $2 million interbank claim. The US court decided that Citibank Manila had wrongfully refused to meet other banks' claims, as it had not sought clarification from the Philippines' central bank as to what the moratorium covered. It appeared to have put a broader interpretation on the freezing order than was intended so as to protect its future banking relationships in that country. The Philippines' government decree did not require the freezing of interbank deposits.

Citibank Manila in its defence also claimed that the interest rate differential of 1.15% between deposit rates in New York and Manila was a risk premium related to the latter centre rather than the result of exemption from reserve requirements on eurodollar deposits. The court rejected risk premium explanation by Citibank as justification for freezing the interbank funds received from Wells Fargo Asia and other banks.

QUICK QUESTION

Are US banks in London subject to US law or English law?

Write your answer here before reading on.

1.3 Jurisdiction risk

One issue which was not fully resolved until 1986 was whether a government could freeze a deposit in its own currency outside its national boundaries. This was basically a question of currency jurisdiction and whether extra-territorial reach by the parent bank's home country had any legality in a host country.

In 1986, President Reagan of the USA exercised his authority under the International Emergency Economic Powers Act to block external dollar deposits held by Libya. Bankers Trust in London refused to repay a deposit of $131 million to the Libyan Arab Foreign Bank.

The UK court in the subsequent case of the Libyan Arab Foreign Bank v Bankers Trust (1987) rejected the extra-territorial reach of the US decree. It maintained that only UK (English) law applied as the bank account was held in London, albeit by a US bank.

There were two aspects to this court case. First, Bankers Trust held that contract performance, i.e. deposit repayment, would involve dollar transfers between nostro accounts in New York which would constitute an illegal act in the USA. The UK court agreed that conventional transfers involving the New York Clearing House were prohibited, therefore Bankers Trust in London had to repay the dollar deposit in cash (either dollars or the equivalent in sterling). Second, Bankers Trust argued that the eurocurrency markets dealt in credit not cash, i.e. not a payments market, and therefore the request for cash repayment was invalid. The UK court rejected this argument.

The significance of this case and subsequent judgements was to remove jurisdiction risk from eurocurrency deposits by the currency country. The case also confirmed that deposit repayments in cash could not be refused by eurobanks, although such requests are unlikely to occur except in rather unusual circumstances.

Summary

In this section we have identified the various types of risk that exist as regards deposits.

First, a eurobank might fail independently of its parent institution, leaving the depositor with a partial or total loss of funds.

Second, a eurobank's assets might be expropriated or frozen by a host government or a moratorium might be declared that deprives the depositors of their funds.

Lender-of-last resort facilities are less clear in the eurocurrency market than in national domestic markets. The provision of emergency liquidity assistance is less probable, especially for a eurobank subsidiary, in the event of a liquidity squeeze in the interbank market. The latter would make the repayment of deposits on maturity less likely in the short term.

These risk factors, plus regulatory/operational differences, may provide most of the explanation for deposit rates for individual currencies being higher in the external or eurocurrency money market.

QUESTION TIME 26

Explain the implications with regard to deposit risk of the following two legal cases:

(a) Sokoloff v National City Bank (1928)
(b) Libyan Arab Foreign Bank v Bankers Trust (1987)

Write your answer here then check with the answer at the back of the book.

1.4 Banks and bonds

Sometimes with capital goods (power stations, rail track/rolling stock, etc) importers demand bonds (or guarantees) from exporters due to the cash payments required under such import contracts. A bond is normally issued by a bank to an importer, guaranteeing the exporter's compliance with his contractual obligations; otherwise the importer must be indemnified for a stated amount. Three main types of bonds are associated with export contracts.

1 **Tender bonds**: these provide an importer seeking competitive bids for a contract with a guarantee that an exporter (or contractor) is making a responsible bid and is technically/financially competent to undertake the contract. If the exporter fails to comply with the tender's conditions or eventually enter into the contract, the bank is liable to pay any costs (limited to the bond's value) incurred by the importer in re-awarding the contract. Such bonds are generally equal to about 5 per cent of the tender's value.

2 **Performance bonds**: this is a guarantee by a bank that an exporter will complete the contract. The bank's liability is generally about 10 per cent of the contract price.

3 **Advance payment bonds**: many export contracts contain provisions for advance payments to meet the exporter's costs. Under this bond, the bank guarantees repayment of such funds to the importer in the event of an exporter's liquidation. These are normally for 20 per cent of the contract value.

Banks have full recourse against an exporter (or contractor) in the event of a bond being implemented, so they are naturally concerned with his/her creditworthiness and commercial/technical expertise. Importers stipulate the wording of bonds and which banks are suitable for the issue of such bonds (guarantees). The banks, in turn, charge customers a fee for providing bonds as they represent a real obligation undertaken by a bank.

2 Foreign currency exposure

As a result of international transactions, it is common for a proportion of a bank's assets and liabilities to be in foreign currencies. As exchange rates are subject to constant change, there is the possibility of loss or gain when a bank changes foreign currency assets or liabilities into sterling.

Case studies

1 Suppose that a bank has an asset in the form of a loan to an importer for the sum of ¥30,000,000. Assuming that the bank had no existing yen deposits and it made the loan when the exchange rate was £1 = ¥200, then it would have sold (30,000,000/200 =) £150,000 on the foreign exchange markets to acquire yen for its customer. However, if sterling depreciated in terms of the yen during the course of the loan to, say, £1 = ¥150, then after repayment, when it came to dispose of the yen which it no longer required, the bank would acquire (30,000,000/150) = £200,000 which would be a gain of (£200,000 - £150,000) = £50,000.

2 Suppose a bank had a liability in the form of $6,000,000 deposited for a fixed period of six months by an American oil company operating in the North Sea. If it had no immediate use for dollars, the bank might choose to utilise the funds within the United Kingdom by converting them into sterling, and if the exchange rate were £1 = $1.65, this would represent ($6,000,000/1.65) = £3,636,363 which it could now lend.

3 At the end of six months, if sterling had depreciated against the dollar so that £1 = $1.50, then the bank would have to sell £4,000,000 to acquire $6,000,000 at a loss of (4,000,000 – 3,636,363) = £363,637, a sum which could wipe out any interest return the bank had made by lending the sterling deposit in the interim.

However, it should be apparent from these examples that if a bank's assets and liabilities in a given currency were equal over a given period of time, then a depreciation of sterling would give rise to both gains (on assets) and losses (on liabilities) which would cancel each other out. The same cancelling out would apply if sterling appreciated, if it was worth more in terms of foreign currencies.

It is the possibility of loss on foreign exchange transactions that banks are most concerned about, and the Bank of England takes the view that British banks should not expose themselves to excessive foreign exchange risks.

A bank's exposure is calculated in terms of each foreign currency in which it deals, and the Bank's concern is that banks should maintain, as near as possible, a balance between assets and liabilities in any currency and so avoid the possibility of loss through exchange rate alterations, although this also precludes the possibility of gain. Banks with net foreign currency exposures hedge their positions in the forward, futures, options and swap markets.

QUICK QUESTION

How could country risk impact on banking operations?

Write your answer here before reading on.

3 Country risk

In the domestic environment, a bank knows its customers and is fully aware of the economic, political and legal framework within which it grants loans and accepts collateral (securities). The international environment, with various different economic, political and social values, represents additional risk for the lending banker. Some risks can be reduced through asset diversification, i.e. a wide spread of loans to various borrowers in different regions of the world.

Banks lending to private sector corporations concentrate on cash flow (cash income and expenditure) projections to generate questions on the use of potential loan facilities and possible repayment sources. Concentration on a corporation's asset values (land, buildings, etc) is of dubious value to a banker, especially if such assets are situated in foreign countries. Asset values are certainly not applicable as security for government loans, as countries cannot be liquidated.

In the case of private sector corporations, the bank's problem is compounded by the lack of international uniformity in accounting and legal standards. To overcome such problems, any available financial statistics must be analysed to ascertain the creditworthiness of the proposed borrower. Additional information may be sought from industry/economic experts and from correspondent banks in the borrower's country. The external residence of a borrower therefore adds new dimensions to bank lending decisions.

3.1 Country risk assessment

Country risk distinguishes international (cross-border) banking from domestic banking. Irrespective of whether the loan proposal is made by a government, state enterprise or public corporation, an appraisal of the economic and political situation of the borrower's country must be made in order to assess the risk involved. Banks deal with loan requests from numerous countries with differing economic/political prospects, therefore the risks associated with each loan must be assessed individually.

Obviously, there is a greater need for banks to carry out country risk assessment when lending to governments and corporations in emerging economies such as Russia or Mexico, than to similar entities in North America and the European Union.

Risk analysis provides a framework for tabulating available information – economic, financial and political – in order to measure risk. As you will appreciate, the degree of risk varies depending on the nature, size and use of each loan, e.g. a three month trade finance loan compared with a twelve year project loan. With the growth of international lending in both domestic and foreign currencies, most banks have increased their staff numbers and resources devoted to the assessment of country risk, although it has to be recognised that such an exercise can never be reduced to an exact science.

Country risk assessment has become more complicated in recent years when assessing countries in the EU. In June 2012, Cyprus applied for financial assistance from the EU. Without an EU bailout, it is almost certain that Cyprus would have defaulted on their sovereign debt obligations and their domestic banks would also have defaulted. The European Central Bank (ECB) has also bailed out four other Eurozone members. Therefore the broader financial climate must also be considered when undertaking country risk assessment.

QUICK QUESTION

Why do emerging economies require external bank loans?

Write your answer here before reading on.

3.2 Economic factors

An analysis of economic facts can provide some indication of a country's stage of economic development and progress. Data used will largely be in the form of statistics – GNP growth rate, per capita real income, inflation rate, economic structure, etc – for the last five or ten years, which should help to make constructive risk assessment. Some additional information is noted below on economic factors.

3.3 Credit ratings

Each country will have a credit rating, called a sovereign credit rating, which is assessed and published by a credit ratings agency such as S&P and Moody's. The rating considers a variety of factors, including GDP growth, budget deficit/surplus and national debt. These factors are analysed to determine the credit quality of sovereign debt, where the higher the rating equals the lower chance of default. The highest credit rating that a country can receive is AAA. Norway has this rating, which means that the ratings agencies forecast very little default risk from sovereign debt issued by Norway.

At the other end of the scale, sovereign debt with a poor credit rating is called junk. This type of sovereign debt has a very high probability of entering into default. For example, the sovereign debt of Cyprus was downgraded to junk when they had to request an ECB and IMF bailout of €10 billion in 2012. The middle ground between AAA debt and junk is a BBB rating, referred to as 'investment grade'. Sovereign debt termed as investment grade has medium credit quality.

A sovereign credit rating is very important because it determines the cost of borrowing for a country. A poor credit rating means that a country will have to pay higher interest rates to investors to entice them into buying their sovereign debt, to compensate them for the higher risk of buying debt that has a higher probability of default.

3.4 Domestic economic factors

Gross national product

Real economic growth rates can be used to assess the expansion in a country's output of goods and services. A high positive rate is nearly always associated with rapid industrialisation and export diversification, both of which enhance a country's credit rating among world bankers.

Per capita real income

This measures a country's ability (or inability) to increase real output at a faster pace than population growth. Statistics over five or ten years will provide definite evidence of increasing, stagnant or declining per capita incomes. It is probably true to state that a country must achieve sustained increases in real GNP per capita to avoid social and political tension. Declining per capita income over a prolonged period of time usually results in a change of government, sometimes after a revolution or a military coup. Such an event might result in the new government being unwilling or unable to service external debt, including bank loans, which means non-payment of interest and /or the principal sum loaned.

A further factor of significance might be the distribution of income (and wealth) in a country. Equality in poverty might mean civil population contentment, whereas glaring inequalities usually sow the seeds of a class struggle or revolution.

Inflation rate

If a country is prone to high inflation, its currency will have to be devalued at regular intervals to maintain the price competitiveness of its exports. Devaluation will increase the local currency costs of servicing foreign currency-denominated debt. However, providing foreign currency receipts from exports are available to service external debt, no real problems should arise.

Economic structure

Agriculture's share in total output and employment can often be taken as a guide to a country's stage of economic development. Those economies which have successfully switched underemployed agricultural labour into manufacturing and service activities have generally achieved significant real economic growth rates.

Another valuable indicator is the ratio of real capital formation (investment) to GNP. A high ratio invariably means output growth and, hopefully, improved external debt servicing capacity through increased exports.

QUICK QUESTION

What do you think a risk analyst can tell from examining a country's exports and imports?

Write your answer here before reading on.

3.5 Balance of payments

Most country risk analysts regard the balance of payments as the most relevant economic statement for assessing a country's ability to service existing (and future) external debt.

1 **Exports**

A steady growth of export income from a diversified product range is the most desirable situation. Most successful emerging economies have increased their share of manufactured goods imported into the OECD countries. If a country depends on one or two primary products, such as bauxite or coffee, for the bulk of its export revenue, then a fall in world demand and prices for these products can have a disastrous impact on export revenues, GNP growth and economic development programmes.

A country can also derive export revenue from service income, such as shipping and tourism, as well as remittances from overseas workers. For many countries (e.g. Pakistan and Turkey) the latter income source is important as large numbers of their nationals are employed in oil-rich states or advanced industrial nations (Saudi Arabia or Germany).

2 **Imports**

The composition of imports will be closely examined by a bank's risk analyst. For most countries, raw materials, food, and oil imports must be maintained at an adequate level to allow the economy to function. Any curtailment of such imports might damage a country's export potential and economic development. Imports of luxury goods (TVs, cars, etc) and military equipment can be severely curtailed to save foreign currency earnings without damaging the economy, although the non-availability of such items can lead to unrest. The interest on external debt is treated as import expenditure, i.e. the service cost of imported capital.

3 **Current account surplus or deficit**

The difference between exports and imports provides a country's current account position. A surplus may be taken as an indication of a country's ability to service its external debt, whereas a deficit might imply, if not corrected or offset by capital inflows, future external debt servicing problems.

4 **Debt service ratio**

This ratio is calculated by combining debt principal repayments and interest payable in a single year and dividing it by the country's exports for the equivalent period. For example, if Utopia has exports of $100 million, and debt interest and repayments of $30 million, its external debt service ratio would be 30%.

$$\text{Debt service ratio: } \frac{\$\ 30 \text{ million} \times 100}{\$\ 100 \text{ million}} = 30\%$$

There is no maximum ratio but, probably, a ratio in excess of 25% can be regarded as indicative of future debt servicing problems. Several major Latin American countries had debt service ratios in excess of 100 per cent in the 1980s that resulted in external debt servicing problems.

Unfortunately, for bankers assessing country risk, this ratio has two major deficiencies. It ignores capital flows which, in the short term, can be used to service existing debt. But, probably more important, available debt statistics often relate only to government-guaranteed debt; details of private debt are not always immediately available.

5 **Reserves**

These consist of gold and foreign currency deposits held by a country's central bank which can be used to finance imports in the event of an export shortfall. A low reserve level in relation to annual imports or debt obligations could signify future problems. Reserves in excess of the value of three months' imports are generally considered adequate. Unfortunately, for some countries (Mali and Tanzania) such reserves can be measured in terms of weeks rather than months.

These various economic indicators (past, present and projected into the future) are used in country risk assessment and thereby aid banks in their loan management. Although such assessments are supposed to be objective, i.e. based on data, the value of such studies is necessarily limited by the availability of up-to-date statistics.

QUICK QUESTION

How can a country's political leadership affect economic conditions?

Write your answer here before reading on.

3.6 Political factors

A lending bank must be concerned about a country's political stability. By its very nature, political risk assessment must be subjective, i.e. not based on numerical data. Despite this, many bankers consider political factors to be more important than economic factors. The major concern is that a loan can be serviced throughout its term, even although fundamental changes might take place in the political system of the country in which the borrower is resident. Many developing countries are apparently vulnerable to political upheavals, perhaps due to the immaturity of their political institutions. In the final analysis, a judgement on the political stability of most countries must be highly subjective. However, having stated this, the following factors – political leadership, political philosophy, social conditions and external relations – are generally taken into consideration.

1 **Political leadership**

Analysis of political risk must include consideration of a country's political structure. Is the country a one person or one party state? Many emerging economies have such governments which can be reasonably stable if they enjoy wide support among the population. Such a political system might be beneficial for economic growth, as industrialisation and agricultural development programmes may be easier to implement. On the other hand, if a country is dependent on the leadership of one person, perhaps their demise through age, ill-health or death might usher in an era of political instability.

The political ideology (philosophy) of a government must also be considered. The strength of political opposition, perhaps underground, must be ascertained, as well as any past or potential future conflicts involving minority, religious or ethnic groups. History has shown that the insensitivity of civil or military rulers to such pressures often results in a civil war, coups or revolutions that can bring about a sudden change in a country's political ideology and attitudes to private enterprise. For a bank this could result in the disruption of debt service payments by a government, state enterprises or private corporations.

2 **Social conditions**

The rate of economic and social advancement of a country's population can influence political stability. An inequitable distribution of wealth, income and employment can result in future political instability. Urban deprivation (overcrowded city slums) and an ossified (permanent) political/social structure are also causes for concern. Information on these factors can be obtained by risk analysts from published material, the media and by personal visits of bank executive personnel to correspondent banks.

3 **External relations**

If a country is under threat from aggressive neighbours, scarce financial resources may be diverted from economic development programmes to defence needs, such as the importation of military equipment. A country's strategic geographical position might invite super-power attention and meddling in its internal affairs. Consideration might also be given to a country's membership of and relations with international agencies such as the IMF or World Bank.

Summary

With the aid of economic, political and social indicators, banks can try to assess country risk. Some factors are given more importance than others by risk analysts. A country's assessed risk will influence loan terms (size, term and loan interest) to its own resident borrowers. Assessment of overall exposure to each country will determine the need for loan portfolio diversification.

Despite the use of country risk analysis, it must be conceded that competition for loan business has sometimes encouraged banks to ignore their own country or regional risk assessments and indulge in what can only be described as imprudent bank lending.

QUESTION TIME 27

Describe and evaluate the main economic and political factors considered by bank loan risk analysts.

Write your answer here then check with the answer at the back of the book.

4 Country risk management

International banks engaged in cross-border lending use a number of techniques to reduce their exposure to country risk. Obviously, country risk assessment is important in determining which countries to lend money to, whether lending to corporations, banks or the country's government. However, other steps can be taken to reduce country risk, including the following:

1. Diversification over a number of countries or regions of the world is advisable; this reduces risk but does not eliminate it, as market risk is always present in a diversified loan portfolio. An extreme global or regional economic shock, even with loan diversification, can result in loan service problems for a bank. If the bank's exposure to one country or region is greater than the capital base of the bank and country (or region) defaults, then the bank is technically insolvent.
2. In order to avoid this situation each bank should use country loan limits to supplement diversification. The maximum amount to be lent to a country (or region) should be expressed as a percentage of the bank's capital base, e.g. Albion Bank's capital £10 billion, maximum 5% to Brazil = £500 million or 10% to South America = £1000 million.
3. Loan maturities can be shortened to higher risk countries so as to effect quicker repayment and this curtails country exposure. Unfortunately, if all banks adopt this strategy, the country's position will become more vulnerable due to its increasing reliance on short-term loans. If all banks cease lending at the same time, the country will default and what were perceived to be short-term liquid loans will become long-term illiquid loans of doubtful value. So shorter loan maturities might work for one bank as a means of reducing country risk exposure but not if all banks collectively take similar action.
4. Third party assistance in the form of the International Monetary Fund (IMF) might be sought by banks as a means of reducing country risk. It must be pointed out that the IMF is not an international economic police force to ensure countries are well managed – it has no compulsory powers. In addition, when IMF assistance is sought by a country it probably already has serious economic problems and any bank loans outstanding will not be serviced.
5. It might be possible to get a domestic government guarantee for some project loan to another country. For a bank this can reduce country risk exposure. In the 1990s, German banks provided loans to Russia, but risk associated with these credits was guaranteed by the German government.

6 A cross-default clause might be incorporated into a loan agreement with a sovereign borrower, e.g. Chilean Treasury. Such a clause prevents selective defaults by a sovereign government, e.g. Chile servicing US bank loans but not Japanese bank loans. Under this clause, a default on one loan is a default on all loans. It means the borrower is faced with the threat of a collective withdrawal of credit.

7 Exposure management sets limits for individual countries, e.g. Albion Bank's £500 million limit for Brazil. This limit is determined on a prudential basis rather than on loan marketing criteria. Loan officers must seek profitable outlets for funds available in various sectors of the country's economy. A mixture of borrower style and maturity must be sought in order to achieve adequate diversification within the country limit.

Country risk exposure management is under constant review by bank regulators within each country. Limits set must be observed and banks must ensure that capital resources are adequate to deal with any potential problems.

5 Country loan defaults

If a country defaults on its external bank loans, then some form of debt restructuring becomes necessary whereby the terms of the original loan agreement are amended. An extension of the loan repayment schedule does not represent new money for the debtor country but it does represent a new credit for the bank (the loan now has a longer maturity).

One of the decisions that have to be made by banks is what to provide in the form of loan loss/provisions on the balance sheet. It is unrealistic to carry a loan at full face value on the balance sheet when it is perhaps standing at a discount in the secondary market. Short of outright repudiation by a debtor country, some form of loan settlement will be agreed with banks, such as Argentina 30 cents in the dollar in 2001.

Finally, some defaulted loans might be converted into equity stakes (or bonds) in a debtor country. In this situation the bank with a defaulted dollar loan converts into, say, local pesos at the debtor country's central bank. The pesos acquired are used to invest in local enterprises which, if successful, will witness a rise in their share price. At some later date the bank can sell its equity stake, hopefully at a profit, and repatriate its funds. Some defaulted loans to Latin American countries were converted into bonds at a discount under the Brady Plan (1989-95); the average discount recovered by most countries was about 40%.

KEY WORDS

Key words in this chapter are given below. There is space to write your own revision notes and to add any other words or phrases that you want to remember.

- Act of State Doctrine
- Sokoloff v National City Bank
- Country risk
- Debt service ratio
- Per capita income
- Country loan defaults

REVIEW

The main learning points introduced in this chapter are summarised below.

Go through them and check back to the learning outcomes at the beginning of the chapter. Only move on when you are happy that you fully understand each point.

- We examined eurocurrency deposit risk with the aid of various legal judgements relating to international banking.
- Close attention was given to the Act of State Doctrine in relation to a eurobank branch's operations.
- The use of bonds (guarantees) in relation to the export of capital goods as well as the management of foreign currency exposure was briefly examined.
- Country risk assessment and management within banks was highlighted as an important factor in successful cross-border loan business.

chapter 9

SECURITISATION AND GLOBALISATION

Contents

Learning outcomes

On completion of this chapter you should be able to:

- Explain securitisation/globalisation and critically analyse how these trends impacted on banks and the financial markets in 2007-09.

Introduction

After studying the role of the syndicated credit market, we will examine sources of direct finance under the broad heading of securitisation. This chapter looks at the development of securitisation, the various forms it can take and its impact on banks. The advancement of securitisation has witnessed the development of commercial paper markets in a number of countries outside the USA, including the euro-commercial paper market. The US commercial paper market has existed since the 1920s, providing a major alternative source of finance to bank loans for US corporations. The chapter concludes with examination of the factors which have encouraged the globalisation of financial markets.

We will consider key aspects of securitisation and globalisation under the following headings:

- Key features of securitisation
- The economic/financial logic behind securitisation
- Commercial paper markets
- Globalisation (or internationalisation) of financial markets
- Securitisation and the global financial crisis

1 International lending: history and development

Pre-1960, most international lending took place via the issue of foreign bonds. Banks provided short-term liquidating finance for exports and imports via bills of exchange. The issue of foreign bonds with fixed coupon rates was in most instances managed and underwritten by merchant/investment banks. Most bonds were acquired by private investors as the interest yield, to take account of risk, was higher than that on domestic government stock of the same maturity.

In the 1960s and 1970s, banks, either individually or in syndicates, began to lend to corporate and sovereign borrowers for terms ranging up to ten years. An examination of the economic and financial environment of that era provides the underlying reasons for this change in the lending strategy of banks.

Some banks saw international lending as a technique for diversifying their asset/loan portfolio and thus reducing their exposure to economic/financial developments in one specific geographic region of the world. The increasing use of syndicated credits also reduced the perceived risk associated with this new departure into international lending.

Smaller banks could rely on the comfort factor provided by the lead manager and could finance participation in international loans via variable rate funds obtained in the interbank market. This ongoing innovative lending process was assisted by the rapid growth of the eurocurrency markets and the need to recycle OPEC's petro-dollar surplus from net creditor to net debtor countries. In addition, banks' risk perceptions were, perhaps, reduced as regards lending to sovereign borrowers due to the perceived policing of the international financial system by the International Monetary Fund. It was a widely held belief that countries of Latin America could not fail and therefore sovereign loans were relatively risk-free.

As a result of these factors, bank involvement in international lending increased, while bond finance experienced a relative decline as a percentage of total global capital flows. Many emerging economies' governments, state enterprises and corporations preferred to use bank or intermediated finance from international banks rather than trying to gain access to bond markets where non-prime names had to pay higher risk-adjusted coupon rates.

The 1980s witnessed a relative shift away from bank finance to bond finance. This trend, often referred to as securitisation, involves the issue of bonds and notes as a means of raising finance. It occurred not only in an international context in relation to financial flows but also influenced domestic financial flows within individual economies.

Three questions we might want to ask at this stage are:

1 Why did securitisation take place?
2 Is the securitisation trend permanent or temporary?
3 Will the securitisation trend accelerate or be reversed with the passage of time?

QUICK QUESTION

How did the Latin American external debt crisis of the 1980s encourage securitisation?

Write your answer here before reading on.

2 Securitisation

The following factors contributed to securitisation in the world's financial markets.

1 **Credit ratings**

The high level of non-performing loans to emerging economies in the 1980s, particularly in Latin America, on the books of banks resulted in a downgrading of bank credit ratings. This meant that prime-rated potential borrowers with higher credit rating could obtain funds in the market place at a lower interest rate than the banks. A displacement of the intermediation role of banks followed as the shift towards direct financing got underway. Bank loans in price (interest) terms could not compete against the issue of paper (bonds and notes). This competitive disadvantage was further reinforced by bank regulators/supervisors demanding higher capital-asset ratios in banks. As a result, the capital costs associated with lending increased; in other words, intermediated funds became more expensive.

2 **Balance of payments trends**

In the 1980s, the OPEC surplus declined and with it the need to recycle petrodollars.

Instead, Japan and Germany had large current account surpluses while the USA incurred a huge deficit which was financed by means of capital inflows from Japan and Germany. This financial transfer did not take place through the banking system; instead, Japanese and German private and institutional investors purchased bonds, equities and real estate in the USA. In other words, their capital exports involved the use of direct finance rather than intermediated (indirect) bank finance. These balance of payments flows provided a tremendous boost to global capital market development.

3 **Financial innovations**

Banks themselves became both issuers and investors in bonds and notes. These financial instruments were issued by banks in order to raise additional capital to meet regulatory requirements and also as a funding source for their lending activities. When banks purchase bonds and notes, these are classified as investments and included in the asset portfolio of the bank as an alternative to loans. Such assets are generally easier to liquefy than loans, although they are subject to greater price volatility. As purchasers of bonds and notes issued by non-bank entities, the banks participated in the securitisation trend; an element of direct finance incorporated indirect finance from banks. In addition, banks were prepared to underwrite note-issuing facilities set up by prime-rated corporations in exchange for fee income. Such facilities oblige the underwriting bank(s) to purchase any unsold notes or provide loan facilities to the issuer. Once again banks assisted the securitisation process by accepting a contingent liability to purchase any unsold notes. Such facilities generate fee income for the banks rather than interest income.

4 **Financial environment**

Securitisation was also assisted by the deregulation and liberalisation of financial markets in most advanced economies. This made it possible not only to introduce new financial instruments, but also to broaden and increase the supply of available capital to potential issuers of bonds and notes. Another government measure which assisted the greater use of direct finance has been the lower levels of inflation and interest rates in most economies. This resulted in investors accepting lower bond yields in exchange for greater price stability in bond markets. A final factor was the information/technology revolution which reduced transaction costs and made the processing/analysis of information available to a wider range of investors. In these ways, the evolving financial environment over the last 20 years has fomented the securitisation trend in national and global markets.

QUICK QUESTION

Which of the above is likely to sustain securitisation in the long term?

Write your answer here before reading on.

Going back to the three questions posed earlier, we have identified some of the main factors encouraging the securitisation trend. Is it likely to be permanent or temporary? Some factors, such as the information revolution, are unlikely to be reversed and therefore must be a permanent support to securitisation. Other factors – balance of payments trends, asset prices, inflation/interest rates – will change and, instead of supporting securitisation, could, if adverse, temporarily hinder the trend, as happened in 2007-09. Will securitisation accelerate or be reversed with the passage of time? To a large extent the answer to this question depends on the economic/financial environment, the demand for credit, potential issuers' credit ratings and the willingness of banks to lend. The securitisation process may decelerate in terms of the amount of paper (bonds and notes) outstanding relative to indirect finance, as part of a gradual maturing of the securitisation process. However, a complete collapse of the securitisation trend in the future is unlikely, either in North America or Europe.

3 Domestic securitisation

In a typical form of domestic securitisation, a pool of assets is transferred from the originating bank to a special purpose company which issues securities backed by these assets in the public debt markets. The securitised assets, typically residential mortgages, are thus separately financed from the remainder of the bank's assets.

If a UK bank decides to securitise £100 million of its mortgage portfolio, this will be transferred to a special purpose vehicle (or a special investment vehicle) which will not be a subsidiary of the originating bank. To finance the purchase of loans, the special purpose vehicle (SPV) will issue bonds or notes in the capital market.

Some form of credit enhancement will normally need to be built in to reduce the risk for the SPV's bond or note holders. This can take the form of an insurance policy to cover any marginal losses resulting from mortgage defaults, or subordinated debt, perhaps purchased by the originating bank. The SPV might issue £10 million of such debt via bonds subscribed for by the originator (selling bank) of the loans.

Interest payments and mortgage repayments received are used to service the bonds and notes issued by the SPV; if any defaults are incurred, these losses are borne by the investors in the SPV's subordinated debt or covered by the insurance company. In theory, the main bond and note holders in the SPV are thus protected from any losses.

The originating bank's risk, after securitisation, is limited to only £10 million of subordinated debt in the SPV. It is no longer responsible for the £100 million of mortgages securitised or the bonds/notes (£90 million) issued by the SPV to investors. The originating bank is neither responsible for any defaults that cause a reduction in income to the bond/note holders nor is it obliged to buy back any of the mortgages securitised (the assumed view until the credit crunch of 2007-09). The originating bank may still have an interest in the £100 million of loans, because it hopes to earn a turn between interest received from the loans (which it continues to administer) and interest passed on to the SPV.

In the originating bank's balance sheet the securitised portfolio of mortgages disappear, to be replaced by the £10 million holding of subordinated debt in the SPV and £90 million of cash, which can be used to make further residential mortgages.

CASE STUDY

Albion Bank decides to securitise £50 million of its residential mortgages from a total asset portfolio of £500 million. It purchases £10 million of subordinated debt in the SPV which finances the rest of the mortgage purchase via the issue of 5 year bonds. The balance sheets of Albion Bank and the SPV pre- and post-securitisation are illustrated below:

Pre-securitisation

A	**Albion Bank**	**L £m**	**A**	**SPV**	**L**
Mortgages	50	Deposits	450	Nil	Nil
Loans	400	Capital	50		
Cash	50				
	500		500	Nil	Nil

Post-securitisation

A	**Albion**			
	Bank L £m	**A**	**SPV**	**L**
SPV				
Bonds	10 Deposits	450 Mortgages	50 5 Yr	
			Bonds	40
Loans	400 Capital	50	Sub-bonds	10
Cash	90			
	500	500	50	50

Although domestic and/or international asset-backed securitisation emerged in a growing number of countries up to 2007, activity outside the United States experienced slower development. Much of the increase in international business resulted from the export of US-originated assets (including sub-prime loans) to the eurocurrency markets.

After 2003, banks and other financial institutions outside the United States participated more in the securitisation trend due to an increasingly favourable legal and regulatory environment in a number of countries. In the UK, an increasing number of banks securitised part of their residential mortgage assets in order to 'liquefy' their balance sheet positions up to mid-2007.

QUESTION TIME 28

Explain the role of SPVs in the securitisation of bank mortgage debt.

Write your answer here then check with the answer at the back of the book.

4 Economics of securitisation

A major factor encouraging securitisation was that the cost of holding a loan on a bank's balance sheet had increased due to higher intermediation costs. This made the issue of paper more attractive than bank finance to a broader range of potential borrowers. Increased intermediation costs were the direct result of:

- Increased capital-asset ratios in banking
- Increased bank funding costs due to a greater reliance on wholesale funds

QUICK QUESTION

How has technology reduced the role of banks?

Write your answer here before reading on.

At the same time, developments in computer and communications technology reduced the economic role of banks and enhanced the function of financial markets. At the heart of financial intermediation is the ability to obtain and use information. The high cost of gathering and using data meant that banks could profit from their cumulative store of knowledge about potential borrowers by making significantly more informed credit decisions than most other market participants. The latter (retail and wholesale depositors) provided banks with funds and permitted them to make credit decisions rather than themselves directly acquiring financial/market instruments.

Computer and telecommunications technology altered this process dramatically. The real cost of recording, transmitting and processing information has fallen sharply in recent years, lowering the cost of information processing and communication for banks. But it also made it possible for borrowers and lenders to deal with each other more directly in a more fully informed way. On-line databases, coupled with powerful computers and wide-ranging telecommunication facilities, can now provide potential investors with virtually the same timely credit and market information that was once available only to financial intermediaries. In this manner the comparative advantage once held by banks has been progressively eroded.

These developments mean that institutional investors, such as money market mutual funds, are increasingly able to make their own evaluation of credit risk, deal directly with borrowers, and with the increased availability of individuals' savings, develop their own portfolios and strategies. Consequently, the advantage that banks held via credit evaluation and the diversification of risk has been made less valuable by the information revolution. Examples of new financial products that resulted from this technological innovation, and challenged traditional bank loans, abound – the explosion in the use of commercial paper, the rapid growth of mortgage-backed securities and the development of consumer loan-backed securities, up to 2007.

As noted earlier, the increased efficiency of issue and trading practices in securities markets *plus* their deregulation/liberalisation encouraged the increasing use of debt instruments tailored to suit the needs of specific investors and borrowers.

QUICK QUESTION

Differentiate between securitisation and bank intermediation in the flow of financial funds.

Write your answer here before reading on.

5 Banks and securitisation

Any definition of securitisation states that it is associated with companies issuing marketable debt instruments (or paper) in the securities market rather than borrowing from banks. Up to 2007, credit flows in the eurocurrency markets, US domestic market and other countries were bypassing the banks because top class borrowers with high credit ratings could obtain funds in the capital markets in many instances at a lower cost than the banks. Bank loans for some borrowers became uncompetitive against the issue of their own paper.

Securitisation thus led to disintermediation in the national and international financial system. However, if banks are issuers or become holders of paper it is not true disintermediation, although it does represent an aspect of securitisation, i.e. banks hold paper rather than loans in their asset portfolio.

In the eurocurrency markets the issue of floating rate notes and medium term notes are alternatives to the use of syndicated credits. Commercial banks became major issuers and purchasers of these securities, as well as arranging and managing new issues for non-bank borrowers. The latter activity generated fee income for banks in place of their traditional interest income from loans.

Securitisation changed the composition of some banks' balance sheets. Evidence seems to suggest that the banks bought a large proportion of notes issued under various issuance facilities together with floating rate notes. In this manner credit flows were replaced by direct paper issues. Many banks also acquired huge amounts of securitised sub-prime loans (mortgages).

Securitisation created new risks within the banking industry, as assets acquired through purchase or underwriting various facilities were always likely to be characterised by much greater price volatility than ordinary commercial loans. Clearly, in turbulent market conditions, heavy losses could be incurred by banks if quick disposals of such assets were required in order to repay depositors. This became a reality in 2007-09.

Furthermore, under general accounting principles, these assets have to be marked to market value, thereby affecting the overall balance sheet figures of individual banks. Large paper losses could and did undermine depositor confidence in banks. It also impacted on the overall solvency position of many banks in 2008-09.

QUESTION TIME 29

Fill in the blanks in the following text.

When a corporation issues bonds rather than using loan facilities, this is known as ________.The use of ________ finance differs from intermediated funds because investors hold a claim on the borrowing corporation in the form of ________ or ________. This trend was encouraged by the________ problems which damaged the ________ ratings of banks in the 1980s, thus prime-rated borrowers obtained market funds more cheaply than the ________ themselves. Banks have also encouraged this ________ trend as a means of generating ________ income and reducing pressure on their balance sheet ratios. This is sometimes referred to as off-balance sheet financing. Other factors encouraging these developments were ________ real interest rates, de _______ of capital markets and the creation of new _________instruments.

Write your answer here then check with the answer at the back of the book.

6 Commercial paper markets

Commercial paper (CP) is a form of direct financing; it is an alternative to the use of bank or intermediated finance. Commercial Paper itself takes the form of a short-term secured or unsecured promissory note which is sold at a discount to face value, with a fixed maturity date of usually less than one year. CP, which is a bearer instrument, is either issued on an *ad hoc* basis or is part of a medium-term finance programme, with maturing paper being met by new issues of CP. In some cases, CP is sold directly by the issuer or is placed by a bank or securities dealer on behalf of the borrower. CP is thus part of the securitisation process.

For borrowers, under normal market conditions, CP has a number of advantages:

- A lower interest cost than bank finance
- Little documentation involved
- Flexibility in meeting financial needs
- Raising publicity/prestige in the financial markets

CP investors (lenders) benefit in a number of ways:

- An interest yield above most bank deposits
- High quality marketable paper
- Anonymity of a bearer instrument

The above comments relate to the common features of CP worldwide.

QUICK QUESTION

Does CP enhance or reduce the role of banks in the US economy?

Write your answer here before reading on.

6.1 United States commercial paper market (USCP market)

- **Key aspects**

  The USCP market is the largest in the world. Total outstanding paper reached a peak of $2200 billion in July 2007. It is a major source of short-term finance for about 15,000 US corporations and financial institutions. CP is used to finance working capital and seasonal credit needs in most sectors of the US economy. It is also used via rollover issue programmes to finance long-term projects such as oil and gas pipelines.

  The main features of USCP are:

  - They are bearer instruments issued on a discount basis (book entries now common)
  - They have maturities of 270 days or less; most CP is for 30 to 60 days
  - Their minimum instrument value is $100000; most in $1 to $5 million range
  - All settlements in same day funds
  - They are exempt from registration requirements under the Securities Act, 1933

- **Issue procedures**

  CP can either be placed directly by the issuer (c. 20% of CP issued) or through a recognised dealer (c. 80% of CP issued). In the former, major corporations and financial institutions use their own CP sales force to place paper directly with investors. In the latter, dealers such as J P Morgan Chase purchase CP from corporations and re-sell it to their clients. CP issuers have to pay a fee to dealers placing their paper with investment clients.

  Most USCP is purchased by corporations and financial institutions with temporary cash surpluses which require to be invested in short-term safe financial instruments. Money market mutual funds (MMMFs), in which retail investors/savers funds are pooled, have become major purchasers of high quality CP issues.

  Prior to a corporation or institution establishing a CP programme, it must be given a good rating by one of the main credit rating agencies, such as Standard and Poor's or Moody's, in the USA. Ratings influence the discount rate applicable to an issuer's CP.

  Various costs are associated with CP programmes. Obviously, the main cost is the discount rate applicable to each issue of CP, which is influenced by market interest rates, the issuer's credit rating and the level of investor demand on the issue date. Other expenses relate to dealer's fees and credit rating fees, etc. These can amount to 0.5% to 1% per annum on paper issued. Economies of scale via large and continuous issues of CP reduce such costs to the lower end of the range stated.

QUICK QUESTION

Why do you think non-US banks issue CP?

Write your answer here before reading on.

- **Foreign entity USCP programmes**

  The entry of foreign issuers has been another significant development in the USCP market over the past two decades. Total outstanding paper by such issuers was approximately $200 billion, or 12% of the USCP market, in 2008. Foreign banks accounted for about 50% of the paper issued by foreign CP issuers. These foreign entities have entered the USCP market to broaden their sources of funds and at times to obtain a cheaper source of dollar financing than the eurodollar market.

  For foreign banks, a USCP programme provides another option for the funding of a dollar loan book other than the eurocurrency market. It also raises the financial market profile of a bank. Dollars raised through the issue of USCP are not restricted to use only in the USA.

  The CP market expanded by July 2007 when total outstanding CP was approximately $2200 billion, of which asset-backed CP was $1200 billion, or over 50% of the total. Asset-backed commercial paper (ABCP) had increased from $600 billion in 2004. Most of the ABCP was issued by SPVs involved in securitised mortgage business in the USA.

  Under the impact of the credit crunch, a loss of confidence by investors in CP resulted in the amount of ABCP shrinking by $400 billion in six months to $800 billion outstanding in December 2007. The collapse in ABCP issuance was the main factor in the overall decline of the USCP market as risk-averse MMMFs, with over $3 trillion in investments in 2007, switched from CP to Treasury bills and bonds.

  At the beginning of 2009, the USCP market was showing signs of recovery, no doubt helped by the Federal Commercial Paper Funding Facility set up in October 2008. This facility has provided assistance to the CP market via the Federal Reserve acting as a buyer of corporate-issued CP, thereby partially replacing the role of MMMFs. It is to be hoped that this recovery in the USCP market continues as it is such an important source of finance in US corporate and financial sectors.

6.2 Other national CP markets

Most other domestic CP markets were established in the mid-1980s. In most countries this necessitated changes in the regulatory and legislative framework applicable to their domestic financial/money markets. Such changes formed part of the general financial liberalisation and securitisation trend in the world's credit and capital markets.

The main non-USCP markets are based in Japan, France and Canada, with other smaller markets in most industrialised countries. As is to be expected, there are variations from one CP market to another. Most have slightly longer maturities than USCP, with consequentially a more active secondary market.

Regulatory regimes applicable to CP markets vary between countries, but most domestic CP markets are restricted to local currency paper.

QUESTION TIME 30

(a) What are the main features of the USCP market?

(b) Why does a British-based bank need to issue USCP?

Write your answer here then check with the answer at the back of the book.

7 Euro-commercial Paper Market (ECP market)

- **Key features**

  ECP is debt in the form of a short-term secured or unsecured promissory note issued by corporate, financial and sovereign borrowers. It is issued without any third party guarantee and is not underwritten by any bank.

  Like most CP, ECP is a bearer financial instrument issued at a discount to face value. Maturities range from 7 to 365 days, although typically most paper has an average maturity of 60 days. The paper has a minimum face value of $500,000 upwards.

  ECP is issued in a currency other than the currency of the country where it is being issued, e.g. $ECP issued in London. This characteristic means that the ECP market is part of the overall eurocurrency market. Not unsurprisingly, the main ECP market is based in London, where about 50% of ECP is euro denominated (c. 30% dollar denominated). International banks act as dealers in the ECP market.

- **USCP v ECP**

  The USCP market tends to discriminate against foreign issuers via higher discount rates; such practices do not apply to the ECP market. In the ECP market the main investors are banks and institutions, whereas in the USCP market most paper issued is purchased by corporations and money market mutual funds.

  Most USCP has a term of less than 60 days, whereas ECP maturities range from 90 to 180 days, and as a result, the latter has a more active secondary market. USCP requires same-day settlement of funds, whereas ECP settlements take two days at least due to the normal time delay associated with eurocurrency transactions.

- **ECP market development**

  The total amount of ECP outstanding was approximately €600 billion in 2008. The smaller size of the ECP market in relation to the USCP market reflects its narrower investor base and the lower liquidity of several currency segments. The market remains hampered by the relatively small size of the European money market fund industry and the traditionally cautious attitude of investors, factors that have limited issuance to highly rated sovereigns and financial institutions.

8 Globalisation of financial markets

In the context of financial markets, globalisation can be defined as the gradual integration of national capital markets into a global market. Although not as yet complete, as is witnessed by different interest rates/yields and real rates of return between major financial centres, the general trend is towards increased integration.

Globalisation has been assisted by policy measures implemented by the financial and regulatory authorities in the main industrial countries and some emerging economies over the last 20 years. This internationalisation of financial markets has also been reinforced by deregulation, securitisation and the information revolution dealt with in the earlier parts of this chapter.

The main policy measures encouraging the globalisation of financial markets are listed below.

- **Removal of exchange controls freed international capital flows**

  This permitted companies to seek out the most convenient and cheapest sources of finance and encouraged a movement of financial resources and facilities across previously sacrosanct national boundaries.

- **Restrictions on non-resident corporations seeking to borrow in many national (domestic) capital markets have been removed**

  To a large extent the borderlines between national and international capital markets are becoming increasingly blurred. Inherent pressures are creating a global capital market.

- **Most countries have removed withholding taxes on interest payments to non-residents**

  This encourages greater diversification of investment holdings by private and institutional investors.

- **Many industrialised countries have liberalised regulations on the establishment of foreign banks in their own countries**

  Examples are Sweden, Canada, Australia and Japan. This acts as a spur to competition and innovation within individual national markets while reciprocity (equal access) internationalises their own domestic banks.

- **Deregulation has encouraged the development of innovatory financial instruments**

  Most of the main financial centres have futures, options and swap markets in addition to the issue of asset-backed securities and global bonds.

- **Information technology has helped the prompt dissemination of information, cut transaction costs and linked individual national markets**

  This has encouraged globalisation by enabling banks and securities houses to trade in a wide variety of instruments on a 24-hour basis. There is now a global market for certain types of financial instruments, such as government bonds, corporate stocks and floating rate notes.

- **Institutions (pension funds, insurance companies) have also contributed to the globalisation trend by pursuing a policy of diversifying their portfolios internationally.**

  This trend has been encouraged by the privatisation of former state enterprises in many emerging economies as governments have sought to raise cash and improve the overall efficiency of their economies. In some cases the direct sale of stakes in industries and utilities has been made to foreign shareholders due to the underdeveloped nature of local capital markets and the need to encourage capital inflows.

- **Emerging financial markets have enhanced diversification opportunities and potential returns**

  About 60 developing countries have stock exchanges and although most are small in market capitalisation terms, they are growing in size and sophistication. A key factor in this development is participation by foreign investors. Privatisation and capital inflow needs have resulted in the abolition of exchange control and dividend remittance restrictions for non-resident investors. Because of the greater market risks involved, the attraction for the latter lies in higher potential returns than are available in long-established capital markets. An additional bonus is that such returns are not always highly correlated to dividend/return trends in the rich industrialised world.

8.1 Results, rewards, risks, risk controls

- **Results**

  The globalisation of financial markets has resulted in a gradual convergence between international (external) and domestic bond markets as regards issue procedures, secondary market trading and interest yields. It has created an environment in which the global bond market is now a reality.

  Globalisation has also increased the pressure for domestic deregulation as banks and other financial institutions sought the right to undertake activities, previously prohibited by domestic regulation, which they could participate in overseas.

- **Rewards**

  Globalisation has benefited investors via improved returns from dividends and capital appreciation. At the same time, borrowers have benefited via lower finance costs and greater flexibility in the range of financial instruments available to them.

  In economic terms, globalisation has improved the overall efficiency of financial markets while, at the same time, achieving a better utilisation of global capital resources. These perceived economic benefits have acted as a further spur to domestic deregulation of banking and financial markets in individual countries.

- **Risks**

  Some fears have been expressed that securitisation and globalisation have increased risks in the banking industry. The decline in the quality of bank loan books via the loss of highly rated borrowers plus lower interest margins has perhaps made banks more susceptible to failure.

  Also, a disturbance in one domestic financial centre can prove to be highly contagious, as globalisation ensures that financial shocks are transmitted internationally at greater speed. Volatile interest rates, asset prices or exchange rates impact immediately upon other countries' financial markets. The dotcom share price collapse in 2000-01 and the credit crunch in 2007-09 are good examples of the global shock transmission process.

  A key question relates to who ultimately assumes responsibility for customer deposits. This poses a risk to bank customers, as highlighted by the collapse of Landsbanki. In 2008, the Icelandic bank Landsbanki was declared bankrupt. A large proportion of their deposits were held by British and Dutch savers. In normal circumstances, the deposits of the British and Dutch savers would have been guaranteed by the Icelandic Depositor's and Investor's Guarantee Fund. However, this fund had been drained by previous claims. Eventually, the British and Dutch Governments agreed to refund the lost deposits. All Icelandic nationals with deposits with Landsbanki were refunded by the Icelandic state.

- **Risk controls**

  In order to reduce the financial risks associated with globalisation, it is necessary to combine sound macro-economic policies in individual countries with an adequate degree of international cooperation. Only in this manner can a stable economic and financial environment be created, but it requires political will to be shown by the major countries to achieve this objective.

  It is also essential that all financial institutions, including banks and securities houses, are adequately capitalised to deal with financial asset losses. Within financial institutions there is also a need for better internal control procedures and systems to deal with crisis management.

QUICK QUESTION

What key benefits have global financial markets brought to those investors and borrowers using them?

Write your answer here before reading on.

9 Global financial crisis and securitisation

9.1 Origins

The financial crisis originated in the US housing market. Up to July 2006 house prices were rising and the overall market was experiencing an asset/market price bubble. This situation was encouraged by financial innovation and large volumes of lending to less than creditworthy borrowers. Much of the sub-prime house loans were packaged up and sold on to financial institutions, investment funds and private investors around the world. As a result, when the bubble burst, the consequences were seen throughout the global banking and financial system.

Four immediate causes of the global financial crisis were:

- Financial liberalisation made it easier for banks to lend and individuals to borrow, for example, asset-backed securities and sub-prime lending.
- Monetary policy focused on inflation in goods and services and ignored asset price inflation, and did not respond to the rapid rise in house prices in most countries.
- Regulatory failures/lapses in a number of countries resulted in some banks relying too heavily on wholesale funds to aggressively expand their balance sheets.
- The growth of the shadow banking system increased leverage and facilitated the creation of credit across global financial markets. Shadow banks are financial intermediaries such as hedge funds that are not subjected to regulation. Shadow banks were able to take very large risks and facilitate trades, particularly in over the counter markets such as Credit Default Swaps (CDS).

9.2 Sub-prime lending

Asset-backed securities (ABS) enabled good and bad loans to be bundled up and sold on by originating banks to other financial institutions/investors. This originate and distribute loan model meant that banks/mortgage providers had little incentive to avoid excessively risky borrowers, while ABS purchasers did not realise the riskiness of the assets acquired.

In the USA, a large amount of sub-prime lending was to low-income households whose chances of paying off a mortgage depended heavily on a continued rise in house prices. Much of the lending was based on over-optimistic assumptions about house prices and/or exaggerated or fraudulent statements regarding borrowers' incomes and employment prospects.

A high proportion of these sub-prime loans were repackaged and resold as mortgage-backed securities which were given a high credit rating and were provided with insurance against default by US government agencies, such as Fannie Mae, and insurance corporations such as American International Group (AIG).

In total, about $7 trillion was repackaged and resold, both in the USA and worldwide. Many European banks and investors bought these mortgage-backed securities as, on the face of it, such investment promised a reasonable rate of return with little or no risk. The sub-prime debt (toxic debt) was thus absorbed into the global banking and financial system. In the UK, most banks, some building societies and investment funds added toxic debt to their asset/investment portfolios.

9.3 The crisis and securitisation

In July 2006, US house prices peaked and then started to fall. One year later, Bear Stearns (US investment bank) reported problems with its asset portfolio of sub-prime repackaged loans. This undermined confidence in the global interbank market in August 2007, as banks became reluctant to lend to one another. Interbank interest rates (LIBOR) rose sharply, thus making wholesale funding less available and more expensive.

The crisis had an immediate impact on US securitisation issuance. In 2002, issuance was $500 billion. By 2006, it had peaked at $1600 billion, only to fall to less than $200 billion in 2008. A similar decline was experienced in other securitisation markets around the world. Globally, issuance in 2006 was $3000 billion; in 2008 it fell to $500 billion. Investors were no longer interested in repackaging residential mortgage debt either in the USA or elsewhere.

The huge losses were incurred by banks (and other investment institutions) and were estimated to be in the region of $3000 billion. This led to the collapse of some banks, such as Lehman Brothers, and the partial insolvency of other banks, such as Royal Bank of Scotland. Only government and central bank support in most of the advanced economies prevented a complete meltdown of the global banking financial system.

Many bankers, financial experts and academics have pondered over the possible future for securitisation. Will it disappear or be regulated out of existence? The overall opinion is that securitisation will survive but on a smaller scale and subject to greater scrutiny and regulatory control. Banks as originators of packaged debt (house loans, car loans, etc) will have to guarantee the integrity of their lending. SPVs will have to be more transparent as regards their operational activities. Investors in ABCP issued by them need to be reassured about the quality of SPV asset books. Finally, SPVs operated in effect an unregulated parallel banking system up to the crisis. Many have been liquidated, with banks and investors incurring huge losses – such an arrangement will not be tolerated in the USA or elsewhere again in the future.

QUESTION TIME 31

Albion Bank plc has dollar euro commercial paper ($ECP) on the liabilities side of its balance sheet. A customer phones up the securities department and asks you, as an employee in that department, the undernoted questions. State how you would answer them.

(a) What are the main features of the ECP market?
(b) Why does a British bank need to issue $ECP?
(c) Is $ECP issued by Albion Bank a worthwhile acquisition for a personal investor?
(d) How does $ECP differ from USCP?

Write your answer here then check with the answer at the back of the book.

KEY WORDS

Key words in this chapter are given below. There is space to write your own revision notes and to add any other words or phrases that you want to remember.

- Commercial paper
- Globalisation
- Credit ratings
- Risk
- Disintermediation
- Securitisation
- Sub-prime lending
- Asset-backed securities

REVIEW

The main learning points introduced in this chapter are summarised below.

Go through them and check back to the learning outcomes at the beginning of the chapter. Only move on when you are happy that you fully understand each point.

- We examined the evolution of securitisation over the last 20 years and how the economic/financial environment, together with new technological developments, assisted this process.
- The economics of securitisation and its impact on banking were explained, along with the role of SPVs in enabling banks to sell off parts of their asset (loan) pool.
- No discussion of securitisation is complete without some mention of commercial paper. The USCP and ECP markets were thoroughly examined and compared from both the issuers' and investors' viewpoints.
- The factors behind financial globalisation were reviewed, along with the results, rewards and risks associated with this process.
- We also considered the interrelationship between securitisation and the global financial crisis.

chapter 10

ECONOMIC AND MONETARY UNION (EMU)

Contents

Learning outcomes

On completion of this chapter, you should be able to:

- Explain the main features of the Eurozone and the case for and against euro membership.
- Critically review current Eurozone problems and policies in relation to the Greek debt problem and its impact on banks and the European economy.

Introduction

In this chapter we will examine the history and development of economic and monetary union in the European Union (EU). We will also examine the case for and against euro membership and recent developments within the Eurozone which impact upon the UK economy and banking/financial systems.

We will consider key aspects of economic and monetary union under the following headings:

- Maastricht Treaty
- Convergence criteria
- EMU benefits and costs
- EMU politics
- Stability and growth pact
- Eurozone crisis

1 The European Monetary System

The European Monetary System (EMS) became operational in March 1979. Its objectives were to stabilise exchange rates between European Union (EU) member states' currencies and to contribute to European integration by creating a zone of monetary stability. A key role in the EMS was played by the European Currency Unit (ECU), which was a composite currency basket of most EU currencies which acted as a denominator for exchange rates.

An exchange rate intervention system was established to preserve stability between different member currencies and was known as the Exchange Rate Mechanism (ERM). Each currency had a central rate in terms of the ECU. These values determined a grid of bilateral central rates between participating member states whose central banks defended these rates within agreed margins of fluctuation.

The EMS/ERM was not a complete monetary union like that of the UK and Jersey. It allowed for currency realignments and incorporated the use of margins. Speculative pressure sometimes resulted in a temporary suspension of the ERM and member currency exits, e.g. sterling in 1992. Also the ECU acted solely as a unit of account; it never attained the status of a replacement single currency for member states' currencies.

Economic convergence did take place as regards inflation rates and long term interest rates, but less so for unemployment rates and budget deficits among ERM member states. The lessons of the ERM convinced many that convergence policies were not sufficient in themselves; what was required was a complete monetary union with the use of a single currency. With this in mind, the EU set up a committee with Jacques Delors (former EU Commission President) as chairman in 1988 to examine the main features of such a union and how it could be achieved over a period of time.

QUICK QUESTION

What do you think the Delors Committee recommended?

Write your answer here before reading on.

2 The Delors Report

This was published in April 1989 and stated that monetary union could only be achieved by means of:

- Absolutely fixed exchange rates with no margins
- The ultimate adoption of a single currency
- A new centralised monetary institution
- Constraints on member states' budgets
- Strengthened regional and industrial policies within the EU

The Delors Report stated that, unlike existing federal states such as the USA, the EU member states were to remain independent nations. However, as regards economic policies, EU members would have to surrender a substantial degree of national sovereignty. Monetary union would be permanent, even although full political union was not envisaged.

3 Maastricht Treaty (1991)

The main points of the Maastricht Treaty on Economic and Monetary Union (EMU) were:

- Agreement to economic and monetary union by 1999 for countries which fulfilled the economic criteria
- The establishment of the European Central Bank (ECB)

The Maastricht Treaty was ratified in 1993 by all the EU members. Both Denmark and the UK obtained an opting-out clause to allow them to reserve their decision on participation.

The Maastricht Treaty established three basic principles as regards fiscal policy:

1 No excessive budget deficits
2 No monetary financing of budget deficits, i.e. unlimited credit from the central bank
3 No bail outs of bankrupt governments

These principles were aimed at ensuring that fiscal mismanagement by one or more member states did not happen in the future. It was accepted that fiscal profligacy could undermine the monetary union. In the late 19th century, the Latin Monetary Union, which incorporated France, Belgium, Switzerland, Italy and Greece, was destroyed by large budget deficits and excessive money creation in the latter two countries.

The Maastricht Treaty laid down the following official convergence criteria for member state participation:

- **Inflation** – no more than $1^1/_2$% above the average of the lowest three country rates in the European Union.
- **Stable exchange rates** – to be within exchange rate mechanism bands for the previous two years.
- **Sustainable government finances** – budget deficit within 3% of gross domestic product and total government debt within 60% of gross domestic product.
- **Interest rates** – no more than 2% above the average on government bonds in three EU countries enjoying lowest inflation.

The convergence criteria were essential to ensure that participants' economies were operating as a single economy as regards inflation, interest rates and budgetary position. Any new or existing EU members, such as Sweden or Hungary, wishing to join the Eurozone will have to meet the above euro convergence criteria. (Note that the convergence criteria on inflation and interest rates now relates to any three Eurozone countries with the lowest inflation rates.)

4 Post-Maastricht: pre-Eurozone

4.1 Dublin Summit: December 1996

This EU Summit resulted in the confirmation of two significant operational aspects of Economic and Monetary Union (EMU).

4.2 Stability and growth pact

The Maastricht Treaty stipulated that countries participating in EMU had to continue to meet the convergence criteria relating to their fiscal deficits and debt, otherwise sanctions would be imposed.

In November 1995 the German finance minister proposed that EMU participants should commit themselves to a Stability Pact for Europe which set out medium term budgetary targets and a scale of sanctions on participants failing to meet the targets. This proposal resulted in a dispute between the Germans and French about the system of penalties for any country in the Eurozone incurring a budget deficit in excess of 3% of GDP per annum.

A compromise was eventually achieved with less onerous procedures for dealing with an excess budget deficit country. In a gesture of Franco-German reconciliation, EU leaders agreed to rename the agreement the Stability and Growth Pact.

The Pact's fines, which moved on a sliding scale from 0.2% to a ceiling of 0.5% of GDP, were intended primarily as a deterrent. Few expected the penalties to be applied in practice because of the explosive political consequences of their implementation.

4.3 ERM 2

In anticipation that some EU member states would not participate in the Eurozone due to failure to meet the convergence criteria or by exercising their opt-out clause, new exchange rate rules were outlined. These new rules applied to newer EU member states, such as Poland and Hungary, and others which intend to apply for Eurozone membership in the future.

As both ins and outs of the Eurozone remain members of the EU single market, it was regarded as important that exchange rate relationships between both groups did not undermine the single market. A high degree of exchange rate stability between all EU currencies was regarded as likely to be beneficial in the future.

At the Dublin Summit, the basic principles for ERM 2 were established:

- EMU 'outs' may select an ERM 2 central rate with target bands for their currency against the euro after consultation with the ECB, e.g. Denmark
- Two years' participation in ERM 2 is a prerequisite for future EMU entry
- Membership of ERM 2 is not compulsory for non-EMU countries, e.g. UK
- A country in ERM 2 must achieve the necessary degree of convergence required before being eligible for EMU membership. The ECB assists and makes recommendations on appropriate economic policies to potential EMU participants

4.4 Brussels Summit: May 1998

In Brussels, the then 15 EU heads of government announced formally the euro's birth. Decisions were taken regarding two important matters:

EMU participants

Using qualified majority voting, the EU decided that 11 member states qualified as first wave participants – Germany, France, Italy, Spain, Portugal, Belgium, Holland, Luxembourg, Austria, Finland and Ireland. Greece initially did not meet the convergence criteria, Denmark and the UK exercised their opt-out clauses, and Sweden decided against participation in the first wave. The selection reflected the economic performance of member states for 1997. The European Commission and the ECB prepared convergence reports which formed the basis of the selection process.

As regards budgetary deficits, the Maastricht Treaty allowed for leniency if countries were seen to be moving in the right direction towards sustainable government finances. The key judgement was which countries were ready to operate within a single exchange rate and uniform monetary policy climate indefinitely. With the benefit of hindsight, we can see that a large element of wishful thinking, or hope, about fiscal positions was incorporated into the EMU selection process.

Irrevocable fixed (bilateral) exchange rates

The Summit also announced that bilateral exchange rates would be the same as the then existing ERM central rates on 31 December 1998. It also decided that one ECU would equal one euro from 1 January 1999 onwards.

On 1 January 1999 the exchange rates between participating currencies turned into 'conversion rates', so that national currencies and the euro became different expressions of what was economically the same currency. The euro came into being as the currency for the then 11 participating members.

EMU participants irrevocably fixed their exchange rates against each other and the euro. National currencies were units of account against the euro.

From these rates, 1 German Mark was fixed at French Franc 3.35386 (6.55957 ÷ 1.95583) until 1 January 2002 when both currencies were completely replaced by one single currency – the euro (€). The mark and franc are now referred to as legacy currencies.

Euro conversion rates

1 euro =

Austrian schilling 13.7603
Belgian franc 40.3399
Dutch guilder 2.20371
Finnish mark 5.94573
French franc 6.55957
German mark 1.95583
Irish punt 0.787564
Italian lira 1936.27
Luxembourg franc 40.3399

Portuguese escudo 200.482
Spanish peseta 166.386

QUESTION TIME 32

What do you think Economic and Monetary Union entails for member state participants?

Write your answer here then check with the answer at the back of the book.

5 EMU: economic benefits, costs and potential

With the benefit of hindsight, you should critically consider the perceived EMU benefits and costs in light of subsequent developments in the Eurozone post-2010.

5.1 Benefits

Prior to the establishment of the Eurozone in 1999, the European Commission's economic/financial experts identified five specific advantages in relation to EMU.

1 **Growth and efficiency**

It was believed that reduced transaction costs for business via the elimination of costs associated with changing currencies would generate a gain of 0.4% of EMU GDP on a once and for all basis. As these costs constituted a net dead-weight loss for society as a whole, their elimination was the most obvious visible benefit to all citizens/firms of EMU, but probably the least important.

It was expected that the removal of exchange risk would encourage more intra-trade and investment between the EMU participants and increased inward investment into the Eurozone, but exchange rate uncertainty is not completely eliminated since the euro fluctuates against non-member currencies. However, this is partially offset by external trade being a far lower percentage of GDP post-EMU than it was for individual EMU countries.

Completion of the single market was to be assisted by use of the euro, as it reduces the possibility of differential product pricing between countries. It makes prices more transparent and hopefully adds to competitive downward pressure on prices in high-cost countries. An additional benefit of closer trading links via EMU is that it should increase the correlation of business cycles between participating countries in the Eurozone and thereby assist further economic convergence.

2 **Price stability**

Low inflation is advantageous for efficient resource allocation; it is also associated with low variability of prices. According to estimates, a 1% decrease in relative price variance could increase real output by 0.3% of EMU GDP on a once and for all basis.

3 **Public finance**

The Stability and Growth Pact was expected to enhance budgetary discipline so that excessive budget deficits financed by inflationary increases in money supply were not permitted. At the same time, it was hoped that increased budgetary stringency would encourage governments to improve the efficiency of tax collection and the provision of public goods and services.

4 **Adjustment without exchange rate changes**

Exchange rate changes with the rest of the world were expected to influence the competitiveness of the Eurozone in relation to the USA, Japan and emerging economies. Within EMU, real exchange rates (competitiveness between participants) would still be possible even with the use of a single currency if individual countries experienced and permitted wage/price flexibility to offset differentials in productivity gains between member states such as Germany and Italy.

5 **Reserve currency status**

It was anticipated that the euro would become a major vehicle/reserve currency in the global economy, which was expected to benefit EMU participants. More euro-denominated trade and finance transactions should generate gains via reduced foreign exchange risk and hedging costs. The Eurozone countries might also have more influence in international financial institutions such as the International Monetary Fund.

QUICK QUESTION

Does the lack of exchange rate and interest rate flexibility pose potential problems for EMU participants?

Write your answer here before reading on.

5.2 Costs

Despite the above benefits, the European Commission's experts recognised that certain specific disadvantages could have a profound effect on EMU participants.

1 **Loss of exchange rate flexibility**

This is the most complex issue raised by EMU and is probably the most 'political'. When allowed to float freely, an exchange rate will tend to respond to economic shocks; in theory such movement is helpful. An uncompetitive country, due to inflation above other union members or a decline in a major industry, will be unable to restore its competitiveness via devaluation in a single currency zone. Such member state imbalances could damage growth and cause high unemployment over a prolonged time period, with resultant political pressures leading to a breakdown of the monetary union. Only real economic convergence could avoid such a possibility in the Eurozone.

However, while devaluation may be a useful economic tool to deal with some specific economic shocks, it is less than successful in dealing with cost price differentials arising from higher inflation. In the latter situation, the benefits of devaluation tend to be short lived due to cost push inflation rapidly eroding any price advantage. In the past, competitive currency devaluations by the UK and Italy did not make them more successful in growth terms than countries which stuck to an exchange rate and used alternative methods to improve their competitiveness.

2 **No independent interest rate policy**

Adopting a single currency entailed countries giving up control of monetary policy to the ECB which sets interest rates and other aspects of monetary policy for the Eurozone rather than for any one country.

This has two implications:

- A loss of power by EMU countries to choose their own short term inflation/unemployment trade-off.
- An inability to deal with country-specific economic shocks via monetary policy; the ECB only responds to shocks affecting all or most members.

However, the loss of monetary sovereignty arguments were assumed to have perhaps lost their significance as all the EMU participants accepted that the prime objective of monetary policy is price stability and not short term output/employment creation.

3 **Fiscal adjustment limited**

In theory, EMU prevents countries using excessive budget deficits and borrowing to try and cure unemployment. To some, the Stability and Growth Pact sterilised all demand management policy tools in EMU and appeared to narrow governmental responsibilities in relation to EU economic welfare. Another longer term constraint on fiscal policy is that EMU is likely to increase pressure for tax harmonisation throughout the Eurozone.

4 **Transition costs**

This was the most readily quantifiable cost of establishing EMU. Direct costs such as producing new notes and coins and a public information/education programme had to be borne by participating governments. Consumers had to adjust to new prices and money; businesses had to change to new accounting systems and issue euro-denominated share certificates. Bankers had to change their systems and note/coin handling equipment. However, transition costs were a one-off EMU expense that was expected to be quickly offset by the anticipated benefits of having a single currency.

5 **Lack of adjustment**

It was widely acknowledged that the EU and Eurozone are beset by structural problems such as large-scale state ownership, excessive subsidies, high structural unemployment and too much regulation. Labour mobility is restricted by culture and language, and national labour markets are rigid. Despite such problems, no machinery exists for transferring income from countries whose demand is high to countries where it is weak, apart from very limited EU regional/cohesion funds.

The economic diversity of EU states poses a unique set of problems. For example, manufacturing accounts for nearly 30% of the German economy, but only 12% of the Greek economy and Greece is also heavily reliant on tourism and agriculture. Therefore the Greek economy is more sensitive than the German economy to cyclical economic factors, but both countries are governed by the same set of economic policies.

In the USA, about one third of a regional economic shock is cushioned by federal taxes and disbursements, which automatically transfer resources from prosperous states to depressed ones.

No such mechanism exists in the Eurozone. Adjustment is further assisted by the US labour force being three times more mobile than in France, while wages are twice as flexible as in the EU.

If adjustment through the EU budget, wage flexibility and migration is limited, then it must come through variations in employment levels. Such adjustment could be prolonged and highly painful via associated economic and social costs, which will only be reduced if EMU participants reform their labour markets to promote greater mobility and real wage flexibility.

5.3 Potential

While the economic benefits and costs of EMU were finely balanced, of far more importance in an overall judgement was whether the potential dynamic benefits outweighed the risks associated with the entire project.

Much of the debate was conducted in national terms as regards convergence qualification, possible benefits and influence over ECB policy, but for corporations, investment institutions and banks which had to cope with the long term consequences of monetary union, the creation of a single currency zone was regarded as crucial to the realisation of a fully integrated continental European economy.

No rational and objective economist in the late 1990s could prove either that EMU did or did not make sense. The straightforward benefits and costs, such as reduced transaction and hedging costs, together with substantial changeover costs, were dwarfed in significance by the uncertainties surrounding the likely impact on output and employment. In the long term it was believed if EMU worked, it would result in a more stable and low inflation environment within the participating group. In turn, this would result in greater investment, enhanced productivity growth, a higher trend GDP growth rate and reduced unemployment.

Whether these hopes and aspirations have been realised or not must be left to the reader to decide. That said, short term problems might be overshadowed by possible long term gains.

QUESTION TIME 33

Briefly examine the economic case for and against EMU membership.

Write your answer here then check with the answer at the back of the book.

6 EMU: political dimension

No one can deny that the EU has made a huge positive contribution to the security and prosperity of Western Europe's people. It is for this very reason that twelve central and east European countries have joined the EU since 2004. The EU is the longest established and most successful free trade area in the world. To achieve this, nation states have been prepared to give up some degree of sovereignty.

European integration has been as much about politics as economics. The EU built up a framework of cooperation, integration and decision taking in order to avoid the rivalry and petty nationalism that led to major conflicts between Germany and France. Whereas the British public/governments have viewed the EU as an economic club, Continental governments have always envisaged a closer political working union. This political dimension is perhaps the main difference between British and Continental perceptions on Europe's future shape and form.

EMU is viewed by many as a further step in the process of European political integration. The risks associated with a single currency were acknowledged, but these were outweighed by the potential economic and political benefits that might materialise. To make monetary union permanent, some degree of political unity may be required. The surrender of some degree of political sovereignty is regarded by many as an acceptable price if it guarantees future European security.

However, it was acknowledged that were some political risks associated with EMU:

- It might result in more centralisation and concentration of power in Brussels over fiscal matters without the consent or approval of the Eurozone electorate. Unelected technocrats might replace democratically elected finance ministers in member states.
- It might engender a Fortress Europe mentality, resulting in renewed protectionism to safeguard jobs and industries from the ongoing process of globalisation.

QUICK QUESTION

What is the UK's current position regarding EMU?

Write your answer here before reading on.

7 UK: EMU policy

In October 1997 the then Chancellor of the Exchequer made a statement to the House of Commons on EMU to the effect that the decision on whether the UK should join the single currency was probably the most important this country was likely to face in the foreseeable future. However, he stated that if a single currency was successful, and the economic case was clear and unambiguous, then the government believed the UK should be part of it; but because of the magnitude of a decision to join EMU, a referendum would be put to the British people.

The government did not seek single currency membership on 1 January 1999. Its decision not to join the first wave of EMU participants might have been influenced by sterling's overvaluation against the German mark and the ECB's interest rate policy being inappropriate for the requirements of the UK domestic economy.

The UK Treasury assessment was that the economy was not ready for entry due to the lack of preparation for entry in the first wave, believing that a period of preparation was required, along with a settled period of sustainable economic convergence between the UK and the Eurozone.

As the years have passed, there has been little evidence of economic convergence between the UK and the Eurozone as regards economic growth and employment levels. This, along with the lack of enthusiasm among the UK electorate for Eurozone membership and the euro instead of sterling has made it extremely unlikely that the UK will seek admission in the near future.

The rise of the UKIP political party has also heightened anti-EU sentiment in the UK. The Prime Minister has also begun talks with the EU to renegotiate Britain's relationship with the EU, due to fears over the UK surrendering rights through the Lisbon Treaty. The Conservative Party have also promised a referendum in 2017 (should the Conservatives be in power) on whether Britain should retain EU membership.

8 Eurozone developments: 2001-2010

1 **Greece**

Greece initially did not meet the convergence criteria in May 1998 and thus was not a first wave participant. In 2000 Greece met the convergence criteria requirements and joined EMU on 1 January 2001. However, it was suspected that the Greek Finance Ministry had 'massaged' some of the public finance data in order to gain EMU entry. ECB officials must now regret that these allegations did not receive more attention at the time in light of subsequent budgetary and debt problems in Greece.

2 **Future member states**

In May 2004 ten new countries (Estonia, Hungary, Cyprus, etc) joined the EU and all expressed a desire to join the single currency area at some future date. Eurozone membership necessitates that these new countries meet the convergence criteria requirements and join the ERM 2 for at least two years.

Up to 2010 five of these new EU members – Estonia, Slovakia, Slovenia, Malta, and Cyprus – met the convergence criteria and joined the Eurozone, thereby increasing the total membership to 17 countries. In 2013, Croatia became the 29th member of the EU, but they have not yet joined the Euro single currency.

At present, ten EU member states outside the Eurozone operate various exchange rate regimes for their currencies – floating exchange rate, ERM 2, a currency board arrangement. Most have large fiscal deficits and require structural reforms to be implemented in their economies. Thus, meeting Eurozone membership requirements is likely to involve a certain degree of economic/social pain over a prolonged period in most future applicant countries. Given the unsettled economic and financial conditions in the Eurozone, none are seeking membership at the present time.

3 **Stability and Growth Pact**

The Pact was suspended in November 2003, primarily due to France and Germany having ongoing budget deficits in excess of 3% of GDP. This suspension removed the prospect of sanctions and fines on these two Eurozone countries, but it meant that, instead of being an 'iron' statute, the Pact had become a voluntary code. This was much to the annoyance of smaller countries such as Holland and Austria, which had complied with the Eurozone's budget/fiscal rules. During 2004, various reform proposals were put forward by member countries and the EU to make the Pact more flexible and workable in light of economic conditions in the Eurozone.

In March 2005, the Pact was reformed after much discussion and negotiation. The main points were:

- The 3% budget deficit and 60% public debt to GDP ratios remained in place
- The aim now was to cut public debt during upswings in economic activity
- Certain types of public expenditure, such as German reunification costs, pension reforms, were exempt in calculating the budget deficit each year

- Any breach of the 3% limit would now initiate talks, with sanctions only being applied after five years or more as a last resort.

Some believed that the new Pact was likely to weaken the fiscal credibility of the Eurozone and thus undermine the long term viability of the single currency area. The ECB stated that the new Pact might entail higher interest rates and undermine investor confidence in the Eurozone.

Subsequent events confirmed that such fears about the new Pact have become a reality within the Eurozone. Some countries, such as Italy and Greece, have incurred huge budget deficits and ever-increasing national debt levels which are far in excess of the criteria set out in the Maastricht Treaty. The German failure to enforce the Stability Pact for Europe in 1996 has now come back to haunt their politicians/citizens and the ECB.

QUICK QUESTION

Comment on recent events in the Eurozone.

Write your answer here before reading on.

9 Recent developments: post-2010

9.1 Eurozone debt problem

Initially, the ClubMed countries (Spain, Portugal, Italy and Greece) had a high credit rating and were able to borrow at a slight interest rate spread over German government bond yields. Prior to 2008, these countries took full advantage of the willingness of investors to buy their apparently risk-free sovereign debt. With the onset of the banking/financial crisis and subsequent recession in 2008-09, the financial markets began to worry about the size of some Eurozone countries' debts and their ability to service them. This was reflected in widening interest rate spreads on ClubMed bonds offered in auctions to global investors.

The Eurozone debt problem started in the first half of 2010 when the Greek government found it difficult to raise funds. It had to offer ever higher interest (coupon) rates on its bonds in exchange for funds from international investors. Most government bonds issued are for a fixed period at a certain interest rate. Where bond yields hit 6% it is seen by investors as a warning signal that a country may not be able to service its external debt. Once 7% is breached, the market's perception is that a debt default or restructuring with IMF assistance is extremely likely to occur. Greece, Portugal and Ireland all sought IMF/EU assistance in 2010-11.

Greece, like Italy and others, after joining the euro, lived beyond its means. In order to finance budget deficits the government borrowed funds until its total debt was about €360 billion or 160% of GDP. The IMF/EU provided financial assistance and the government introduced austerity and privatisation programmes, while the ECB propped up the Greek banking system for almost two years by providing loans secured by Greek bonds. Finally, in October 2011, a €130 billion bail-out package was put in place which involved a debt write-off of up to 50%; thus Greece became the first developed country to default on its debt since 1945.

A default means a country is bankrupt and can no longer service its debt. Even before October 2011 Greek debt had been trading at less than 50% of its face value in the bond market. Such a large discount had an impact on European banks holding Greek debt in their asset portfolios. It has been estimated that French banks have an exposure of over €40 billion to Greece and will be forced to raise new capital to cover losses. The RBS in 2011 wrote down its Greek debt by 50%, which involved a book loss of over £700 million.

The total exposure of European banks to ClubMed countries is estimated at €1.5 trillion and thus failure to resolve the debt problem and implement a plan for economic recovery could result in a new banking crisis. Banks could be frozen out of wholesale money markets which would instigate a new credit crunch and thereby reduce lending to industry and commerce. Such a scenario will deepen the recession in the Eurozone and EU.

After six years of economic contraction, Greece has forecasted that their economy will grow by 0.5% in 2014. The Greek economy has been steered by the European Union, the International Monetary Fund and the European Central Bank (known as the 'troika'), as these parties provided the funding for the Greek bailout. Under the guidance of the troika, Greece has managed to reverse the decline in consumption and raise finance through the privatisation of national assets. Despite this progress, the recovery is still very fragile – the political landscape in Greece has become fragmented and there are continuing tensions between the Greek government and the troika. Therefore while Greece looks set to remain a member of the EU for the short-term future, the long-term future is still unclear.

9.2 Eurozone rescue plan: Brussels Accord, October 2011

At this 14th euro crisis summit in 21 months, the Brussels Accord was agreed upon, after lengthy debate and argument, on 26 October 2011. It was aimed at protecting the single currency union, preventing a deeper recession in the EU and stabilising the banking system. The Accord had three main financial elements plus a proposal to work towards fiscal union within the Eurozone.

The main financial elements of the rescue plan are explained (with comments) below:

1 **Greek debt**

It was agreed to write off 50% of Greek government debt. This is aimed at reducing Greek debt from 160% to 120% of GDP by 2020. It was acknowledged that Greece was effectively bankrupt and could never pay off its huge debt. For banks that had lent to Greece, a 50% loss has been incurred by them. Private investors in bonds in principle face a similar loss.

Doubts existed about the political will of the Greek government to see through the necessary spending cuts and tax rises required by the rescue plan. Some economists questioned if a debt target of 120% of GDP was realistic given the weak state of the economy, with output expected to fall by over 10% in 2012. As we now know, a second bail-out package was agreed in February 2012.

2 **Bank protection**

It was agreed that European banks must raise about €115 billion in new capital by mid-2012 in order to insulate themselves against sovereign debt exposure to ClubMed countries. The fear is a major default by one or all of these countries could result in a new banking crisis. If selling bank shares to investors fails, then government injections of capital will be required, which will entail the partial or full nationlisation of some major Eurozone banks. British banks, hopefully, will avoid the need to raise fresh capital.

Some commentators believe that the sum involved is inadequate in relation to potential problems faced by banks. The IMF estimated in September 2011 that European banks had a capital shortfall of over €200 billion in relation to possible sovereign debt write-offs or restructuring. The voluntary Greek debt write-off alone might cost the banks €100 bilion.

3 **EU bail-out fund**

The European Financial Stability Facility (EFSF) which was established at a previous euro summit meeting, is to have its funds increased to €1 trillion to deal with any future crises in big economies such as Italy and/or Spain. It already had €440 billion but €150 billion has been used buying Greek and Portuguese bonds. As no core countries such as France and Germany or the ECB were prepared to put up the extra funds, the remaining €290 billion in the EFSF is to be leveraged four or five times to attain the €1 trillion of funds. It is hoped that sovereign wealth funds from the Middle East and China will fill the gap.

The basic idea is that the EFSF sells triple A rated bonds to China and Saudi Arabia etc, and then uses the cash to purchase lower-rated Eurozone sovereign debt. If some defaults occur, the EFSF will be able to use its own funds to cover losses. So far China and others have expressed no interest in participating in this Eurozone SPV. It is widely acknowledged that this leveraged EFSF, even if it came about, would not have enough money to bail out Spain and Italy.

4 **Cyprus**

Although one of the smaller states within the EU, Cyprus found itself embroiled in a financial crisis in 2012. Cyprus has a large off-shore banking industry, with many loans and deposits with Greek and Russian customers. Due to bad debts, Russia gave Cyprus an emergency loan of €2.5 billion in January 2012 to cover its budget deficit. However, this loan did not make any provisions for the recapitalisation of Cypriot banks, who were reeling from writing off bad debts.

Therefore, in March 2013 Cyprus agreed a deal with the ECB, EU and the IMF to receive a €10 billion bailout. However, this bailout resulted in a one off bank levy on domestic bank accounts, resulting in Cypriot savers taking a financial loss. Like Greece, the Cyprus economy is now being steered by the troika.

5 **Fiscal union**

In order to avoid future budget deficits and rising debt from threatening the entire Eurozone, Germany and France proposed a super-Treasury with power to dictate tax and spending policies to Eurozone member states and apply financial sanctions for non-compliance. Such a step would require limited EU Treaty changes for what looks like the re-birth of the original Stability Pact.

Many commentators have questioned whether greater fiscal and budgetary integration can be achieved between 17 member states with different corporation and personal tax rates. An additional problem is that, in some countries, tax fraud is a part of their culture. Can Germany impose its tax rules (and inspectors) on Italian or Spanish citizens?

The European Commission completed a review of the all the proposed budgets of the EU members for 2014. They concluded that most EU governments are on course to gradually lower their deficits and reduce debt. The question of fiscal union has become more complicated as Germany now has a debt level that is above the level allowed under fiscal compact rules. From an economic perspective, it is widely agreed that the productivity gap between Germany, France and the other states would have to narrow to enable fiscal union to be successful.

The last main piece of legislation regarding fiscal union was the European Fiscal Compact in 2012, which implemented restricted caps on government spending, with sanctions for countries that break the rules. All EU members apart from the United Kingdom and the Czech Republic signed the European Fiscal Compact.

6 **Banking Union**

While the debate over fiscal union rages on, another controversial proposal has been put forward by the EU – Banking Union. The primary purpose of the Banking Union would be to ensure that taxpayers would never again have to bail out banks.

It has already been agreed that by the end of 2014 the ECB will have assumed responsibility for supervising the major banks in the eurozone. The next stage of Banking Union is where opinions differ – who should pay to bail out a bank? One proposal is for each country to pay for any of its domestic banks that fail. To do this, a fund would have to be put aside (paid for by banking fees) to cover any failed banks. However, there is still much debate about what would happen should a country not be able to bail out one of its banks.

7 **ECB interest rates**

Like the US and the UK, the eurozone has had a historically low interest rate since the financial crisis. The rate has steadily declined from 1.5% in 2009 to 0.5% in May 2013. However, where as the USA is looking to halt quantitative easing and tighten the money supply, the eurozone reduced their interest rate again to 0.25% in November 2013. This is in response to the strength of the Euro against other currencies. With French business activity slowing and the threat of recession, the eurozone is once again struggling to set its monetary policy to suit all of its members.

10 Future of the Eurozone

The Maastricht Treaty envisaged the Eurozone as a zone of economic/monetary stability in a volatile and uncertain global economy. It was also hoped that, in the monetary union, no one country would dominate its overall policies and operations. It was believed that the single market for goods, services and capital would be fully realised via the single currency, the euro.

Now, 13 years later, the reality is that EMU poses a threat to the global economy via currency instability and a lack of confidence undermining European economic prospects. The Eurozone is dominated by its most populous country and strongest economy – Germany – which sets the agenda for crisis talks and resolution schemes. At the same time, the Eurozone has all but split into two groups of nations — the core countries and ClubMed.

Perhaps the central flaw is the exchange rate and interest rate philosophy/policy of 'one size fits all' which was always going to pose a problem among 17 diverse member states. The reality was that, from 2001 to 2010, unit labour costs rose by 5% in Germany, whereas in the ClubMed countries it rose between 20% and 30%. Without the possibility of exchange rate depreciation, Germany got wealthier while Greece, Italy and others got poorer through their deteriorating balance of payments current account positions. The deficit-prone ClubMed countries borrowed to maintain their expenditure or finance house price bubbles. So what is to be done to resolve this in-built problem?

One solution is to accept that a single currency requires a unified fiscal policy, i.e. a pan-European budget on public spending, taxation and government borrowing. At the Brussels Accord, euro members committed themselves to achieving balanced budgets and to enter consultations with the EU Commission and other member states before adopting major fiscal/economic reforms. On 24 November 2011, the European Commission President, Jose Manuel Barroso, stated that without stronger economic governance in the Eurozone it will be difficult, if not impossible, to sustain the common (single) currency. However, such fiscal centralisation in Brussels for the survival of a crisis-free Eurozone in the future may not be matched by the democratic accountability of Brussels to the citizens of the 17 member states. This could prove to be troublesome from a political perspective as framing fiscal policy without political representation could question the legitimacy of Brussels edicts and thereby create a political crisis.

Will the Eurozone break up? Well, some suspect it will, and, as a result, some banks outside Europe have already issued guides for their customers on how to handle legal disputes arising from countries seceding from the Eurozone. What is more likely, if the rescue packages fail to solve underlying debt problems, is a radical overhaul of EMU. This would probably involve the exit of weaker member states and thereby a smaller monetary union based on the core countries of Germany, France, Benelux and Austria. The euro would still exist as a single currency for a smaller geographical region, while the non-euro countries would manage their currencies in relation to the euro or allow them to float independently of it. Thus, the EU would be made up of two distinct blocs – the euro in-crowd and the outsiders.

QUICK QUESTION

What problems might a country encounter if it exits the euro?

Write your answer here before reading on.

10.1 Eurozone exit

With large external debts, a lack of competitiveness and a decline in economic activity, some peripheral Eurozone countries have two options – stay the course, which means austerity and high unemployment for the foreseeable future with all important economic decisions affecting them taken in Brussels or Berlin, or default on their debt, exit the euro and go back to their own national currency.

Austerity and reform packages need time to work, so in the meantime the recession will get worse in peripheral countries. At the same time, deflationary policies imposed by Germany and the ECB might make existing debt more unsustainable. Even debt restructuring will not restore economic growth and external competitiveness. What is required is a real currency depreciation which cannot occur in the Eurozone as deflationary policies and structural reforms take too long to reduce unit labour costs. Therefore to achieve real depreciation, the only option for a country is to leave the euro, default on external debt and set an independent monetary policy to suit the needs of their economy. Obviously, if a number of countries resorted to this option, it would destroy the Eurozone or reduce it to a few core countries.

The Maastricht Treaty did not incorporate a legal procedure for a country to exit the single currency area. In fact the EU Treaties mandate all members to eventually join the Eurozone as part of a deepening integration process towards completion of the single market. It was believed establishing a legal means to leave the euro would have invited the possibility of countries making use of an exit clause, and this in turn could have cast doubt on the permanence of the EMU project and the lasting value of the currency.

However, leaving the Eurozone would be fraught with legal and non-legal difficulties for any country. It would involve renegotiation of large euro payments/receipts from Brussels under agricultural subsidy schemes and the cohesion fund. Euro-denominated domestic contracts (loans, salaries) would have to be redrafted into local currency in the exit country. All this would involve lengthy negotiations between lenders/borrowers and employers/employees. There would be litigation from foreign creditors refusing to accept repayment of cross-border obligations (loans/bonds) in a new currency with a value probably less than that of the euro against the dollar or sterling.

Loans from the EU and ECB in euros would become more expensive to service and repay in local currency terms, although hopefully higher economic growth and exports would ease this burden.

An exit strategy could involve a run on a country's banks as citizens sought to withdraw their euro deposits and transfer them to banks in Germany and Switzerland. Some euro deposits could be used to buy gold. Controls to limit withdrawals to a specific daily/weekly amount plus exchange controls to prevent euro transfers abroad could be used, but this would contravene EU rules on the free movement of capital. The printing and distributing of a new currency, initially in secret, would be no easy task, as the introduction of the euro involved extensive planning over four years. In addition, bank computer/payment systems would have to be re-programmed while notes/coins were put in position in banks in the exit country's cities and towns. However, such transition difficulties must not be overstated: the Czech Republic and Slovakia took only a few weeks to terminate their monetary union.

For peripheral countries, the risks of re-introducing a legacy currency, such as the drachma or lira etc, might be preferable to years of austerity and high unemployment. We should not forget the pound's exit from the ERM in September 1992 when the UK government was unwilling to accept a Bank of England discount rate of 15% and a deeper recession in an effort to retain a fixed parity (£ = DM 2.90) between the pound and the German mark. Yet some urge caution as an exit country might have no access to the international bond market and would probably need long term assistance from the IMF. It would also weaken the EU concept, and although a weaker currency would boost exports, it might cause higher inflation, thereby wiping out any external competitiveness gains.

To avoid the exit of countries from the EMU, the ECB would have to become a lender of last resort to deeply indebted countries. This would involve printing money, zero interest rates and a competitive depreciation of the euro against other currencies. To ensure success of such action, a fiscal stimulus in Germany and a gradual equalisation of unit labour costs in the Eurozone would be essential. Only the implementation of such policies will prevent an exit disaster, as perceived by some, taking place in the future.

QUICK QUESTION

Why did David Cameron veto an EU fiscal treaty?

Write your answer here before reading on.

10.2 Brussels Summit — Fiscal Compact: December 2011

At this Summit, David Cameron used the UK's veto to block a new European Treaty proposed by Germany and France for greater fiscal convergence in Europe. He sought exemption for the UK from the imposition of a Financial Transactions Tax on the activities of the City, which is important for the UK in terms of economic growth, employment and tax revenues. His request was refused and the other 26 EU members decided to go ahead without the UK in framing a new treaty for fiscal stability union. The new fiscal compact will provide tighter budgetary rules to restrain government deficits with automatic penalties for spendthrift member states.

The fiscal compact is more intrusive than the Stability and Growth Pact as regards taxation and spending policies of the Eurozone members. If a deficit exceeds 3% of GDP, it will result in automatic penalties unless other euro member states vote against such action. Structural deficits are to be capped at 0.5% of GDP and each country must establish an automatic correction mechanism if the overall budget deviates from pre-set targets. The overall objective is for each member state government to have a budget surplus or balance.

Any member state with a deficit will have to submit plans on how this is to be eliminated, and such plans will be monitored by the EU Commission. Government debt issuance plans must also be submitted and approved by Brussels. The fiscal compact also envisages overall national debt being 60% or less of GDP, which will be a hard objective for some euro members to achieve in the near future. The EU Commission will have the power to request draft budgetary plans, question tax and spending policies as well as ensuring that each member state's plans are aimed at working towards a common economic plan. Any major economic policy reforms by a euro member state will have to be discussed against a benchmark of best practice policies for government finance ministries.

This Summit also agreed to establish a European Stability Mechanism with funds of €500 billion by July 2012. This will ultimately replace the EFSF by mid-2013.

10.3 ECB liquidity support: December 2011

In mid-December 2011, the ECB took action to improve the liquidity position of Eurozone banks and thereby try to avoid a new credit crunch. It provided €490 billion through a three year liquidity operation which resulted in 523 banks accepting cut-price loans (funding) secured against sovereign bonds in their asset portfolios. The interest rate on these funds is fixed to the ECB's main interest rate which at the time of the deal was one per cent. It was hoped some of these funds would be invested by banks in ClubMed bonds or lent to firms and consumers in the euro area.

However, in January 2012, banks in the Eurozone had deposits at the ECB of about €450 billion, an increase from the average €100 billion monthly balance held by them throughout 2011. This might indicate a reluctance by banks to lend to one another or to the non-bank sector, as these deposits earn little or no interest compared to overnight interbank loans.

In the UK in December 2011 the Bank of England announced that plans had been put in place to prop up British banks if the Eurozone collapsed. Temporary loans will be made available to banks if their operational activities are threatened by their interbank exposures to French and German banks.

10.4 Brussels Summit: February 2012

On 21 February 2012, Eurozone finance ministers agreed upon another bail-out for Greece in an attempt to save the country from bankruptcy. Under this second bail-out, Greece will receive further loans of €110 billion (first bail-out €130 billion) through to 2014 from Eurozone governments and the International Monetary Fund (IMF); the latter's contribution is expected to be about €25 billion. Taken together, the bail-outs mean that every Greek citizen owes Eurozone governments and the IMF approximately €22,000 (£18,500). In return for these loans, the Greek government has promised to reduce its debt ratio from 160% of GDP in 2012 to 120% by 2020.

In addition to the loans, it was decided that €107 billion of Greek debt will be written off. This represents an immediate loss to private bond holders and banks of 54%, and still leaves Greece with debts of €352 billion. Under the proposed bond swap, the average interest rate will fall from 4.8% to 3.7%, and the term of such bonds will extend to 30 years rather than the present average of 7 years. For bond holders the debt write-off plus concessions linked with the new bonds will represent a real loss of over 70%. Of course this assumes banks and private investors will take up the bond swap deal. This bond swap constitutes the biggest sovereign debt restructuring in recent times, if not history.

To assist Greece, the Eurozone countries have agreed that loans under the first bail-out package are to cost 1.5% over market rates rather than the 2% to 3% as originally agreed in 2011. In addition, the ECB and national central banks have decided to forgo any profits on Greek debt held up to the year 2020, which eases debt service costs for the Greek government.

However, all this benevolence to Greece comes at a cost of diminished national sovereignty, as Greek economic management will be subject to permanent monitoring by troika (EU, ECB, IMF) officials based in Athens. The troika has set out 79 measures which are to be implemented by the Greek finance ministry. Not unsurprisingly, priority is to be given to debt repayments over the funding of government services such as health and education. In addition, a special account is to be kept by the finance ministry which is to be managed separately from the main budget. This account must have funds available to it in order to service debts for at least three months on an ongoing basis. The Greek government also agreed to further austerity measures involving reductions in public spending and wages, pension cuts and a reduction in the minimum wage.

In conclusion, this second bail-out was required to enable Greece to meet bond repayments of €15 billion in mid-March 2012 and perhaps to shore up the euro so that Europe can experience a return to economic growth. Whether it works or not remains to be seen, but the omens are not good. Greece, with 21% unemployment and negative economic growth of 7% in 2011, now faces a decade of austerity which many regard as an unsustainable position and might result in some sort of social revolution. Some regard the bail-outs as a waste of good money and that Greece should default on its entire debt and leave the single currency area. Rumours already exist in the markets of the possible need for a third bail-out of up to €100 billion in the near future. So watch this space for the unfolding Greek Tragedy!

10.5 Keeping up with developments

The European scene is changing very rapidly and you are advised to keep up with new developments by reading quality newspapers and paying attention to news reports on radio, television and the internet.

QUESTION TIME 34

Critically evaluate the present situation in the Eurozone as regards economic activity and the solvency position of banks.

Write your answer here then check with the answer at the back of the book.

KEY WORDS

Key words in this chapter are given below. There is space to write your own revision notes and to add any other words or phrases that you want to remember.

- European Monetary System
- Exchange Rate Mechanism (ERM)
- European Currency Unit (ECU)
- Delors Committee/Report
- Maastricht Treaty
- European Central Bank
- Convergence criteria
- Stability and Growth pact
- ERM 2
- The euro
- Eurozone

REVIEW

The main learning points introduced in this chapter are summarised below.

Go through them and check back to the learning outcomes at the beginning of the chapter. Only move on when you are happy that you fully understand each point.

- We have reviewed the Delors Report, Maastricht Treaty and EU Dublin Summit, with particular emphasis on the convergence criteria and the single currency – the euro.
- We looked at EMU economic benefits, costs and potential, and the current UK EMU position.
- Recent developments in the Eurozone include the ten new entrant countries wanting to join the single currency area and the reform of the Stability and Growth Pact.
- Greek sovereign debt problems have serious implications for the future stability of the Eurozone.

chapter 11

PUBLIC FINANCE

Contents

Learning outcomes

On completion of this chapter, you should be able to:

- Examine underlying tax principles and the need for government spending
- Critically evaluate recent budgets and the establishment of the Office for Budget Responsibility
- Comment on the money burden and real burden of the UK national debt which now exceeds £1 trillion

Introduction

Public finance deals with the expenditure and revenue of the state. In this chapter we'll be examining only central government tax revenues and expenditure. Local authorities also raise council tax and provide some community services. The state collects money from taxpayers in order to spend on goods, services and transfer payments, so that public finance involves a process of income redistribution in the economy.

When a state raises funds and spends them, it is directing the productive efforts of the community into channels different from those which would have been followed in the absence of public finance operations. People whose private expenditure is reduced through having to contribute to funds for public expenditure resent taxes and often ignore the benefits – which are often indirect and hidden – of such expenditure (for example, the police provide protection to all peaceful citizens).

Public finance is raised for two main purposes:

- To provide community services such as defence, education, health and road infrastructure, the expense of which is beyond the means of any one citizen.
- To assist members of the community unable to provide for themselves because of poverty, ill health, old age or unemployment. This involves a deliberate redistribution of national income and is associated with the development of the welfare state post-1945. The proportion of public expenditure devoted to this purpose has risen steadily over the last 30 years.

We conclude with a closely related theme of the national debt and whether it imposes a real burden on present and future generations.

In summary, we will consider some key concepts in relation to fiscal policy under the following headings:

- Direct and indirect taxation
- Taxation principles
- Public and merit goods and services
- Fiscal stabilisers
- Budget policies
- National debt components
- Internal and external national debt

1 Taxation

Compulsory taxation constitutes the state's most important source of revenue. States also raise some revenue by charging prices on a limited number of public services. Taxes are payments made by the taxpayer without receiving anything directly in return. In some situations it might be possible to avoid tax (such as VAT on goods or services) but otherwise the individual has to sacrifice the pleasure of possession or consumption to avoid payment of tax.

A tax system incorporates all the taxes contributing to state revenue. Under a multiple tax system, revenue is collected by means of direct and indirect taxation.

1.1 Direct taxation

Direct taxes are collected from private individuals, corporations and other legal entities that are intended to bear the burden of the tax charge. Tax is deducted from sources of income.

1.2 Indirect taxation

Indirect taxes are mainly collected from business entities but the tax burden falls either in part or wholly on others; for example, a car importer pays customs duty which is then added to the car's price and charged to the end buyer.

The perceived advantages/disadvantages of direct and indirect taxation are summarised below. Keep this in mind when we consider the main forms of UK taxation.

Direct Taxes	**Indirect Taxes**
Advantages	
The cost of collection is low.	The method of collection is simple.
The taxpayer knows exactly how much they have to pay.	The taxpayer does not feel the impact directly.
As the state can calculate the size of the source of revenue, it can estimate source of revenue, it can estimate the yield.	Payment is convenient.
Evasion is difficult, but not impossible.	Evasion is difficult.
	Small incomes can be reached.
	Yield can be quickly increased if demand for a product is inelastic.
Disadvantages	
It is difficult to calculate a just basis of assessment.	The cost of collection is generally higher than that of direct taxes.
The taxpayer feels the burden directly and is prone to exaggerate it.	They are inequitable when imposed on necessities such as food or fuel.
The taxes may reduce the incentive to work and save.	Yield is uncertain.
	The tax may be shifted on to people not intended to bear the burden.

QUICK QUESTION

What do you think are the main principles of a good taxation system?

Write your answer here before reading on.

1.3 Taxation principles

In his book *The Wealth of Nations* (1776) Adam Smith laid down four principles (or canons) for a good taxation system:

- Equality
- Certainty
- Convenience
- Economy

These have been adapted and added to over the years. The main principles of taxation are as follows.

Equality

Although it is impossible to compare the sacrifice imposed on various individuals, it is generally agreed that taxation should be related to a person's ability to pay and that the proportion of income which a person pays as tax should rise as their income increases. Any tax which satisfies this principle is a progressive tax.

The opposite – a regressive tax – imposes a larger proportional burden on poor persons than on rich persons. A person receiving twice another person's income does not, generally, buy twice as much tobacco or any other taxed commodity. Therefore, a larger proportion of the poor person's income will be taxed away by a regressive tax than in the case of a rich person.

This is the reason why many economists and politicians favour income tax as it can be progressive, whereas indirect taxes are rarely progressive. However, from a political point of view, a limited number of regressive taxes may be favoured, since they will ensure that even the poorest members of the community pay some taxes, and thus contribute towards the maintenance of that community.

Certainty

This principle implies that the rate of tax, where it should be paid and when, should be well known and publicised.

Convenience

The inconvenience of paying tax should be kept to an absolute minimum; for example, PAYE tax deducted from wages or salaries which reduces the administrative burden for individual taxpayers.

Economy

Most of the tax collected should be available for the intended public expenditure. If a tax costs nearly as much to collect as it yields, it is not a good tax. Income tax via PAYE schemes is one of the cheapest taxes to collect in relation to revenue.

Yield

Even though the standard rate of direct tax may be fixed, it should automatically produce a larger yield as national income rises. Inflation will also increase tax yield for the government, especially where a sales tax is a fixed percentage of the sale price of goods or services purchased by the general public, e.g. VAT at 20%.

Elasticity

A tax should be elastic in its yield. A tax which, when increased, gives an increased revenue is to be preferred to one which produces only a fixed or diminishing revenue. A tax on a commodity which is subject to a sensitive demand is likely to be elastic in its yield. A tax on whisky, increased beyond a certain point, could be followed by a decline in the demand, reducing the revenue from the tax, although the government might wish to encourage this reduction in consumption for health reasons.

QUICK QUESTION

What is a nation's taxable capacity?

Write your answer here before reading on.

Although advanced industrial countries can support a large amount of taxation, excessive tax burdens can damage an economy. Each government must endeavour to ascertain the taxable capacity of the nation. This is the maximum amount which can be deducted from a country's income, consistent with maintaining national income in the future. A minimum sum must remain with the public to ensure people's continued ability and willingness to work.

It is not enough to estimate the consequences of taxation on the income of the people taxed; instead, the effect on the wealth-producing capacity of the economy must be considered. If this is damaged by taxation it may reduce national income and thus tax yields, together with the quantity and quality of community services.

Taxable capacity is influenced by a number of factors:

- Taxes which arouse the least resentment and interfere as little as possible with business enterprise tend to raise the taxable capacity of a nation.
- The greater the inequality of income distribution, the greater is taxable capacity. Progressive taxation seeks to reduce this inequality.
- Where taxation proceeds are returned to the pockets of the country's taxpayers, taxable capacity may not be diminished and may increase if the tax revenue is devoted to productive purposes, such as improving the country's economic infrastructure.

- The taxable capacity of a country might be greater in a war or national emergency, as people are willing to make greater sacrifices for patriotic reasons.

From the above comments it will be obvious that it is impossible to measure the upper limit of taxable capacity accurately. While keeping these principles in mind, a country's government can only achieve a practical assessment of taxable capacity by experiment and experience.

2 UK taxation

We'll now review the two main types of taxation used in the UK – direct and indirect taxes. You must keep up to date with current tax developments via the media and also literature received from HM Revenue and Customs with your personal tax return. The Budget each year (in March or April) usually features changes to tax rates and allowances, the main details of which appear in the media.

QUICK QUESTION

What at present is the lowest and highest income tax rate?

Write your answer here before reading on.

3 Direct taxation

3.1 Income tax

This form of taxation was introduced in 1842. Low incomes are exempt, various allowances are granted and tax is charged at higher rates on successive slices of taxable income. It is a progressive form of taxation.

The PAYE system of weekly or monthly tax deductions was introduced in 1944. It is paid by approximately 30 million people and provides tax revenues of over £150 billion in each fiscal year (national insurance contributions are around £100 billion). Income tax is still technically a temporary measure and has to be renewed by Parliament each year.

Although progressive in nature, some economists and politicians believe that income tax, particularly at high rates, can have a damaging impact on the UK economy. It discriminates against saving, as tax is imposed both on capital when first earned and then again on income flows from subsequent investment of this capital. It may also discourage work, as the bulk of the population work for financial reward and not pleasure. A reduction in net reward, after deduction of tax, may make leisure more attractive. Thus, high income tax rates may discourage production and reduce national income growth.

It is important to distinguish between the average rate of taxation and the marginal rate of taxation. The average rate is found by dividing gross income by the total tax paid. The marginal rate is the rate payable on any additional earnings. Under the British progressive system, marginal rate is always above average rate.

Realisation that progressively larger proportions of additional earnings are taken away in tax may induce a taxpayer, at a certain level of income, to prefer not to work or save.

The UK operates a single graduated income tax system with various tax-free indexed allowances depending on age. The undernoted table relates to taxpayers below 65 years of age.

Income tax rates 2014/15

£	%
0 – 31,865	20
31,865 – 150,000	40
150,001 and over	40

Personal allowance 2014/15 = £10,000

Age related: Born between 6/4/35 and 5/4/38 £10,500; born before 4/4/36 £10,600
www.hmrc.gov.uk/incometax (or CGT etc)

3.2 Capital Gains Tax (CGT)

It was regarded as inequitable for income to be taxed while capital gains from the appreciation of assets went largely untaxed. To rectify this situation, capital gains tax was introduced in 1965. Assets subject to CGT are shares, second homes, business premises and land.

As a tax, CGT probably fails in satisfying the basic principles of taxation. It does not generate a huge amount of tax revenue. A further shortcoming is its unusual complexity. A capital loss is normally allowable if a gain on the same transaction would have been chargeable. An exemption limit – £11,000 in 2014/15 – on capital gains is allowed; this allowance is indexed. Capital gains tax is 18% for basic rate taxpayers and 28% for higher rate taxpayers. Various items are exempt from CGT – household goods, gilts, cars, houses (first home only) – which perhaps distorts investment in the economy.

3.3 Inheritance tax

This taxes the estate of a deceased person and is thus a tax on the transfer of wealth. Some believe that it discourages saving and enterprise and thereby harms national income growth. As with other taxes, some exemptions are permitted, such as gifts between husbands and wives.

In 2014/15 any estate in excess of a threshold (allowance) of £325,000 (married couples £650,000) is liable to inheritance tax at 40%.

3.4 Corporation Tax (CT)

Corporation tax was introduced in 1965 to replace income tax and profits tax on company profits. The rate is fixed for each fiscal/financial year. In 2014/15 the rate is 25%, and it is to be reduced by 1% per annum over the next two years to 24% by 2015. Small companies with annual profits of less than £1.5 million pay 20% corporation tax. Corporation tax has raised over £40 billion in recent fiscal years.

4 Indirect taxation

4.1 Value Added Tax (VAT)

Introduced in 1973, VAT is levied on all goods and services at the point of sale (about 2 million business firms collect VAT for the government this way). There is a standard rate of 20% and a lower rate of 5% which applies to a number of goods and services including domestic fuel and power supplies. VAT raises over £80 billion in each fiscal year. In 2009, VAT was cut to 15% for thirteen months in a bid to boost economic demand.

Zero-rated supplies include most foods, water services, books and newspapers, passenger transport, bank services, children's clothing and prescribed drugs. In addition, there are a number of exempt goods and services such as the sale and lease of land and buildings, burial and cremation services, and health and welfare services.

The regressive nature of the tax is modified because many of the day-to-day purchases of poorer people are exempt from the tax. VAT is a tax on expenditure, not on income. People do have a choice whether they want to pay it or not. Any increase or decrease in VAT has an immediate impact on the prices of goods and services, i.e. the rate of inflation.

4.2 Excise and other duties

These are levied at particular rates on tobacco, alcohol, petrol and cars. Customs duties are payable on imports from outside the European Union. Tobacco, fuel and excise duties (beer, wines and spirits) are generally increased each year in line with inflation or by a greater percentage amount. Such taxes raise about £50 billion in each fiscal year.

4.3 Transaction taxes

These are taxes usually associated with the transfer of property, such as shares, houses and land. Exemptions are granted: national savings certificates, gilts. The documentation involved in the title transfer is subject to stamp duty. Variable stamp duty is charged with different thresholds on the purchase of residential and business property in excess of £125,000 and £150,000 respectively.

Summary

If a government decides to raise revenue by indirect taxation, it will choose products the demand for which will fall only a little in response to an increase in price. However, these products may be basic purchases that form a large part of the spending of the poorer sections of the community. Such taxes, for example on beer and cigarettes, apart from being unpopular, have in the past led to demands for higher wages and have thus increased cost push inflation.

On the other hand, if a government seeks to make indirect taxes progressive by taxing articles considered to be luxuries and bought by more wealthy people, the tax may simply reduce the quantity produced, harm industrial production and cause unemployment, without raising much additional revenue or reducing the spending power of the wealthy.

Like direct taxation, an indirect tax structure has a tendency to become more complex and costly to administer with the passage of time. The government must also ensure that people do not resort to smuggling (cheap beer and cigarettes in excess of import duty limits) to avoid indirect taxes on goods; again prevention of this form of tax evasion involves costs.

QUICK QUESTION

What are the effects of moving from direct to indirect taxation?

Write your answer here before reading on.

5 Direct versus indirect taxation

In 1979 the new Conservative government's first Budget incorporated a major switch from direct to indirect taxation. Income tax rates were reduced while VAT was increased to ensure total tax revenues remained unchanged. This supply-side measure had an impact on the total economy. The shift to indirect tax was intended to increase saving while at the same time providing an incentive to work and enterprise. Its initial impact on the economy was contractionary in terms of output. The shift to VAT also increased inflation and reduced real incomes. In the long run it did increase work, output and enterprise. The Labour government (1997-2010) did not reverse the trend of switching from direct to indirect taxation. Neither has the Conservative-Liberal Democrat coalition government post-2010.

We have to recognise that a movement from income tax towards indirect taxes – from taxing income towards taxing spending – might bring about changes in the work/leisure preference, the pattern of consumer demand and the structure of the production system. What these precise changes are cannot be firmly stated because of the large number of other factors influencing national income and output.

QUESTION TIME 35

What factors must be considered by a government before altering an existing tax or introducing a new tax?

Write your answer here then check with the answer at the back of the book.

6 Government expenditure

6.1 Government expenditure (1980 - 2011)

	£ billions
1980	117
1988	155
1998	331
2002	394
2005	520
2011	700

The above table illustrates the huge increase (500%) in government expenditure both in nominal and real terms over the last 30 years or so. Part of this upward progression can be explained by inflation but real expenditure has also increased due to the following reasons.

Displacement effect

New legislation and economic/social developments have resulted in higher expenditure. Once such expenditure becomes established, it is difficult to reduce. Social security (welfare) systems which become ever more extensive are more or less impossible to rein back as greater use is made of benefit schemes by the citizens of a country. As a result, the public may tend to become more tolerable of a higher level of taxation.

Concentration process

Government expenditure also increases due to a continuous levelling-up in welfare state facilities and provisions. The best hospital becomes the norm that the whole country expects. This tends to create a general upward pressure on government expenditure.

Let us now examine the main categories or types of government expenditure.

Public goods and services

It has always been the role of the state to provide goods which are collectively consumed. These goods confer indivisible benefits which are shared equally by the whole community. Private enterprise could not produce and sell these goods individually because a consumer could refuse to pay their share and still benefit, for example, from defence, police, street lighting, etc. and so these goods have to be provided communally and financed from taxation of the community.

From the earliest days, defence has been a major item in this category. It is still a large item of expenditure but is falling as a proportion of total government spending.

Internal law and order involving the police, law courts, justice and prisons is another item which has traditionally been provided under this heading, together with the costs of Parliament and the Civil Service.

In recent years the scope for such expenditure has increased with overseas aid, environmental programmes, trade regulation and consumer protection.

QUICK QUESTION

Give examples of what you think merit goods and services are.

Write your answer here before reading on.

Merit goods and services

Merit goods and services differ from public goods because they provide personal benefits which could be supplied through the market. However, in the UK it has been decided as a matter of policy that these goods should be provided free, or almost free, to individuals on the basis of merit (need).

The two largest items in this category are education and health, both of which now absorb a larger share of tax revenues (and national resources) than defence. The principle behind free primary/secondary education is that of equality of opportunity. It is argued that a universal system of education will provide everyone with a good start in life, irrespective of their ability to pay for the service.

Similarly, medical treatment should depend solely on need and not be linked to ability to pay. Thus, medical care through the National Health Service is virtually free of charge, apart from prescriptions for medicines and the costs of dental treatment and spectacles. Other items provided on merit include roads, welfare clinics and facilities for old people.

Note that merit goods and services, apart from providing personal benefit, also provide an element of public benefit. For example, a healthy and well-educated working population raises general living standards via increased national output.

Subsidised services

Sometimes the state subsidises a service provided by the market sector. The government provides funds to enable loss-making rail services to remain open if they are essential for a community or assist in easing road traffic congestion and pollution.

Transfer payments

These arise when the state raises taxation and redistributes it within the community. Transfer payments take the form of old age pensions, unemployment benefit, sickness benefit, child benefit and family income supplement. This is the fastest growing component of public expenditure.

These transfers do not affect the overall level of demand in the economy but they alter the distribution of demand from the free market pattern in so far as the type of goods bought by old age pensioners will differ from that of taxpayers in the 21-45 years of age group.

Another form of transfer payment is interest on the national debt which is mainly held by UK residents and institutions.

7 The Budget

The Budget is the annual plan of the government's income and expenditure for the next financial/fiscal year commencing at the beginning of April. It outlines the services the government is going to provide and how it proposes to raise tax revenue required to pay for those services.

Unlike a private person, the government first decides how much is to be spent during the ensuing year, and then decides on the steps to be taken to raise the necessary money to pay for this expenditure. This separation of expenditure from income or, in parliamentary terms, of supply from Ways and Means, is rooted in the history of Parliament's control of finance.

Future expenditure is based largely on the services provided during the previous year, adjusted for inflation and any real increase in expenditure on services. These plans are presented each November/December to Parliament as estimates for the forthcoming year.

7.1 Budget practice

From 1945 to 1976, Budgets were based on Keynesian demand management principles which attempted to fine-tune the economy (see Chapter 3). It was believed that in a market economy any variations in employment or inflation caused by fluctuations in private investment or consumption could be offset by variations in government expenditure and taxation. The Budget could be used to reflate or deflate the economy. The government's aim was no longer a balanced budget, but a balanced national economy.

However, stagflation in the mid-1970s resulted in fine-tuning policies falling out of favour. A return to the more orthodox or balanced budget concept was adopted in the UK from 1979 onwards; most other advanced economies have done likewise. An unbalanced budget is now regarded as a sign of government extravagance which may cause inflation and increase the national debt. The Budget is no longer primarily concerned with offsetting the business cycle; instead, it concentrates on raising sufficient tax revenue to cover essential government functions. Fluctuations in output, employment and prices are primarily the concern of the Bank of England, although in a severe recession the government might resort to budgetary action, for example a temporary VAT reduction from 17.5% to 15% in 2009.

7.2 Fiscal drag or built-in stabilisers

Whatever budget management and practice prevails in a country, alterations in the national income of a country will alter total tax revenue, even though direct and indirect tax rates remain unaltered. A rise in economic activity will result in higher personal incomes and thus greater tax liability. At the same time, higher company profits will result in more corporation tax being paid at the end of each fiscal year. During a recession, the opposite will occur and total tax revenues will be depressed, providing a stabilising influence on the level of demand.

The tax effect provides an automatic stabilising service in the economy. In a boom, the tax leakage will help to slow down the rate of expansion in the economy as it approaches full employment, while a recession reduces the tax leakage and may prevent the deepening of the recession into a slump (although it creates an automatic budget deficit).

Fiscal drag could have a damaging effect on the economy, as inflation rates push up people's incomes into higher tax brackets. Tax leakages reduce the level of real demand in the economy. Constant tax rates and personal allowances will bring in additional tax revenue but might add to the general state of deflation. In order to offset this effect, governments have reduced fiscal drag by increasing (indexing) personal tax allowances in most Budgets.

7.3 2013 Budget

The 2013 budget predicted that economic growth would be strong in the UK from 2014 to 2017. Corporation tax was reduced to 20% as of 2015, National Insurance bills for companies were reduced and investments in shale gas were announced. Although the budget was generally well received, it was also announced that national debt as a percentage of GDP would rise from 75.9% in 2013 to 85.6% in 2014. The on-going challenging of managing the national debt is covered later on in this chapter.

QUESTION TIME 36

Assess the likely impact of a balanced budget on UK financial markets and the economy.

Write your answer here then check with the answer at the back of the book.

8 Code of Fiscal Stability

In 1998, the then new Labour government published the *Code of Fiscal Stability* to emphasise its commitment to managing public finances in the long term interests of the UK. The Code was motivated by three key considerations:

- A stable environment is vital if economic growth and employment are to prosper
- The conduct of fiscal policy is a critical influence on economic stability
- In the past, fiscal policy had failed to deliver a stable economic environment

Under the Code, fiscal policy was to be based on two fiscal rules:

- The Golden Rule: over the economic (business) cycle, the government would borrow only to invest, i.e. capital budget expenditure, and not to finance current expenditure, such as health, education and welfare.
- Public debt as a proportion of national income was to be held over the economic (business) cycle at a stable and prudent level, i.e. less than 40% of GDP.

QUICK QUESTION

How does public debt impose a burden on future generations?

Write your answer here before reading on.

The Golden Rule's aim was to promote stability and responsibility as regards taxation and expenditure. It also aimed to promote fairness between generations as the cost of public investment would be met by those who benefit most from such investment. A stable and prudent debt ratio would ensure fiscal policy was managed in a responsible manner. The UK Treasury, in theory, was committed to medium term fiscal responsibility, with an overall aim of current budget balance or surplus, together with a gradual decline of national debt as a percentage of GDP.

8.1 Code outcome (1998-2010)

Initially, the Golden Rule was adhered to with budget surpluses and a reduction in the national debt in the late 1990s. However, with the passage of time, tax revenue shortfalls due to lower than expected economic growth and increased public expenditure resulted in ever-larger budget deficits and national debt. By 2006, many economists outside the Treasury stated the Golden Rule was no longer of any relevance as the economic cycle appeared to be totally elastic as regards its exact duration.

The banking/financial crisis of 2007-09 resulted in a huge increase in the budget deficit, and so destroyed the entire concept of a Golden Rule. It ceased to be mentioned in Budget Statements after 2008. In June 2010, the new Chancellor of the Exchequer stated that the Golden Rule test had failed by the sum of £485 billion over a 10 year business cycle.

QUICK QUESTION

What do you think are the main areas of public expenditure in any Budget?

Write your answer here before reading on.

9 Emergency Budget 2010 – 11

The newly elected Conservative-Liberal Democratic coalition government decided on the need for an emergency budget which the Chancellor of the Exchequer announced on 22 June 2010. It emphasised the need to reduce the budget deficit from £150 billion (11% of GDP) to £20 billion (1% of GDP) by 2015-16. A large part of the deficit is what is termed as a structural deficit, the estimated size of which was £110 billion in 2010. A structural deficit is the share of a budget deficit that would remain even after an economy recovers to normal levels of output; it is the result of fiscal profligacy. In order to tackle this problem, the government announced a plan of fiscal retrenchment to balance the budget. Tax increases are to account for 20% of the retrenchment over the next four years, while planned public expenditure cuts will account for 80%. The latter involves a 25% reduction in planned expenditure over four years in all government departments, excluding health and foreign aid. This will amount to about £80 billion and will entail a reduction in the public sector workforce of half a million, or 8% of employees.

The main components of the Emergency Budget, in summary, were as follows.

9.1 Taxation

VAT was raised from 17.5% to 20%. The income tax threshold personal allowance was increased by £1,000 to £7,475; however, the tax bands were adjusted downwards, with the starting figure for 40% income tax frozen until 2013-14. Insurance premium tax was increased and a new bank levy based on balance sheet size was announced. To encourage enterprise and economic growth, corporation tax is to be reduced from 27% to 24% by 2015.

9.2 Spending

A freeze on public sector pay for two years for 4 million employees earning over £21,000 per annum was instituted, along with a review of pension provisions. As the social security budget of over £240 billion had doubled in 10 years of Labour government, it is to be trimmed back by up-rating welfare payments (excluding state pension) to the CPI instead of the RPI. This should save £15 billion by 2015. Cuts in defence, education and other departmental budgets will all take place over four years.

9.3 Budget balance

The Chancellor set a new target to balance the budget, excluding investment, by the end of five years, adjusted for the economic cycle. The Office for Budget Responsibility (OBR) will determine the length of the economic cycle and by stripping out the business cycle will determine whether the budget deficit has been eliminated or not.

9.4 Autumn Spending Statement: 29 November 2011

In the Autumn Spending Statement, the Chancellor of the Exchequer announced that the OBR had revised downwards economic growth forecasts for 2011 and 2012 to less than 1% per annum and, as a result, government tax revenues will be lower and spending higher than anticipated in the Emergency Budget (2010). This means that the budget deficit in 2014-15 will be an estimated £75 billion, or 4.5% of GDP. Between 2011 and 2015, the government will have to borrow an extra £110 billion, and the structural deficit, now larger than first thought by the OBR, will not be eliminated until 2017. In summary, the government austerity programme has been extended from 2015 to 2017 – in other words, beyond the next general election.

Another major announcement related to the public sector where, after the pay freeze of 2011-12, annual pay increases will be restricted to 1% per annum until 2015. Public sector job losses are now anticipated to be over 700,000 by 2016, while at the same time, national pay deals will be terminated in favour of local negotiations which will take account of regional labour market conditions and the cost of living in different parts of the country.

The Chancellor tried to offset the gloom surrounding this statement by promising further infrastructure investment of £20 billion to be financed by pension funds and a new loan guarantee scheme of £40 billion for small businesses.

You should try to keep up to date regarding future Budgetary Statements and OBR economic and deficit forecasts. For more information on the Budget, visit the Treasury's website at: www.hm-treasury.gov.uk.

9.5 Office for Budget Responsibility (OBR)

The OBR, set up in 2010, is housed within the Treasury. It is a financial forecasting body ostensibly free from political interference. Its main aim is to restore creditability to government forecasts about the budget, the national debt and the economy, after the financial markets lost confidence in the Golden Rule. It also issues assessments on whether the government will meet its self-imposed fiscal goals. The reason for the OBR's independence is to stop the Chancellor tweaking the figures, actual and forecast, to suit political needs and the electoral cycle.

QUESTION TIME 37

Why has government intervention increased in most market economies over the last 30 years?

Write your answer here then check with the answer at the back of the book.

QUESTION TIME 38

Discuss the present UK economic environment and various policy options available to the government.

Write your answer here then check with the answer at the back of the book.

10 The national debt

Each fiscal year, the government makes substantial expenditures which are financed by the following techniques:

- Taxation
- Printing money
- Borrowing via internal and/or external bond and certificate issues

Taxation or printing money enables the Treasury to avoid the need for interest payments and loan redemptions. However, the country might be at the limit of its taxable capacity, while excessive money creation may result in higher inflation. As a result, most governments since 1945 have borrowed funds in order to finance budget deficits.

An increasing national debt has raised questions on whether or not it imposes an economic and financial burden on society. Any discussion on the national debt burden requires a distinction to be made between the money burden and real burden of debt, and internal and external national debt.

QUICK QUESTION

Do wars increase or reduce the national debt?

Write your answer here before reading on.

11 National debt growth

UK National Debt
(Market Holdings)

Year	£ billions
1914	1
1938	7
1946	24
1986	170
1996	344
2005	475
2013	1160

These figures testify that UK national debt, which started in 1693, has grown with war-time borrowings and peace-time budget deficits. In the case of the former, no asset exists except the intangible one of freedom and saving the world from Nazi tyranny. Peace-time budget deficits have mostly arisen from fine-tuning the economy, financing public sector investment needs and social security payments. As regards the latter type of expenditure, no tangible asset exists, as the recipients of such funds used them to meet basic consumption needs.

More recently, the banking crisis increased the budget deficit due to a decline in tax receipts and increased welfare payments. The government was also obliged to inject capital into the Royal Bank of Scotland and Lloyds Banking Group in order to keep both banks solvent. As regards this type of expenditure, a tangible asset does exist in the form of government shareholdings in these banks.

12 National debt components

Government stocks (or gilts) account for the largest component (over 70%) of UK national debt. Most of this consists of stocks which must be repaid after a set number of years at full face value, or in the case of index-linked stock, at a value which takes account of inflation since the date of issue.

Stock requiring repayment is sometimes referred to as unfunded debt. Funded debt consists of stocks which have no repayment date. Holders of such stock, such as 3½% War Loan, who wish to realise their capital, must sell the stock in the market at its current market price.

National savings represent the second largest component. Such debt is not marketable like gilts. Instead, fixed repayment dates exist or repayment is at the holder's option, such as with national savings certificates and premium bonds.

Foreign currency debt consists in the main of bonds and notes issued by the UK Treasury in order to raise foreign currencies to supplement the UK's international reserves. Interest must be paid and repayment dates have been fixed. Such debt constitutes a real economic burden for the UK, albeit small at present.

The largest holders of sterling national debt are insurance companies and pension funds with over 40% of marketable debt. Sizeable amounts are also held by the Bank of England, overseas residents (approximately 35%), UK residents and private trusts.

QUICK QUESTION

What might result if taxation were used to finance government expenditure entirely?

Write your answer here before reading on.

13 National debt burden

Taxation reduces the net wealth of an individual. However, if the government borrows funds, no reduction in wealth takes place, provided the bonds are issued on terms similar to private sector loans. The payment of interest on such loans represents a money transfer from future taxpayers to bond/certificate holders, who are basically the same people. The funds raised are used to switch resources from the private to the public sector, and if any burden does arise it could be at this point, such as with war expenditure between 1939-45.

Interest on the national debt represents a money burden, but it might result in a real burden if taxation to finance the debt servicing cost acts as a disincentive to work, enterprise and saving (private capital formation); in which case, reduced national output and income per head in the future could be regarded as the real burden of the national debt.

If taxation, not borrowing, were used to finance government expenditure entirely, this would reduce consumption of the present generation. The use of borrowing would curtail private investment which might reduce the nation's future private capital stock. This might bring about a transfer of the real burden of the national debt on to future generations. A higher level of consumption at present might be at the expense of lower future output, but this assumes that all government expenditure is wasteful. Government borrowing might be used to increase the country's stock of capital goods (roads, schools, hospitals, etc) in which case future generations should benefit from a higher level of economic welfare.

13.1 How do economists assess the burden of the national debt on society?

The most common measure is to express the national debt as a percentage of Gross Domestic Product (GDP). The national debt burden declined from 55% to 30% of GDP between 1975 and 1990 to reach its lowest ratio since 1914. The main reason for this was that the rise in money national income exceeded the growth of the national debt. Although some of the rise in national income was attributable to higher real output, most was accounted for by higher inflation in the economy.

It is important to realise that inflation reduces the *real* value of non-index linked national debt. Ultimate repayment is made in depreciated currency to the holders of government bonds/certificates at redemption.

In the late 1980s, the government had a budget surplus due to buoyant tax receipts and the proceeds of privatisation issues, which resulted in an overall decline in the nominal size of the national debt and the debt ratio. Unfortunately, the early 1990s recession and subsequent slow economic recovery increased government borrowing to record levels; as a result, the ratio of net debt to national income had risen to 47% by 1997. The then new Labour government set a fiscal rule that debt should be held at a sustainable level, below 40% of GDP over the economic cycle. It fell to 34% in 2001-02.

This remarkable improvement was the result of three factors:

- Economic growth – higher tax receipts
- Lower unemployment – reduced social security benefits
- Fiscal prudence – generation of a budget surplus

After 2002, the government incurred ever larger budget deficits which resulted in increased borrowings and thus a rise in the national debt. By the end of 2004 national debt as a percentage of GDP was about 42%.

Q **QUESTION TIME 39**

(a) Describe the main features of two components of UK national debt.
(b) How might the government during this decade reduce the debt ratio to 40%?

Write your answer here then check with the answer at the back of the book.

14 External national debt

It is generally accepted that external national debt – foreign currency funds borrowed by a government – imposes a real burden on future generations. Interest (and repayment) on external debt requires the export of goods and services, thereby depriving the country of output which could have been consumed at home or exported abroad in exchange for tangible benefits; such interest appears as an adverse invisible item in the balance of payments current account.

Also large external debts increase the possibility of foreign interference in the domestic economy; for example, loans may be conditional on the implementation of specific fiscal or monetary policies.

However, external borrowing can be beneficial because the creation of such debt can take place without a decline in private domestic investment. In fact, foreign loans can be used to increase a nation's productive capacity, thereby reducing the real burden of interest and capital repayments, but if the loans are used to finance excessive consumption of foreign goods without any increase in the nation's productive capacity, then a real burden is placed on future generations.

The proportion of UK national debt denominated in foreign currencies has declined to less than 1% of national debt. This is the result of a substantial growth in sterling denominated national debt and the repayment of official external debt.

15 UK Debt Management Office

On 6 May 1997, the Chancellor announced that the Bank of England's role as the government's agent for debt management, cash management and oversight of the gilts market was being transferred to HM Treasury. This formed part of his announcement granting the Bank operational independence to set interest rates. The transfer was deemed necessary to ensure that debt management decisions could not be perceived as being influenced by inside information on interest rate decisions.

The UK Debt Management Office (DMO), an executive agency of HM Treasury, was established on 1 April 1998 and is responsible for all official operational decision making in the gilt market. The DMO aims to carry out the government's debt management policy, thereby minimising the long term cost of meeting its financing needs, while ensuring that debt management is consistent with the objectives of monetary policy. DMO issues gilts and Treasury bills on behalf of the government.

The DMO has a number of strategic objectives:

- Meeting the government's gilt remit
- Maintaining market liquidity
- Responding to the demand for new products
- Providing a high quality service to customers (investors)
- Developing a successful cash management function on behalf of the Treasury

15.1 National debt: 2011-15

By the end of fiscal year 2010-11, the national debt was over £1 trillion, or 63% of GDP, with resultant debt interest payments of £43 billion. The national debt increased rapidly from 2008 due to the economic recession which caused large budget deficits. However, the UK national debt must be kept in perspective as most rich western nations struggle with budget deficits and rising national debt. In 2011 the US national debt was over $15 trillion, or 100% of GDP, Japan's national debt was 220% of GDP, while the better managed Australian economy's national debt was a mere 20% of GDP.

George Osbourne set a target of eliminating the UK deficit by 2015, this was not achieved and the target date was moved to 2018, by which time interest payments on the national debt will total over £70 billion per year. Progress in reducing the deficit has been very slow. 2012/13 net borrowing is forecasted to be around £116 billion, which is slightly below the original forecast of £120 billion.

David Cameron has clearly stated that reducing the deficit is a main aim for the coalition over the coming years. Therefore the size of the deficit is likely to be a key factor in the 2015 UK General Election.

You should keep up to date with national debt forecasts from the OBR and the resultant debate in the financial media.

15.2 UK credit rating

A constant worry for the UK Treasury and DMO over the past three years has been the threat of the UK's AAA credit rating being downgraded. Poor economic growth and a rapidly growing deficit have resulted in credit ratings agencies considering issuing a credit downgrade. In March 2013, Standard and Poor's reconfirmed the UK credit rating as AAA, however, both Moody's and Fitch have downgraded the UK rating to AA+, reflecting a weaker economic and fiscal outlook. This could have severe consequences, as it would further increase the financial cost burden of the UK's deficit.

Summary

Whether you consider the national debt to be a burden depends on your own judgement of the arguments set out here. Obviously, if the UK national debt increased 100% in one year, most economists, politicians and people would question the advisability of such a policy.

In 1997 the UK government adopted a policy of no further substantial increases in the nominal size of the national debt. Any further borrowing was to be used solely to finance public sector investment, i.e. real assets, for the future benefit of the economy. Unfortunately, recent large budget deficits have resulted in an increase in the size and burden of the national debt.

KEY WORDS

Key words in this chapter are given below. There is space to write your own revision notes and to add any other words or phrases that you want to remember.

- Welfare state
- Direct taxation
- Indirect taxation
- Equality
- Certainty
- Convenience
- Economy
- Progressive tax
- Regressive tax
- Taxable capacity
- Displacement effect
- Merit goods and services
- National debt
- Funded and unfunded debt
- Golden Rule
- Emergency budget
- Office of Budget Responsibility

REVIEW

The main learning points introduced in this chapter are summarised below.

Go through them and check back to the learning outcomes at the beginning of the chapter. Only move on when you are happy that you fully understand each point.

- We have examined the main aspects of public finance, including the main sources of tax revenue, along with the advantages and disadvantages of each one in relation to the basic principles of taxation.
- We defined and reviewed the concept of a nation's taxable capacity.
- We explained various categories of government expenditure – public and merit goods, transfer payments – in order to seek justification for the state's redistribution of national income.
- We examined the UK Emergency Budget in June 2010 in relation to prevailing economic philosophy and orthodoxy.
- We studied aspects of the Code of Fiscal Stability – the Golden Rule – and its subsequent demise.
- We examined the national debt and distinguished between the money burden and real burden of this debt on present and future generations.

In summary, we looked at:

- Direct taxation versus indirect taxation
- The six main taxation principles
- Economic and social objectives of government expenditure
- The Code of Fiscal Stability
- The emergency budget and the establishment of the OBR
- The national debt

chapter 12

FINANCIAL CRISIS 2007-2009

Contents

Learning outcomes

On completion of this chapter, you should be able to:

- Examine the causes and consequences of the financial crisis in 2007-09 and how this resulted in bank failures and problems.
- Critically analyse the implications of government shareholdings in banks.

Introduction

You will already be familiar with some key aspects of the banking/financial crisis in 2007-09. This chapter attempts to explain the underlying reasons for the crisis and the resultant aftermath. We will also consider the reasons for bank problems and failures and summarise the problems that afflicted the Royal Bank of Scotland (RBS) and Lloyds Banking Group (LBG).

We will examine the existing and future role of UK Financial Investments and UK asset resolution agencies and conclude with some comments on the Eurozone sovereign debt problem and its potential impact on UK banks.

1 Financial crisis 2007-2009

1.1 Origin

The financial crisis originated in the US housing market. Up to July 2006 house prices were rising and the overall market was experiencing an asset price bubble. This situation was encouraged by financial innovation and political initiatives to encourage home ownership for most citizens, and large volumes of lending to less than creditworthy borrowers. Much of the sub-prime house loans were packaged up and sold on to financial institutions, investment funds and private investors around the world. As a result, when the bubble burst, the consequences were experienced throughout the global banking and financial system.

Three immediate causes of the global crisis were:

- Financial liberalisation, which made it easier for banks to lend and individuals to borrow, i.e. asset-backed securities and sub-prime lending.
- Monetary policy focused on inflation in goods and services prices and ignored asset price inflation, and not responding to the rapid rise in house prices in most countries.
- Regulatory failures/lapses in a number of countries resulted in some banks relying too heavily on wholesale funds to aggressively expand their balance sheets.

Asset-backed securities (ABS) enabled good and bad loans to be bundled up and sold on by originating banks to other financial institutions/investors. This originate and distribute loan model meant that banks/mortgage providers had little incentive to avoid excessively risky borrowers, while ABS purchasers did not realise the riskiness of the assets acquired.

In the USA, a large amount of sub-prime lending was to low-income households whose chances of paying off a mortgage depended heavily on an increase in house prices. A large percentage of the lending was based on over-optimistic assumptions about house prices and/or exaggerated or fraudulent statements regarding borrowers' incomes and employment prospects.

A high proportion of these sub-prime loans were repackaged with sound loans and resold as mortgage-backed securities which were given a high credit rating and provided with insurance against default by US government agencies. For example, Fannie Mae and Freddie Mac guaranteed $5 trillion, along with insurance corporations such as the American International Group (AIG).

In total, about $7 trillion was repackaged and resold, both in the USA and worldwide. Many European banks and investors bought these mortgage-backed securities as on the face of it such investment promised a reasonable rate of return with little or no risk. The sub-prime debt (toxic debt) was thus absorbed into the global banking and financial system. In the UK, most banks, some building societies and investment funds added such toxic debt to their investment portfolios.

1.2 Crisis begins: credit crunch 2007 - 08

In July 2006, US house prices peaked and then started to fall. A systemic risk problem arose from the fact that when a bubble bursts, risk management fails, as risk cannot be diversified away. One year later, Bear Sterns (US investment bank) reported problems with its asset portfolio of sub-prime repackaged loans. This undermined confidence in the global interbank market in August 2007, as banks became reluctant to lend to one another. Interbank interest rates (LIBOR) rose sharply, thus making wholesale funding less available and more expensive.

In September 2007, a UK mortgage bank known as Northern Rock ran into financial trouble, as it could no longer raise wholesale funds to finance its asset portfolio. It had to receive lender of last resort support from the Bank of England. Unfortunately, the announcement of this central bank assistance resulted in a panic among Northern Rock's depositors, which caused a run on the bank. The UK government was forced into providing a guarantee that all deposits were safe in the institution. This liquidity problem and the subsequent admission of loan losses led to the nationalisation of Northern Rock in February 2008.

The reluctance of banks to lend to one another and their customers was generally referred to in the media as the credit crunch.

1.3 Crisis spreads: bank liquidity/solvency problems

In March 2008, Bear Sterns, now almost bankrupt, was taken over by J P Morgan for almost nothing. This development prompted a further decline in confidence in the interbank market and the global banking system. In the first quarter of 2008, house prices started to fall in the UK and elsewhere. To deal with prospective losses on their own house loans and US sub-prime loans purchased, a number of UK banks made rights issues of shares in order to improve their capital-asset ratios. The Royal Bank of Scotland made a £12 billion rights issue; the shareholders paid £2 for each new share.

As the size of the sub-prime loan problem/losses became apparent, the US government was forced to bail out its own mortgage agencies, which guaranteed and bought sub-prime debt, e.g. Fannie Mac, in early September 2008. This did not stop the panic in the US and global banking system. On 15 September, Lehman Brothers (a major US investment bank) filed for bankruptcy due to large sub-prime losses of $14 billion, an inability to renew wholesale funding and a collapse in its share price. The US government refused to bail out Lehman Brothers, but on 16 September it was forced to bail out AIG (a major mortgage insurer) with the aid of a $85 billion capital injection.

With the collapse of Lehman Brothers, the global credit markets seized up in the form of financial cardiac arrest as banks stopped lending to each other. Fears about the stability of the global financial system began to spread to the real economy as companies began to find it hard to get working capital finance. In October 2008, the UK government injected capital (equity) into a number of UK banks, e.g. RBS, to prevent a complete meltdown in the UK financial system and a loss of confidence in London as an international banking/financial centre. Similar action was taken by the USA and other countries, such as Germany, France and Ireland, to shore up their own banking/financial systems. Most large global banks incurred huge losses and thus dividends were cut or suspended for shareholders. Such dividends will not recommence until adequate profits are made and government assistance has been repaid.

1.4 Impact on the real economy

In October to December 2008, the financial crisis hit the real global economy as consumers reduced their spending due to a loss of confidence, and firms cut back on investment and production. Economic growth forecasts were revised downwards for the developed world and emerging economies. The impending global recession encouraged US and UK governments to cut taxes and increase government spending and thereby incur huge increases in their national debt. At the same time, most central banks reduced their interest rates in order to stimulate their economies. As the size of debt write-offs in the global banking system reached over $1 trillion by the end of 2008, many governments were forced to make further injections of capital into their banks. As a consequence, a number of major banks in Europe are now partially or almost wholly owned by their governments. In effect, the financial crisis brought about the partial nationalisation (state ownership) of the global banking system – something which was not previously contemplated by most governments.

You should endeavour to ascertain the impact of this global banking/financial crisis on your own bank or financial institution.

QUESTION TIME 40

How might the banks avoid large loan losses in the future?

Write your answer here then check with the answer at the back of the book.

1.5 Bank of England/UK Treasury action

The Bank of England became involved in actions relating to the credit crunch over the period from October 2008 to March 2009. In October 2008, the Bank implemented special liquidity schemes which provided increased liquidity assistance of approximately £400 billion to the banking system. It also provided loan guarantees up to £250 billion for the issue of short term bonds by banks which enabled them to refinance wholesale funding obligations. In addition, the Bank allowed banks to swap mortgage-backed securities for Treasury bills in order to improve the overall liquidity position of the UK banking system. At the same time, the UK government was injecting capital into a number of banks via preference shares and underwriting ordinary share issues. Most of the latter shares were subsequently acquired by the UK Treasury. The taxpayer thus became a major shareholder in the Royal Bank of Scotland and Lloyds Banking Group.

In January 2009, the government implemented another rescue package of £410 billion for the banks. It was forced to take this action when the Royal Bank of Scotland announced losses of £28 billion and its ordinary share price fell to just 11 pence, compared to a £6 share price in 2007. The UK Treasury provided a £100 billion guarantee for new mortgages to encourage banks to lend and slow down the fall in house prices. It set up an Asset Purchase Facility worth £50 billion to purchase corporate and financial institutions bonds. A further £260 billion insurance facility was set up to deal with toxic debt on the balance sheets of banks. For the payment of a cash fee or more bank shares, the UK Treasury is liable for 90% of the losses from such debt. The banks are responsible for the remaining 10% of potential losses. This latter action of insuring toxic debt was aimed at restoring confidence in the UK banking system and encouraging the banks to lend money again to personal and corporate customers. It was hoped that such action would result in increased economic activity and recovery from recession. Evidence suggests this was partially successful in 2009-10.

After August 2008, the Bank of England reduced its interest (discount) rate to 0.5% in order to assist banks and the economy. In March 2009, the Bank announced the launch of quantitative easing to create money via the purchase of assets, mostly gilts, thereby lowering the risk-free cost of borrowing for the government. At the same time, the sellers of such assets received cash from the Bank and deposited it in retail banks to increase their reserve balances. Banks were now in a position to expand their loan portfolio via the bank deposit multiplier and thus encourage more spending in the economy. By the end of 2009, £200 billion of new money to purchase assets was approved. In effect, quantitative easing by the Bank is akin to open market operations on a large scale.

QUESTION TIME 41

What measures might be taken by retail banks to resume dividends to ordinary shareholders?

Write your answer here then check with the answer at the back of the book.

Summary

The financial history of the last 200 years, from the South Sea Bubble (1720) to the sub-prime lending bubble (2007/09), confirms that an asset price bubble burst nearly always results in a contraction in credit and the liquidation of assets. These two factors result in asset price falls and wealth destruction, which can lead to negative economic growth and a deflationary environment. In such a situation, the weight of debt borne by over-geared/ leveraged corporations, institutions and private individuals, if no remedial action is taken, can sink a banking system through large loan losses and result in an economic depression.

Most governments and central banks took actions to try and avoid a meltdown of the global financial system and economy. Banks were re-capitalised with governments acquiring equity stakes in some of the largest institutions. Bad loans were written off (approximately $1 trillion by 1st quarter 2009) and the remaining toxic debt, estimated at $2 trillion, was being insured by government agencies or transferred to some form of debt resolution bank. Unfortunately, a large part of cleaning up banks' balance sheets was borne by taxpayers in the USA, UK and elsewhere.

It is thus no surprise that governments are seeking to avoid a repetition of the sub-prime lending crisis in the future. This involves new regulations for banks/financial systems, greater transparency as regards banks' operational activities and better corporate governance.

QUICK QUESTION

How did the crisis affect the price of bank shares?

Write your answer here before reading on.

2 The aftermath

The UK committed more than £840 billion in various bail-out measures to support the British banking sector, with capital injections and loans for four banks totalling almost £125 billion. Hopefully, at some future date these capital injections will be repaid and the contingent liabilities will be unwound via liquidity support repayment and guarantees/asset insurance no longer being required by the UK banking sector.

Institutional investors suffered huge losses on pre-2008 bank shareholdings, while small investors (including many past and present employees of the troubled banks) suffered huge damage to their financial wealth. A £5,000 stake in RBS or HBOS or LBG in January 2007 was worth only £400, £340 and £200 respectively by October 2010. Further sharp falls in the share price of RBS and LBG have added to the misery of such investors who are unlikely to receive any dividends from these two banks in the foreseeable future.

QUICK QUESTION

Why was the financial crisis not foreseen?

Write your answer here before reading on.

The question that has been asked many times is 'how did this catastrophe to the UK banking system occur?' Her Majesty the Queen summed it up in 2008 on a visit to the London School of Economics when she asked banking/finance professors: 'If these figures were so large, how come everyone missed them?'

A partial answer has already been provided in the highlighting of some of the main causes of the crisis, such as securitisation/sub-prime lending, weak regulation of banks, a house price bubble and lax monetary policy. Yet warnings about unsustainable house prices in many countries and global imbalances were ignored by governments, central banks and chief executive officers of banks. Why were the warnings ignored?

Sometimes there is a human aversion to forecasts incorporating bad news. The financial pressure is to go with the flow – onwards and upwards – especially if it involves the payment of bonuses and fees associated with large deals. It might also be put down to memory loss about the last boom-bust cycle – a situation, perhaps, made possible by a new generation of executives in a bank with no or a cleansed folk memory. This might explain how the loan losses experienced in the early 1990s by banks from a collapsed housing bubble did not ring bells in the mid-2000s. It also has to be stated that a number of chairmen and chief executives of British banks were not professionally qualified bankers and had never studied banking history and past bank failures. For example, the City of Glasgow Bank failed in 1878 due to fraud and speculative investments in US railroad shares and bonds.

It is now widely accepted that bank remuneration policies fuelled the credit bubble in a number of countries. The rules governing executive bonuses created perverse incentives for banks to expand their balance sheets but not their equity base, as such action increased the return on equity. The latter was a key factor in determining chief executive officers' bonuses with the approval of appreciative shareholders who received increased dividends and a rise in shareholder values. Therefore to a certain extent the credit bubble was driven by greed which overcame fear of an asset price correction. Politicians connived in this expansionary cycle (asset growth/bonuses up) because increased profits, often illusory, generated increased tax revenues to pay for unsustainable social/welfare programmes.

QUICK QUESTION

How might rapid expansion of a bank cause problems?

Write your answer here before reading on.

3 Bank failures and problems

It might be useful at this stage to consider bank failures and problems in general and not just as the result of the banking/financial crisis of 2007-09. A brief summary of some key causes/factors are noted below.

1 **Rapid expansion**

Sometimes banks expand their balance sheets too rapidly and as a result become very reliant on wholesale funding from the money markets which can suddenly dry up if risk perceptions suddenly change about a bank. This, together with inadequate management expertise and lack of proper internal controls within an initially small bank, can cause a potential problem, especially if bank supervision/regulation is lax.

2 **International operations**

Over the last 30 years, globalisation of financial markets has encouraged banks to establish branches and subsidiaries in offshore centres. In some instances lack of proper internal controls and the division of supervisory responsibilities have caused substantial losses from fraud and poor management decisions. A number of British banks have paid excessive prices in acquiring foreign banks only to discover few synergy gains and, in some cases, asset portfolios stuffed full of dubious loans and/or derivatives.

QUICK QUESTION

What caused the failure of Barings Bank in 1995?

Write your answer here before reading on.

3 **Derivative markets**

Futures, options, swaps and securitised debt etc, have been a cause of problems or complete failure for many banks. In many cases, the top management were oblivious to the risks associated with such complex financial instruments until huge losses were revealed. Other situations have arisen where the lack of proper controls has enabled rogue traders such as Nick Leeson in Barings Bank to be encouraged by the potential for large bonus payments to undertake fraud on a massive scale by gambling the bank's capital on the financial markets. Such fraud is hard to detect and can result in huge losses from which a bank might succumb (Barings Bank) or never fully recover, only to be taken over at a knock-down acquisition price.

4 **Economic factors**

Bank directors and chief executives sometimes choose to ignore the business cycle and assume the good times will last forever. An adverse interest rate and/or exchange rate development can quickly undermine many assumptions made in the credit appraisal stage of granting loans. Budgetary changes by a government can also have a similar impact. In many instances, banks have huge exposures to boom sectors such as energy, mining, telecoms or property, and thus incur strategic risk. An adverse development such as an economic sector price collapse can result in huge losses and insolvency for a bank(s). In the 1980s, an oil price collapse resulted in many bank failures in Texas.

5 **Political interference**

Sometimes bank liberalisation has taken place but without adequate regulation/supervision of banks' enlarged activities. This has been compounded in some cases by unlimited deposit insurance which has encouraged reckless behaviour by banks – safe deposits, but unsafe banks! In other situations, the state has asked bank regulators to exercise forebearance and not close insolvent banks for political reasons. The outcome of such action is almost invariably delayed bank closure, with huge losses being borne by the taxpayer. In some countries, nationalised/state-owned banks have been set their policy objectives and had their top management appointed by politicians. The simple lesson is that politics and money do not mix well and often result in the taxpayer underwriting a dubious loan portfolio and then bearing the loan losses as they materialise.

6 **Insufficient capital**

To increase shareholder returns, banks relied on high leverage. By the end of 2007, the US investment bank Bear Sterns had an assets to common equity ratio of 38-1. This meant that banks had insufficient capital to soak up losses. Regulators conceded that banks were holding insufficient tier one capital (common equity and reserves)to cope with stressed financial markets. Regulatory initiatives to increase the capital of banks have resulted in numerous rights issues by banks in Europe and the US. In 2013, Barclays announced a rights issue of £12 billion to bolster its capital base in order to meet regulatory requirements.

CASE STUDY

Halifax Bank of Scotland (HBOS)

HBOS was formed in 2001 by a £30 billion merger between the Halifax and Bank of Scotland; it became the fifth largest bank in the UK. It pursued an aggressive form of brand banking in competition with Northern Rock and others to retain and expand its share of the deposit and mortgage markets. It also expanded its corporate banking division via involvement in commercial property lending and mergers/acquisition activity. This division indulged in some dubious lending deals even after the onset of the credit crunch. HBOS also expanded its operations in Ireland in order to participate in the booming property market there. Unfortunately, this strategy of gung-ho expansion by the top management of the bank was at the expense of ignoring basic banking principles as regards funding and lending.

The credit crunch, combined with problems in the commercial property market, resulted in the financial markets making comparisons between HBOS and Northern Rock as regards wholesale funding needs and possible loan impairments. The HBOS share price had been £10 in October 2007 and by September 2008 it was £1.50, which ruled out a rights issue of shares to raise additional capital to deal with forecast losses of £10 billion for the financial year 2008. Lloyds TSB saw an opportunity for a takeover of HBOS, on the face of it, at a knock-down share price. The subsequent £12 billion takeover created a high street banking giant with about one third of the savings and mortgage markets in the UK.

QUICK QUESTION

What does the term due diligence mean?

Write your answer here before reading on.

3.1 Lloyds Banking Group (LBG)

The credit crunch impacted on the share price of Lloyds TSB, which fell from £5.50 in October 2007 to £3 in September 2008. Despite this fall in value, HBOS shareholders accepted a share exchange worth £12 billion. The creation of LBG was approved by the government and regulatory/competition agencies because it was hoped that the merger would restore banking and financial stability in the UK. The top management of Lloyds TSB believed that the two banks were a good mix and that large synergies existed to be exploited to enhance shareholder value.

Subsequent events resulted in the exact opposite outcome. It proved to be a disastrous takeover deal which was compounded by the lack of due diligence by Lloyds TSB directors who failed to audit the HBOS balance sheet and assess its financial prospects. All too late, it was discovered that HBOS had a horrendous loan book and required large scale funding. The now enlarged LBG had to receive capital injections of £20 billion from the government which, as a result, acquired a 41% stake in the bank.

Under European Commission rules, in exchange for state assistance, LBG was forced to dispose of 632 branches in order to encourage competition in the UK banking market. With no prospect of a resumption of dividend payments in the near future, LBG is still reliant on massive wholesale funding and has inherited from HBOS a toxic Irish loan portfolio of £27 billion, of which over 60% is thought to be impaired. LBG has also had to set aside £3.2 billion for compensation payments to customers who were mis-sold payment protection insurance by the component subsidiaries of the group. For the original Lloyds TSB shareholders, the takeover of HBOS has been an unmitigated disaster, as evidenced by a share price of 25 pence at end-2011, while taxpayers are nursing a paper loss of £10 billion on their stake in LBG.

In February 2012, LBG announced an overall loss of £3.5 billion for 2011, despite making a profit of £3.6 billion in the retail banking division. Loan write downs amounted to just under £10 billion, of which £8 billion were attributable to the former HBOS. The total final bill for integrating Lloyds TSB and HBOS was disclosed at £3.8 billion; this included the cost of integrating IT systems and staff redundancy payments, but excluded loan write-offs.

A recovery of LBG's fortunes because of its largely domestic loan portfolio is very much linked to a recovery in the UK economy over the next five years. LBG hopes to resume dividend payments to its shareholders within three years.

LBG has re-branded 600 bank branches as TSB (a brand name that has not been used for 18 years). These branches are currently up for sale as part of the European Commission to increase competition. LGB has come under the spot light in December 2013 due to receiving a £28 million fine from the FCA for bonus schemes which induced staff to mis-sell financial products to customers. Both the reputational and financial damage of such a fine will further impede the efforts of the UKFI to return LBG to private ownership.

Q

QUESTION TIME 42

Explain what causes of bank failures/problems are applicable to LBG.

Write your answer here then check with the answer at the back of the book.

QUICK QUESTION

Why did the government partially nationalise RBS in 2009?

Write your answer here before reading on.

3.2 Royal Bank of Scotland

RBS was founded in 1727 and failed in 2009 when the government had to inject £45 billion of capital into the bank to keep it solvent and prevent a complete collapse of the UK banking system. At its peak, the RBS balance sheet size was larger than the entire UK GDP for 2007. During the last ten years before the government acquired a 83% stake in RBS, it had pursued an aggressive policy of expansion through takeover deals for other banks. It became a multinational Scottish bank through acquisition of the National Westminster Bank (1999), Charter One in the USA (2004) and part of ABN-Amro in Holland in 2007. Citizens Bank, a wholly owned subsidiary, had expanded its operations in New England and RBS Greenwich Capital, also in the USA, and was heavily involved in sub-prime debt deals.

The RBS certainly made the headlines in 2007 to 2009: "the biggest takeover in banking history (ABN-Amro deal), the largest failed rights share issue (£12 billion) in corporate history, the biggest loss (£24 billion) in banking history, the biggest banking rescue In history, the biggest share price collapse – from £7 in January 2007 to 11 pence in January 2009".

The real question is: how did this happen to RBS and what lessons can be drawn from the catastrophic collapse? Financial journalists and analysts, as well as a 500 page report by the FSA, provide some answers. The undernoted is a very brief review of the key factors which caused the downfall of RBS.

- Aggressive expansion had weakened its capital position and it was over-reliant on short term wholesale funds; in other words, RBS was short of capital and liquid assets.
- The underlying asset portfolio incorporated good and bad assets. The latter had been accumulated through an aggressive acquisition policy in the USA. The Global Banking and Markets division, which regularly accounted for over half of RBS annual profits in the mid-2000s, was heavily involved in sub-prime debt deals.
- The ABN-Amro acquisition in October 2007 for £47 billion by a consortium of RBS, Santander and Fortis Bank was a disaster from the outset, as the Dutch bank had a large portfolio of defunct sub-prime loans. The RBS share of the acquisition price was about £22 billion, £3 billion paid in RBS shares and £19 billion in cash, largely funded by short term loans. The write-down of ABN loans cost RBS approximately £20 billion in 2008.
- Corporate governance deficiencies also contributed to the failure of RBS. The Board of Directors were ineffective in challenging and restraining the CEO Fred Goodwin. As far back as 2003, the FSA had concerns about his robust management style. In 2007 his relentless desire to acquire ABN resulted in little due diligence being undertaken as regards the Dutch bank's assets. It was assumed that the rival bidder, Barclays Bank, had done its "homework' before putting in its own bid for ABN.

- Other contributory factors were the systemic banking crisis and the light touch regulation of RBS by the FSA. It assigned only four staff members to monitor RBS at the time of the ABN deal. The FSA wrongly assumed that basic risk controls were in place and thus paid a regulatory dividend to the bank in the form of less regulatory scrutiny. It must also be stated that no politician north or south of Hadrian's Wall ever voiced any objections or concerns about the RBS-ABN deal.

With the benefit of hindsight, we can see that RBS was not a robust institution when it launched its takeover bid for the badly run Dutch bank. In 2008, ABN was demerged from RBS and nationalised by the Dutch government so that most of the price paid by RBS was lost. In exchange for a state capital injection, RBS was forced to dispose of 318 branches which were acquired by Santander in December 2011. Over 30,000 jobs have been lost in RBS since 2007 and it has incurred operating losses since 2008. In late 2011, with its share price at about 20 pence and taxpayers nursing a £20 billion paper loss on their stake in RBS, the government instructed the bank to run down its investment banking division and return to operating mainly as a retail bank in the UK. RBS also intends to dispose of its insurance subsidiaries in order raise additional capital funds.

In February 2012, RBS announced an overall loss of £2 billion for 2011, despite the core part of its business making a profit of £6 billion. The financial accounts revealed that its core capital and liquidity positions had improved, and there was reliance on wholesale markets for funding its balance sheet. It also disclosed that scaling back its balance sheet by £712 billion to £980 billion had cost the bank £43 billion so far in redundancy costs, loan write downs and selling off businesses at a loss.

Like LBG, the fortunes of RBS are very much linked to the UK economic recovery. With further balance sheet disposals it is hoped that the bottom line of its operating statement will show a profit in two to three years. Meanwhile the taxpayers are in for the long haul as regards recovering their initial stake (£45 billion) or making a profit from their involuntary investment in RBS.

In December 2013, the RBS share price was 320p, 180p short of the price required for the UK government and tax-payer to break even on the money invested to bail out RBS. In 2013 RBS made some steps towards exiting state ownership. The Contingent Capital Fund gave RBS the option to gain an extra £8 billion of government funding if required. RBS also exited the Asset Protection Scheme that provided government insurance for their toxic assets. RBS still faces many challenges, not least the £1 billion required to upgrade its IT infrastructure in light of continued customer complaints over online banking problems.

QUICK QUESTION

What do you understand by the term bad bank?

Write your answer here before reading on.

3.3 Toxic assets

Some financial analysts and experts have argued that the toxic assets of RBS and LBG should be transferred to a bad bank. This is common practice in the USA when a major bank fails. Such assets would be purchased at a discount from both banks and realised over time by a resolution agency. This would clean up the balance sheets of RBS and LBG. So far the government and Bank of England have only employed such a scheme for smaller banks such as Northern Rock and Bradford & Bingley. Instead, the two large banks have benefited from an asset protection scheme whereby, for a fee or more shares, the government insures 90% of their doubtful loans, with the first 10% of any loss borne by the bank. It is to be hoped that both banks can work their way out of their weak loan portfolios through write-offs over a number of years.

QUESTION TIME 43

Discuss the lessons that might be learned from the downfall of RBS by bank regulators.

Write your answer here then check with the answer at the back of the book.

QUICK QUESTION

What does the government propose to do with its shareholdings in RBS and LBG?

Write your answer here before reading on.

4 UK Financial Investments (UKFI)

UKFI was set up in November 2008 to manage the government shareholdings in Royal Bank of Scotland (RBS) and Lloyds Banking Group (LBG). HM Treasury is the sole shareholder in UKFI, whose basic aim is to create and protect value for taxpayers as shareholders in both banking entities. UKFI has a wholly owned subsidiary known as UK Asset Protection, which deals with the management of the closed mortgage books of Bradford & Bingley and Northern Rock.

The decision to sell shareholdings in RBS and LBG ultimately rests with the UK Treasury. Any recommendation to sell by the UKFI will be based on a variety of criteria such as expected sale value, competitive issues in the banking sector and the impact on financial stability; it will not be based solely on the original cost of the investments. At present there is no pre-defined timetable for an exit programme or method of sale. It might be that the disposal of RBS and LBG shareholdings will take several transactions – share auctions and/or offers for sale – over an extended time period.

With a staff of about sixteen and income of about £4 million per annum, the UKFI has no remit to make a profit and pay dividends to the Treasury. Its present role is to manage the government's shareholdings and to have plans in hand to sell shares at the most propitious time. As this may be unlikely in the immediate future, some financial experts would like to see a change in its role from just selling shares to influencing corporate governance decisions on issues such as remuneration and bonuses in the two banks. Some politicians would like to see the UKFI cast its votes in RBS and LBG on behalf of the taxpayers who involuntarily have invested £65 billion in these two banks.

QUICK QUESTION

Is the government at present showing a profit or loss on its shareholdings in RBS and LBG?

Write your answer here before reading on.

4.1 Government shareholdings

Through UKFI, the government owns 90 billion shares in RBS, which is equivalent to 83% of the total share capital. This investment cost the taxpayer £45 billion, and the average buy-in price was 51 pence per share. UKFI also owns 41% of LBG's share capital through the ownership of 28 billion shares which cost £20 billion in capital injections. The average buy-in price in LBG was 74 pence.

So far, apart from in mid-2010, the market price for both banks' shares has been well below the buy-in prices. In November 2011, the government's paper loss on its £65 billion taxpayer stakes was £40 billion, due to the low share prices of approximately 20 pence for RBS and 25 pence for LBG.

To a certain extent the fate of both banks is linked to the fortunes of the UK economy and conditions in the banking market. Both banks are faced with a subdued demand for credit, a battle for retail deposits and problems as regards wholesale funding and its cost. In a recessionary economic environment there appears to be little prospect of a profitable exit from these shareholdings in the immediate future. The coalition government would like to sell the state's stake in both banks in 2013 or 2014 and use the proceeds to reduce the budget deficit before the next general election. Such a share disposal could be by an offer for sale to the general public (re-privatisation) and/or an auction to institutional investors including overseas sovereign wealth funds. The latter could entail the Chinese Investment Corporation and Middle East investors having substantial future shareholdings in both banks.

The UKFI has seen multiple personnel changes since its inception in 2009, with four different heads. The main challenge of the UKFI has been to manage the relationship between taxpayers, the government and LBG and RBS – not always easy when trying to break up large banking groups.

QUICK QUESTION

Should the government buy out the 17% stake held in RBS by private investors and thus fully nationalise the bank?

Write your answer here before reading on.

Alternative proposals have been put forward by some politicians and bank/financial analysts as regards the state's stakes in both banks. Some argue that the government should buy out the remaining 17% stake in RBS and thereby complete the nationalisation of the bank. A wholly state owned RBS could then be directed by the government to adhere to financial and social policies it sets down, such as more lending to small firms, ending the bonus culture and keeping branches open with adequate staffing levels, etc. However, given the track record of nationalised banks in Europe (France, Italy) in past decades, there appears to be little enthusiasm for such action by the main political parties. The UK Chancellor George Osborne has encountered many problems when trying to handle the government's interest in RBS. Osborne has ignored advice from industry experts such as John Redwood on how to break up RBS and has struggled to balance the national interest with the commercial interests of RBS. He has encouraged RBS to sell-off profitable investment banking operations and insurance units, but no definitive plan to break-up RBS has been executed. It is quite significant that the US government in 2010 off-loaded its investments in US banks when a temporary rise in share prices on Wall Street made this a profitable option. The prospect of partially or fully nationalised banks over a long time period did not appeal to the US public or politicians.

Another interesting proposal from the Liberal Democratic party in the UK is for a share give-away in RBS and LBG to the general public. This would widen share ownership and give the public a personal stake in the re-privatised banks. It might also enable the taxpayers to profit from their enforced investment in both banks, with the state itself recovering its £65 billion investment. Of course, such a win–win outcome would depend on the market share prices of both banks.

Under a share give-away proposal, each UK adult on the electoral register (46 million) would receive about 1,400 RBS shares and 400 LBG shares. They would be able to sell their shares once the buy-in prices of 51 pence and 74 pence respectively were being quoted on the stock exchange. The higher the market share price, the greater the profit for each adult shareholder. So if RBS shares rose to £1, a member of the public could sell their shares, with 51 pence going to the Treasury and 49 pence profit to the shareholder. The government would thus get back the funds it invested in RBS. A new electoral shareholder is not obliged to sell their RBS shares so could hold on to them and receive any future dividend payments. If at some future date the new shareholder did sell their shares for £2.51, then 51 pence would still go to the Treasury and £2 profit to the shareholder.

Needless to say, such a give-away share scheme has been criticised by various financial pundits. They state it would be costly to administer due to the need to open and manage 46 million new shareholder accounts at either the Treasury or UKFI. Some believe it would be too complex for Joe and Joan Public to understand, while others believe it should be restricted to pre-2009 taxpayers (30 million). It would also mean less certainty of funds for the Treasury, especially if large numbers decided to hold on to the shares and funds were not provided through share sales to reduce the budget deficit. A final criticism is that it would result in a hybrid ownership structure (private/institutional investors and a diminishing state stake) over a prolonged time period.

QUICK QUESTION

What happened to Northern Rock's toxic assets?

Write your answer here before reading on.

4.2 UK Asset Resolution (UKAR)

UKAR is 100% owned by the UK government through UKFI, and was established in October 2010 to facilitate the orderly management of Bradford & Bingley's (BB) closed mortgage book and Northern Rock Asset Management (NRAM) mortgage and loan book. Its aim is to maximise the value of such debt for the benefit of taxpayers who bailed out both of these small banks.

UKAR does not deal with customers directly but instead continues to service their debt with BB and NRAM. The total mortgage book is about £110 billion. This asset book is gradually being reduced by loan redemptions as BB and NRAM customers find suitable re-mortgaging facilities with other lenders. This enabled the UKAR to repay £2 billion of a government loan in 2010-11. Further reduction of £20 billion still outstanding to the government and repayment of other creditors depends largely upon economic conditions.

The BB and NRAM are two separate entities under the control of UKAR, although management functions of both were integrated in October 2010. In 2010, UKAR made an overall profit of £477 million (BB £200 mil. and NRAM £277 mil.).

QUICK QUESTION

Why was Northern Rock the first bank to succumb to the credit crunch in 2007?

Write your answer here before reading on.

4.3 Northern Rock: nationalisation and privatisation (2008-11)

As previously noted, Northern Rock was the first British bank to succumb to the banking/financial crisis in 2007-09. Its liquidity and asset problems caused the first UK bank run in over 150 years and, despite Bank of England liquidity support and government guarantees to depositors and other creditors, it had to be nationalised in February 2008 at a cost to the taxpayer of £1.4 billion.

Northern Rock (NR) was a Newcastle-based building society which demutualised in 1997, and thereafter experienced rapid expansion and became the fifth largest mortgage lender in the UK. At its peak, it had assets of £110 billion, 6000 employees and over one million customers, of which 800,000 had a mortgage. The demutualisation created over 180,000 shareholders who witnessed NR's share price rise to £12.50 in February 2007, only to fall to zero pence in February 2008.

So how did this banking disaster come about? One key factor was that, with only 76 branches, NR's rapid expansion, through buying market share in house loans, was financed in part by wholesale funds, and when the credit crunch occurred in mid-2007, the reckless nature of their business model was exposed. With limited cash resources and no bilateral credit lines, it had an immediate liquidity problem which, once in the public domain, caused a customer run on the bank. Various schemes to save the bank came to nothing and, as already stated, it was nationalised in February 2008. In January 2010, NR was split into a good bank and a bad bank. NRAM acquired the latter, retaining the majority of the pre-existing mortgage and loan book with a book value of £20 billion.

In November 2011, NR (good bank) was sold to Virgin Money for £747 million up front, plus potential add-ons of £250 million. This sale price was estimated to be equivalent to 90% of NR's book value. Assuming the Treasury receives about £1 billion from Virgin Money, it will be less than the £1.4 billion taxpayers sunk into the bank, so the deal represents a loss of over £10 for each UK taxpayer. A stock market floatation of the bank was considered unrealistic by the government as it was still incurring losses at the time of sale, while re-mutualisation proposed by some would not have generated any funds for the Treasury.

With £16 billion of deposits and £14 billion in mortgages/loans, NR will probably be re-named Virgin Money to make people forget the demise of the bank which is etched in people's memories forever.

Since Northern Rock became Virgin Money, much progress has been made. In 2011, losses of £59 million were reported. The loss dropped to £8m in 2012 as the bank edges towards profitability. Virgin Money is also launching current accounts as they look to increase their market share.

QUICK QUESTION

What were self certification mortgages?

Write your answer here before reading on.

4.4 Bradford & Bingley (BB)

Bradford & Bingley was a former building society which had de-mutualised in 2000 and, as a result, had over one million shareholders. By 2006 it was valued at £3.2 billion and had about 200 branches and 2,800 employees. It provided mortgages and sold mortgages for other financial services providers, and was also heavily involved in the buy-to-let house market and the provision of self-certified mortgages. In addition, it purchased mortgages to boost its balance sheet size and earnings. In 2007-08, the onset of the credit crunch and the decline in the buy-to-let market raised questions in the financial markets about the quality of its loan/mortgage book and overall solvency. It tried to raise new capital through a rights share issue in mid-2008, but the decline in its share price made this impossible. Throughout September 2008, BB's financial position deteriorated and its share price collapsed to just 20 pence.

To avoid another bank run, the government nationalised BB in September 2008 and split it into two parts – a good bank and a bad bank. The former, which consisted of the branch network and £20 billion of deposits, was sold to Abbey (a Santander subsidiary) for £600 million. It was subsequently re-branded Santander in January 2010. The bad bank, still known as Bradford & Bingley, took the mortgage book of the bank into public ownership. It is now closed to new mortgage business and deals only with interest and principal repayments on existing 200,000 mortgages. As already noted, BB operates under the auspices of the UKAR entity, whose prime aim is to recover taxpayers' funds used to bail out the defunct bank.

QUESTION TIME 44

Discuss what lessons can be drawn from the failure of the two former building societies.

Write your answer here then check with the answer at the back of the book.

QUICK QUESTION

How could a sovereign debt default by Greece or Italy damage UK banks?

Write your answer here before reading on.

5 Eurozone debt problem and banks

The European sovereign debt problem has become the new sub-prime debt problem, except this time its origin is in Europe. As noted in chapter 10, various Eurozone governments have borrowed too much and this has created debt service problems in ClubMed countries. Unfortunately, bank regulators permitted banks to treat such sovereign government debt as risk-free, and no distinction was made between German bonds and Italian bonds. International capital accords for banks also treated all European sovereign debt as risk-free and thus requiring little bank capital to be held against it.

The Basel 2 Capital Accord mandated banks individually to determine the risk on sovereign debt held in their asset portfolios. At the same time, after the sub-prime debt problem/crisis in the USA, national bank regulators instructed EU banks to hold more safe assets such as Eurozone sovereign debt, which provided a satisfactory yield, i.e. 4-5% in 2008. Such debt was seen as a prudent way of diversifying asset risk and with an active secondary market it was regarded as a relatively liquid asset. The banks and financial markets chose to ignore that excessive borrowing was financing house price bubbles in Spain and Ireland and ever-increasing budget deficits in Greece, Italy and Portugal. Investment banks which made large fees and staff bonuses did not signal potential problems to banks or investors. The resultant debt problem and loss of confidence in the euro has had a severe impact on the European banking system, especially as regards interbank funding.

On 1 December 2011, the Bank of England and five other central banks joined forces in a coordinated effort to provide limitless supplies of cheap funds to credit-starved banks which were being frozen out of the wholesale money markets. This situation had arisen due to banks becoming reluctant to lend to one another because of underlying solvency problems in many banks with high levels of ClubMed debt. This concerted central bank action, similar to that taken after the collapse of Lehman Brothers in 2008, was aimed at preventing a new credit crunch. This liquidity squeeze was not helped by the credit agencies down-rating a number of European banks. The ECB also recycled around €300 billion from banks depositing funds in it as a safe haven to other banks desperately short of funds.

In December 2011, the Bank of England published its half-yearly Financial Stability Report on the British financial system. It highlighted that British banks hold £15 billion of sovereign debt and £175 billion of loans to banks and corporations in the ClubMed countries and Ireland. The Bank's Governor, Sir Mervyn King, urged banks to cut bonus payments and dividends in order to shore up capital reserves to deal with more debt write-offs, exit of stricken euro members, or, at worst, a complete collapse of the Eurozone.

KEY WORDS

Key words in this chapter are given below. There is space to write your own revision notes and to add any other words or phrases that you want to remember.

- Sub-prime debt
- Capital adequacy
- Loan write-offs
- Asset resolution
- Credit crunch
- Asset price bubble
- Corporate governance
- Due diligence
- Equity stakes
- Regulatory failure

REVIEW

The main learning points introduced in this chapter are summarised below.

Go through them and check back to the learning outcomes at the beginning of the chapter. Only move on when you are happy that you fully understand each point.

- We reviewed the causes and aftermath of the banking/financial crisis in the context of the present structure of UK banking.
- Individual bank failures and problems were examined, together with the role of the government and agencies established to manage and attempt to resolve the problem.
- We considered the Eurozone sovereign debt problem and analysed the implications of potential exposure to this issue of UK banks.

In summary, we looked at:

- The financial crisis of 2007-2009
- Bank failures and problems
- Government action and entities to resolve the crisis
- Detailed accounts of some problem UK banks
- Potential euro debt problems for the UK banking system

chapter 13

BANK REGULATION

Contents

Learning outcomes

On completion of this chapter, you should be able to:

- Critically evaluate the need for bank regulation and prudential controls together with deposit insurance.
- Explain the importance of capital adequacy and liquidity adequacy for banks and the international accords on these issued by the Basel Committee on Bank Supervision.
- Comment on the Independent Commission on Banking Report's recommendations for ring-fencing banking activities and its suggestions for greater competition in the UK banking market.

Introduction

You will already be familiar with the main operational aspects of UK retail banks and other deposit takers, so we will now look at the regulatory regime that determines under what constraints financial organisations operate. We will be referring frequently to the Bank of England, which is often known simply as the Bank.

To be authorised, an institution has to satisfy the Bank that its business is conducted in a prudent manner, which includes having adequate capital and liquidity, a realistic business plan as well as sound systems and controls. Adequate provision must be made in the accounts for bad and doubtful debts and the institution's business must be conducted with skill and integrity. The directors, managers and controllers must be fit and proper for the positions they hold in the organisation.

We will examine capital adequacy and liquidity adequacy in relation to banks in the context of the Basel III Capital Accord, which is to be fully implemented by 2019. In considering the UK bank regulatory framework, we will include a review of the Vickers Report and the recommendations it contains for revision of the banking system.

In summary, we will examine the key concepts and internal/external developments relating to UK bank regulation under the following headings.

- Bank regulation and prudential controls
- Capital adequacy and Basel III
- Liquidity adequacy and management
- Reform of UK bank regulation
- Independent Commission on Banking (Vickers Report)

QUICK QUESTION

What are the reasons for bank regulation?

Write your answer here before reading on.

1 Bank regulation

Most banks accept deposits, provide loans and are part of the payments mechanisms in a country and consequently are subject to some form of regulation by the state. There are four main reasons why banks are regulated.

1 Bank deposits represent the main component of money supply in an economy. The size and growth of money supply influences economic activity and the inflation rate, thus central bank control via reserve requirements is essential for economic stability.

2 Banks are a depositary for public savings which must be secure to retain public confidence. This makes banks a target for consumer protection legislation/regulation.

3 Banks control a large proportion of national financial resources, which can result in a concentration of financial power in a limited number of institutions. Governments put in place restrictive Acts and/or agreements to limit the potential abuse of such power.

4 Banks are vulnerable to financial problems or complete collapse and, as such, are subject to prudential regulation to safeguard the banking system of a country. Prudential regulation can be regarded as a public good.

Taking the last point further, banks are vulnerable to failure due to the composition of their balance sheets. On the liabilities side, high gearing/leverage is most evident, with capital only funding up to 10% of the assets, the remainder being provided by mainly short term deposits. Such deposits are not automatically renewable, especially if confidence in a bank is undermined by bad publicity or rumours about its overall solvency. On the assets side, loans that are mostly illiquid make up 60% to 70% of total assets. Most loans are not quickly marketable and if a quick disposal is required to obtain liquid assets, this can only be brought about at a substantial discount to face value. Any resultant losses erode the capital base of a bank. The quality of the loan book is also influenced by economic conditions which can quickly change and thus undermine the bank's solvency.

As seen in the banking/financial crisis (2007-09), one bank's liquidity/solvency problem or failure can quickly become contagious and result in a general banking crisis or collapse. A systematic crisis caused by multi-bank failures can have a severe economic impact on a country. It is for this reason that prudential controls on banks and their activities are put in place.

QUICK QUESTION

How might a government ensure the stability of its banking system?

Write your answer here before reading on.

1.1 Prudential controls

Prudential controls put in place by the state and/or bank regulatory authority take two main forms – protective regulation and preventative regulation.

The main aims of protective regulation are to limit damage to depositors due to bank failure, stabilise the banking system (reduce systemic risk) and the overall economy. To achieve these aims, most countries operate some form of deposit insurance scheme as well as lender of last resort support from the central bank. Deposit insurance is a form of consumer protection and is a matter of social policy in most countries. It should help to prevent runs on a bank by the public. Lender of last resort support represents an infusion of liquidity to help a solvent bank that is suffering an unwarranted outflow of funds.

Unfortunately, both types of protective regulation create a moral hazard problem in a banking system due to the fact that depositors cease to monitor the overall soundness of banks and bank management incur excessive risks to their asset portfolio on the assumption that deposit insurance and central bank liquidity support will resolve any problems.

QUICK QUESTION

Why might a bank's size make the moral hazard problem worse?

Write your answer here before reading on.

This lack of caution may be influenced by the size of the bank and its (mistaken) belief that central bank and government support will be provided automatically as the bank is too important to be allowed to fail. This is sometimes referred to as the 'Too Big To Fail' doctrine.

The moral hazard problem presents the state and bank regulators with a dilemma as banks operate in a financial environment of unbalanced incentives, made worse by the engrained bonus culture of recent years. Banks can take on excessive risks on and off their balance sheets to make large profits, but if their market positions go wrong, the losses/cost will be met by the deposit insurance agency and/or taxpayer. Therefore banks can socialise losses and privatise gains – this alone is a major incentive for banks to engage in potentially destabilising behaviour. In order to deal with the moral hazard problem, most countries limit deposit insurance to a specific amount, while lender of last resort support is at the central bank's discretion; it is not automatically provided. Regulators also use preventative regulation to curb excessive risk taking by banks with depositors' funds and thereby try to reduce the moral hazard problem.

QUICK QUESTION

Using your knowledge from previous chapters, what might preventative regulation entail?

Write your answer here before reading on.

Preventative regulation is effected through liquidity adequacy and capital adequacy rules and ratios which may reduce the potential for liquidity and solvency problems in banks. Liquidity adequacy is ensured by specific minimum ratios being set for liquid assets in relation to total assets on a bank's balance sheet. In most cases the regulators define the types of suitable liquid assets, e.g. cash, operational balances at the central bank, Treasury and commercial bills of exchange. By holding such liquid assets, it is hoped that banks will avoid forced asset sales, not use lender of last resort facilities and that depositor panic will thus be avoided.

Capital adequacy rules set minimum capital – asset (solvency) ratios for banks. This is to ensure that losses incurred by a bank can be borne by its capital funds and that depositors' funds will be safe and secure. This is sometimes supplemented by limits on the size of loans a bank can make to any one customer, and this is generally expressed as a percentage of the bank's capital resources. To a certain extent, this is official encouragement of loan diversification within a bank's asset portfolio. Most countries now accept and enforce an internationally agreed minimum capital assets ratio of 8% in respect of their banks.

QUICK QUESTION

Why does a bank require adequate capital resources?

Write your answer here before reading on.

2 Capital adequacy

When a bank incurs bad debts or makes a loss, these are written off against shareholder funds, therefore the paid-up capital and reserves of a bank must be adequate to cover anticipated bad debts and losses. Losses must be borne by the shareholders, not the depositors. For protection of the latter, each bank must have enough capital to make any risk to deposits a remote possibility. Under the provisions of the Banking Act 1987, the Bank of England has responsibility for ensuring that UK banks maintain sufficient levels of capital adequacy.

Capital is also required to finance part of the bank's lending operations, meet expenditure on new equipment or refurbishing offices, and to maintain the confidence of depositors in the bank. Capital must be adequate because the value of a bank's assets is subject to risks of depreciation in value from three main areas.

1 **Credit risk** – the possibility of default by borrowers. This is not just default on the total amount of a loan, but also the possibility that a loan will not be repaid in full. There is the further possibility that repayment will be delayed beyond the agreed term. (The possibility of default loss can be reduced by requiring security – collateral – on an advance.)

2 **Investment risk** – the possibility that market assets, such as shares, gilts, securitised debt and derivatives, held on the balance sheet may depreciate in value, thus involving the bank in a capital loss.

3 **Forced sale risk** – this occurs when a bank is forced to sell an asset at a time when its market value is less than that at which it appears in the bank's books.

With the rapid growth of international banking, the case for convergent capital adequacy requirements on both prudential (soundness of banking systems) and competitive grounds was regarded as essential. The resultant Basel Capital Convergence Accord in 1988 was not dissimilar from the then existing Bank of England approach which measured the credit risk of total assets against capital by assigning risk weights to different asset categories, ranging from nil on bank notes to unity (100%) on advances.

QUICK QUESTION

Why do you think there is a need for international agreement on something like capital adequacy?

Write your answer here before reading on.

3 Basel Capital Convergence Accord

Until 1987, bank regulators rejected any attempt to harmonise national regulations; the emphasis was on coordination within a framework of regulatory diversity. In July 1988, the Basel Committee on Banking Supervision (BCBS) announced the phased introduction of a Capital Convergence Accord (now known as Basel 1) which represented a shift towards harmonisation and the creation of a level playing field in international banking, thereby allowing banks to compete on an equal basis.

Variations in required capital ratios had meant that banks from high capital standard countries were less able to compete with banks from low capital standard countries. This had tended to depress interest margins on loans, thus diminishing returns for all banks. As a result, some banks indulged in riskier lending in order to boost their earnings, while banks and/or supervisors in any given country found it difficult to raise their capital adequacy ratios in isolation.

In 1988 the central banks of ten major economies/countries, including the United Kingdom, signed an agreement which standardised the criteria to be used when assessing a bank's capital adequacy. The Basel Capital Accord, which took account of bank domestic and international operations, incorporates:

1 A definition of what constitutes the capital of a bank – equity capital, reserves, general provision and certain types of loan capital.

2 A specification of the minimum capital requirement – capital is divided into three categories:

- Tier One: Core Capital – equity capital and reserves
- Tier Two: Supplementary Capital – provisions, loan capital, etc
- Tier Three: Trading Capital – loan capital and accumulated trading book profits

3 A formula for calculating the amount of capital necessary to cover assets with different degrees of risk, including assets held offshore – four risk weights:

- 0% for cash, balances at central bank
- 20% interbank claims

- 50% mortgages fully secured
- 100% advances and premises

4 A requirement that assets should include items in addition to straight lending, i.e. off-balance sheet exposures – contingencies such as bill acceptances or unutilised credit facilities.

5 Specification of a minimum capital to risk asset ratio of 8%:

- Tier One = 4% (minimum 2% equity capital)
- Tier Two/Three = 4%

This agreement became fully operational at the end of 1992 and means that banks in the major developed countries compete with each other on more or less equal terms as regards capital adequacy.

In addition, as there is a strict ratio between capital and risk assets, once the ratio is reached, further lending is impossible without the bank in question being in breach of the agreement. The only way for a bank to increase its lending under such circumstances would be for it to increase its capital. Given that the issue of further shares is not likely to be resorted to, very often the main source of additional capital will be ploughed-back profits, those not distributed to shareholders in the form of dividends. This encouraged banks worldwide to become more profitable by charging realistic loan interest rates in relation to risk and increasing fee income. At the same time, costs were reduced via new technology, reduced staff and smaller branch networks.

The minimum capital to risk assets ratio is 8%. Each bank publishes its ratio on its balance sheet date. Bank regulators in each country set minimum ratios for each institution to take account of its strengths and weaknesses. This ratio, which is usually higher than the common ratio of 8%, is adjusted over time and remains confidential in most cases.

Overall, the Basel Capital Accord equalised the impact of supervision on the competitive positions of banks in different countries in terms of capital adequacy. It also strengthened the international banking system by making it more able to deal with global economic/financial shocks.

The Bank of England's method of calculating how much capital is required by each bank is based on a system which assigns different risk weights to different categories of a bank's assets. The capital base is measured against the weighted portfolio of risk and calculated as a percentage of it.

CASE STUDY

Albion Bank (£)

Assets		**Liabilities**	
Bank of England	20	Capital	70
Market Loans	120	Deposits	730
Mortgages	260		
Advances	400		
	800		800

Calculate the capital-assets ratio using the four risk weights noted in the Basel.

1 Accord.

Asset	**x**	**Risk Weight**	**=**	**Risk Weighted Asset**
20	x	0%	=	0
120	x	20%	=	24
260	x	50%	=	130
400	x	100%	=	400
				554

Therefore:

$$\text{Capital-asset ratio} = \frac{\text{Capital}}{\text{Risk weighted assets}} \times 100 = \times\%$$

$$= \frac{70}{554} \times 100$$

$$= 12.6$$

This technique only measured credit risk, such as the failure of a bank counterparty to repay, but did not reflect market risk (potential losses) from financial instrument price declines. The latter type of risk takes account of the fact that many banks have diversified their activities; they no longer simply make loans, but also trade for profit in a range of financial instruments. Items held in a bank's trading book are subject to capital charges, the amount of which varies depending on the nature of the risk, such as foreign exchange risk, or equity position risk.

Such capital charges are converted into Notional Risk Weighted Assets to enable the capital adequacy requirement of the whole of a bank's business (banking and trading books) to be expressed as a single risk asset ratio by dividing the capital base by the sum of weighted risk in both books. However, for supervisory purposes, each UK incorporated bank is set a separate target capital adequacy requirement for both the trading book and the banking book, below which it should not fall.

The Bank does not set uniform capital requirements for all banks; instead, individual requirements are set which take into account other risk factors arising from the nature and business of a particular bank (such as the quality of control systems, the nature and concentration of its business and operational and legal risks). The absolute minimum capital requirement is 8%.

With the passage of time, the Basel 1 framework became less effective due to financial, technological and institutional developments. Its treatment of banking risks was regarded as too simplistic – country risk was almost ignored; apart from house purchase mortgages, collateral was given no consideration; the use of one risk bucket for all loans (British Gas or the small corner shop) was regarded as unrealistic. To deal with such risk issues, the BCBS decided that a new Basel Capital Accord was required.

QUESTION TIME 45

(a) What are the main aspects of the Basel Capital Convergence Accord (Basel I)?

(b) Calculate the capital-assets ratio using the Basel I Accord's risk weights for the undernoted bank.

Write your answer here then check with the answer at the back of the book.

National Bank (£)

Assets		**Liabilities**	
Bank of England	50	Capital	50
Market Loans	100	Deposits	650
Mortgages	200		
Advances	350		
	700		700

3.1 Basel II (B2)

Basel II was first issued in 2001, only to be substantially revised in 2004. Implementation of the new capital accord only began to take place in some countries during 2007-09; it is still an ongoing process. The basic aims of B2 were to strengthen the solvency position of banks, encourage a more sophisticated approach to risk management and extend market transparency into the operational aspects of banks. The B2 Accord had three main pillars:

1 **Minimum capital requirement**

B2 increased the number of risk categories for corporate/business loans. Low grade borrowers were given a 150% risk weighting, while other less risky loans could be given a risk weighting of 20%, 50% or 100%. This new risk scale reflected a more risk-sensitive approach to default risk. Differential risk weighting was also introduced for interbank lending and sovereign lending. Operational risk, such as systems failures, legal threats and internal/external fraud were also to be given consideration in determining the capital requirement of a bank.

2 **Supervisory requirements**

Bank regulators were now obliged to ensure each bank had sound internal procedures to assess capital adequacy in relation to their risk profile and operational environment. Regulators/supervisors were required to know new risk management techniques and consider strategic risk, business cycle risk and interest rate risk in relation to each bank and the entire banking sector.

3 **Market discipline**

This aspect required banks to make a full disclosure of all financial facts so that the financial markets could price risk properly in relation to the funding of a bank's activities. Greater transparency would mean a bank with a higher risk profile would be subject to an increase in its funding costs and this was expected to act as a constraint on excess risk taking by a bank. Other facts to be disclosed by banks were economic and geographic credit exposure and the estimated value of impaired loans.

Although B2 was a more sophisticated and inclusive approach to capital adequacy for banks, it still retained the minimum capital assets ratio of 8%. With the benefit of hindsight, B2 did not comment enough on how easily banks could access cash, as Northern Rock was technically solvent but ran out of cash when the markets froze over. To deal with the deficiencies of bank regulation revealed by the 2007-09 banking crisis, the BCBS decided to update B2 by issuing a new capital accord – Basel III – in December 2009. This incorporated new capital adequacy proposals and a standardised monitoring system for liquidity risk. It should be noted that some countries are still incorporating B2 into their bank regulatory systems, while others are merging the implementation of B2 and B3 over the next few years.

QUICK QUESTION

What additional features do you think were necessary to be incorporated into Basel 3?

Write your answer here before reading on.

3.2 Basel 3 (B3)

After consultations, the new regulatory framework was agreed and approved by the G20 nations at their Seoul Summit in South Korea in November 2010. B3 will become applicable after 2013, and although the implementation timetable stretches through to 2019, UK banks hope to fully implement it by 2015. The minimum capital to assets ratio of 8% remains, although the composition and quality of Tier 1 and Tier 2 capital has been improved, while Tier 3 capital is to be gradually phased out by 2019. Tier 1 capital is to exclude hybrid types of capital such as preference shares, and a higher proportion of it is to be constituted by core capital in the form of equity and reserves. Risk weightings have been adjusted to take account of complex financial transactions and a new leverage ratio has been adopted.

B3 is aimed at strengthening the three pillars of B2, especially pillar 1 via enhanced capital and liquidity requirements. New capital buffers will be put in place to force banks to hold more capital of a higher quality to cope with volatile financial conditions. Pillars 2 and 3 are also upgraded to improve supervision and market transparency as regards risk exposures. Counterparty credit risk, which arises if small banks deposit cash reserves in larger banks, has been given its own risk weighting. However, the main aspects of B3 relate to capital cushions to be held by banks by 2019.

The core capital ratio is to rise from 2% to 7%, which includes a 2.5% capital conservation buffer. In a crisis, a bank will be allowed to let its capital ratio drop temporarily to as low as 4.5%, but all dividends and employee bonuses must stop until the ratio is rebuilt to 7%. An extra counter-cyclical buffer of between 0% and 2.5% will allow national regulators to raise the core capital ratio to 9.5% in periods of economic boom. These new capital rules are to be phased in and be fully operational by 1 January 2019. The capital conservation buffer will only apply after 2016, and special allowance has also been granted to banks rescued during the financial crisis – they have been given ten years to comply with B3. This dispensation was granted because some governments feared that the quick implementation of B3 would result in rescued banks restricting their lending and thereby damaging economic recovery.

As usual, national bank regulators can set higher capital standards if they so wish. Discussions are still taking place about higher capital requirements (possible core capital ratio of 9.5% by 2019) for global systematically important banks as their failure could wreck the entire financial system. Finally, a leverage ratio (equity capital to total assets) of a minimum of 3% will become mandatory by 2018. This will be a non-risk based measure to supplement the risk weighted minimum capital requirements.

Capital Requirements: 1 January 2019

	%
(i) Minimum equity capital ratio	4.5
(ii) Capital conservation buffer	2.5
(i)+ (ii)	7.0
Minimum Tier 1 capital	6.0
Minimum total capital (Tier 1 & 2)	8.0
Minimum total capital and counter-cyclical buffer	10.5

QUICK QUESTION

How might higher capital asset ratios impact on banks?

Write your answer here before reading on.

B3: summary

B3 will significantly and progressively increase capital requirements for most banks, which will have to raise more equity (core) capital or cut risky lending and investments. However, if this is achieved by the banks, the new higher capital asset ratios will also create potential problems for a country's financial system. Firstly, they impose an increased obstacle on the entry of new banks in an economy and thus may result in less competition. Secondly, an economy will incur higher intermediation costs as banks raise interest margins and service costs to meet their increased capital costs. Thirdly, the latter might encourage more disintermediation and the renewed growth of a parallel banking system as the ingenuity of bankers finds ways to conduct business beyond the regulator's remit.

Historical evidence confirms that national and international regulatory edicts to establish a fail-safe regime have been largely unsuccessful, although they might have ameliorated crisis situations.

QUICK QUESTION

What do you understand by the term liquidity in relation to banks?

Write your answer here before reading on.

4 Liquidity management

In arranging the distribution of assets, retail banks are pulled in opposite directions – on the one hand towards liquidity, and on the other, towards profitability. As operators of the payments systems, the banks cannot allow their liquidity to fall too low, even though liquid assets offer a poor return. Cash and operational balances at the Bank of England pay no interest. In fact, when allowance is made for the cost of protecting cash from theft, it can be said to have a negative yield.

Nonetheless, with 70% of their deposits virtually payable on demand (at least in theory), the banks must keep sufficient cash or its equivalent (balances at the Bank of England) to meet all likely withdrawals. This does not mean that banks keep 70% of their deposits in cash. If they did, they would earn very little profit indeed. From experience, banks know that only a small proportion of deposits will actually be withdrawn at any given time. Provided the banks maintain sufficient cash to meet these likely withdrawals and a margin of liquid assets which can be converted into cash rapidly to meet any unexpected demands, they can lend the remainder of their funds for longer periods.

Banks are companies operated for profit on behalf of their shareholders. They earn income from money transmission service charges, investment and insurance fees and loan interest. The more the banks lend, the more interest and profits they can make.

Profit is of major importance to a bank as it provides for future growth and a return for shareholders. A bank considered to be earning inadequate profits could be subject to a takeover bid by a competitor. A management unable to earn sufficient profit could well be replaced. This pursuit of profit conflicts with the need for liquidity, since the most profitable loans tend to be the least liquid. Up to 2007, banks were moving towards term loans of a longer maturity while operating on lower cash and liquidity ratios. The asset structure of all banks is a compromise between the desire for profit and the need for liquidity. Success depends on striking the right balance between the two.

Liquidity thus represents the ability of a bank to convert its assets into cash quickly and without loss. Government securities can be speedily converted into cash via the stock exchange, but the price of these securities fluctuates and losses might be incurred if sold at an inopportune moment. It is for this reason that government securities are regarded as illiquid.

Advances are slow to realise, because it is not normal practice to call them in and so drive the borrower into liquidation or bankruptcy. The usual way of contracting advances is to slow down the granting of new advances while allowing repayments of existing advances to continue, thereby reducing the total outstanding. Advances are therefore slow to liquidate and convert into cash for the purpose of deposit repayment. Because of the importance of liquidity to a bank, assets are always listed in order of ease of realisation or closeness to cash. As liquidity decreases, profitability increases, as shown in the following diagram.

Asset	**Liquidity**	**Profitability**
	Increases ↑	Decreases ↑
Notes & coins		
Balances with Bank of England		
Market Loans		
Bills of exchange		
Investments		
Advances		
	Decreases ↓	Increases ↓

5 Liquidity adequacy

Banks must be capable of meeting their obligations (cash withdrawals/interbank debts) when they fall due or are called, which they do by holding cash, liquefiable assets and by arranging a suitable pattern of maturing assets. In this context, banks' obligations are mainly deposits at sight or short notice, deposits with fixed maturity dates and commitments to lend. Although the former category is unpredictable in terms of individual customers, experience allows reasonably accurate estimates of the aggregate amount during any given period. The difficulty with lending commitments is that banks have to estimate the value of advances to be made in a given future time period.

Indeed, as lending is the most profitable activity, there will be pressure to maximise lending and branches will be assigned targets in this respect. Such a procedure presupposes adequate inflows from deposits and repayment of past loans. If the inflow of funds is less than anticipated and loans to customers have been negotiated beyond the sum available, then, if lending facilities are not to be withdrawn – which would have a very adverse effect on the prestige of a bank – there must be liquid reserves to fall back on to make up any deficiency. There must also always be sufficient liquidity to cover the take-up of existing overdraft facilities, particularly if there is a downturn in the economy.

For each institution the mix of obligations will vary. In the Bank of England's view, a bank's ability to meet these obligations rests on two essential elements:

- Sufficiency of immediate available cash or liquefiable assets, subject to the qualification that marketable assets may vary in price when sold.
- A suitable future picture of known cash inflows and outflows.

Banks also derive some protection by their ability to bid in wholesale deposits, such as large time deposits, or by issuing certificates of deposit, although such a capacity and its cost depend on a bank's credit rating and standing in the money markets. A bank must also have a suitably diversified deposit base.

The Bank's supervisory objective is to ensure that all banks maintain a prudent mix of different liquidity forms at all times. This is one which offers security of access to liquidity, without undue exposure to suddenly rising costs from liquefying assets or bidding for deposits. The Bank's approach to meeting this objective is that primary responsibility for a bank's liquidity rests with its own management. It does not seek to impose across-the-board liquidity ratio requirements.

The Bank also requires to be satisfied that banks have both prudent policies and adequate management systems. To ensure this, the Bank monitors banks' liquidity management during the normal course of supervision. In determining what is prudent policy, the Bank takes full account of each bank's particular characteristics. For example, a bank with immediate obligations should have sufficient cash or maturing/ liquefiable assets.

Banks have to complete quarterly liquidity returns to the Bank and are expected to maintain an adequate level of liquidity on a day-to-day basis.

5.1 Basel 3: liquidity requirements

To ensure adequate funding is maintained in case of a crisis, two new liquidity requirements are to be put in place. The first, which is to be in place by 2015, is a new short term liquidity coverage ratio whereby banks must hold sufficient liquid assets to cover 30 days of their net cash flow needs. In other words, a bank must be capable of one month's survival in case of a new credit crunch in the money markets. The second requirement is a net stable funding ratio, which means that banks must have long term or stable fund sources to finance medium term loans and investments by 2018. In addition, regulators have to monitor more closely maturity mismatching, funding concentration and available free assets. Regulators will be expected to demand and receive liquidity risk reports each month from all banks.

6 Large exposures

The capital adequacy approach works well when a bank has a diversified portfolio of loans and investments. However, particular risks can arise when a bank puts too many of its eggs in one basket and becomes heavily exposed to a single customer or counterparty, which might mean it would be unable to meet its commitments. The Banking Act 1987 requires banks to report such large exposures, and the Bank considers that no single counterparty (or related group of counterparties) should account for more than 10% of a bank's capital base without thorough justification; also that no borrower or group should account for more than 25% of the capital base other than in the most exceptional circumstances. Account can be taken of good quality collateral held against loans.

The Bank also requires banks to report their exposures to individual sectors, such as property and manufacturing, and to individual countries. It sets no specific target percentages for these exposures but will discuss significant concentrations of risk with the bank involved.

7 Provisions

Banks must make provision in their accounts for any bad and doubtful debts. While the Bank is not usually involved in the process of determining the precise level of provisions which should be held by a bank (this being primarily a matter for the management of the bank and their auditors), the Bank has to be satisfied that the provisions arrived at are adequate. If they are not, then banks will be overstating the value of their loans and presenting a misleading view of the adequacy of their capital.

In assessing provisions, the Bank looks at the provisioning policy of the bank involved, its methods and systems for monitoring credit risk and recoverability, arrears patterns, and practices for taking and valuing security. Often judgements will be subjective, but in some areas objective tests may be possible.

8 Systems and controls

A bank cannot be run prudently without adequate systems for keeping up-to-date records of all its transactions and commitments, in such a way that management are continuously aware of the bank's condition and the risks to which it is exposed. Moreover, internal controls should ensure that assets are safeguarded, and that commitments and payments are properly authorised in accordance with management intentions. External auditors report periodically on management control systems to the Bank, as well as on the accuracy and completeness of the statistical returns submitted to the Bank.

Reporting accountants and (where different) external auditors are also enabled by the terms of the Banking Act to report direct to the Bank, should the need arise, about any worrying development that they may have noticed in the course of their work. In addition, they have a statutory duty to report to the Bank any concerns which cast doubt on whether a bank should remain authorised.

8.1 Repercussions of insufficient systems and controls

Two high profile scandals have caused shock waves across the financial world in recent years. In 2011, UBS announced that it had lost over $2 billion due to fraudulent trades executed by a rogue trader. The rogue trader was sentenced to seven years in prison. The UBS CEO resigned and UBS was fined $47 million by regulators.

In 2012, JP Morgan announced that it had lost $5.8 billion due to trades executed by a star trader called the 'London Whale'. The trading strategy used by the London Whale was described by the JP Morgan CEO as poorly reviewed and poorly monitored.

Both of these scandals highlight that continuing importance of risk and controls in banking. While the financial losses are staggering, the reputational damage can be much more severe and far reaching.

QUESTION TIME 46

Explain the importance of capital adequacy and liquidity adequacy in relation to UK banks.

Write your answer here then check with the answer at the back of the book.

9 The Banking Act 1987

The main purpose of the 1987 Act was to improve the Banking Act 1979 in light of regulatory experience and to make banking law consistent with the Financial Services Act 1986. One of the central aims of the 1987 Act was to formalise the Bank of England's position as the UK's banking supervisory authority and to strengthen its statutory powers to prevent unauthorised institutions taking in illegal deposits. The Act's basic objective is to protect bank depositors.

The main aspects of the Banking Act 1987 are as follows.

1. Under the Act, any licensed deposit taker with capital (or undistributed reserves) of more than £5 million can call itself a bank, an authorised institution. Overseas institutions can use their banking names without any restrictions. The Act sets stringent requirements for capital, liquidity, loan loss provisions, internal control systems and accounting records.

2. The UK Treasury can amend the definition of deposit and deposit taker in line with changes in the financial markets/services industry. There is a general restriction on the taking of deposits except by authorised institutions. The Bank can revoke the authorisation of a deposit taker to take deposits from the public.

3. Limitations on the amounts of money expressed as a percentage of capital that banks can lend to a single customer were introduced. Automatic notification is required of any exposure to an individual customer in excess of 10% of a bank's capital base. Exposures in excess of 25% of the capital base require prior notification to the supervisory authority.

4 Nobody can take a stake of 15% or more in a bank without notifying the Bank in advance. The Bank has powers to object to or block parties from gaining a controlling stake in a bank. Foreigners cannot acquire a controlling interest in a UK bank – defined as 15% or more – unless UK banks are given reciprocal access to the purchaser's home banking market. Prospective controllers of banks must undergo a fit and proper test (considerations: probity, competence, diligence, sound judgement) before being authorised to accept deposits from the public.

5 The Bank was granted greater information gathering powers. In particular, auditors will not be in breach of their duties if they inform on banks. Prudential statistical returns must be examined periodically by external qualified accountants who prepare yearly reports on banks, their internal controls and the adequacy of their records.

10 UK deposit protection

The Financial Services Compensation Scheme (FSCS) operates under a set of rules made by the FSA under the terms of the Financial Services and Markets Act 2000. The FSCS became operational on 1 December 2001, is independent of the government and financial services industry, but is accountable to the Treasury.

The Scheme operates when an authorised deposit taker (bank, building society or credit union) goes out of business and is unable to repay depositors. If a bank fails, the FSCS will compensate depositors up to £85,000 (holders of joint accounts £170,000). This cover is per banking licence and many banking groups share a licence, for example RBS and NWB. This means in practice that if a depositor holds £50,000 in each bank, they are only insured up to £85,000. If a depositor has more than £85,000 deposited in a bank, the extra sum above the limit is not eligible for compensation. Such a depositor (as an ordinary creditor) will have to recover the excess amount from the realised assets of the insolvent bank.

The FSCS is funded by the financial services industry. Every authorised bank, building society and credit union is obliged to pay an annual levy which is based on total deposit size. This ensures that large banks pay more than small banks. The annual levy is based on expected compensation payments forecast for each year. In 2009-10 the total levy was £23 million, while in 2010-11 it was considerably less at £4 million. If large compensation payments materialise, the FSCS has the power to raise additional funds through supplementary levies.

11 The Financial Services Act 1986

This Act affected some functions of banks, such as investment advice/management, as well as those of all other institutions/firms in the investment sector. The main purpose of the Act was to ensure that those involved in providing financial services are fit and proper to do so. The actual requirements of clients must be investigated and the best possible advice given. Banks (and other financial firms) must state clearly whether they are agents for one financial product, or whether they are qualified to give independent advice on a range of financial products.

QUESTION TIME 47

Comment on the main features of deposit protection for UK bank customers.

Write your answer here then check with the answer at the back of the book.

12 Financial Services Authority (FSA)

On 1 June 1998 the FSA assumed responsibility from the Bank of England for bank supervision. Staff of the supervisory division of the Bank took up their new posts as FSA employees.

The Financial Services and Markets Act received Royal Assent in June 2000, and was implemented during 2001. The FSA was then the single statutory body for financial business in the UK. The new legislation also gave the FSA new responsibilities, such as regulating certain aspects of mortgage lending and monitoring compliance with a code of conduct in relation to house purchase loans.

In summary, the FSA's responsibilities were to regulate and supervise all financial businesses and investment exchanges, and in doing so maintain confidence in the UK financial system and secure an appropriate degree of protection for consumers.

QUICK QUESTION

Why do you think the government decided to replace the FSA?

Write your answer here before reading on.

12.1 New regulatory regime

On 16 June 2010, the Chancellor of the Exchequer announced that the FSA would cease to exist by the end of 2012 as it had failed in its basic tasks. Firstly, it had allowed an unsustainable increase in debt to take place and, although the balance sheets of UK banks had trebled over five years, no FSA official noticed or made a comment especially as only one fifth of all credit went into the real economy. Secondly, it failed to anticipate the scale and complexity of the problems that banks faced at the outset of the banking crisis in 2007-08. Thirdly, there was a lack of communication between officials at the Treasury, Bank and FSA (the tripartite regime) which directly contributed to regulatory failure. Finally, it failed to take account of the development of a shadow (parallel) banking system which was created through securitisation and complex derivative instruments.

The Chancellor introduced a new system of regulation under the Financial Regulation Act 2012, which is more specialised and focuses specifically on financial services providers. This Act establishes three new regulatory entities as subsidiaries of the Bank of England. These are listed below, along with a short summary of their respective remits.

1 **Financial Conduct Authority (FCA)**

The FCA's main aim is to protect financial services consumers and fight financial crime. In supervising the conduct of both retail and wholesale banks, it will attempt to ensure that future mis-selling scandals are prevented, if at all possible. In the last 20 years the latter has cost banks and other financial institutions about £15 billion in compensation payments and has undermined public confidence in the ethical standards of the banking system. To achieve these aims, the FCA also regulates the provision of credit cards, motor vehicle insurance and personal loans.

2 **Prudential Regulation Authority (PRA)**

The PRA is responsible for the prudential supervision of banks, building societies, credit unions and insurance companies, including 200 of the most powerful financial institutions in the UK. The main objectives are to ensure the safety and soundness of institutions and help maintain the stability of the financial system.

The PRA has moved away from the FSA box ticking approach to regulation towards a principles-based system based on forward looking judgements about the solvency of banks and focusing in particular on capital adequacy and business models, and thereby the liquidity position and loan book quality of each institution. A ranking system is used to identify potential problems. The PRA tries to create greater transparency for markets and customers by publishing bank returns and has promised to publish reports on any future failed banks, building societies, credit unions and insurance companies.

3 **Financial Policy Committee (FPC)**

The FPC's main aims are to monitor banks and identify any threats to financial stability such as asset price bubbles. To act effectively as a lender of last resort, the Bank of England must be familiar with every aspect of an institution and so this aspect of micro-prudential regulation can be achieved through the FPC.

The FPC's main tasks are to monitor trading risks, cash reserves held, the level of borrowings and quality of the assets. The FPC decides on the necessary capital buffers and can lay down lending rules such as caps on mortgage lending and ceilings on loan-to-value ratios. The FPC is also required to question financial innovations that might create illusory profits in banks. If any risks are identified as regards a bank, the FPC can refer the said institution to the PRA for investigation. The FPC can also block any bank takeovers if they are perceived to be too risky and/or an excessive acquisition price is being proposed by a bank's directors.

Finally, the FPC operates in parallel with the MPC to provide the Bank with a broad macro-economic understanding of the financial system, thereby reinforcing the Bank's authority and knowledge to make macro-prudential judgements.

QUICK QUESTION

How might the government recover some of the economic/social costs of the banking crisis?

Write your answer here before reading on.

12.2 Bank levy (tax)

From January 2011, UK banks and UK operations of foreign banks have been subject to a bank levy on the liabilities on their balance sheets. The levy is set at 0.04%, rising to 0.088% of liabilities, and is expected to raise £2.5 billion per annum for the UK Treasury. Banks receive reductions on the computation of total liabilities for Tier One capital and insured deposits, while long term funding is subject to a lower tax charge. The latter allowance is to discourage an over-reliance on short term funding of assets. Due to its reliance on short term borrowing, Lloyds Banking Group (LBG) is expected to face a bank levy charge of about £350 million. Small institutions and building societies with deposits of less than £20 billion are exempt from the bank levy. The bank levy is regarded by some people as a justifiable punishment imposed on big banks for the social costs incurred by the country as a result of the banking crisis.

The levy was originally only intended for UK banks. However, in the 2013 Autumn Statement it was announced that the levy would also begin to effect foreign banks. This was introduced to take the burden off UK lenders and share it with non-UK banks. The changes are estimated to double the size of the levy payable for HSBC, who are now likely to pay over £1 billion per year. The legislation behind the levy has also been amended to make it more flexible, allowing the government to quickly make changes to the levy as necessary.

QUICK QUESTION

Given your knowledge and understanding of the banking crisis (2008) what actions would you suggest to avoid a future crisis and use of taxpayer funds?

Write your answer here before reading on.

12.3 The Independent Commission on Banking Report (ICB Report or Vickers Report)

In mid-2010 the government set up the ICB, under the chairmanship of Sir John Vickers, to examine UK banking. After 15 months of deliberation and an interim report (in April 2011), the ICB published its final report in September 2011. The Report contained a number of recommendations for restructuring the UK banking sector. The Report's main aspects relating to the separation of retail and investment banking and competition in the banking market are summarised below.

1 **Ring fencing**

The Report recommended that retail banking operations (deposit taking;, personal loans, small and medium sized enterprise loans, mortgages) be ring fenced from investment bank (casino) activities in order to avoid a taxpayer bail-out of banks in the future. It was also recommended that the government legislate for 'firewalls' around banks' high street operations.

The ring-fenced retail operations will have their own balance sheet and capital buffers and will be a separate legal entity from the rest of the banking group, with its own board of directors. If profits are made, dividends will be paid to the parent bank. Such a retail banking entity will have limited exposure to global markets, although it will be able to lend to large corporations outside the financial sector and trade in derivatives to hedge its own exposures. It will be required, as a subsidiary, to have core capital ratio of 10%, compared to the 7% set by Basel 3, by 2019.

The overall aim is to safeguard customers' deposits and ensure that loans to firms in the real economy do not dry up in a crisis. If investment banking, which will be conducted through a separate subsidiary entity, incurs large losses, it will be allowed to fail without disrupting the retail subsidiary's supply of credit to the economy.

Given the scale of such reform, the ICB decided that banks should be given eight years to implement ring fencing. The deadline of 2019 was chosen due to the fragility of the UK economy, the implementation of the new bank regulatory framework and the adoption of the Basel 3 capital requirements.

2 **Competition**

The ICB decided that LBG did not need to dispose of more than 632 branches as a condition for state assistance (capital injection) under a European Commission competition ruling. These branches were acquired by Co-operative Bank Group (CBG) which implies a challenge to the big four – RBS, LBG, HSBC, Barclays Bank – in the retail banking market. The latter have 77% of all personal customer accounts and 85% of small/medium enterprise loans.

The Report also recommended that a new system be introduced to allow personal and business customers to switch their current/cheque accounts more easily and within 7 days. At present, about three quarters of the number of customers never switch their accounts due to inertia, the hassle involved, and fear of automatic payments being missed. The ICB hope that easier switching will encourage more competition.

3 **Other aspects**

As regards bank regulation, the ICB supported the new arrangements concerning the FCA. It also wants long term unsecured debt to absorb some of the losses if a bank fails or has problems in the future. This will increase the loss-absorbing capacity in most banks to somewhere between 15% and 20% of their assets.

In mid-December 2011, the Chancellor of the Exchequer stated in Parliament that he accepted the Vickers Report proposals and planned to implement the changes in full. Much of the necessary legislation will be debated and voted on in 2015. Banks are expected to comply as soon as possible thereafter. The Chancellor also indicated that RBS will have to close its casino banking division in order to reduce riskier banking activities and return to basic banking.

QUICK QUESTION

What costs might be associated with the Vickers Report recommendations?

Write your answer here before reading on.

12.4 Comments on the ICB proposals

The ICB hopes that its ring fencing proposal will reduce the likelihood of another banking crash in the UK economy. A more stable financial services sector should contribute to renewed economic growth and thereby offset the financial and social costs of implementing ring fencing. However, critics point out that ring fencing would not have prevented Northern Rock's failure due to reckless lending or the disastrous merger between RBS and ABN-Amro. There is also no guarantee that ring fencing will prevent contagion between a failed casino subsidiary and the retail subsidiary, so that a public run on the latter could still take place. It has to be accepted that the total elimination of risk in banking is not possible unless a bank invests all its deposits in risk-free gilts.

The large banks have estimated that the total cost of ring fencing will be somewhere between £4 billion to £8 billion due to the lost benefits of universal (conglomerate) banking. It will also reduce the UK's annual output by £1 billion to £2 billion. Critics believe that the banks will attempt to recover these costs by increased loan charges and service fees, or perhaps cater only for high net worth customers.

Some argue that the ICB went for the safer and less costly options – easier account transfers, a new competitor from LBG branch disposals – rather than forcing the break-up of the big four banks. It might be with the passage of time that the Competition Commission will come to a similar conclusion.

Finally, some bank/financial analysts believe that ring fencing will only partially solve the Too Big To Fail problem as a casino subsidiary will be allowed to fail if it gets into financial difficulties. The state will no longer be confronted by the moral hazard problem – the shareholders/bondholders are to be wiped out, but no state bail-out will be required to keep a retail bank subsidiary intact and operational. However, some experts believe that such an outcome can only be guaranteed by full separation of retail banking and investment banking into totally separate legal and financial entities, each with their own shareholders.

12.5 Parliamentary Commission on Banking Standards

The Parliamentary Commission on Banking Standards was led by Andrew Tyrie and published in June 2013. It was driven by calls to overhaul UK banking in light of the numerous scandals (such as LIBOR and PPI mis-selling) that have already been mentioned. It contained eighty recommendations that were intended to fundamentally improve UK banking standards. The recommendations were not just limited to banks, but also considered changes required by the government and regulators. The key recommendations were:

- The break-up of RBS
- An audit of the number of female staff working on trading floors, as it is suggested that more female staff could help to reduce risk
- Measures to increase competition between high street banks, including making it easier to switch between bank accounts
- Measures to make bankers more accountable for their actions

The report also looked at UK banking cultural and concluded that cultural changes are needed to improve banking problems. During the LIBOR investigation, regulators decided that the LIBOR manipulation at Barclays was largely driven by cultural factors. The UK Treasury is prepared to make amendments to the finance bill to incorporate recommendations from the Commission, highlighting that UK banking could be forced to undergo a dramatic transformation in the near future.

12.6 Banking Reform Bill

In December 2012 MPs gave their approval to the Banking Reform Bill that would implement the recommendations made by the Parliamentary Commission on Banking Standards and other recommendations (such as the Vickers Report) that have been undertaken in the wake of the financial crisis. The two most significant parts of the bill are measures to force banks to separate investment banking from retail banking activities. Senior bankers will be held more accountable for their actions, including criminal sanctions if their institution fails. Another key part of the bill is to put a cap on the overall cost of credit charged by short-term lenders and pay-day loan companies.

The only issue not fully addressed by the Banking Reform Bill is proprietary trading – but regulators are set to put forward proposals on how to prevent excessive risk taking through proprietary trading after the separation of retail banking has taken place.

KEY WORDS

Key words in this chapter are given below. There is space to write your own revision notes and to add any other words or phrases that you want to remember.

- Capital adequacy
- Credit risk
- Investment risk
- Forced sale risk
- Liquidity adequacy
- Banking Act 1987
- Basel Capital Convergence Accord
- Financial Services Authority (FSA)
- Risk asset ratio
- Financial Conduct Authority (FCA)
- Prudential Regulation Authority (PRA)
- Financial Services Compensation Scheme
- Financial Services and Markets Act 2000
- Moral hazard problem
- Vickers Report

REVIEW

The main learning points introduced in this chapter are summarised below.

Go through them and check back to the learning outcomes at the beginning of the chapter. Only move on when you are happy that you fully understand each point.

- We examined the need for bank regulation and prudential controls.
- We looked at a number of key concepts including capital adequacy and liquidity adequacy.
- We discussed the content and implementation of the Basel Capital Accords, including the impact on bank balance sheets.
- We examined the main aspects of past and present UK bank regulation.
- The Vickers Report contains proposals for the separation of retail banking and investment banking and for increased competition in banking.

In summary, we looked at:

- The main aspects of bank regulation/supervision
- Key aspects of capital and liquidity adequacy
- The main points of the Banking Act 1987
- The UK bank regulatory system
- The Vickers Report

chapter 14

BANKING/FINANCIAL ENVIRONMENT

Contents

Learning outcomes

On completion of this chapter, you should be able to:

- Critically assess the competitive environment in which banks operate and the role of social banking.
- Explain the single banking market in Europe and the development of cross-border banking.

Introduction

In this chapter we will review the financial services sector environment as an understanding of the development and evolution of today's highly competitive financial services market is essential background knowledge within the context of the organisation in which you work.

Due to income and cost pressures as well as the financial crisis, banks have been forced to restructure their operations and re-assess the role of staff and branch networks. Government involvement in banking via shareholdings and acceptance of the Vickers Report recommendations will result in fundamental changes to the structure and operations of banks.

Building societies face similar issues due to greater competition in the mortgage market and must diversify to remain competitive and survive in the financial services market.

We will examine the role of other, smaller competitors in the banking market, such as credit unions, who see their role as reducing financial exclusion in society, and also the government-backed national savings movement.

Added to these domestic developments is the creation of a single EU banking/ financial services market which presents both opportunities and challenges for all banks.

In summary, we will consider key aspects of banking operations under the following headings:

- Branch networks and staff levels
- Mutualism versus plc status
- New competitors in the banking market
- Social banking via credit unions
- The single banking licence (passport) in the EU

QUICK QUESTION

Why do you think the financial services sector expanded in most countries up to 2007?

Write your answer here before reading on.

1 The banking/financial environment

Largely due to income and cost pressures, as well as the financial crisis of 2008, banks and other financial institutions in most countries have been forced to re-assess the contribution to profits made from their branch networks and loan/asset operations. Staff levels and branch networks are constantly being examined with a view to improving customer services and overall profitability.

2 Trends in the financial services sector

Between the mid-1980s and 2008, the financial services sector, which includes banks, building societies, securities houses and fund management, was one of the most successful in terms of employment creation and output growth in the UK economy. This expansion in financial services activity was probably the result of two major trends.

1. The consumption (or use) of financial services tends to increase with income, but at a faster rate. As consumers become wealthier, they want both to save and to borrow more, at different stages in their life cycle. Financial services can be viewed as an alternative to consumption; apart from banking-type services, consumers also need advice about investment, insurance and housing.

2. A major objective of government policy was to liberalise the provision of financial services. The banks were allowed to move into the mortgage market while building societies provided a broader range of financial services. Political philosophy and policies created a more market-orientated framework for the provision of financial services.

British banks were among the UK's most successful enterprises. Five of the largest sixteen banks in the world (e.g. RBS) were based in the UK. Competition was intense, and there was pressure on banks to increase efficiency and provide better services.

The financial sector provided jobs for more than one million people, around 4% of the UK workforce. The financial sector was a major taxpayer, contributing around one third of corporation tax collected by HM Revenue and Customs. Overall, financial services were a huge contributor (over 8% of GDP) to the UK economy in 2007.

A major feature of the financial services sector was that customers were demanding more and better services – in other words, looking for more value for money. With a much broader range of financial products and institutions, customers were prepared to switch their financial assets from one provider to another. Customer loyalty to banks started to decline as competition increased among financial services providers.

QUESTION TIME 48

Why do individuals switch their holdings of financial assets?

Write your answer here then check with the answer at the back of the book.

3 Bank strategy pre-2008

3.1 General overview

The overall strategy of banks in most countries up to 2008 as regards the range and delivery of products and services was influenced by a number of related developments. You should be aware of some of these at first hand, and major changes also attract much media attention.

1 **Problem loans**

In the early 1990s, problem loans resulted in some retail banks reporting operating losses and reducing dividend payments to shareholders. Some commentators blamed deregulation and excessive competition which, perhaps, encouraged banks to expand their balance sheets too rapidly at interest margins that did not reflect the risks taken on.

Others blamed the government's faulty economic management for creating an unstable economic environment of 'boom-bust' in the property market, which fatally undermined many financial arrangements made between banks and their customers.

Whatever the causes, banks faced major problems regarding commercial property loans, personal mortgages and small business sector advances. The extent of the loan book problem was confirmed by British banks increasing their annual domestic loan loss provisions in the early 1990s.

2 **Financial market environment**

The operating environment for UK banks was influenced by a conflux of major trends – innovations, technology, deregulation, and securitisation – which forced every bank to continuously re-assess its overall operating and marketing strategy.

QUICK QUESTION

What impact do you think the new financial environment had on net interest income and fee income for banks?

Write your answer here before reading on.

3 **Income and costs**

Competitive pressures eroded interest margins on all types of bank lending, while increased reliance on wholesale funds increased funding costs. To deal with this twin threat to profitability, the banks endeavoured to reduce their costs and enhance their non-interest income.

Cost cutting was implemented via a reduction in staff levels and branch network cuts, both made possible by investment in technologically advanced processing and delivery systems.

On the income side, banks switched from low margin corporate business to higher margin and thus more profitable personal sector business via the provision of more lending/mortgage facilities. Non-interest or fee income was boosted by charging for services previously provided for free and by selling an increased range of financial products, such as insurance policies, pension schemes, investment facilities, etc.

In many instances, banks adopted more stringent cost control procedures as a means of achieving sustainable profits. One of the most effective methods of cost reduction was via a centralisation of branch back-office tasks.

4 **Staff levels and the branch network**

It is worthwhile making a few further comments on bank staffing levels and the branch network. For most large retail banks, staff and premises/equipment costs usually account for between 40% and 60% of total operating costs. Both were obvious targets in the efforts to reduce costs.

a) **Staff**

Reduction in staff levels was achieved through natural wastage, early retirement, low recruitment levels and compulsory redundancies. Using part-time staff to match workload requirements and outsourcing non-strategic functions also enabled banks to reduce costs. However, the resultant saving on staff expenditure costs was partially offset by the need to upgrade the skills of the remaining staff via expensive training programmes and the introduction of bonus payments.

Post-2008, the banking crisis and economic recession has accelerated staff reductions in the big four banks. LBG alone has axed over 33,000 jobs since its merger with HBOS. Even investment banking divisions of the big banks are reducing their staff levels as income from trading bonds and derivatives declines.

b) **Branch networks**

Rationalisation of bank branch networks was also an ongoing process between 1990 and 2010. About 7,400 branches were closed in Britain. Although this process was motivated by the need to reduce costs, it was also encouraged by the broad range of products and services that can now be delivered through automated facilities (see chapter 15).

With the lowest branch density among major European nations (160 branches per one million population in the UK, 470 branches per one million in Germany), UK rationalisation has probably eliminated overcapacity and now the branch is seen as complementary to the call centre, online and mobile channels. Given the bankruptcy of the Icelandic banks, such as Landesbanki, which has perhaps dented credibility in the direct banking model, the physical presence of an office may have enhanced branch banking as an outward sign of security.

3.2 Retail banking sector consolidation

The key requirement in the UK retail banking sector was, and still is, to control costs. However, staff reductions are to some extent offset by the expense of investment in information technology (IT), which tends to yield cost savings to retail banks over the longer term. High IT expenditure and the need for a critical mass of customers to make it viable, together with the need to reduce administration and branch overlaps, encouraged mergers and consolidation in the UK retail bank sector (e.g. HBOS).

Studies in the USA have indicated that bank mergers, if managed properly, have the potential to reduce total expenditure by up to 20%. Such cost savings, rather than any increase in total revenues, are the main source of increased profits resulting from bank mergers. However, the downside is that consolidation and restructuring of the banking industry in any country is fraught with difficulties. Supposed organisational, marketing and information synergies such as between banks, building societies and insurance companies, sometimes fail to materialise because of a lack of coherent leadership or a clash of management styles.

Such diseconomies often encourage subsequent disposals of acquired assets and staff, along with renewed specialisation in a narrower known range of activities. Shareholder dissatisfaction as regards returns on the enlarged asset base has often played a key role in the de-merging process.

In most banks up to 2008, the top management were very conscious of the need to maximise shareholder value. Any acquisitions had to add to shareholder value, i.e. increased dividends and a rise in the enlarged bank share price. Unfortunately for some banks, such as RBS/ABN-Amro and Lloyds TSB/HBOS, it had the exact opposite effect in 2008-09.

3.3 Banks and their customers

As noted above, branch closures have accelerated over the last 20 years and now many communities have no bank or only one to facilitate their financial needs. This loss of access to bank branches has been compounded by the centralisation of decision making on loan applications where computerised box ticking has become the norm. The days of experienced and knowledgeable local bank managers has long since disappeared, with the result that the general public feel disenfranchised from banks which, in many cases, indulged in investment banking with disastrous consequences for their profitability and solvency.

The announcement of derivative and sub-prime losses impacted on the retail side of banks' operations as attempts were made to restore profits by more branch closures and front line staff reductions. All this affects the economic and social fabric of a country, in particular the ability of small firms to access local banks for advice and the financial support that is so vital to economic recovery.

The desire for more competition and better customer service has been supported by the compulsory branch disposals of government-assisted banks such as RBS and LBG, and by the recommendations of the Vickers Report. It is therefore most likely that the face of UK banking will change considerably over the next few years. This will create new opportunities for personal/business customers and bank employees via more banking institutions and a re-orientation of banking towards meeting the retail needs of the economy.

3.4 PPI mis-selling

The relationship between banks and their customers has been badly affected by the Payment Protection Insurance (PPI) mis-selling scandal. PPI policies were introduced in the 1990s. PPI policies are used by customers to ensure that they can pay back loans, credit cards and mortgages should they fall into financial hardship. It is estimated that customers will claim around £4.5 billion in compensation from UK banks for the mis-selling of PPI policies. Regulators found that banks were aggressively selling PPI policies that were inappropriate and insufficient to meet the needs of customers. Regulators have introduced strict new PPI guidelines to ensure that policies are sold in the best interest of the customer.

3.5 Youth unemployment

A concern for European banks is the high levels of youth unemployment across Europe. 5.5. million people aged under 24 are unemployed in the EU. This is a worry for banks as it means that a generation of potential customers may never have the need to use a variety of banking products (such as savings accounts and pensions) and services. High unemployment also reduces the amount that people save, potentially reducing the deposits that banks will have to lend in the future.

4 Building societies: current trends and prospects

Building societies in the UK were extremely successful up to the 1980s because banks chose to ignore two of the fastest growing and most profitable sectors for deposit takers – mortgage lending and personal savings. As societies secured these areas for themselves, due to the oversight and/or legislative problems encountered by other institutions, they expanded their balance sheets, branch networks and numbers of staff. For all their apparent success, the building societies now face a number of uncertainties regarding the future.

1 **Owner-occupied housing market**

The proportion of owner-occupied dwellings has risen from under 25% in 1945 to about 70% in 2011. It is thus likely that the pool of untapped potential home owners is set to decline in the future. As mortgages represent the main asset held by the societies and have been the chief source of balance sheet growth over the last forty years, a deceleration of growth is now widely expected, unless other assets such as personal loans can be expanded.

2 **Long-run share of mortgage market**

Competition in the mortgage market has intensified, with traditional retail banks capturing at least 50% of the market. Along with competition from insurance companies, overseas banks and mortgage corporations, the building societies have witnessed a steep decline in their mortgage market share in recent years.

3 **Interest margins**

As already noted, competition in the mortgage market intensified up to 2008, with an increased number of mortgage lenders. In order to retain market share, reduced margins between shareholders' (depositor) interest rates and borrowers' interest rates was inevitable. Thus, the maintenance of surplus income and adequate reserve levels now depends on additional income sources and a tight control over costs.

4.1 Number of building societies

Building societies since 1990

Year	**Number of Societies**	**Total Assets £billion**
1990	110	220
1998	70	140
2006	63	270
2010	47	330*

Source: Building Societies Association
**Mortgage Assets £210 billion; Savings Balances £215 billion*

As the table shows, the last twenty years have witnessed a marked increase in the total assets of building societies but an equally marked decline in their numbers. Underlying the decline in numbers are three factors.

1 The closure of some small building societies.

2 The process of amalgamation via mergers.

3 Under the Building Societies Act 1986, a building society has the right to convert from mutual to company status. The Abbey National converted in 1989, to be followed by other major societies (e.g. Halifax and Woolwich) in 1997. Once company, i.e. plc, status is achieved, a building society is reclassified as a retail bank. This conversion trend inevitably reduced further the number of societies and their share of personal sector deposits and mortgages.

The number of societies has declined, thereby leading to the concentration of business into fewer but larger societies. The two largest societies (Nationwide £190 billion, Yorkshire £33 billion) accounted for over 67% of the movement's total assets at the end of 2010.

The trend towards increased concentration can be expected to continue between the remaining mutual building societies for a number of reasons.

1 Increased competition from both within and without the building society movement may force weaker societies to re-assess their position and seek a merger with a larger partner, e.g. Yorkshire Building Society acquired the Barnsley (2008), Chelsea (2010) and the Norwich and Peterborough (2011) Societies.

2 Small societies will be unable to offer the full range of services allowed under the Building Societies Act 1986.

3 Increased administrative burdens and the need to keep up with developments in information technology may prove difficult for smaller societies.

4 Economies of scale will continue to benefit the larger societies and encourage further mergers.

5 Higher capital adequacy requirements are difficult to comply with for smaller building societies.

6 Losses incurred by some smaller building societies as a result of the credit crunch/economic recession.

Taking the last reason, the Nationwide Building Society acquired the Cheshire, Derbyshire and Dunfermline Societies in 2008-09. These three societies had run into financial difficulties as a result of diversifying into riskier assets in order to boost their earnings. The Derbyshire had invested in sub-prime mortgages, while the Cheshire and Dunfermline had lent substantial sums to commercial property companies that had defaulted on their loans. The FSA encouraged these quick takeovers by the Nationwide in order to retain confidence in the building society movement. All three societies still operate under their brand names.

Not everybody favours this increased concentration. Critics have complained that it is growth for its own sake and that it detracts from the achievement of the societies' social and economic goals. Others have stated that too many societies in the past, perhaps, led to wasteful competition, a proliferation of branches and unwise investments in related financial services areas.

4.2 Conversion versus mutualisation

Advantages of conversion

A major advantage claimed by the supporters of conversion to plc status is that it enables an institution to carry out rationalisation of its mortgage lending and diversification of its financial services. It also enables the converted society to issue more shares to acquire other financial institutions.

Other advantages claimed for conversion are that societies such as banks have greater operational freedom and the plc form of ownership engenders greater accountability of the managers to the shareholders. Poor management and bad decisions are punished by a share price fall or takeover bid.

Advantages of mutualism

Despite the advantages of demutualisation (conversion), 47 societies (end-2011) have decided to remain mutual institutions. One advantage is that they do not have to pay dividends on capital or satisfy the expectations of investment analysts. Many societies have now taken the view that they can pay a dividend to their customers via higher savings rates and lower mortgage rates than converting societies.

The Building Societies Act 1997 has also enhanced mutual status by giving societies a more liberal operating regime, while removing the five year takeover protection from converting societies. This increases the likelihood of bids from other financial institutions, such as banks, which may discourage conversion to plc status. The 1997 Act means that societies are allowed to do anything, unless it is expressly prohibited by legislation.

New mutualism has rediscovered the ethic of being a mutual institution, of realising that building societies exist to serve customers and their local communities, rather than any other group. A number of societies have taken various initiatives such as special benefits to long term mortgage customers or providing assistance to charitable and community organisations.

QUESTION TIME 49

(a) Comment on the potential advantages and disadvantages of building society mergers.
(b) How might such mergers affect the economy and depositors/borrowers?

Write your answer here then check with the answer at the back of the book.

Summary

In 2011, the FSA identified a number of problems confronting building societies, the main ones being as follows:

- A high fixed cost base due to an extensive and sometimes underutilised branch network
- Shrinkage in their mortgage market share (currently 20% of residential mortgages)
- Higher funding costs plus being less able to raise capital for solvency requirements
- A prolonged housing market downturn, together with increased mortgage arrears
- Intense competition in the house lending market from banks

Legislation in the 1980s and 1990s broke down the strict demarcation lines between traditional banking and building societies' business. Both now offer a wider and more sophisticated range of financial services attuned to user needs in a competitive market place. At the same time, as a direct result of intensive marketing and advertising, personal customers have become more selective and sophisticated in their financial needs. They now demand improved services, better information and higher returns on their money.

However, although points of contrast between retail banks and building societies have narrowed in recent years, some differences still remain:

- Banks still offer a wider range of financial services.
- Banks lend to the industrial and commercial sectors of the economy, while building societies at present lend most of their funds to the personal sector.
- Banks are profit-making public limited companies while building societies are non-profit distributing mutual societies.
- Banks are regulated by Banking Acts; building societies are subject to Building Societies Acts.

QUICK QUESTION

What are the advantages and disadvantages of demutualisation?

Write your answer here before reading on.

4.3 Co-operative Banking Group

The mutual Co-operative Banking Group (CBG) was formed in 2002 as the result of a merger between the Co-operative Bank and the Co-operative Insurance Society. In 2009 the CBG and the Britannia Building Society, which was then the second largest building society with assets of over £30 billion, merged to create the UK's most diversified mutual services provider.

In 2011, this super-mutual had assets of about £70 billion, 341 branches with a full-time staff of about 8,500 and approximately 8 million customers availing themselves of CBG banking, mortgage and insurance services.

5 Other banking competitors

5.1 Banco Santander Group

Santander was founded in Spain, operates in 40 countries and has over 12,000 branches. In terms of market capitalisation (€53 billion) it was the eleventh largest bank in the world in September 2011. At that date it had total assets of €1.25 trillion, with UK operations accounting for about 20% of the group's profits.

Its strategy has been to be a significant local participant and achieve a sizeable market share of retail banking in each country where it undertakes business. In the UK, it acquired Abbey in 2004 and the Alliance and Leicester in 2008. Both were demutualised building societies. The former had incurred heavy losses in a failed attempt to enter investment banking, while the latter was badly affected by the turbulent financial market conditions in 2008. The fall in the share price of both institutions made them a worthwhile acquisition for Banco Santander, which wished to secure entry into the UK retail banking market. In 2008 it also acquired the deposits and branches of Bradford & Bingley, which had been nationalised by the government. This was followed by the purchase of over 300 RBS branches, mainly in England.

Santander now has over 1300 branches (over 25,000 employees) in Britain, which means that it has the fourth largest branch network. It is now a major deposit taker, with 25 million UK customers and a major mortgage provider (one in six new mortgages sold) and is thus a major competitor in the banking market. Santander plans to float its UK arm on the London stock market in late 2013 or 2014, although the exact timing will depend on the UK economic environment.

5.2 Metro Bank

This new bank commenced operations from four outlets in London in 2010. It offers current and savings accounts as well as mortgages and loans. The basic aim is to offer the public a more straightforward and convenient banking service. It also provides business banking facilities. Metro Bank hopes to have over 200 outlets in the Greater London area by 2020. Similar banks might be established in other conurbations in England in the future and thereby increase consumer choice.

5.3 Virgin Money

Virgin Money was founded in1995, and is 70% owned by Richard Branson's Virgin Group. It has about 500 staff and offers credit cards, savings and investment products, plus general insurance, to its 3 million customers. At present, no mortgage or current account facilities are on offer, but this is likely to change in the near future as the intention is to lend at least £45 billion to customers by 2016.

It has recently acquired Northern Rock which adds an additional one million customers and £14 billion of mortgages to their overall operations. The enhanced Virgin Money hopes to achieve a stock exchange flotation in 2014 in order to access additional capital funds for expansion.

5.4 Supermarket banks

Tesco Bank is the trading name for Tesco Personal Finance which was founded in 1997. It is a telephone and internet bank which uses its customer base to cross-sell financial services; this is supplemented by bank branches in its largest stores. With total assets of about £10 billion, it is still a relatively small financial services provider.

Sainbury's Bank, also founded in 1997, is a joint venture owned by Sainbury's and LBG. With around 1.5 million customers, it has total assets of over £5 billion, which makes it a minor financial services provider compared to the large retail banks.

Although small in terms of asset size, supermarket banks have the advantage that customers can conduct banking business online, by phone or in-store, with the latter having extended hours and ample free car parking space. A number of store groups also offer various financial services and products, such as Marks & Spencer Money and Harrods Bank, but given the scale of their operations, these are also unlikely to become major competitors in the UK banking market in the foreseeable future.

6 Private banks

Private banking, which has expanded over the last few years, tends to be associated with names of long standing, such as Coutts & Company, Cater Allan, Hoare & Company or the relative newcomer, Adam & Company. The latter is a wholly owned subsidiary of the Royal Bank of Scotland plc, but it operates under a separate licence and has its own board of directors.

Private bank clients are people with high incomes or substantial net assets and, in many cases, private banks will be bankers to an entire family. They mostly prefer to have clients introduced to them by existing customers. The club atmosphere and informal networking is beneficial to both the bank and its clients.

Key features of private banking services are the assignment of an experienced relationship manager to look after a client's range of financial needs. There is also added value in the form of itemised statements and full narratives of income and expenditure. The relationship manager will also coordinate the various financial interests of a client, which might involve managing and advising clients about their investment portfolios. Long-term success for private banks lies in their ability to combine relationship management and personal service with modern technology. The plastic card, with its access to credit and cash throughout the world, together with the telephone, gives clients of private banks the best of both worlds.

QUICK QUESTION

What can NS & I bank facilities offer to customers compared to those of retail banks?

Write your answer here before reading on.

7 Quasi banks

7.1 National Savings and Investments (NS & I)

The idea of a national savings bank operating through the post office was proposed in the UK as long ago as 1807. However, it was not until 1861 that the National Savings Bank (NSB) was established. Deposits at the NSB were guaranteed by the state, so there was no risk of default. All deposits were placed in an account at the Bank of England and subsequently invested in government securities.

Around 2000, the NSB was absorbed into the National Savings and Investment (NS & I) department of the UK Treasury. NS & I raises funds for the government by offering a broad range of savings products to the general public. This has included fixed interest savings certificates, index-linked savings certificates, capital bonds and retirement bonds. Some of the facilities on offer provide various tax concessions or exemptions for personal savers.

NS & I also offers two types of bank accounts for use by the general public. A direct saver account (minimum deposit £1) can be managed online or by phone, offers 1.50% interest gross and withdrawals can be made at any time without penalties. An investment account is also offered with a variable tiered interest rate on outstanding balances. Interest is paid gross but is taxable. Income bonds (minimum £500) pay monthly income to holders, and can be applied for online or by phone. Only premium bonds can be purchased over the counter at post offices.

NS & I manages over £100 billion of savings (approx. 9% of the UK savings market) which is loaned to the UK Treasury and thereby accounts for about 10% of the UK's national debt.
The Post Office Bank is owned and licensed by the Bank of Ireland (UK), and provides various savers' accounts that can be accessed at the counter of almost 12,000 post offices or by phone or online.

QUICK QUESTION

What do you think is meant by financial and social exclusion?

Write your answer here before reading on.

8 Social banking

A large section of UK society is socially and financially excluded from the mainstream of economic life. Many people in poorer communities are unbanked and make little or no use of basic financial services. Most of the unbanked are unemployed or engaged in part-time work, with a cash culture reliant on benefit payments.

8.1 Social exclusion

Financial exclusion is both a symptom and a cause of social exclusion. Combating social exclusion is a government priority. Over the last 20 years, the gap between rich and poor has widened in this country. Most people in Britain benefited from rising living standards pre-2008, which was reflected in the growth and prosperity of the financial services industry, but for the poorest people, concentrated in the most deprived neighbourhoods, it was, and still is, a different story. They do not share in the increased wealth and greater opportunities that are available to others. The risk of long term poverty is high for such people, along with the prospect of poor quality health, housing and education.

In many deprived areas of cities, financial services all too often mean benefit cheques and illegal loan sharks. Many have no access to bank accounts and other financial services; in effect, they are locked into a cash economy with no access to affordable credit or mainstream savings opportunities. Accessing appropriate finance to support any type of business start-up is effectively zero.

The government believes that banks and the financial services industry as a whole should provide this section of our society with basic banking/financial services which should help to reintegrate them and improve the overall social environment of the country.

8.2 Financial exclusion

The government alone cannot overcome the problems of social exclusion, particularly in the area of financial exclusion, but they have tried to improve access to retail banking and insurance services for people living in poor neighbourhoods, along with the encouragement of enterprise. The latter necessitates better access to small firm finance and appropriate advice; obviously, this impinges on the banking industry, including credit unions.

QUICK QUESTION

Why do you think about the fact that 10% of adults do not have a current account?

Write your answer here before reading on.

8.3 Unbanked public

The government has expressed concern at the number of people without bank accounts. There is a conspicuous unbanked minority, predominantly poor and not in regular full-time work, for whom life without a bank account is inconvenient. The number involved could be about 3 million, concentrated in the most deprived neighbourhoods.

In the past it was thought that banks had turned down such potential customers, but research sponsored by the British Bankers' Association (BBA) revealed that a large number of poor people thought traditional bank facilities were not for them, the so-called self-excluded. To overcome this self-exclusion, the government believes that banks must redesign their products to better suit the circumstances and preferences of those currently without access to them. Some banks now offer new accounts where an online debit card replaces the cheque book, while access to credit is withheld until a proper banker-customer relationship develops. Credit unions in the UK have an important role to play in tackling financial exclusion.

9 Credit unions

Credit unions are relatively new to the British financial scene, although they have been around in some countries for a long time. It is estimated that over 40,000 credit unions exist in about 80 countries, with a total membership of approximately 120 million members. Credit union services are extremely popular in North America, the West Indies and Ireland. In Northern Ireland there are over 170 credit unions with 400,000 members, which is equivalent to 24% (Britain less than 2%) of the population.

Credit unions are mutual savings and loan societies providing a basic low cost banking service for people who might otherwise find it too difficult or too expensive to obtain credit. Members finance their personal borrowing from their own combined resources.

Until relatively recently, members in a credit union had to share some common bond, such as being members of the same church, living in the same locality, or working for the same employer. One possibility is for a firm to support a credit union for its staff and deduct its employees' savings automatically from their pay. In London a local taxi drivers' association has formed its own credit union, while British Airways has a credit union for its own employees. The Glasgow Credit Union is the largest in the UK with assets in excess of £60 million and over 21,000 members.

QUICK QUESTION

What sort of income group do you think credit unions cater for in the UK at present?

Write your answer here before reading on.

Each credit union is a self-governing club owned by the members themselves and run on cooperative principles. Administration is through a board of directors, a credit committee and a supervisory committee elected by and from the members Many credit unions rely to some extent on voluntary support. Members must be regular savers and can apply for small loans at moderate rates of interest to meet such expenses as holidays, weddings or even, in the winter, high fuel bills. Borrowers must continue to save while repaying their loans. Loan requests are treated in confidence and dealt with by the credit committee.

Part of the strength of credit unions is their size. Managers and members should be known to each other and loans can be granted on the basis of personal knowledge of the borrower. This is important for low income families with no financial assets to offer as security. It is also important for those groups, such as the unbanked public, whose needs and culture are outside the experience of the established financial institutions.

The operations of over 400 credit unions in the UK are governed by the Credit Unions Act 1979. The minimum permitted membership is 25. Under recent deregulation measures, the maximum permitted membership is 10,000, although this may be exceeded with permission from the Prudential Regulatory Authority.

A member's savings may exceed £5000. Credit union savings earn a dividend and the maximum rate is 8% per annum. The dividend is decided at the annual general meeting. Most mature credit unions pay a dividend (interest) of between 4% and 6%. Savings in credit unions are covered by the Financial Services Compensation Scheme. The basic rules for loans are:

1. The maximum loan is £5000 above the member's savings balance with maximum loan rate of 12.6% per annum (some of the larger credit unions do not insist on prior savings before granting small loans).
2. Loans cannot run concurrently; the first loan must be repaid before a second loan.
3. Repayment of unsecured loans can be over 4 years, while secured loans can be repaid over 5 to 10 years.
4. Business loans and mortgages are not permitted.

Free life insurance cover is provided for both loans and deposits. In the event of a member's death, outstanding loans are cancelled, while the next of kin receives twice the value of accumulated savings. Until the recent recession, less than 1% of credit union loans resulted in bad debts. This was attributed to moral suasion among the members and the common bond.

The Association of British Credit Unions Limited (ABCUL) is the main trade association for credit unions in England, Wales and Scotland, and provides advice, training and development services to help member credit unions. It has also undertaken active political lobbying to try and get legislation altered to enable credit unions to offer a wider range of financial services, such as credit cards and mortgages, to their members. ABCUL's aim is to put in place a growth-orientated strategy for credit unions so that they can play a greater role in society. In order to achieve this objective, ABCUL has sought changes to the Credit Unions Act 1979 via a Legislative Reform Order (LRO). In November 2011, this regulatory reform was approved by Parliament and came into effect in January 2012.

This reform enables credit unions to recruit new members without the need of a common bond, and also to provide loans to small businesses, community groups and social enterprises. Some larger credit unions that meet the necessary criteria will be allowed to pay regular interest on savings instead of an annual dividend and can also offer interest-paying, tax-free ISAs.

The government is investing £73 million up to 2016 to help credit unions with modernisation and expansion programmes. This should improve access for savers via online and phone banking. In addition, the Post Office has agreed to allow credit union members access to their accounts through its branch network. These measures should reduce the reliance of credit unions on taking deposits at small branches, church halls and community centres.

The economic recession in 2009 caused a number of credit unions to fail, and, as a result, regulators have encouraged mergers among credit unions in order to strengthen their overall financial position. One recommendation is that credit unions should keep at least 20% of their assets in a liquid form as deposits at a major bank. Under normal economic circumstances only about five credit unions fail each year due to bad management or fraud, and savings in credit unions are protected by the FSCS.

Q **QUESTION TIME 50**

Could credit unions pose a serious threat to retail banks and building societies in the future?

Write your answer here then check with the answer at the back of the book.

10 Peer to peer lending

Since the mid-2000s, a number of money exchange websites have been established which, by the end of 2011, accounted for over 2% (£240 million) of the UK unsecured personal loan market. These social lending websites are organised by money exchange companies such as Zopa, RateSetter, Lending Well and Funding Circle, which basically operate an online money exchange service. In exchange for their assistance in fixing up deals, they charge both lenders and borrowers a small annual fee based on the amount lent and borrowed.

These money exchange websites enable people (savers) with money to lend/provide funds to potential online borrowers. The savers, who, in many cases, are disillusioned with low rates of return from banks and other institutions, can fix their own rate of return and allow potential borrowers to access their funds if they are prepared to pay the interest rate set for the loan. Such loans can be for various time periods, but the most common loan terms are 36 or 60 months. The requests to borrow are matched to the offers to lend. In effect, this is a form of disintermediation (as described in chapter 1) – the banks are omitted from the process of recycling of funds in the economy. The omission of banks, apart from transferring funds between lenders and borrowers, eliminates the overhead costs of branch networks, and thus enables a higher interest rate to be paid to lenders and lower loan charges for borrowers. However, this parallel, or shadow, banking system is not covered by the Financial Services Compensation Scheme which guarantees deposits up to £85,000. Therefore, if borrowers default or the money exchange company fails, lenders (savers) have no protection.

In order to protect lenders, all potential borrowers are graded for risk by a credit referencing agency. Various risk bands exist and it is up to the lender to decide which risk band he/she wishes to lend their funds to and what interest rate they are prepared to offer their savings to potential borrowers. In order to reduce risk, a lender's loan is spread over many borrowers, sometimes as many as 50 clients, to reduce default risk. Lenders are more or less committed to the duration of their loan while borrowers are provided with flexible loans that can incorporate variations in monthly loan repayments and early repayment without any financial penalty. Lenders can get higher rates of return for accepting more risk if their savings are lent to less creditworthy borrowers. It is up to the lender to state what interest rate they are prepared to lend at to would-be borrowers. So far the returns for most lenders, after any bad debts and fees, have been higher than those offered by any bank, building society or the NS & I. If a lender wishes to lend more than £25,000, they must apply for a Consumer Credit Licence (which costs £110).

Bad debt risk is factored into the interest rate/price offered to potential borrowers. If a borrower defaults, the debt is normally sold to a debt collecting agency and any money recovered is paid to the lender. It is generally believed that money exchange applicants have a slightly worse credit profile in their respective risk bands than the UK average.

The money exchange companies involved in this form of direct finance have formed a Peer 2 Peer Finance Association to represent their interests in the financial services industry. Zopa (zone for possible agreement) was founded in 2005 and accounted for about 60% of the funds lent at the end of 2011. In the first quarter of 2012, RateSetter was offering a one year savings bond with an interest rate of 5% before tax, with a minimum investment of £10. It was thus targeting disgruntled savers with limited financial resources looking for a higher return on their funds. However, once again, there is no government insurance cover. It will be interesting to note over the next few years how this shadow banking system performs and whether it represents a major challenge to the banks for personal savings. It might prompt regulatory action to re-intermediate such e-Bay lending/borrowing activity within a broadened banking system in order to prevent a re-run of the Icelandic bank deposit debacle.

11 Pay day loan companies

It is estimated that around 1.2 million in the UK have used the services of pay day loan companies. This industry started to grow in the aftermath of the credit crunch, when short term credit was in short supply. Companies such as Wonga and Peachy offer short-term loans (usually for small amounts), at very high rates of interest. Typical customers using pay day loans companies are people who cannot get credit from high street banks and building societies.

These companies have caused controversy, because there is no limit on the amount of interest that they can charge customers. Annual percentage rates (APR) can be in excess of 1,000%. Pay day loan companies heavily advertise on the TV and radio to attract customers. Despite the high cost of payday loans, the industry is rapidly growing and generates more than £250 million a year in revenue.

12 Co-op Bank scandal

The Co-op Bank was plunged into crisis in November 2013 when they revealed that they would require an extra £1.5 billion of funds to recapitalise the bank. This led to the bank being taken over by two hedge funds. To make matters worse, a former chairman was accused of supplying illegal drugs.

The scandal posed some difficult questions for the UK financial regulators: Firstly, how was the former chairman given approval by the then regulator the FSA to help run a bank, when it was revealed he had very limited prior banking experience? Secondly, in light of the tougher regulations introduced in the wake of the 2008 financial crisis, how did a high street bank manage to find itself with a £1.5 billion black hole on its balance sheet? Both of these questions are currently under public scrutiny as Parliament awaits the results of a pubic enquiry.

13 The return of TSB

In September 2013 a familiar name returned to the UK high street – TSB, the Trustee Savings Bank. The TSB name was phased out 18 years ago when TSB merged with Lloyds. 600 Lloyds branches became TSB branches, as part of the process ordered by the European High Commission to increase competition in banking. This will result in TSB being broken away from Lloyds and sold in 2014. The resurgence of TSB has resulted in five million Lloyds customers becoming TSB customers. So far, no buyer has been found for TSB. Co-op was a potential suitor, but had to withdraw due to their aforementioned funding issues.

14 Islamic banking

Islamic banking is a growth area for UK banks. More than twenty banks currently offer Islamic banking products and services in the UK. While some of these products are designed for UK Muslims, the UK is also making strides in becoming a global Islamic banking hub. David Cameron, the UK Prime Minister announced in December 2013 that the UK will launch a £200m Sukuk Government bond. This is a bond that complies with Islamic law and will enable the UK to become the first non-Muslim country to tap the growing pool of Islamic investments that is forecast to top £1.3 trillion by 2014.

This will allow the UK government to offer its debt to a wider range of investors and will offer stimulus to the City of London. The London Stock Exchange is also set to unveil some Islamic finance indices, with the goal of enabling London to compete with Dubai as a leading Islamic finance centre.

15 A single banking/financial market in Europe

The European Union (EU) is by far the world's largest banking market; it has a denser branch network than the USA. Despite this, the creation of a single banking market has taken a considerable time to achieve. A first step was taken in 1977, with the adoption of the First Banking Co-ordination Directive which applied to banks and building societies in the UK. It required all such institutions to be authorised and regulated. This Directive applied the host country rule, which permitted branching by EU banks throughout member countries but authorisation/supervision was undertaken by the regulators in each host country where branches were sited.

The Second Banking Co-ordination Directive (2 BCD) became effective on 1 January 1993. It was decided from the outset that there was no hope of standardising the vast and diverse range of banking legislation and practice in the different EU countries. Instead, the Directive is based on mutual recognition by member states of each other's system of authorisation and supervision.

This step necessitated increased cooperation among the supervisory and regulatory agencies of the member states. In effect, the emphasis was shifted from host country to home country for all a bank's activities throughout the EU. The essential mechanism is a Single Banking Licence, which means that bank authorisation in one country endows an institution with a passport enabling it to operate throughout the EU.

A solvency directive has been adopted which sets the minimum capital ratio for EU credit institutions. Shareholders' funds (capital plus reserves) have to be at least 8% of risk weighted assets. An own funds directive defines capital for EU credit institutions. Both directives are similar in content to the international capital accord standards established by BCBS.

2BCD is made up of 23 Articles.

- Article 3 sets the minimum capital for a bank at €5m.
- Article 4 states that substantial shareholders must be vetted by supervisory authorities.
- Article 12 allows host countries to control bank liquidity for monetary control purposes.
- Articles 16 to 18 state that credit institutions can branch or sell services directly from their home base throughout the EU without host country authorisation. This covers the provision of core banking activities, e.g.
  - Deposit taking
  - Loans
  - Money transmission
  - Leasing
  - Portfolio management
  - Safe custody
  - Securities trading
  - Provision of financial advice
  - Travel cheques

These activities are regulated by each bank's home country central bank or supervisory agency. This provides a single banking licence (or passport) for expansion throughout the EU (an analogy is a UK driving licence enabling you to drive in the EU without taking a driving test in European countries).

The single licence, plus competitive pressures, will result, in theory, in the creation of a common market in bank services throughout the EU.

Deposit guarantee systems are compulsory and member states must provide at least €50,000 of cover for any given depositor.

QUICK QUESTION

How might customers benefit from a single banking market?

Write your answer here before reading on.

15.1 European financial integration: impact on banking

The main objective of a single EU banking market is the creation of additional benefits for consumers of banking services. These benefits are derived from two related sources.

1. The consumer benefits from increased freedom of choice via redirecting business to institutions offering lower prices for financial services or obtaining services not previously available.

2. Prices of most financial services are expected to fall over time following the creation of a larger internal market for banking products. Estimates of such possible price decreases vary for different financial products and countries, but could amount to as much as 50%. Experts believe that competition, rather than economies of scale, will be the main cost-reducing factor for customers.

Banks may try to reduce their costs by selling several services rather than individual ones. Distribution networks might thus be more fully exploited and fixed costs spread over a wider array of products. Most banks, as previously stated, now offer banking, investment and insurance services under one roof in order to benefit from the economies of scope by cross-selling financially-linked products.

Some retail banks might use mergers/acquisitions in other EU member states in order to achieve economies of scale and increase their distribution network.

It is also worth remembering that customer/client loyalty and inertia, informational advantages concerning the local economy plus the capacity to offer tailor-made services, probably provide ample room for the continuance of small, locally-based institutions within a unified banking market.

QUICK QUESTION

What factors might prevent the creation of a complete single banking market in the EU?

Write your answer here before reading on.

15.2 European cross-border banking

Overall within the EU, many financial firms – banks, insurance companies, securities firms, etc – have succeeded in identifying opportunities for cross-border acquisitions at an acceptable price. It appears that a significant proportion of these opportunities have arisen where the company or unit being acquired has been performing poorly (e.g. Santander's acquisition of Abbey).

Other options include the establishment of new operations via branches or subsidiaries in EU member states, or by the direct selling of services from the home base into foreign markets.

Whatever approach is adopted, the selling of banking and financial services by any EU retail bank is likely to prove difficult in the short run because of differences in languages, traditions and customs among the residents of the member states. Despite such problems, some banks in the EU have been quite active in forging cross-border alliances in recent years.

The single banking market is still in its preliminary stages and banks will no doubt take time to review their overall strategies to take advantage of the opportunities of a single banking market. Overall, it would appear that the expected benefits of the single market programme, (lower costs to consumers via more open markets and increased competition), have yet to be fully realised.

It seems that, as in other areas of EU development, this process may take rather longer than its proponents had originally anticipated; ultimately, however, the single market programme will have a profound impact on the financial services sector within the EU.

QUESTION TIME 51

Outline briefly the main aspects of the European Community Second Banking Directive.

Write your answer here then check with the answer at the back of the book.

15.3 Single financial services market

On 1 January 1996, a single securities market in the EU became a reality. Banks and non-banks can now receive a passport from their home regulator to deal in securities throughout EU capital markets. A single insurance market had already been created on 1 January 1994.

However, a single financial services market is still regarded by many to be a myth, due to the failure of governments to observe the spirit of EU law. Governments can still protect local institutions via the general good rule which enables them to restrict harmful competition. This has provided a loophole for protectionists in member states. Different tax regimes are also a legal barrier to a single financial services market, making it difficult to sell life assurance policies and pensions from the UK throughout the EU. However, the most entrenched barrier to a single financial services market comprises cultural and psychological factors such as brand names, customer attitudes and the risk of the unknown.

With the euro in place, the EU has a clear priority on the financial front: completing the single market in financial services. Despite various European Commission statements and plans to speed up the process, a single financial market is still not reality. On the retail side, the amount of activity in cross-border financial services is limited, mainly the result of local rules and regulations. This causes a disparity in the price of financial services in different countries.

15.4 European Banking Authority (EBA)

The EBA was established in November 2010 and became operational on 1 December 2011, taking over the tasks of the Committee of European Banking Supervisors. The EBA aims to ensure the stability of the financial system in the EU, improve market transparency and protect depositors. In order to achieve these aims, it hopes to create a level playing field as regards competition in banking, strengthen supervision and provide advice to EU banks. The latter entails setting minimum capital-asset ratios for banks, as well as ensuring that more publicly-held information on the asset portfolios of EU banks is available to investors and clients.

KEY WORDS

Key words in this chapter are given below. There is space to write your own revision notes and to add any other words or phrases that you want to remember.

- Rationalisation/restructuring of bank operations
- Government intervention in banking market
- Building societies
- Co-operative Banking Group
- Mutual institutions
- Santander and Virgin Money
- Supermarket banks
- Co-op Bank and TSB
- National Savings and Investment
- Financial exclusion
- Social banking and credit unions
- Single banking licence
- Cross border banking
- European Banking Authority

REVIEW

The main learning points introduced in this chapter are summarised below.

Go through them and check back to the learning outcomes at the beginning of the chapter. Only move on when you are happy that you fully understand each point.

- We have examined the current banking, financial and economic environment. Increased competition between existing and new deposit takers, along with the need to make adequate profits, has encouraged the rationalisation and restructuring of the banking industry.
- Trends in the banking sector indicate that further rationalisation/restructuring is likely to take place that will have an impact on the number of branches and staff levels. Competition and new technology are likely to reinforce this trend.
- Mutual building societies will be subject to the same pressures with the possibility that more mergers will take place.
- We considered a number of new competitors – Santander, supermarket banks, etc – in the banking market and how they might increase competition and consumer choice.
- We also examined the concept of social banking, the basic aim of which is to reduce social and financial exclusion in our society which marginalises a large number of our fellow citizens.
- We concluded with an examination of various aspects of the single European banking and financial market, and the obstacles to its attainment at present.

chapter 15

INNOVATION AND TECHNOLOGY IN BANKING

Contents

Learning outcomes

On completion of this chapter, you should be able to:

- Examine the impact of technology on the branch network.
- Review developments in internet banking and mobile phone technology together with associated risks.
- Assess the use of expert systems in banks and how these might affect staff levels and delivery systems.
- Critically evaluate technological risks/cyber crime in banking and how banks seek to control such threats.
- Describe hardware/software developments in banking.

Introduction

At this stage in your studies you should be aware that there has been a huge growth in the volume of services available from banks, and this has led to more active selling policies. Of necessity in a rapidly changing global technological environment, banks have to constantly review their distribution channels, which entails developing new delivery modes using modern technology such as e-banking and m-banking. Such technology has had and will continue to have a significant impact on the more traditional ways of delivering financial services, such as the bank branch.

The use of computers in banking has assisted the development of expert systems whereby a computer can undertake tasks and solve problems previously only undertaken by highly skilled staff. This speeds up decisions and helps to reduce costs.

Although computer technology is hugely beneficial to banks, the accompanying downside is increased technological risk such as cyber crime, which requires banks to invest in appropriate systems of protection. International guiding principles have been devised for banks and their supervisors to follow in order to protect the global banking system.

Financial services organisations must constantly update their computer systems and be fully aware of innovations/developments in hardware and software, with the primary aim of improving customer services.

In this chapter we will consider some of the key aspects of delivery of bank services and the impact of technology on banking, including:

- Distribution channels and remote banking
- Impact on the number and operations of bank branches
- Expert systems in banking
- Technological risks in banking
- Developments as regards hardware/software and digital banking

1 Distribution channels and remote banking

Banking as an industry has experienced a great deal of change over the past thirty or so years. Some of this change can be attributed to the arrival of technology, but a great deal is also about the changing demands of customers. Up until fairly recently, the branch was the bank, and the customer's own branch was the centre of their banking universe, whether they needed to carry out any activity on their account, arrange a loan, withdraw or pay in cash – all of this had to be channelled through the branch.

The beginning of the shift away from this rather restricted culture was evidenced by the introduction of ATMs in the early 1970s. The ATM was developed primarily to reduce the amount of time each cashier spent on cash withdrawals, and was therefore essentially a cost-saving initiative. However, it did give the customer an alternative route for obtaining cash from their account, and despite some initial distrust, very quickly became a popular service.

One consequence of this extra distribution channel is that customers have less need to visit their branch. As technology allows more and more customers' needs to be dealt outside the branch environment, customers are becoming less and less dependent on their home branch.

QUICK QUESTION

Which banking services do you regularly use? How many of these necessitate a visit to your branch?

Write your answer here before reading on.

Like many people, you will probably find that a great deal of your banking activity is either:

- Automated – like salary payments, direct debits and standing orders
- Carried out outside banking hours through an ATM or a telephone banking service unit or via the internet

The automation of much of our requirements has made banking a simpler and more convenient experience for many of us; however, the impact of these changes has made banking more remote. Remote banking means that the customer becomes physically distanced from the providers of the service. On many occasions, the customer will not even need to speak with a member of staff, as the technological interface allows all of their instructions or requests to be carried out without human intervention. It also means that the customer has a choice of outlets, and is not tied to just one location or one bank.

1.1 Delivery channels

In banking there are now several ways to provide the customer with access to their account. Each delivery, or distribution, channel will appeal to a different set of customers at a different time, and many customers will make use of several of them, depending on their needs at that point in time. There are several ways by which customers can access their accounts and carry out transactions:

- Visit their branch in person
- Use an ATM
- Telephone their branch or telephone banking services
- Use a personal computer or mobile phone to access their account details

Branch visit

Bank branches enable customers to conduct their personal banking business face-to-face with the bank staff, whether it is seeking advice or paying/drawing cash from their account. The branch still provides customers with a one-stop shop of banking services which allows them to access the full range of banking activities. As customers' lifestyles change, visiting branches is now less common.

Using the ATM

A very popular way for customers to access their bank account is through the Automated Teller Machine (ATM). The ATM reduces the amount of time and resources spent on cashier activities within the branch network. Most ATMs are usually located just outside or actually inside the branch, which allows customers to self serve without having to go into their branch. Customers can also use the ATMs of any bank within a linked network, and are therefore not restricted to using only the ATMs of the bank where their accounts are held.

Realising that the cash machine was becoming an accepted method by which customers could access their accounts and that it requires very little in the way of maintenance, the banks decided to capitalise on this channel of delivery and add increased functionality to it.

QUICK QUESTION

What functions can ATMs now perform?

Write your answer here before reading on.

Many ATMs can now:

- Accept deposits
- Process a cheque book request
- Send out marketing information
- Print out the customer's balance
- Pay bills
- Change the customer's Personal Identification Number (PIN)
- Transfer money between the customer's accounts
- Top up mobile phones

Far from being mono-functional, ATMs are now a delivery channel in their own right and can be located in a wide variety of places. Customers can withdraw cash at their local petrol station, supermarket, railway station or shopping precinct, thus giving them access to their accounts when they are likely to need it most. This represents a significant step forward in customer service.

Telephone banking

Although customers have used the telephone for many years to contact their branches, it is only in the last 15 years that this service has developed as a delivery channel in its own right. The service is now comprehensive, and offers customers almost all of the functionality that they would expect to get from an actual visit to their branch.

PC banking

Many banks have developed a personal computer (PC) based version of their telephone service units which allows customers to access their accounts using a PC. The bank's computer and the customer's computer connect with each other through a secure gateway and the customer can then view and transact on their account online. The service offers all the convenience of the telephone service, with the added advantage of being able to view the account on-screen.

QUICK QUESTION

What are the advantages and disadvantages to banks of telephone banking?

Write your answer here before reading on.

2 Telephone banking

A major electronic development in recent years has been the advent of telephone banking. Customers call in to a central call centre to make enquiries about their accounts, pay bills, make transfers, and so on. Nearly all banks now operate direct banking services with telephone access 24 hours a day. These services operate on the customer's existing account and thus have the advantage that they do not need a new account to be opened. The customer's identity is established by way of a personal identity number and a password to ensure that information is not given out to unauthorised parties.

Using telephone banking helps to achieve two objectives:

- It removes the task of responding to customer enquiries from the branches, enabling staff there to concentrate on tasks that have to be branch-based.
- Provision of a better service to customers through the use of specially trained staff using specialist computer software.

2.1 Telephone banks

A number of banks have been established whose only contact with their customers is over the telephone. Customers have access to the normal range of account services – cheque books, plastic cards, standing orders, direct debits, etc, while cash withdrawal facilities are available through ATM reciprocity agreements with other banks.

In the UK, the first major development of this type of bank was First Direct by the Hong Kong & Shanghai Banking Group (HSBC). This is operated as a separate bank which undertakes all dealings with customers over the phone or by correspondence. Customers can ring in 24 hours a day to speak to someone about the transactions they wish to make. After a slow start, this operation gained momentum and has now attracted a substantial number of customers.

Other players have now entered the field, including large retailers, such as Tesco. Not only do these organisations offer their customers very competitive interest rates because of their highly cost-effective way of conducting banking business, they also offer innovative forms of account which combine the features of several traditional account types.

QUESTION TIME 52

(a) What is the difference between direct banking and offering a telephone service?
(b) Explain the term remote banking.

Write your answer here then check with the answer at the back of the book.

QUICK QUESTION

What type of customer is most likely to use telephone banking?

Write your answer here before reading on.

The general profile of a telephone banking customer includes the following characteristics:

- Usually 24-55 age group
- Financially astute
- Salaried professionals

Although a generalisation of typical users, such a profile is useful to the bank to identify potential users of telephone services.

Despite telephone banking being popular, some customers still have concerns regarding it. Many customers prefer personal contact with their bank, which is a legacy of the way that banking services were delivered in the past. Before the advent of telephone banking, most financial products were sold to customers after an interview with a bank official so some customers regard the process now as rather impersonal. What banks have to do is convince the customer that they will receive the same quality of service via a telephone. Another concern is security, as many potential customers fear their personal account details might be obtained and used fraudulently by some other person. To deal with this problem, each customer must be able to verify their identity and provide the password and/or number to access the system. Bank employees must not be able to by-pass the security system and indulge in fraud. For additional security, telephone calls with customers are recorded. In this way, banks are taking measures to reassure their customers that telephone banking is secure.

More customers are now using this delivery system because of the widespread use of phones to purchase a wide range of services. Increased familiarity with other information technologies is also encouraging the use of phone banking. Similarly, changes in customers' lifestyles and working practices are motivating them to seek a bank service that is convenient and cost effective.

The huge growth of the call centre has facilitated the development of technology that harnesses the capabilities of the computer and the telephone simultaneously. Computer Telephony Integration (CTI) enables computers and telephones to be linked to help improve the effectiveness of the call centre. CTI shows the customer's details on-screen and puts the call through to an adviser at the same time. Thus, an enhanced level of service can be provided to the customer by combining the processing power of computers with the accessibility and convenience of the telephone. CTI can also be used for outbound calling to automatically dial a number while simultaneously inputting the customer's details on-screen. This saves adviser time from the need to search for the correct customer record.

QUICK QUESTION

What are the main benefits of internet banking for both customers and the banking services provider?

Write your answer here before reading on.

3 Internet banking

The internet/worldwide web, a global online communications system, can be accessed through a personal computer. By subscribing to an internet services provider, users can access the internet to make use of a vast range of services, including electronic mail, news services, social networking, online shopping and so much more. The first place to look for information on just about anything is now, for many people, the internet. It is absolutely essential in the 21st century for any individual or organisation that wants to publicise their activities or sell their products and services to the global online community to have a website. This applies equally to financial services organisations, especially when competing globally with other financial services providers, where an informative, easy-to-use, well-designed website can provide potential customers with all they want to know about products and services. Nearly all banks have now developed their own versions of PC/ online banking.

There are two types of internet banks:

- Standalone banks which, due to lower overheads, are sometimes able to offer competitive interest rates and service charges.
- Clicks and mortar banks which provide branch and telephone accounts plus internet facilities.

Interest rates on offer under such facilities are similar to branch deposit account rates. It is possible that the lower operating costs of online banking might be passed on to customers using such facilities for most of their banking business.

Initially the number of internet bank users was lower than expected for a number of banks. This was attributed to the following factors, some of which are still evident.

1 A number of households were/still are without PCs, particularly among the over 65s. There is still a large segment of the population who do not use the internet through choice or a lack of interest.

2 Delays in conducting banking business at peak times, which results in prolonged time spent on the internet, thus increasing user cost.

3 Adequacy of immediate technical support if assistance is required by online users. A supplementary telephone helpline can prove to be expensive. Thus, difficulties as regards 'real time' assistance and associated costs can perhaps defeat the purpose of using the internet as a banking channel.

4 Bank computers are sometimes subject to failure, which can also hinder the online users' access.

5 Worries over the safety of financial information have been a major concern to existing and potential users of online banking facilities. Some bank customers fear that adequate security measures have not yet been put in place.

3.1 Internet banking benefits

Internet banking generates considerable cost savings for banks as it is a cheaper delivery channel than the main traditional physical channels such as branch and telephone banking. Such cost savings are derived from the more efficient utilisation of the workforce, equipment and office space.

Bank consultants in the USA have found that the cost of an average payment transaction on the Internet is $0.13 or less, compared to $0.54 for telephone banking service and $1.08 for a transaction conducted in a bank branch. That means that costs of internet banking are only 15% of income compared to the banking industry's average cost-income ratio of 60%. This fact, combined with the low set-up costs of establishing an internet bank, means that the traditional retail banking sector could face severe competition from standalone internet banks.

Internet banking also has the potential to increase a bank's customer base by attracting new customers, particularly those who are educated in the use of the internet. It also enables banks to conduct marketing campaigns without incurring charges associated with the traditional media such as TV and newspapers. The costs of designing a web page are limited to its development costs and customers can be guided through a catalogue of products and services, including insurance and share dealing facilities, offered by a bank. Due to the global dimension of the internet, a bank can expand into markets beyond the UK.

A bank can collect information on the customer automatically and so adapt its offerings to suit the changing needs of the customer, as well as using such information to identify any potential cross-selling opportunities and thereby targeting the right products to the right customers at the right time.

Faster Payments

A key breakthrough in UK internet banking occurred in 2008, when the Faster Payments Service (FPS) was launched. FPS is a free service designed to reduce the time it takes to transfer money between different banks. Prior to FPS, it typically took around three working days to transfer money online between different banks. FPS facilitated payment within the same day and usually completed transactions within a few hours. FPS can be used for one-off payments and standing orders and is supported by most major UK banks and building societies.

Problems with internet banking

NatWest customers were plunged into chaos in June 2012 when an IT meltdown resulted in them not being able to view their bank balances and make and receive payments into their bank accounts for a week. The problem occurred due to a software release that caused the online banking system to shut down. NatWest had to extend the opening hours of its branches to deal with the huge volume of customer queries and complaints. Customers were not able to pay their bills or access their wages.

Although NatWest did agree to waive any charges that arose to customers in this period, it highlighted the high risk associated with online banking.

Internet banking customer services

Banking services offered over the internet vary from bank to bank. The main service is instant and up-to-date access to account information. Some banks offer only deposit accounts and credit cards via the internet. In most cases it is possible to transfer funds between accounts, initiate/alter/cancel standing orders and direct debits, activate electronic bill payment and apply for loans.

Those customers who use internet banking find it convenient and cost efficient, and fees are often lower than traditional banking fees. Information from an account can be transferred onto a spreadsheet and personal finance software packages enhance the ability of internet bank users to more actively manage their financial affairs.

Banking via the internet has a number of benefits for customers.

- Convenience and up-to-the-minute availability – instant access to current information and banking services on a 24 hour basis, 7 days a week, without the need to visit a branch.
- Easier money management – transfer of funds between accounts; activate standing orders and direct debits; make automated payments; cheques and regular payments can easily be verified, etc.
- Sharing of information means that a customer and an adviser can look at the same information on screen and interact online.
- Use of e-mail (rather than a letter) to resolve a problem or initiate some action quickly.
- With the advent of digital technology it is now possible for customers to access the web through their TV in an easy-to-use format.
- Customers can chat directly with bank staff online to resolve any queries or questions.
- Customers can apply for new banking products online, such as credit cards and Individual Savings Accounts (ISAs).

3.2 Mobile phone technology and m-banking

The use of mobile phone technology has increased rapidly in recent years. Most banks offer mobile banking via an iPhone, iPad, Android or Blackberry. M-banking users download their bank's app and must already be registered for online banking. The service is free, secure and easy to use, although a charge may be made by the mobile network operator. Mobile phone top-ups are debited directly to m-banking users' accounts.

A personal customer can use their iPhone, etc to make payments such as utility bills, credit cards or transfer funds. The balance in the account can be checked, plus recent transactions. A weekly balance alert can be arranged for a particular day and time. Limit alerts can also be made if the balance in the account goes above or below a set amount. A mobile banking helpdesk can also be available to assist customers with any problems they may encounter using m-banking, as well as extensive guides on how to conduct m-banking in a safe manner, with many security hints on how to prevent fraud.

Mobile phone banking (m-banking) is also available to business banking customers and can assist greatly in the management of cash flow within a firm. The ready access to information on a business account as regards inflows and outflows of funds, regular payments and limit alerts enables owners/managers to concentrate their minds on ensuring the success of their business venture.

Another consequence of digital banking becoming more sophisticated is that mobile banking and online banking together will perhaps take over from the branch network as the main means of conducting banking business. Already with the rapid growth of mobile technology, financial services companies are evaluating how to integrate apps into their marketing plans. In addition, with people spending 25% of their time online on social networks such as Facebook (30 million users in the UK) and Twitter, the banks are giving consideration as to how this form of social media can be used to market their banking services to potential customers.

3.3 Other related technology

Some smart phones with a sticker on the back of the handset can be swiped over a till in order to make a payment; in effect the mobile becomes a digital wallet and makes obsolete the need for cash, credit cards and cheques while shopping or eating out, etc. If adopted on a large enough scale, this could herald a move towards a cashless society, although such predictions have been made for over two decades and yet people still use cash.

Attempts have been made to encourage people to purchase hi-tech watches containing a chip which is loaded up with spending power from an online account. The watch is tapped on a special terminal to pay for goods and services acquired by the watch owner and thus avoids the need for a direct debit from a bank account. It is envisaged that such watches would initially be used for relatively small payments. Again the aim is to reduce the use of bank notes and coins in society. Only the passage of time will confirm whether such technology will actually create a truly cashless society.

3.4 Banking in the future

Without a crystal ball, it is very difficult to map the path which customers' expectations and technology will create for the banking world. It is only possible to indicate the likely future direction of banking as a whole, but with technology advancing at such a pace the actual possibilities for the future are hard to quantify.

Some certainties do exist, however:

- The customer will demand more and more flexible access to their accounts, and technology, in whatever shape or form, will help them to achieve this.
- The level of service given to customers will be what differentiates one bank from another. In order to remain competitive, banks must always keep customers at the forefront of everything they do. Developing a customer service culture impacts on every aspect of the business, from product design to staff training to service delivery, and it is the key to the future.

QUICK QUESTION

What factors do you think have impacted on the role of the branch network?

Write your answer here before reading on.

3.5 Impact on the branch network

The role of the bank branch has had to adapt and change in line with each bank's strategy and changes in its external and internal operating environment. Several factors have helped to reshape the role of the branch network in retail banking in the UK, the three most important of which are as follows.

Technology

Technological enhancements plus alternative delivery channels mean that the branch is no longer the hub of the banking industry. New technology has given customers the ability to access many services outwith a branch and the core banking hours.

Relationship or transactional banking?

Technology advances in the 1980s and 1990s led to a cultural shift in banking: Where as banks used to pride themselves on creating strong relationships with customers through their branch network, they began to concentrate on reducing costs and focusing on providing low-cost transactions. The reliance on technology to automate credit scoring and lending applications is attributed by some as a reason behind the financial crisis in 2008. Therefore, banks must decide if their future strategy will be based on purely transactions, or perhaps a step back to rebuild traditional relationships with customers.

Centralisation of back office tasks

There has been a move towards centralisation of routine branch tasks in order to streamline bank processes and reduce operating costs. This has delivered economies of scale to the banks and allowed branch staff to concentrate more on sales and customer service. However, this has had an adverse effect on jobs in the UK, as banks often decide to locate centralised back office centres in locations with cheaper labour costs, such as India and Singapore.

The end of free banking

Some banking critics have hailed that the era of free banking is over and that all banks will start introducing charges for even basic bank accounts. This is because of the current low interest rate environment (which reduces a banks margin between loans and deposits) and the cost of banking regulation. Some banks, such as HSBC actively market their fee-paying accounts, due to the additional benefits that they provide to customers, such as travel insurance. However, some customers may choose to use other financial services providers such as Credit Unions should banks start to introduce fees across the board.

Customer behaviour

As customers have adapted to and become regular users of new technology available, they no longer need to visit branches within certain time constraints. As many customers no longer routinely visit a branch, it becomes more difficult to increase sales through an incidental encounter at an enquiries desk.

The combination of these factors has led to a redefinition of the role of the branch network and, as a result, many branches have been closed. However, few banks will close all their branches because well-sited ones are a valuable source of income for banks. Branches are also used to maintaining a bank presence in the high street which is a form of marketing by keeping the bank's name in the public arena. What most banks have done in their remaining branches is to completely upgrade the facilities available to customers, with the aim of making banking more friendly and appealing. Many branches are now open plan, with more space devoted to the customer and less to the staff.

QUICK QUESTION

How could expert systems enable banks to increase their operating profits?

Write your answer here before reading on.

3.6 Expert systems in banking

Conventional computer programs use algorithmic routines and repetitive processes to perform tasks which require the use of conventional decision-making logic. Expert systems use expertise knowledge as data or rules within the computer to solve problems. Although not replicating human intelligence, an expert computer program mimics the reasoning capability of human experts and therefore there is a wider distribution and access to scarce human knowledge. It is for this reason that such programs are also known as knowledge-based systems. Program knowledge is often embedded as part of the programming code to reason through a problem(s) using appropriate knowledge.

Expert systems provide the technology to handle large volumes of transactions at an ever-decreasing cost. A platform for new products and delivery costs is thereby created, while at the same time costs are reduced by the computer program performing tasks previously undertaken by highly remunerated employees. The system seeks to exploit specialised skills or information held by a group of people on specific aspects of banking such as credit card applications. Expert systems do not replace people, but instead augment them and makes their contribution to the bank more effective. It means that minor or major problems can be solved by non-experts within a reasonable timeframe. Thus, expert systems enable banks to achieve improved economies of scope and scale.

Expert systems use heuristics (learning by investigation) and inferential processes to perform difficult and specialised tasks at the level of a human expert. Heuristics is a judgemental knowledge acquired through personal experience by experts such as that of experienced loan officers and other experts in a bank. An inference mechanism or engine controls the reasoning operations of the expert system. Most expert systems are developed via the use of specialised software tools, referred to as shells, which are equipped with inference mechanisms, Knowledge is entered according to specified formats with special features such as interfaces with external programs.

An expert system is basically a computer program designed to use appropriate knowledge/rules to produce and make decisions and is based on logic. Extensive analysis is required by experts before developing rules that result in the building of expert systems. In lending decisions, for example, there is a high element of subjective assessments required which must be considered and given appropriate weighting in the development of an expert system. The expert system's purpose is to provide a bank with a consistent, thorough and objective decision-making process that can be used by staff, regardless of their skills or lack of expert knowledge/experience. The expert system recommends specific actions by applying uniformity of knowledge and decision rules that attempt to replicate the way decisions are made by human experts in relation to particular problems. In this sense, expert systems are a form of artificial intelligence which allows highly technically skilled tasks to be undertaken by less skilled people within a bank.

Although expert systems cannot completely replace human intervention in making decisions, when joined to human resources they increase the likelihood of the correct decision being made as regards a loan request, for example. A loan manager can always interview a potential borrower and therefore still make a subjective judgement on whether or not to provide the loan facility. An expert system, as of yet, cannot provide such interaction. This does not mean that expert systems will never be able to completely replicate such human intervention.

Advances in computing power and the further development of artificial intelligence systems might be able to provide expert systems that are so highly accurate and reliable that complex human decision making is replaced. Such expert systems in the future might be used to detect fraud and money laundering in the banking system more effectively than existing computer programs and human input. However, before the advent of thinking, listening and talking machines – banking terminators – that will provide a fully automated bank with no human involvement, the development costs and recognition that expert systems will not be completely infallible will have to be taken on-board by banks. Would the general public seeking the provision of financial services wish a completely de-humanised banking system?

At present, expert systems have a number of applications within banks:

- Credit evaluation/scoring, particularly in relation to mortgage and personal loan requests

- Dealing with requests for online insurance quotes and credit card applications
- Investment portfolio management/evaluation in relation to optimal holdings and market price movements
- Financial planning within the bank whereby statistics can be analysed and forecasts made to assist with asset-liability management
- Assisting top management in problem solving and decision making in order to improve overall performance/profitability
- Evaluating economic and financial conditions impacting upon the bank's operating environment.

Expert systems also provide a bank with innumerable cost savings and other benefits:

- Such systems generate considerable cost savings through the better utilisation of staff who do not need to be paid the salaries of highly skilled experts
- Better use is made of available data which improves overall efficiency within the bank and also improves the service quality delivered to customers
- Human expertise, apart from being expensive, is also scarce and is ultimately lost through retirement. Expert systems enable such knowledge to be stored and used by average practitioners in the future without the need for extensive thought processes to be undertaken
- Risk management systems should be improved, which hopefully leads to increased profits and shareholder value

QUICK QUESTION

From your own personal experience, what are some technology risks in banking?

Write your answer here before reading on.

3.7 Technology risks

To a great extent, banking is about the management of risks – credit risk, liquidity risk, and market risk – but these types of risk can be managed separately in the various divisions of a bank. Technological risk, however, is all encompassing as technology impacts upon the entire operations of a bank. Technology enables a bank to develop and deliver products and services to customers and to manage credit risk, for example, more effectively. An understanding of the key role of technology in a bank enables top management to look at potential risk from this source in the overall business strategy.

Technology risk assessment must consider what role technology plays in the gathering, processing and storing of information. It is here that potential risks must be identified, especially in the interconnections with other internal and external systems. Information flows – data entry, transfer and storage – must be fully understood as this is where potential weaknesses might be uncovered. It is also essential to classify data as being highly confidential, confidential or 'in the public domain, as this will determine what transmission path should be used and how the data should be stored. Highly confidential data should only be transmitted over very secure pathways and stored in tightly controlled servers. The outsourcing strategy must also be considered, particularly relationships with service providers where the role and responsibilities of each party must be clearly set out. Overall assessment of technology risk must consider outsourced systems as extensions of the organisation's own internal networks.

Once the information flows are fully understood, senior management should be able to identify any potential gaps in the system so that improvements can be made to the security system and any vulnerable areas eliminated. However, this can be complicated by the introduction of new hardware and software to improve customer services, which will add to the complexity of the information system and perhaps create new security flaws. A bank must keep abreast of such technological developments by continually up-dating the security systems. This should include the processes in place at service providers/partners and ensuring that these are sufficiently secure from threats. Data transfer points require special attention to identify weaknesses that may compromise critical or sensitive information. Outsourced service providers must be viewed to a certain extent as a component of a bank's system and thus be evaluated for the technology risk they may pose to the internal system.

Any identified weaknesses in existing controls and security processes must be addressed as they can be exploited by unscrupulous parties and inflict great harm. Are appropriate controls in place as regards highly classified information? Has more advanced hardware and software compromised the security systems of older models? Can service providers neutralise vulnerabilities in their own systems? Positive answers to these questions are required to reduce information risk.

Threats arise when active agents exploit weaknesses in the control and security of technology systems. Sometimes the threats are internal – from disgruntled or incompetent employees, contractors or service providers – whereas external threats come from hackers, competitors or terrorists. Up to the year 2000 most threats came from former insiders who exploited retained information or previous access rights to data. Now, with increased internet use, external threats from malicious hackers and recreational hackers have become more common. Hackers can infect programs via a worm which replicates itself and clogs up networks, destroying data in the process. Such an occurrence raises questions about the integrity of the systems, with a resultant cost involved in solving the problem. The capability, motivations and likelihood of such hacker attacks must be assessed and appropriate action taken to mitigate their impact on genuine customers, a bank's reputation and overall financial position. Obviously, significant and potentially damaging threats must been given urgent attention, especially where weak internal controls have allowed fraudulent transactions to take place.

Broadly, there are three approaches – not mutually exclusive – to managing technology risk: use internal processes/controls, or outsource such activity, or transfer risk via an insurance policy. Each approach has benefits and costs, thus whatever is the optimal mix for the particular organisation needs to be determined. The first depends on the organisation's own internal resources and ability to develop/administer the necessary in-house controls. Some form of information technology audit might be required to test transactions and internal supervisory procedures. The second involves outsourcing, on either a temporary or a permanent basis, to contractors with the required expertise. This option might be suitable for a small bank or the provision of security mechanisms for a particular project in a large bank. The third option is some form of cyber insurance. The final decision of which approach, or mixture of approaches, to adopt will be influenced by the organisation's own internal capabilities and level of risk acceptance. What is essential is that all banks offering internet banking services must have sound and robust risk management systems capable of identifying, measuring and responding to technology risk.

QUICK QUESTION

What is cyber crime?

Write your answer here before reading on.

3.8 Digital banking risks

Digital banking of course refers to the provision of banking services via electronic delivery channels, based on computer networks and the internet, online using a PC or some mobile device. Banks reliant on information technology and the internet to operate their business and interact with other participants in the banking/financial markets implies increases risks which must be countered by robust risk management systems. There has to be recognition of the fact that the internet network is intrinsically insecure. For an information service that is basically one-way, involving advertisements and promotional material, the potential risks are relatively low, as long as it is not subjected to hacking. A transactional service, on the other hand, where customers can execute online transactions, is significantly more at risk of penetration by outsiders if the internal and external threats to the system are not identified and controlled.

Cyber crime is an ongoing threat to digital banking, particularly as financial data is stored and transmitted online, where the crime of identity theft, for example, is a constant threat. Although data in transit can be attacked, the biggest threat from hackers relates to the storage of data in desktops and servers. Organised crime targets servers, remote users and hosting companies. All these potential threats have to be countered by layered security, firewalls and intrusion detection systems, etc. In an attempt to reduce identity theft, banks are already testing multiple factor authentication via additional components of personal identification such as palm or iris scans (biometrics) as well as a password. In addition, it is essential to have incident response plans in place in order to maintain customer confidence in the integrity of online banking services.

Mobile phone banking (m-banking) poses additional risks:

- A handset can be easily lost or stolen.
- The security of data messages and instructions from the handset to the bank is dependent on the level of information security put in place by the mobile network operator.

Obviously, banks must issue strict instructions to their m-banking customers regarding access to their phones or what to do in the event of losing their handset. Online security lies in recognising shared responsibilities between banks and their customers. Network operators' systems must be thoroughly checked to ensure that security of the system is given highest priority. As the functionality of handsets increases, m-banking/financial services is converging ever closer to straight internet banking and the risks associated with this type of banking must receive increased attention from the banking services providers.

QUESTION TIME 53

Discuss how the increased use of expert and digital systems in banks might affect their staff recruitment policy and need for branch networks.

Write your answer here then check with the answer at the back of the book.

3.9 Basel risk management principles for e-banking

The Basel Committee on Banking Supervision (BCBS) has recognised the risks associated with e-banking and, as a result, has issued a set of Risk Management Principles (RMPs) specifically relating to electronic banking. These RMPs note the increased dependency of banks on third parties that provide the necessary information technology. This in turn has modified some of the traditional risks associated with banking, such as operational, legal and reputational risks, and has thereby affected the overall risk profile of banking. The BCBS believes it is necessary for the senior management of banks to continually review and modify their existing risk management policies to cover existing and planned e-banking activities.

The BCBS has identified 14 RMPs relating to electronic banking. These are not so much requirements but rather supervisory expectations in recognition of the fact that setting detailed requirements would be counter-productive and would soon become outdated due to rapid technological advances in e-banking services. The BCBS also realised that each bank's risk profile is different and thus management must tailor risk control policies to suit their own particular needs.

The RMPs are to be used by national bank regulators with adaptations to suit individual banks and country circumstances. Apart from national variations, certain key risks must be addressed, such as outsourcing arrangements, security controls and implications of legal and reputational issues specific to the use of internet distribution channels.

The RMPs can be classified into three categories.

1. Management oversight – banks must ensure that the security infrastructure provides proper safeguards for e-banking systems against internal and external threats.
2. Security controls – banks must protect customer stored data and the integrity of transactional data; audit trails for e-banking must be in place, together with measures to preserve confidentiality.
3. Legal/reputational risk management – banks must ensure that e-banking services are delivered in a consistent manner to customers and have incident response plans in place to deal with continuity issues and external/ internal threats.

These RMPs are under constant review by the BCBS to ensure their relevance in light of technological developments in relation to e-banking services, both on a national and global scale.

3.10 Hardware/software developments

Hardware

A wide range of computers is used in banks to carry out day-to-day operations, such as activating transactions, processing customer requests, preparing forecasts and internal/external reports and so on. Banking-specific hardware to drive and support information systems can be classified into three main types: mainframe computers, minicomputers, and a variety of microcomputers from PCs to digital assistants.

Mainframe computers are large in size and can occupy an entire room. These have tremendous storing, processing and computational capability and can handle large volumes of data, performing thousands of transactions per second. If you use an ATM to withdraw cash you are linked to the bank's mainframe computer. The head office of a bank is linked to the branch terminals through the mainframe computer. Thus, multiple users can access the same computer simultaneously, processing customer needs quickly at a reduced labour cost.

Faster and more powerful mainframe servers are being developed all the time, although they are not quite in the league of supercomputers which can perform complicated calculations used in weather forecasts and complex scientific computations associated with astrophysics. With mainframe computers, some applications were written years ago, while new applications being continually developed are also able to work with existing programs – in other words, there is compatibility.

Minicomputers come in sizes somewhere between a mainframe and personal computer. Their main functions are as internet servers and network servers to file storage systems and run email systems. Such computers are capable of supporting over 60 terminals.

Personal computers, or microcomputers, come in a variety of forms such as a desktop, laptop or hand-held personal digital assistants. Such devices are used for word processing, spreadsheet work or accessing the mainframe computer, depending on the software.

Software

Software is the programming that in effect tells the computer what it can do. Banking software is becoming ever more sophisticated, driven by the need for banks to stay ahead of competitors in the financial services industry and the necessity of utilising the latest innovations in software to provide the best possible customer service. The only constant in software is change and innovation. Banking software companies, such as Misys in the UK, tend to lack longevity themselves, as new companies replace or supersede existing ones.

Banking software, geared to meet customer needs, provides easy-to-use menus, automatic updates and facility to view account transactions, sometimes also including an option to assist customers, both personal and business, with active money management. However, as with other areas of e-banking, security of systems is an absolute priority and the software has to be constantly developed to tackle the threats of cyber crime.

Developments in software enable banks to operate more efficiently and more cost effectively, which is a major consideration in the current economic/financial environment. Software comes in various forms, such as those used for core banking services, loan origination, cross-selling financial services and internal risk management, etc. Some software is designed to meet the niche needs of banks, such as electronic transactions between banks and stock markets, or the need for continuous rebalancing of asset portfolios. Such software must of course be compatible with other programs and the hardware that a bank uses.

With vast numbers of software companies producing new innovative products, there is the need for financial services providers to remain alert for updates. This technology professionals can log into bank software sites through trade groups or subscribe to software application publications/ newsletters. Although saving resources and speeding up transactions, purchase of new software is a major expense, so research to find the best software for specific applications should always be undertaken. Up to 2012 the state of uncertainty in the banking sector has made many institutions put off making decisions on new products, including market-leading trading programs.

QUESTION TIME 54

Using text material and your own personal experience both as a customer and employee of a financial services organisation, critically evaluate technological risk and its control.

Write your answer here then check with the answer at the back of the book.

KEY WORDS

Key words in this chapter are given below. There is space to write your own revision notes and to add any other words or phrases that you want to remember.

- Distribution/delivery channels
- ATMs
- Cyber crime
- Digital banking
- Expert systems
- Internet banking
- Mobile banking
- Rationalisation
- Hardware
- Software
- Technological risks

REVIEW

The main learning points introduced in this chapter are summarised below.

Go through them and check back to the learning outcomes at the beginning of the chapter. Only move on when you are happy that you fully understand each point.

- Examination of trends in the financial services industry and how further rationalisation and restructuring is likely to take place with the need to make adequate profits.
- The key aspects of delivery of bank services and the impact of technology on banking, including delivery channels and remote banking.
- The impact of increased use of technology on the number and operations of bank branches.
- The role of telephone and digital banking (e-banking and m-banking) in the distribution of bank services to customers was evaluated.
- The advantages of the use of expert systems in banking.
- The identification of the threat of cyber crime and how financial services providers can combat the threat.
- The implications of technological risk, the nature of that risk, and how such risk can be identified and managed.
- The paramount need for security of computer systems.
- Hardware and software developments for application in banking services.

SOLUTIONS TO QUESTION TIMES

QUESTION TIME 1

Utopia (£ billions)

	Ind/Com Sector	Public Sector	Personal Sector	Total
Physical assets	25	**75**	50	**150**
Financial assets	**50**	30	100	**180**
	75	**105**	150	**330**
Less				
Financial Liabilities	25	**95**	60	**180**
Net Worth	**50**	**10**	90	**150**

QUESTION TIME 2

Your list of why people save could include:

- For large items of expenditure
- For old age
- Fear of unemployment
- To give their family an inheritance
- Habit
- Virtue
- Because they are so rich or have limited needs that they cannot spend all their money

QUESTION TIME 3

The main attributes of physical and financial assets should be related to:

	Ford Focus	**National Savings Certificates**
Return	Utility/pleasure	Interest rate
Liquidity	Second-hand market	Few days' notice
Selling expenses	Depends on sale price	No expense
Risk of loss	High	None (except inflation)
Depreciation	Yes	No
Insurance	Yes	No
Taxation	Tax on purchase/MVL	No
Ongoing costs	Repairs	None

QUESTION TIME 4

(a) The rise in Utopia's personal sector's saving ratio from Yr 1 to Yr 5 may be regarded as a return to norm, as the average over the nine-year period is 9.6%.

At 5.7% in Yr 1 the savings ratio had declined below its long term trend. This could have been the result of excessive spending during an economic boom. The subsequent recession, fear of unemployment and need to reduce debt perhaps encouraged a higher level of savings over the period Yr 3 to Yr 5.

The subsequent decline by Yr 9 might be the result of improved economic conditions, as well as the personal sector being satisfied with the total amount of savings held.

(b) The increase in the UK's personal savings ratio might be attributable to the banking crisis and subsequent recession which have created uncertainty in people's minds and thereby encouraged increased savings. Of course, such action has reduced consumer spending in the economy.

QUESTION TIME 5

(a) Bank deposit multiplier value = Liquidity Ratio

therefore $\frac{1}{12.5\%} = 8$ therefore $\frac{1}{6\%} = 16.6$ therefore $\frac{1}{4\%} = 25$

(b) Liquidity ratio 4%, therefore bank multiplier 25. Liquid assets 280 x 25 = 7,000

Balance Sheet

Deposits	7000	Liquid assets	280
		Advances	6720
	7000		7000

QUESTION TIME 6

The circular flow of income emphasises the basic economic concept that total income equals total output (or expenditure). Households supply firms with the factors of production which are used to produce goods and services. In return they receive income – wages, rent, interest and profit – which is spent purchasing total output.

In the real economy the circular flow suffers from leakages and injections. The main leakages are savings, taxation and imports, which mean that total income generated is not returned to firms. Fortunately, such leakages are offset by injections into the circular flow of income – investment, government expenditure, exports – which ensure that national income equilibrium is roughly maintained at all times.

QUESTION TIME 7

National income can be measured by three different methods; the circular flow of income ensures the same total for each method.

1 Total Expenditure – this incorporates total spending on consumption, investment and by the government, plus exports minus imports, i.e. C + I + G + (X – M).

2 Total Output – this measures the value added, i.e. output value, of the various economic sectors, i.e. agriculture, manufacturing and services. It also takes into account net income from overseas.

3 Total Income – this includes all forms of factor payments plus net income from overseas.

In all three methods of measurement, a figure is deducted for estimated capital consumption in the economy. This represents depreciation of equipment which has to be replaced. After such adjustments, a figure for net national product (income or expenditure) is derived.

As expected, various problems are encountered in measuring national income. A major problem is incomplete information which tends to be associated with tax evasion. Another problem relates to unpaid services such as housework or DIY. Double counting must also be avoided, for example the value of steel output must be reduced by the value of coking coal used. Estimates must also be made for capital consumption and stock valuation, together with imputed rents. Finally, the GDP figure arrived at must be adjusted for inflation which raises the money value for the same level of output of goods and services in the economy. National income must be deflated to a base year by measuring it in constant or real prices.

QUESTION TIME 8

If national income figures on their own can be misleading, we need to be aware of other figures that can help us judge changes and comparisons in living standards. There are, of course, many. The actual choice must depend on what aspect of living standards we are examining.

If we are interested in health, we would wish to examine figures for birth and death rates, average life expectancy, the infant mortality rate, the rate of heart disease, and so on. We would also wish to examine the number of hospitals, the number of doctors in relation to the population, and the proportion of total national income spent on health and social welfare.

If we are interested in education, we would look at the number of illiterate, the proportion of the population with graduate or equivalent qualifications, etc.

If our interest is in material goods, we would look at the ownership of private cars, the number of independent housing units, the ownership of television or household appliances, and the use of electricity.

Other factors to be examined are the length of the working day or crime levels.

Thus, simply looking at GDP statistics might not be sufficient in itself.

QUESTION TIME 9

(a) The multiplier is the ratio of the change in the equilibrium level of national income resulting from the initial injection. It is ascertained by the equation $k = {}^1/s$ where 's' is equal to the marginal propensity to save. If an increase in investment of £10 mil takes place and the mps is $^1/_5$ then the increase in national income will be £50 mil. The national income will be at a higher equilibrium level.

(b) The multiplier concept is important in national income analysis because it enables the government to ascertain the impact of a tax cut or increased expenditure. If it injects too much, it may result in inflation. It is necessary in this situation to know the full multiplier value, i.e. $k = \frac{1}{s + t + m}$ where 't' is the marginal propensity to tax and 'm' is the marginal propensity to import. This results in a lower multiplier value.

(c) The accelerator measures how much investment increases with each successive increase in GDP. Rises in national income and the prospect of increased demand (and profits) encourage increased investment in the private sector.

QUESTION TIME 10

There are various types of unemployment and for each one suggested cures are available:

1 Seasonal unemployment – certain people follow employment where seasonal demand exists, such as tourism, or where production, such as agriculture, is affected by the weather. The first type can be alleviated by prolonging the tourist season, the latter is of declining importance due to the relatively small number of hired workers in agriculture.

2 Residual and frictional unemployment – this comprises those who are unable to work or are moving between jobs. The government tries to alleviate this with social security payments and improved information services in job centres. Grants may also be provided to improve the mobility of labour.

3 Structural unemployment – this can be quite a serious form of unemployment in certain areas of the country and is caused by demand changes, technological developments and foreign competition. It has impacted, in particular, on coal mining, shipbuilding, steel and heavy engineering industries and thus tends to be concentrated in specific regions and towns, such as the west of Scotland, north-east England, Wales. Government policy to deal with this type of unemployment includes regional grants/allowances to attract an inward flow of new investment/industries and employment, such as microtechnology or call centres. Even when the rest of the economy is working at full capacity with labour shortages in some areas of the UK, this type of unemployment persists due to lack of occupational/geographic mobility.

4 Demand deficiency unemployment – this arises due to the business cycle in the UK economy. Areas of the country that have been dependent on heavy/capital goods industries, for example, where demand fluctuates the most, are those most affected by economic downturns. The solution to this problem is to reduce the impact of the business cycle by having a more broadly

diversified economy, with encouragement of local enterprise, particularly firms in new technologies and services, via inward investment.

QUESTION TIME 11

(a) You should answer this question with a brief description of the main phases of the trade cycle – slump, recovery, boom, recession – including comments on output, employment and prices. Something should be stated on what, perhaps, causes turning points in economic activity around the general growth trend in an economy.

(b) Two explanations are required – psychological factors or fluctuations in investment or interest rate developments or economic mismanagement by the government. You must make your own value judgement as to the validity of these theories and relate this to the current UK economic environment.

QUESTION TIME 12

(a) You should expand on the following points:

Balanced Budget	**Demand Management Budget**
Budget equated with sound financial practice (good housekeeping)	Budget used to balance the national economy, avoid unemployment and inflation if possible
Surplus (profit) used to repay national debt	Deficit financed by borrowing; therefore increase in national debt, therefore increased transfer payments in future budgets
Unbalanced budget source of inflation and economic instability	Deficit spending not inflationary if the economy has spare capacity
Economic management is the responsibility of central bank	Economic management is the responsibility of the state; the central bank operates monetary policy as a support for fiscal policy
Expenditure on public goods and merit wants; subsidies to private sector kept to a minimum	Expenditure adjusted to ensure maximum output in economy and steady economic growth
Unemployment due to trade cycle, automatic correction in economy via measures – deficit budget, regional flexible wages/prices	Unemployment tackled by budgetary transfers, etc

Keynes envisaged the budget as part of a dynamic financial system which could be managed in the interests of a high and stable level of economic activity. In other words, it could be used as a correction to a condition of rising or falling prices and output of undesirable proportions. The present government probably prefers financial orthodoxy, i.e. the balanced budget concept, as it views inflation control as the chief priority of macroeconomic management by the Bank of England. Steady economic growth and rising employment is to be achieved by various microeconomic measures, such as tax measures to stimulate investment and enterprise.

(b) A critical evaluation of government economic management over the last 10 years requires some form of value judgement on budgetary and monetary policies over the period. Obviously, this requires consideration of the banking crisis and the subsequent economic recession. Alternative policies to the ones adopted by governments should be reviewed in your answer.

QUESTION TIME 13

The move to de-politicise the monetary policy process has been widely welcomed, but it does not in itself guarantee that the quality of monetary policy making will improve. There is no substitute for judgement, luck is important, and policy mistakes are inevitable by the Bank's Monetary Policy Committee.

The arrangements should help reassure financial markets of the commitment to achieving low inflation and result in a permanent narrowing of the risk premiums on medium and long dated gilts and bonds.

To the extent that inflation expectations are moderated, the new policy framework could result in a lower average level of short term interest rates over the economic cycle.

QUESTION TIME 14

The Bank of England has a number of weapons at its disposal to restrict the growth of money supply. Its principal weapon is its ability to influence short term interest rates. Other rates of interest tend to follow the Bank of England's discount rate. By raising interest rates, the Bank of England can discourage borrowing and make credit tighter.

Through its operations in the gilt-edged market, the Bank could sell securities to the customers of banks and so drain cash out of the banking system as these customers draw on their accounts to meet their purchases. As the banks lose cash they are less able to lend and expand money supply. This could be reinforced by gilt repo market operations.

In the past, the Bank has also used directives and various controls over credit creation, although these have now been abandoned as such actions interfere with the free market.

QUESTION TIME 15

(a) The investment demand function illustrates that the return rate of investment declines as the level of investment increases. This is due to the marginal efficiency of investment declining on each extra pound invested. In interest rate diagrams it is shown as a downward sloping curve.

(b) Equilibrium interest rate is established at the point where the supply of savings (plus money supply) equals investment demand (plus hoarding).

(c) Nominal interest rate is the published interest rate, while the real interest is ascertained after taking the current inflation rate into account.

(d) Normal yield curve illustrates that similar securities with differing maturities will generate a lower yield in the short term than in the long term.

QUESTION TIME 16

(a) Successful control of inflation depends on identifying and dealing with its causes.

Economists identify two types of inflation – demand pull and cost push inflation.

Demand pull inflation occurs when the total demand for goods and services exceeds the productive capacity of the economy at current prices. The simple solution is to reduce the level of total or aggregate demand, although this may not be easy. Cuts in government expenditure could be attempted, but may be difficult to achieve. Private spending may be held in check by higher taxes, tighter credit and higher interest rates – all of which would be unpopular.

Cost push inflation occurs when increased costs are passed on as higher prices. The answer to cost push inflation is to prevent costs from rising. In many industries, wages form a major part of costs and so much effort has gone into controlling labour costs. If pay rises are matched by increased productivity, there is no inflationary pressure.

In the 1960s and 1970s in the UK, governments tried to control cost push inflation by prices and incomes policies. Limits were placed on wage increases to keep down costs and price rises were restricted to make incomes policies more acceptable to the workers. In practice, incomes policies met with limited success and were not very popular.

Most economists now believe that the real cause of inflation is the money supply growing at a greater rate than output. Their solution is to limit the growth of the money supply. This raises questions as to which measure of money is to be controlled and how this is to be achieved.

(b) Trying to predict the future inflation rate is risky. It is dependent on the level of economic activity, personal savings ratio and sterling exchange rate. A sharp fall in the latter could lead to higher import prices and thus cost push inflation. However, if this is combined with a domestic recession, the longer term inflationary prospect would be mild; but if the economy was experiencing a stronger recovery when the exchange rate depreciates, this could be inflationary. Higher energy prices could also have an impact on the inflation rate, especially if heating and petrol prices increase enough to encourage workers to ask for higher wages and salaries.

Much also depends on the government's political will and commitment to setting a low inflation rate target, i.e. 2% pa. The Monetary Policy Committee at the Bank of England is empowered to adjust interest rates in order to ensure that inflation remains within a narrow range of the 2% pa target.

(c) QE could have an inflationary impact on the economy as increased money supply could lead to higher prices. However, the recession in the economy is likely to delay this possible outcome. Once recovery commences, QE may have to be reversed by the Bank.

QUESTION TIME 17

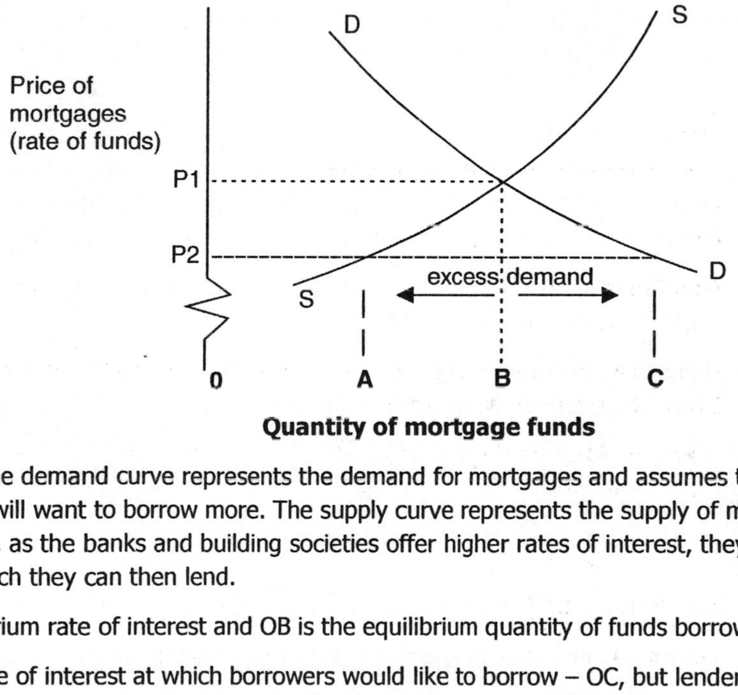

Quantity of mortgage funds

In the diagram, the demand curve represents the demand for mortgages and assumes that, as interest rates fall, people will want to borrow more. The supply curve represents the supply of mortgage funds and assumes that, as the banks and building societies offer higher rates of interest, they are able to pull in extra funds which they can then lend.

OP1 is the equilibrium rate of interest and OB is the equilibrium quantity of funds borrowed.

OP2 is a lower rate of interest at which borrowers would like to borrow – OC, but lenders are only willing to supply OA.

AC represents an excess of demand when the interest rate is OP2.

QUESTION TIME 18

Your answer will be based on local and/or regional knowledge. Key factors to be taken into account are:

Unemployment rates
Disposable income levels
Government policies in region
Housing stock
Inflow and outflow of people
Company closures and openings
Level of public service employment
Manufacturing vs services employment

QUESTION TIME 19

Principal amount $1,000,000	Interests
First Interest Calculation $1m @ 10.5% (LIBOR on 1 Jan + 0.5%) for 3 months	$26,250
Second Interest Calculation $1m @ 8.5% (LIBOR on 1 Apr + 0.5%) for 3 months	$21,250
Third Interest Calculation $1m @ 14.5% (LIBOR on 1 Jul + 0.5%) for 3 months	$36,250
Fourth Interest Calculation $1m @ 12.5% (LIBOR on 1 Oct + 0.5%) for 3 months	$31,250
Total	$115,000

QUESTION TIME 20

The German subsidiary could use a number of techniques to fund its euro Swiss franc loan book. It could issue in London euro Swiss franc CDs, notes and bonds. The interbank market would probably be the major source of euro Swiss franc funds. Time deposits in euro Swiss francs could be sought from non-bank customers. If it has a Swiss subsidiary, the former could raise Swiss franc funds in Switzerland and transfer them to its London operation. Finally, it could convert sterling deposits via the forex market into euro Swiss franc funds.

QUESTION TIME 21

The eurocurrency interbank market is the result of eurobanks having either a surplus or deficit of funds in a particular currency. The interbank market enables eurobanks to eliminate or minimise non-earning assets. Although little or no profit is generated from such activities, it enables a liquidity smoothing process to take place in the international banking system. The importance of the market is highlighted by the fact that 50% of the eurocurrency market's gross size is accounted for by outstanding interbank balances. Within the market, eurobanks are subjected to interest rate tiering which in turn depends upon the nationality, size and creditworthiness of the eurobank.

The market transfers non-bank deposits via a chain of banks from lenders to borrowers and also enables eurobanks to collect information on other banks, acts as a form of insurance via the virtual assurance of funds, if required, and provides a general barometer of market conditions. It also engages in various transformation roles – geographic, credit, currency, maturity, market.

QUESTION TIME 22

(a) Demand and supply of funds in the eurocurrency interbank market. This depends on the funding positions of eurobanks and the needs of their clients. Capital flows and interest arbitrage influence LIBOR.

(b) Derives income to cover the expense of arranging the loan plus (hopefully) profit, together with any provisions for doubtful loans.

(c) Differentials due mainly to risk and maturity of loan. The less creditworthy the borrower, the higher the spread charged on a loan. Return made on a loan is related to risk incurred by the lending bank(s).

QUESTION TIME 23

Convertible eurobonds are issued by large corporations. Most have a fixed interest rate and maturities of 10 to 15 years. The attraction of convertible stock is the security it offers plus the option open to the investor to treat the stock as an investment for income purposes or capital appreciation. The convertible element allows the holder to benefit from growth in the value of the underlying shares.

Conversion prices and dates are predetermined at the time of issue. If the market value of the ordinary shares declines, at some point the price of the convertible is stabilised when the yield offered is comparable to that of straight bonds.

In the market, the price of a convertible eurobond and underlying share are closely correlated. Convertible eurobonds are attractive to investors who wish to participate in the growth of the company through an equity stake, but also desire a relatively high yield.

QUESTION TIME 24

(a) To finance $ loan book or operations in the USA. It is an alternative means of raising $ funds on a medium/long term basis instead of using interbank credit lines.

(b) FRNs – variable coupon rate related to LIBOR + spread, fixed repayment date.

(c) Investment aspects – relatively secure, particularly for a risk-averse investor. Interest yield correlates with current interest levels, therefore FRN remains relatively stable in value at more or less par. The LIBOR aspect ensures that the FRN interest yield matches market interest yields in the dollar market.

(d) MTN facilities are a more flexible means of raising funds for a borrower. Notes can be issued for various maturities in excess of one year to suit particular cash flow requirements. Most MTNs have a fixed coupon rate.

QUESTION TIME 25

(a) London's main natural advantages as a financial centre are:

- English language
- Geographical position
- Climate
- Political stability
- Telecommunications
- Time zone
- Expertise

(b) Benefits for the UK from London's role:

- Employment
- Income
- Council or local tax
- Central government tax

- Financial facilities for UK industry and commerce
- Prestige
- Invisible earnings

QUESTION TIME 26

(a) Sokoloff v National City Bank (1928)

The general principle of law is that the parent or home office of a bank is responsible for its branch's liabilities if the latter wrongfully refuses to repay a deposit. Sokoloff had a rouble deposit at City's Petrograd branch in 1917. Anticipating nationalisation by a new Communist government in Russia, the National City Bank closed its doors without giving the depositors a chance to withdraw their funds. The NY Court held that the assets of the branch belonged to the parent bank that also had responsibility for the deposits. This was a fundamental judgement in international banking, although it is subject to qualifications related to the Act of State Doctrine.

(b) LAFB v Bankers Trust (1987)

The US President, using American law, attempted to freeze Libyan financial assets worldwide. Bankers Trust in London refused to repay a deposit of $131 million to the LAFB. The UK court rejected the extra-territorial reach of the US decree, as only English law applies in London. The other key aspect of this case was that Bankers Trust had to repay the eurodollar deposit in cash, i.e. the equivalent in sterling bank notes.

QUESTION TIME 27

Loan risk analysts take various economic and political factors into account when assessing country risk. An analysis of economic facts can provide some indication of a country's economic and financial stability. Data can be used to illustrate trends and highlight particular problems – GNP figures can give some indication of economic growth rates and per capita income along with the underlying economic structure. Balance of payments figures/trends give some indication of present/future foreign exchange sources which are vital to the servicing of external loans by a country, i.e. debt service ratio. Such assessments based on available data (economic statistics) are objective and can be used to provide a "definite" score for a country.

Political factors and their assessment tend to be subjective as they are based more on value judgements made by bank analysts. Aspects to be considered under politics are country leadership, form of government and overall political/economic philosophy.

Social conditions and external relations must also be assessed and scores awarded under the country risk assessment system being used. Different analysts could draw different conclusions from reviewing such factors.

The important point to remember is that country risk assessment is not a precise exercise – it is a rough grading system.

QUESTION TIME 28

A bank can raise cash and/or improve its capital-assets ratio by selling part of its mortgage pool to a special purpose vehicle (SPV). The SPV must not be a subsidiary of the bank and must have its own funds via the issue of bonds and notes. In order to protect the investors in these financial instruments, the SPV may purchase enhancements from insurance companies or issue subordinated debt which is purchased by the originating bank. Such steps should, in theory, ensure that the bond/note investors are protected against any shortfalls in interest or principal repayments from the mortgage pool of assets acquired from a bank. The originating bank continues in some cases to act as the collector of interest and principal payments on behalf of the SPV in return for a fee or spread margin. Cash received by the bank from the SPV in exchange for part of its mortgage pool can be re-lent or invested by the originating bank.

QUESTION TIME 29

The missing words: securitisation, direct, bonds or notes, bad loan, credit, banks, securitisation, fee, positive, deregulation, financial.

QUESTION TIME 30

(a) USCP takes the form of secured and unsecured promissory notes with a minimum face value of £100,000 and maturity of 270 days or less. Most CP issued now takes the form of book entries for security purposes. Funds raised by the issue of USCP are used for working capital purposes by corporations and financial institutions. Some CP is issued on a continuous basis to finance investment in fixed assets. Large issuers of CP, such as Exxon, have their own CP sales staff and sell paper directly to potential investors. Medium-sized corporations use the services of investment banks to place their CP with investors. To issue USCP, an investment grade rating is essential. Backstop facilities with a bank or banks are required in order to ensure funds are available for the repayment of CP at maturity at all times. Investors in USCP are financial institutions, corporations and investment funds with short-term cash surpluses.

(b) A British-based bank might issue USCP as an alternative source of dollar funding for its loan book. Dollar funds raised might also be used to finance the operations of a subsidiary or branch operation in the USA. The establishment of USCP programmes also results in raising the financial profile of a bank, both in its own domestic market and overseas.

QUESTION TIME 31

(a) The ECP's market size is €c600bn. ECP is issued at a discount to face value. It is a bearer instrument with maturities ranging between 7 and 365 days, with the average being 60 days. ECP is issued by corporate, financial and sovereign borrowers. The main ECP market is in London. At present about 50% is denominated in €s. Investment/commercial banks act as dealers in the secondary ECP market.

(b) A British-based bank may have issued $ ECP for the following reasons:
- as a source of $ funding for a $ loan book
- to finance operations in USA via a branch/subsidiary
- as an alternative to raising funds via USCP or offshore dollar time deposits.

(c) ECP as an investment represents low risk short-term paper with a limited secondary market. The minimum note value is $500,000 up to $5 million; thus it is mainly purchased by institutional investors. It carries no third party guarantees.

(d) ECP v USCP: the latter discriminates against foreign issuers via a higher discount rate; ECP is purchased by institutional investors, whereas USCP is acquired by corporations and money market mutual funds (MMMFs); USCP average maturity is 30 days while ECP is 90-180 days.

QUESTION TIME 32

For the 17 participating EU member states, economic and monetary union entails:

- The use of a single currency
- A common central bank (ECB) based in Frankfurt
- A common monetary policy, i.e. interest rate
- Constraints on member countries' budgets and public sector deficits
- A single exchange rate against other currencies

QUESTION TIME 33

EMU debate centres on arguments for and against:

FOR: reduced transaction costs; currency risk reduced; completion of the single market; lower/stable interest rates; improved price stability; economic growth; reserve currency status, etc.

AGAINST: transition costs; fiscal policy curtailed; loss of exchange rate policy; no independent interest rate policy; reduced economic sovereignty; increased political integration.

QUESTION TIME 34

A critical evaluation of EMU will require consideration of past and current developments as regards the euro; debt problems; budgetary positions; fiscal integration; bank solvency and economic growth, etc. Obviously, reflection on points raised in QT33 in light of experience of EMU must be considered in any answer which critically appraises the single currency area.

QUESTION TIME 35

A government must always keep Adam Smith's canons of taxation in mind along with making some assessment of the taxable capacity of the country.

Some taxes are imposed primarily for revenue purposes. Some are raised to redistribute income. Others are part of a deflationary or reflationary policy. The decision whether to adopt a tax depends not only on its immediate purposes, but also on other factors.

If the tax is intended to redistribute income, one must calculate not only the influence on the propensity to save (on the part of those parting with a proportion of their income), but also whether the economy would benefit. Indirect taxes have a bearing on the cost of living and may provoke wage demands.

If imposed on necessities, they may be regressive, unless carefully graduated, and may cancel out benefits of a graduated direct taxation system. Further, they may change the pattern of spending and consequently the industrial and commercial structure of the country and of localised employment.

If taxes are introduced as part of a deflationary or reflationary package, the aim will be to influence both spending and saving. Taxes on income, for instance, may be used to increase or decrease purchasing power or to stimulate or damp down business activity. The question is, not only what taxes are to be introduced, abolished or changed, but also, taking the multiplier into account, the amount of taxation needed to achieve the objective without provoking unintended inflation or deflation.

QUESTION TIME 36

A balanced Budget means PSNB is zero. Such a situation has an impact on money supply growth and gilt issues. It will affect interest rates in the bond market. Private sector savings will not be subject to crowding out by public sector needs; instead, funds will be used for private investment in the productive capacity of the economy.

Business confidence might be raised by the prospect of lower taxation and inflation plus some possible repayments of the national debt. These prospects should encourage investment and thus economic growth. Lower interest rates will also stimulate the mortgage market and thus housing demand within the economy. Fiscal responsibility should engender business optimism about the future and thus enhance employment prospects.

QUESTION TIME 37

You should discuss the reasons for increased government intervention along the following lines:

- Displacement effect and concentration process – a natural phenomenon of public finance.
- Public goods – defence, law and order plus new forms of expenditure on the environment, consumer protection, etc – people expect the state to do more for them and their community.

- Merit goods/services – health/education needs/expectations increase with passage of time – NHS is a victim of its own success, (more people living to an older age).
- Redistribution of income – welfare objectives/safety net expenditure – creates a dependency culture and an army of social workers/bureaucrats.
- Economic stabilisation policies – Keynesian policies increased state share of GDP – proved difficult to roll back in recovery/boom periods.

QUESTION TIME 38

You must make some comment on employment, output, economic growth and inflation. The sterling exchange rate, interest rate and external trade position should be mentioned, as should major international economic/financial developments impacting on the UK economy.

The budgetary position and stage of the business cycle require comment.

Policy options available to the government are generally dealt with by the media on a continuous basis. Keep abreast of such developments and debates.

QUESTION TIME 39

(a) The two main components of the UK's national debt are government stocks – indexed and non-indexed gilts, i.e. 70% of nominal value, and national savings certificates, premium bonds, etc. Foreign currency debt is negligible at present. So the UK's national debt is basically internal sterling debt held by insurance companies and pension funds, etc.

(b) The government could attempt to reduce the debt ratio to 40% by running a budget surplus and using this to retire part of the national debt. A budget surplus, unless generated automatically by higher economic growth, could be achieved via higher taxation and/or curtailment of public expenditure programmes. The government could also privatise any remaining state assets (e.g. RBS 83% shareholding) and use the proceeds to reduce the national debt.

QUESTION TIME 40

In order to avoid large loan losses, the banks must learn from their past mistakes. It is essential that:

- Tighter and more sophisticated systems of credit control are in place.
- Better credit quality control is instigated.
- Loan portfolios must be diversified without an over commitment to any sector.
- Loan portfolio risks must be assessed and rewards must be adequate.
- Better staff training and information are provided.
- The herd instinct, i.e. excessive lending to the property sector, is avoided better knowledge of the risks associated with derivative instruments.
- Perhaps a greater emphasis is placed on ethical practices.

The banks must also be assisted by sound macroeconomic policies by the government and Bank which avoid excessive monetary expansion. In the past, the latter has created easy money with resultant excessive lending on false assumptions which have been quickly shattered by the need to deal with inflation in the economy.

QUESTION TIME 41

Various operational measures can be taken by a bank to increase its profits and thereby its dividends to ordinary shareholders. The most common measures are:

- Cost-cutting programmes
- Rationalisation of staff/admin/branches
- Attraction of new business
- Improved marketing
- Charges related more closely to the cost of services
- An improvement in interest margins, i.e. wider margin between deposit and loan rates
- Use of new technology and delivery systems

The above measures increase shareholder value but in the longer term rationalisation of staff and branches may provide reduced rewards as a basic core of resources is attained. Government, media and consumer attitudes may also influence bank profitability via charges for services etc.

QUESTION TIME 42

Various lessons can be learned from the problems at LBG. Firstly, the bank failed to carry out due diligence on HBOS, which must be regarded as a management failure. The top management's desire for expansion and market dominance over-ruled commonsense as regards investigating thoroughly the asset composition and problems at HBOS. Secondly, the merger was encouraged by politicians and regulators as a means to solve a bigger problem of financial stability in the UK. As a result, the interests of the shareholders in Lloyds Bank were ignored to their ultimate cost via a share price collapse and the termination of dividends. Thirdly, the reliance of LBG on the UK house and domestic loan market linked the new enlarged bank's success to that of a slow growth or recessionary economy. Finally, EU competition rules forced the sale of various units of the bank, thus depriving the bank of any future synergies from its enlarged size – a major reason used by Lloyds Bank directors to justify the merger with HBOS.

QUESTION TIME 43

The lessons for bank regulators from the demise of RBS could be:

- Rapid expansion funded by inadequate capital resources
- International expansion in the USA that lacked adequate HQ internal controls
- Corporate governance was weak due to the CEO's robust style of management
- Regulatory failure through inadequate scrutiny of overall operations
- Failure of risk management controls as regards sub-prime debt position in USA
- Inadequate due diligence and too high an acquisition price paid for ABN-Amro

Hopefully the new UK bank regulatory system will ensure these lapses do not occur in the future.

QUESTION TIME 44

The failure of Northern Rock and Bradford & Bingley highlights some key problems for small institutions wanting to become major players in the UK banking market. Both were relatively small local institutions that, once demutualised, embarked on rapid expansion in order to increase their share of the house mortgage market. This resulted in a number of problems, such as over-reliance on wholesale funds and a lack of adequately qualified top management to control the expansion of their activities. Both institutions were swept along in the credit boom and resorted to lower and lower credit standards as regards granting mortgages and loans to their customers. Northern Rock used securitisation to expand its balance sheet, while Bradford & Bingley used self certification mortgages and sub-prime debt to achieve the same result of grossly extended balance sheets. The credit crunch and recession undermined both institutions and exposed their inherent weaknesses to the financial markets. The latter stopped funding flows and made share issues a non-option for both banks; to prevent customer panic both banks were nationalised.

QUESTION TIME 45

(a) The Basel Capital Convergence Accord (Basel 1) established a minimum capital-assets ratio of 8% for international banks. It defined various classes of capital into Tier 1 and 2. Assets, on and off the balance sheet, were given specific risk weights, i.e. 0% cash, 50% mortgages, 100% advances, etc. The Accord's main objective was to improve the solvency position of banks and create a level playing field to ensure equality of competition as regards capital.

(b) Capital - Asset Ratio

Asset	×	%Risk Weight	=	Risk Weighted Asset £
	×			
50	×	ø		ø
100	×	20		20
200	×	50		100
350	×	100		350
				470

therefore capital – asset ratio $= \dfrac{50 \times 100}{470}$

$= 10.6\%$

QUESTION TIME 46

Any losses made by a bank must be written off against its capital and reserves. Losses must be borne by the shareholders and not depositors. The bank must have enough capital resources to make any risk to depositors' funds a remote possibility. Thus capital adequacy is something which bank regulators set down guidelines for and to ensure that a minimum capital to risk weighted assets is adhered to at all times. With the Basel Capital Accords a minimum ratio of 8% was established for most banks worldwide. National regulators might request banks in their own countries to hold a higher capital-assets ratio.

A bank must also be capable of meeting its obligations such as repayment of deposits as they fall due. Liquidity adequacy is maintained by each bank holding sufficient cash and liquefiable assets. Again, regulators set basic liquidity standards for banks. Insufficient liquidity can cause a loss of customer (and market) confidence and encourage a run on a bank, e.g. Northern Rock. A liquidity problem can quickly become a solvency problem for a bank as it is forced to dispose of assets at a loss in order to generate required liquid funds.

QUESTION TIME 47

The FSCS provides deposit insurance protection in the UK. If a bank fails, the FSCS pays up to £85,000 (joint account £170,000) compensation to any depositor; any sum in excess of these limits is uninsured and thus recovery of funds can only be made out of the assets of the insolvent bank.

QUESTION TIME 48

People switch their financial assets for a variety of reasons. It might to enhance the potential yield or reduce risk.Liquidity preference might also be another important factor in deciding on a specific term investment or having instant access to funds. A person may prefer to hold a savings account balance rather than a long term bond. Ordinary shares might have to be sold to raise cash for some use such as house improvement or to pay for a wedding.

QUESTION TIME 49

(a) Building society mergers should in theory bring about substantial cost savings. Benefits should be derived from staff and branch economies, i.e. overlaps can be eliminated.

A larger society can afford more effective advertising and will have the resources to use the most up-to-date technology to deliver existing and new products to its customers. It might be able to attract the best managers while at the same time achieving a greater diversification as regards its home loan (mortgage) portfolio.

The drawbacks are that the enlarged society might be bureaucratic and slow to react to customer needs. It might suffer from communication problems, while its sheer size makes it more impersonal for staff and customers. The technology, management styles and product range of two societies might be incompatible.

(b) Mergers might benefit the economy through more efficient societies. It might also lead to a better utilisation of financial resources within the economy. The downside is that an overall lack of competition could be to the disadvantage of depositors/borrowers via a lower return on funds and higher borrowing charges. Consumer choice of financial services will be reduced.

QUESTION TIME 50

Credit unions, if successful, will reduce social and financial exclusions in our society. Apart from providing banking and financial services to "poor" people at a reasonable price, they might help to regenerate deprived communities via business start-ups. This would result in a higher level of employment and income, together with a general rise in morale in poorer sections of the community.

For the wider community, such success would result in less government expenditure on unemployment and social benefits, as well as a reduction in crime, police and prison costs. It might make society as a whole more at ease with itself.

QUESTION TIME 51

The EU Second Banking Directive (2BCD) became effective on 1 January 1993 and consists of 23 Articles. Article 3 sets the minimum capital for a bank at euro 5m. Articles 16 to 18 allow banks to branch or sell services directly from their home base throughout the EU without host country authorisation. This covers the provision of core banking activities. In effect, a bank will now be granted a single banking licence by its supervisory/ regulatory agency.

QUESTION TIME 52

(a) The term direct banking implies that the product is offered through one central distribution channel, such as the telephone, and that this is the only way to access the account. Offering a telephone service implies that it is an additional way of accessing the account and that there are other delivery channels available to the customer.

(b) Remote banking means that the customer is distanced from the source of the product or service they are using; for example, they can access their account without visiting their branch.

QUESTION TIME 53

Expert systems are likely to reduce the need for large numbers of highly qualified staff, which will result in cost savings as regards staff remuneration. A total replacement of customer services staff is unlikely, but what expert systems will enable is for such staff to meet customer needs in a more efficient and speedier manner. It might make the branch network more cost effective as specialised knowledge incorporated into computer/expert systems can be more easily accessed. However, with the direct handling of loan, insurance and credit card requests, particularly by online technology, as well as further development of expert systems, the need for a large branch network might be reduced in the future.

Digital banking will probably reduce staff and branch requirements in the future. With the passage of time, an ever-increasing percentage of bank customers will become comfortable with e-banking and m-banking, and this fact, along with the desire of banks to reduce their cost structure, will bring about a major change in the delivery of bank services. Any move towards a cashless society will definitely reduce the branch network as pure cash transactions disappear.

QUESTION TIME 54

Technological risk is of paramount concern in banking services. Computer systems can be hacked into by cyber criminals who are becoming increasingly well organised. A particular problem for banks is outsourcing and reliance on the internet system. Stored data can give banks the most cause for concern as any intrusions by hackers could give rise to major problems and losses. Banks must be constantly alert to new, sophisticated methods of attacks on their internal mainframe computer. Risks have to be assessed and dealt with whatever the cost of putting security procedures in place. Customers must also be educated on how to reduce digital banking risks. (Note the procedures used in your own financial institution.)

Technology risks can be managed by the use of internal procedures or by outsourcing to specialist risk management companies. The BCBS and national bank regulators have also laid down guidelines for banks. However, it must be stated that this is no easy task either for banks or regulators. (Note any risk management techniques you are aware of in your institution.)

GLOSSARY

Glossary

Accelerator

A rise in national income means increased consumption. In order to satisfy the extra demand, firms undertake increased investment in order to increase productive capacity. This action will further increase aggregate demand and national income.

Act of State Doctrine

Courts in all countries must give effect to the law or Acts of a recognised government in its own country. Such Acts might relieve a parent bank of its liability to repay deposits of its foreign branch in a host country.

Agent bank

The agent bank in a syndicated eurocredit or a eurobond issue handles the distribution of interest payments and principal repayments. Such a bank ensures that various conditions and terms are complied with by the borrower.

Aggregate demand

In an economy this equals consumption + investment + government expenditure + (exports – imports), i.e. C + I + G + (X – M) = national income or product.

Asset price bubble

This is an unsustainable rise in asset prices (houses, shares, etc) generally caused by excess supply of credit in an economy – mainly the result of economic/monetary mismanagement.

Asset transformation

The switching of assets from one particular use to another, e.g. turning cash into investments or switching from one kind of deposit to another.

Authorities (The)

In the UK the authorities in economic matters are the Bank of England and the Treasury. The Bank has responsibility for monetary policy, while fiscal policy is the responsibility of the Treasury.

Balance of payments

This is a financial statement which records a country's trade and financial flows with other countries. Trade in goods and services is included in the current account section, whereas capital flows and money transfers into and out of a country are recorded in the capital account. Components of the statement may be in deficit or surplus, but overall the statement is in balance.

Balance sheet

Lists the assets and liabilities held by a corporation or financial institution. Both must sum up to an equal amount.

Bank for International

The BIS was established in 1931 and is based in Basel, Settlements (BIS) Switzerland. Its objectives are to promote central bank cooperation, provide funds for international financial operations and to act as trustee or agent in international financial settlements.

Banking Act 1987

Provides the supervisory/regulatory framework for banks in the UK. It formalised the regulatory powers of the Bank of England.

Bank levy	This is a tax imposed on banks by the UK government as their contribution to paying for the economic/social costs of the banking crisis and recession. It is based on the balance sheet size of a bank.
Basel Capital Convergence Accord	An international agreement which provides standardised criteria for assessing the capital adequacy of banks. Three Accords have been issued which have become more sophisticated as regards risk weights for assets, but have maintained the minimum 8% capital ratio.
Basel Committee on Banking supervision	This Committee was set up to harmonise the regulation and supervision of international banking. It issued the Basel Concordat and the Basel Capital Accords. Its aim is to strengthen countries' banking systems and create a level playing field for regulatory costs imposed on banks.
Bond	A document issued by a government or company borrowing money from the public, stating the existence of a debt and the amount owing to the bond holder. Bonds are usually long term (greater than five years maturity) and pay fixed rates of interest.
Budget (The)	Annual plan of government expenditure and taxation, presented to Parliament by the Chancellor of the Exchequer in March or April of each year.
Building society	Financial institution which issues shares (i.e. accepts deposits) and lends to borrowers, mainly for home mortgages.
Capital	Generally regarded as shareholders' equity plus debentures, i.e. loan stock.
Capital adequacy	This is the ratio of a bank's capital resources (share capital plus reserves) to its total assets. Deductions are made from the capital resources for goodwill, etc. A high ratio is generally regarded as an indicator of a financially sound bank.
Capital adequacy ratio	The ratio of a bank's capital resources (share capital plus reserves) to its total risk-weighted assets.
Capital conservation ratio	A ratio of plus or minus 2.5% in relation to the 7% core ratio for banks. It is adjusted to take account of the overall capital position of a bank and the economy.
Capital exporter	A country with a balance of payments current account surplus can finance a capital outflow via direct or portfolio investment overseas. This should increase the net worth of the country.
Capital markets	Markets where capital funds (bonds and ordinary shares) are issued and traded.
Central bank	The key financial institution in a country, responsible for the note issue, implementation of monetary policy and, in some countries, supervising/regulating the banking system.

(The) City

The City is the square mile in London in which most financial deals take place. It centres on Lombard Street and Threadneedle Street, where the Bank of England, the Stock Exchange and the head offices of some major retail banks are situated. The close proximity of financial institutions and markets facilitates the completion of financial deals.

ClubMed

This term refers to those countries in southern Europe (Italy, Greece, Spain, Portugal) which have debt service problems and large budget deficits. All pose a threat to the continuance in its present form of the single currency area.

Code of Fiscal Stability

Introduced by the Labour government in 1998, it adopted an orthodox philosophy to budgetary policy. Current expenditure was to be financed out of tax revenues and borrowing kept to a minimum or zero. Borrowing was only permitted to finance public investment in the infrastructure. Unfortunately, the Code was ignored with the passage of time and was official scrapped in 2010.

Commercial bank

A retail banking institution which carries on traditional banking activities such as deposit taking, granting loans and offering cheque accounts.

Consumer credit

Loans and other forms of credit extended to the personal sector.

Consumer Prices Index (CPI)

CPI measures the average change from month to month in the prices of consumer goods and services. The CPI is a useful tool for indicating the general trend in UK prices.

Convergence criteria

The Maastricht Treaty outlined the economic convergence criteria for EMU participants. There are four criteria:

(a) Price stability – average consumer price inflation in 1997 had not been more than 1.5% above that of the three best performing countries.

(b) Sustainable Government finances – government budget deficits had not to exceed 3% of GDP and total debt was to be no more than 60% of GDP.

(c) Interest rates – long term interest rates in 1997 had not exceeded by more than 2% the long term interest rates in the three countries with the lowest inflation rate.

(d) Stable exchange rates – each participant had to maintain their exchange rate within normal fluctuation margins for at least two years prior to entry.

Convertible bond

A convertible bond issued by a corporation is convertible at a predetermined future date into ordinary shares in the corporation at a predetermined price.

Convertible currency

This is a currency which is freely convertible into other currencies for non-resident holders. Most of the world's major currencies are also freely convertible for residents (non-residents), as exchange control has been abolished in most rich countries.

Corporate governance This term relates to the board of directors in a bank and whether they act in a robust enough style to protect shareholder interests. This requires the directors to have adequate experience, qualifications and inquisitive minds to question the CEO and top management of a bank.

Correspondent bank A bank which either receives or makes money payments plus other services for another bank in another country. A bank's currency accounts held with correspondent banks in foreign countries are known as nostro accounts. Correspondent banks are essential for the conduct of foreign trade and finance.

Country risk This is associated with cross-border banking, i.e. deposits in one country, loans in another country. The economic and financial situation of a country in which a potential borrower resides need to be assessed. Shortages of foreign exchange in the borrower's country may prevent interest and principal payments.

Coupon rate This is the stated interest rate payable on a bond. Interest must be paid at least once per annum.

Credit crunch The interbank market ceases to provide the necessary amount of short term funding for banks due to a crisis of confidence in the liquidity/solvency position of banks.

Credit risk The risk that a counterparty defaults on some or all of its contractual obligations. Credit risk in lending operations is the likelihood that a borrower will not be able to repay the principal or pay the interest on a regular basis.

Credit unions These are mutual savings and loan societies which provide low cost banking services to people with a common bond, i.e. church or workplace, etc.

Cyber crime This is a continuous threat to digital banking and arises through computer intrusions that enable criminals to access stored and processed data.

Debt service ratio This ratio is calculated by combining debt principal repayments and interest payable in a single year and dividing it by a country's exports for the equivalent period. A ratio in excess of 25% is sometimes taken as indicative of future debt service problems.

Default A country (or corporation) is in default of its financial obligations when it fails to pay interest on the due date and/or fails to make scheduled repayments of the debt principal. This is generally followed by the announcement of a moratorium which leads to negotiations between the lender and the defaulting borrower.

Deflation	Deflation is generally associated with rising unemployment and low or negative economic growth. In most cases it is the result of restrictive government economic policies (increased taxation, public spending cuts or higher interest rates). The policy objective is to reduce inflation, excessive imports or a large budget deficit. Such policies might be implemented on the instructions of the International Monetary Fund in order to stabilise an economy and before receipt of IMF financial assistance.
Deposit insurance	This occurs where bank deposits of retail customers are insured against loss in the event of bank failure. In the UK this task is undertaken by the Financial Services Compensation Scheme (FSCS).
Devaluation (depreciation)	A country devalues its exchange rate when its currency is reduced in value in terms of other currencies. Its exports become cheaper abroad, whereas its imports are more expensive for domestic consumers. Depreciation achieves the same result, except that the new lower rate is determined by market forces.
Digital banking	This refers to the provision of banking services by electronic means, e.g. e-banking and m-banking.
Discount	This refers to the purchase of financial instruments at a price below their face (nominal) value.
Disposable income	This is income after deduction of income tax and national insurance, which is available for discretionary spending by the personal sector.
Due diligence	The need to investigate the quality of assets on a bank's balance sheet and its overall operations. This is an essential requirement for any bank pursuing an acquisition/merger of another bank.
Economic and Monetary Union (EMU)	Monetary union between EU member states involves no capital controls, a single currency and the ECB to formulate monetary policy. This should accelerate progress towards economic union via the completion of a single market for goods, services, capital and labour.
Economic growth	This results in a greater output of goods and services in a nation, i.e. a larger GNP. If output growth exceeds population growth, then a country's living standards should rise. Such a development is generally the result of a better utilisation of a country's economic resources.
Eligible liabilities	Sterling deposits with less than two years' maturity held by a bank. Bank of England reserve requirements are based on the resultant figure.
Emerging economies	New industrial economies which have developed a manufacturing base and diversified their exports. Most have experienced rising per capita income and reductions in poverty. Over time, most emerging economies have liberalised their capital market and banking system.

Entrepôt	An entrepôt financial centre, such as New York or London, makes its domestic financial markets available to foreign lenders and borrowers. They are attracted by the depth and liquidity of its markets and the various financial instruments traded.
Equity	In the context of capital markets, equity refers to an ordinary share.
Euro	The agreed name for the single currency in European member states. Euro bank notes and coins are available in a variety of denominations. The ECB has issued euro notes and coins since 1 January 2002.
Eurobank	A term used to define a bank operating in the eurocurrency market(s) in an offshore centre. Eurobanks can take the form of subsidiaries and branches.
Eurobond	This bond is sold by a borrower outside of their own country in other countries' capital markets, other than the capital market of the bond's currency, e.g. German corporation issues eurodollar bonds in London. Foreign bonds issued in the capital market of the bond's currency.
Eurocredit	A loan granted by a bank(s) operating in the eurocurrency markets. Most eurocredits have a variable interest rate charge which is adjusted every few months. Large loans are handled by syndicates of banks. Loans are provided to governments and corporations.
Eurocurrency	A eurocurrency is a time deposit held in a bank located outside the country, or the jurisdiction of the central bank, responsible for the currency in which the deposit is denominated. A dollar time deposit held in any bank's branch in London or Singapore, etc. Eurodollars are held by US residents and non-residents.
Eurozone	This constitutes the 17 member states of the EU which participate in EMU.
European Central Bank (ECB)	This is the independent central bank of the Eurozone which has responsibility for monetary policy and thereby sets interest rates. It is owned by the member state central banks. Profits are distributed on the basis of shares held in the institution by each EMU participant central bank. The national central banks have transferred part of their foreign exchange reserves to the ECB.
European Union	At present it consists of twenty-seven member states in Europe (one of which is the UK). Most customs procedures, tariffs and quotas have been eliminated, thereby encouraging the free flow of goods, services and labour.
Exchange Rate Mechanism (ERM)	Each ERM currency has an official central rate in terms of the euro, which central banks defend within agreed fluctuation margins. Devaluation or revaluation of central rates is permitted under this system of adjustable exchange rates.

Financial assets	A financial asset should provide some form of return to its holder, i.e. interest, dividend payment. The return on a financial asset is usually related to the risk associated with it.
Financial Conduct Authority (FCA)	The FCA's main aim is to protect financial services consumers from future mis-selling scandals.
Financial exclusion	Many poorer members of society do not have access to banking and financial services due to their income position.
Financial Policy Committee (FPC)	The FPC's main aims are to monitor banks, identify threats to financial stability and review takeover bids by banks.
Financial Services Act 1986	Established the regulatory framework for investor protection in the UK.
Financial Services Authority (FSA)	Established in 1997 to regulate/supervise the entire financial services industry in the UK. It was replaced by Bank of England regulatory subsidiaries in 2012.
Fiscal drag	A progressive form of taxation will generate increased tax revenues from a rise in national income. A fall in national income will result in a smaller tax leakage in the economy. Fiscal drag thus acts as an automatic stabiliser in the economy.
Fixed exchange rate system	A system where the exchange value of currencies is fixed in terms of some common standard such as the dollar, with only limited fluctuations allowed. The IMF adjustable peg-rate system (1945-73) was based on fixed exchange rates.
Floating exchange rate system	A system where the exchange value of currencies is determined by the interplay of market forces in the foreign exchange market. Sometimes it is referred to as a clean float. If central bank intervention occurs to restrict movement, it is known as a dirty float.
Floating rate note	A short term bond issued with a variable coupon rate which has a fixed margin over (or under) LIBOR or prime rate. Interest is usually paid twice a year to the bond (note) holder. FRNs are popular with international banks both as issuers and holders.
Foreign bond	A bond issued by a foreign corporation or government in another country's capital market. The bond will be denominated in the latter's currency. The bond issue will be subject to the capital market regulations of the country in which it is issued, e.g. Spanish corporation issues £ bond in London are subject to UK regulations.
Foreign exchange intervention	This occurs when the central bank, such as the Bank of England, intervenes in the foreign exchange market in order to manage its country's currency exchange rate against other currencies. Such operations have an impact on the level of foreign exchange reserves held by a country. Support for the pound involves the Bank of England in selling part of its foreign currency reserves.

Gilt-edged securities (gilts)	UK government stock (abbreviated to gilts). Such stock or gilts are regarded as risk-free securities because the UK government has always paid interest and the principal back on the due dates (excepting irredeemable stocks such as War Loan which carry no repayment obligation).
Globalisation	This is the integration of the world's money and capital markets, a process assisted by deregulation, innovative financial instruments and the information revolution.
Grace period	This is the period of a loan when no repayment of the principal is required from the borrower. Only interest payments on the outstanding debt require to be paid.
Gross National Product	A measure of the value of a nation's output of goods and services in a particular time period. Nominal GNP measures output value in present day prices. Real GNP measures output value in constant prices. The latter measure is the best indicator of economic growth.
Hardware	This is associated with mainframe computers which store, process and perform thousands of transactions per second. It also refers to minicomputers and microcomputers.
Inflation	This is a rise in prices within a national economy due to internal economic mismanagement or external factors, e.g. higher oil prices. Between 1945 and 1995, inflation was a persistent economic problem in most countries. Hyperinflation is associated with high levels of inflation, e.g. 100% price increases per month; ultimately currency becomes worthless.
Inflationary gap	This occurs in an economy when total demand exceeds total potential supply or output; as a result, prices rise to ration out available supplies.
Injections	Increase the flow of income and can take the form of additional investment, exports and government expenditure.
Institutional investors	Non-bank financial institutions which are mostly involved in the long term investment of their clients' funds, e.g. pension funds, life offices, etc.
Interest spread (margin)	Difference between interest paid and interest owed, e.g. if interest paid on deposits averages 5% and interest earned on assets equals 8%, then the interest spread (or margin) is 3%.
Interest yield	This is the nominal rate of annual interest paid on a bond divided by the market price of the security; e.g. if the coupon or interest rate on a bond is 9% and the market price is 95, the current yield is 9.47% (9 ÷ 95 x 100).
Intermediation	Financial intermediation is an important role performed by banks (and other financial institutions).Banks recycle funds between deficit and surplus units in the domestic (and international) economy. Direct claims are purchased by banks from deficit units; secondary claims are issued to depositors.

International liquidity — This constitutes the international reserves, i.e. gold and foreign currency holdings, of a country.

International liquidity is held to defend an exchange rate and deal with external economic shocks.

International Monetary Fund — The IMF was established in 1944 to supervise the international monetary system. It provides a source of funds for members experiencing balance of payments and external debt problems. Loans are conditional on the implementation of specific fiscal and monetary policies.

Keynesian economics — This is a wide-ranging term used to describe demand management or fine-tuning of the economy. A deflationary gap or unemployment could be cured via fiscal policy, i.e. increased government expenditure or reduced taxation. Used by UK governments (and others) between 1945 and 1976 to maintain full employment, but was less successful with the passage of time.

Lead manager — A major bank which organises a syndicated eurocredit or bond issue with the help of other banks.

Leakages — These occur in the circular flow of income in an economy via savings, imports and taxation.

Lesser developed countries — These are countries which are backward in economic and social terms relative to advanced industrial nations. About 120 countries in the world fall into this category. Most have a low per capita income.

LIBOR — This refers to the London Interbank Offered Rate at which funds are offered on overnight and short term loan in the interbank market to first class banks. This rate is used in loan roll-over agreements in relation to variable rate eurocredits. It is determined by the demand and supply of eurodollar (or any other eurocurrency) funds in the market. The bid and offer rates are obtained each day from at least eight banks in London.

Liquidity — This is the ease with which a financial asset can be turned into cash for immediate use by a bank or other financial institution. It also relates to assets which can be easily converted into a spendable form without a capital loss.

Liquidity adequacy — This is the ability of an institution to pay its obligations such as deposits or interbank loans when they fall due. It is essential for retaining customer and market confidence in an institution.

Liquidity risk — This is the risk that a solvent institution is temporarily unable to meet its monetary obligations, i.e. repay customer deposits. Such an occurrence usually results in a bank run.

M-banking — As an aspect of digital banking this refers to the use of mobile phone technology via iPhone, iPad, Android and Blackberry.

Maastricht Treaty — The European Council met in Maastricht (Holland) in December 1991 and concluded the Treaty on European Union, which amended the Treaty of Rome, to enable EMU to take place among the member states. By 1993 all the EU states had ratified the Treaty in their own parliaments.

Marginal propensity to consume (mpc) — This is the portion of any change in disposable income which is spent on consumption. The mirror image of the mpc is the marginal propensity to save (mps), i.e. mpc + mps = 1.

Maturity — The length of time elapsing before a debt (bank loan or bond) is to be redeemed by the bank borrower or bond issuer.

Maturity transformation — A technique used by banks whereby short term deposits finance longer term loans, e.g. 3 month time deposits used to finance 5 year loan.

Merit goods and services — Health and education services which could be provided through the market mechanism but are deemed so essential that the government makes public provision of these services.

Monetarism — Monetarists believe that economic policy should be concerned solely with money supply management. A non¬-inflationary environment must be created against which supply-side policies, e.g. lower taxation, can be used to promote output and employment growth.

Money market — Short term financial market usually involving lending and borrowing of funds with less than one year to maturity. It is extremely important for asset-liability management in banks.

Mortgage — The lender, i.e. bank or building society, has a claim on the property which acts as collateral, i.e. security, for the mortgage (loan) granted.

Multiplier — The mechanism whereby an autonomous change in a component of aggregate demand has a more than proportionate effect on the national income. The size of the multiplier in an economy is determined to a large extent by leakages, i.e. marginal propensity to save, tax and imports, and injections, i.e. government spending, investment and exports.

Mutual society — One owned by the members, e.g. share account investors in a building society. Profits made are transferred into general reserves for use within the society and are not distributed as a dividend (as is the case in most banks with shareholders).

National debt — Money the government has borrowed in the main from its own citizens to finance government spending not paid for by tax revenues. It represents debt owed in a collective capacity to people in an individual capacity.

National income — Equals the total income in an economy. Income is derived from two main sources: the provision of personal services and from the ownership of land and capital. It equals the value of the output of goods and services of a country in any time period.

Nationalisation	State ownership of assets. In the case of a bank, it generally arises when a capital injection is required to replace private capital absorbed by loan defaults.
Net national product	Gross National Product minus an estimate for capital consumption in the economy, i.e. depreciation of the existing capital stock.
New industrial economies	This is a country (Brazil, India, China, etc) which has developed its industrial base to satisfy domestic demand and diversify exports. Such a country is generally classified as an emerging economy. Most Asian NIEs have experienced rising per capita income and reductions in poverty.
Nostro account	Currency accounts held by banks with their correspondent banks in other countries. Such accounts are essential for the conduct of foreign trade and finance, together with transfer and settlement of operations in the eurocurrency markets.
OECD	The Organisation for Economic Cooperation and Development represents 30 industrial nations, such as USA, Japan, Germany. Its headquarters are in Paris and it carries out economic surveys on member countries and makes recommendations at regular intervals.
Office of Budget Responsibility	This independent unit of the UK Treasury is responsible for making budget, national debt and economic forecasts to assist the Chancellor of the Exchequer in framing overall economic policy.
Offshore financial centre	This is an offshore financial centre which participates in the eurocurrency market. In such a centre banks intermediate in external currencies different from the locational currency of the centre, e.g. banks in London borrowing/ lending dollars or yen.
OPEC	This is a price cartel (arrangement) which seeks to maximise its members' oil export revenues. It attempts to fix the market price for oil and sets output quotas on the oil production of its members. This can have influence on national and global inflation rates.
Operational balances	Funds kept by banks in their accounts at the Bank of England to settle imbalances between themselves, resulting from daily cheque and giro clearings.
Ordinary shares	This is a security which represents a claim to ownership in a company. Ordinary shareholders receive dividends and can vote at AGMs.
Paradox of thrift	In a recession, due to the fear of being made unemployed, people generally save more, and the marginal propensity to save increases. Such action, by reducing aggregate demand, deepens the recession and increases the probability of unemployment.
Pension fund	A fund which collects and invests contributions from its members. At some subsequent date, pensions are paid to the beneficiaries. Pension funds are major institutional investors.

Per capita income	The total income in a country (Gross National Product) is divided by the total population to derive per capita (per head) income figures. When adjusted for the effects of inflation and exchange rate changes, the resultant real per capita income can be used to assess the standard of living in individual countries.
Preventative regulation	This form of bank regulation relates to specific minimum capital and liquidity ratios that must be adhered to by banks. The basic aim of such ratios is to reduce calls on the deposit insurance fund and lender of last resort facilities, as well as necessitating state capital injections.
Project finance	A term used to describe the provision of finance (bonds, bank credits, etc) for a specific project. Project finance is used to develop oil fields, mines, electricity generation, etc.
Protectionism	A country can use various protectionist techniques to reduce imports and to protect domestic industry. The most Protective regulation popular forms of protectionism are tariffs and quotas.
Prudential controls	Protective regulation takes two main forms – deposit insurance and lender of last resort facilities – to safeguard customers' deposits and provide emergency liquidity support to banks.
Prudential Regulatory Authority (PRA)	The PRA is responsible for the prudential supervision of banks, credit unions and insurance companies.
Protective regulation	Bank regulatory measures which are put in place to avoid liquidity and solvency problems in the banking system. The two main forms are protective regulation and preventative regulation.
Public goods and services	Government expenditure on defence, law and order. Generally, goods and services that cannot be supplied by the market mechanism.
Public sector	Central government, local authorities, public corporations and nationalised industries.
Public sector net borrowing	This the amount the government needs to borrow in any one time period to cover the financing needs of the public sector.
Rationalisation	A term used in banking where activities are being re-organised within a bank in order to improve efficiency and reduce costs. It almost inevitably means reduced staffing levels and fewer branches.
Recession	An economic term used to describe a decline in the level of economic activity within a country, region or world economy. It is generally associated with low (or negative) economic growth, rising unemployment and declining rates of inflation.

Reschedule	Debt rescheduled implies that the creditors and the borrower have managed to negotiate a deal which generally reduces the debt service burden on a country. In most debt reschedules the debt principal is paid off over a longer period than was originally envisaged. Rescheduling might also involve a lower interest rate and the provision of new funds to assist economic recovery.
Reserve currency	This is a currency held by central banks as part of their official reserves which will be universally accepted in international debt settlement. The US dollar is the main reserve currency.
Retail banking	Banking services provided to the household (consumer) sector and small/medium sized enterprises.
Revaluation (appreciation)	A country revalues its currency when it is increased in value in terms of other currencies. Its exports become more costly, whereas its imports become cheaper for domestic consumers. Appreciation achieves the same result, except that the new rate is determined by market forces in the foreign exchange market.
Ring fencing	The separation of casino and retail banking divisions into separate subsidiaries so that if one fails, the other can continue its operations.
Risk asset ratio	The is the ratio between an institution's capital and its risk-weighted assets The weights assigned are related to the degree of risk attached to each asset.
R/M ratio	This measures the ratio of reserves to imports over a year. A ratio of 25% implies 3 months' import cover.
RPI	Retail Price Index
Saving	Basically, disposable income which is not used for consumption expenditure by households.
Securities Exchange Commission	This agency is responsible for the regulation and supervision of securities markets activity in the USA.
Securitisation	This is the provision of direct finance to borrowers via the issue of bonds or notes to investors. It is an alternative to raising funds by means of bank loans.
Self certification mortgages	The potential borrower fills in the mortgage application form and certifies details on income, assets and outstanding debt. This system is wide open to abuse from uncreditworthy borrowers and was a major factor in the downfall of Bradford & Bingley.
Single financial market	The Second Banking Co-ordination Directive in 1993 laid the framework for a single EU banking/financial market. It is anticipated that EMU/euro will act as a catalyst to bring about a truly single banking market. This will probably involve the restructuring/ consolidation of continental banking systems. On completion, the user of financial services should benefit from lower prices and a greater range of products.

Software	Computer programmes that tell a computer what to do. Software is designed by software engineers for banks and other users.
Social exclusion	That part of society which is removed from the mainstream of economic and social life due to low income, unemployment and reliance on state benefits for prolonged periods of time.
Solvency	This relates to the ability of an institution to absorb losses without endangering depositor funds. It depends on the capital resources of the bank.
Sovereign debt	Debt issued or guaranteed by a sovereign government.
Spread	This is added on to LIBOR at the appropriate reference dates to determine the total interest cost on a variable rate loan. It compensates the bank for providing the loan. The spread meets the management costs, provides for bad debts and contributes to the bank's profits.
Stability and Growth Pact	At the Dublin Summit in December 1996 it was decided that EMU participants had to continue to meet the convergence criteria relating to their fiscal deficits and debt, otherwise sanctions would be imposed. The Pact was basically aimed at maintaining stability within EMU.
Stagflation	Occurs where an economy is experiencing cost push inflation while output is stagnant or declining.
Structural economic problems	Relates to basic deep-seated problems in an economy. In most cases these result from economic mismanagement by the government or economic problems caused by the rundown of a basic industry such as ship building, or exhaustion of a raw material or energy resource within an economy.
Sub-prime debt	Generally associated with house loans in the USA that were defaulted on due to the lack of income by borrowers to service such debt. Much of it was packaged up or sold on to unsuspecting banks and investors. It was a key factor in the global banking crisis of 2007-09.
Syndicate loans	The size of some eurocredits necessitates their provision by a number of banks. A syndicated loan is managed by a lead bank(s) which assesses the borrower's needs and tries to get other banks to participate in the loan. The syndicate leader receives a management fee.
Taxable capacity	Relates to the burden of tax that can be imposed on an economy without it being detrimental to work, saving and enterprise. In other words, tax must not damage GDP growth.
Taxation principles	The main principles when altering or introducing a new tax are equality, certainty, convenience, economy, yield, elasticity. Adherence to these should result in a sound tax system for a country.

Technological risk	Unlike other types of risk in banking which can be assigned to certain factors, technology risk can be all-pervasive, potentially affecting all systems and parts of the organization. It is essential for a bank to continually update its security systems in relation to the technology used.
Tombstone	An advertisement in the world's financial press announcing the arrangement of a successful bank credit or placing of a bond. It provides some details on the financial deal.
Toxic debt	Impaired loans held on the balance sheet of a bank. Such loans are unlikely to be repaid at full face value. In some cases such loans are transferred to a bad bank to enable the first bank to carry on business and recover.
Trade (or business) cycle	All market economies experience fluctuations in economic activity around a long term rate of economic growth. Extreme trade cycles have four phases: recovery, boom, recession and slump. Output, prices and employment vary during the course of the cycle. There is no standard length for the cycle; it can be four or eight years, etc.
Transfer payments	A government raises tax revenues and then redistributes them within the community, e.g. old age pensions, unemployment benefit, etc. Payment of interest on the national debt is also a form of transfer payment.
Transparency	This relates to information released by the bank regarding the quality of its assets and overall operations. It enables investors and interbank lenders to assess the risk associated with a bank and request an appropriate return in exchange. Regulators hope this will restrain banks from indulging in risky lending and over-reliance on wholesale funding.
Treasury bill	A security issued by the government as a means of borrowing money for short periods of time, usually three months.
UK Asset Resolution	A government agency responsible for managing the mortgages and loans of the now defunct Northern Rock and Bradford & Bingley.
UK Financial Investments	This government agency holds/controls the state shareholdings in RBS and LBG. It aims to dispose of these stakes in the future at a profit for the UK Treasury.
Unemployment	This refers to part of a country's workforce not employed in the production of goods and services. Unemployment arises due to a lack of demand for labour (or a specific skill) in an economy. A recession in a national (and world) economy is a prime cause of unemployment.
Universal bank	A universal bank undertakes the whole range of banking activities – deposits, loans, portfolio management, underwriting, mergers and acquisitions advice/finance, etc.
Vickers Report	A shorthand reference for The Independent Commission on Banking (ICB) which reviewed the UK banking structure and competition issues. It recommended the ring fencing of casino banking from retail banking operations in an effort to avoid any future banking crisis.

INDEX